Those who cannot remember the past
are condemned to repeat it.
—George Santayana (1905)

More than three decades after the final withdrawal of American troops from Southeast Asia, the legacy of the Vietnam War continues to influence political, military, and cultural discourse. Journalists, politicians, scholars, pundits, and others have used the conflict to analyze each of America's subsequent military engagements. Many Americans have observed that Vietnam-era terms such as "cut and run," "quagmire," and "hearts and minds" are ubiquitous once again as comparisons between U.S. involvement in Iraq and in Vietnam seem increasingly appropriate.

Because of its persistent significance, the Vietnam War era continues to inspire vibrant historical inquiry. The eminent scholars featured in *The War That Never Ends* offer fresh and insightful perspectives on the continuing relevance of the Vietnam War, from the homefront to "humping in the boonies," and from the great halls of political authority to the gritty hotbeds of oppositional activism. The contributors assert that the

(CONTINUED ON BACK FLAP)

The War That Never Ends

The War That Never Ends

New Perspectives on the Vietnam War

Edited by
David L. Anderson
and John Ernst

THE UNIVERSITY PRESS OF KENTUCKY

Publication of this volume was made possible in part by a grant
from the National Endowment for the Humanities.

The University Press of Kentucky

Scholarly publisher for the Commonwealth,
serving Bellarmine University, Berea College, Centre College of Kentucky, Eastern
Kentucky University, The Filson Historical Society, Georgetown College, Kentucky
Historical Society, Kentucky State University, Morehead State University, Murray State
University, Northern Kentucky University, Transylvania University, University
of Kentucky, University of Louisville, and Western Kentucky University.
All rights reserved.

Editorial and Sales Offices: The University Press of Kentucky
663 South Limestone Street, Lexington, Kentucky 40508-4008
www.kentuckypress.com

Map by Dick Gilbreath

11 10 09 08   5 4 3 2

Library of Congress Cataloging-in-Publication Data

The war that never ends : new perspectives on the Vietnam War / edited by David L.
Anderson and John Ernst.
     p. cm.
  Includes bibliographical references and index.
  ISBN 978-0-8131-2473-5 (hardcover : alk. paper)
  1. Vietnam War, 1961-1975. 2. Vietnam War, 1961-1975—United States. 3. United
States—History—1945-   4. Vietnam—History—1945-1975. I. Anderson, David L.,
1946-   II. Ernst, John, 1962-
  DS557.7.W3675 2007
  959.704'3—dc22   200702642

Contents

Dedications vii

Introduction: Why Vietnam Still Matters   1
  Marilyn Young

1. No More Vietnams: Historians Debate the Policy Lessons of the
   Vietnam War   13
   David L. Anderson

2. The United States and Vietnam: The Enemies   35
   Walter LaFeber

3. With Friends Like These: Waging War and Seeking "More Flags"
   55
   Gary R. Hess

4. The Perspective of a Vietnamese Witness   75
   Luu Doan Huynh

5. Ho Chi Minh, Confucianism, and Marxism   105
   Robert K. Brigham

6. Vietnam during the Rule of Ngo Dinh Diem, 1954–63   121
   Ronald B. Frankum Jr.

7. The Buddhist Antiwar Movement   143
   Robert Topmiller

8. The Long-Haired Warriors: Women and Revolution in Vietnam
   167
   Sandra C. Taylor

9. Military Dissent and the Legacy of the Vietnam War   191
   Robert Buzzanco

10. Unpopular Messengers: Student Opposition to the
    Vietnam War   219
    Joseph A. Fry

11. Vietnam Is Here: The Antiwar Movement   245
    Terry H. Anderson

12. The Media and the Vietnam War   265
    Clarence R. Wyatt

13. Congress and the Vietnam War: Senate Doves and Their Impact
    on the War   289
    Kyle Longley

14. In the Valley: The Combat Infantryman and the Vietnam War   311
    Yvonne Honeycutt Baldwin and John Ernst

15. The War That Never Seems to Go Away   335
    George C. Herring

16. A Speech for LBJ with Comments on George W. Bush   351
    Howard Zinn

List of Contributors   357
Index   361

Dedications

This anthology of essays on the complex and continuing historical significance of the American war in Vietnam is dedicated to my colleague and friend Professor George C. Herring of the University of Kentucky. His book *America's Longest War: The United States and Vietnam, 1950–1975,* currently in its fourth edition, has served as the basic textbook on the war for thousands of students since it first appeared in 1979. What has given his work on the war such an enduring quality, gaining it the respect of students and scholars from across a broad spectrum of ideological and cultural backgrounds, is the clarity and force of his logical, well-documented analysis.

Professor Herring is internationally recognized as one of the preeminent authorities on the history of the Vietnam War, and his writings (seven books and scores of book chapters, articles, and reviews) have earned numerous academic awards. He is in frequent demand as a guest lecturer. His colleagues at the University of Kentucky have honored his teaching and service with many special designations. He has mentored some three dozen Ph.D. students. In 2002, the Society for Historians of American Foreign Relations (SHAFR) awarded him the Norman and Laura Graebner Prize for career achievement in recognition of his significant contributions to the profession through scholarship, teaching, and service. He helped build SHAFR into a highly regarded learned society through his leadership in every major office, including his terms as president in 1989 and as the editor of *Diplomatic History* from 1982 to 1986. He has also held major committee positions in the American Historical Association and the Organization of American Historians and provided valuable service to the profession on the State Department and Central Intelligence Agency historical documentation committees. His career is a model for all historians of American foreign policy.

—David L. Anderson

George Herring represents the best of academe, a scholar invested in the community. A Virginia gentleman who made Kentucky his home, he is devoted to family, friends, and his profession. Dr. Herring gladly gave over thirty years to his beloved University of Kentucky and, in the process, either trained or directly influenced a generation of Vietnam War scholars. This compilation of original essays on Vietnam, designed for college students, is dedicated to him and, in part, reflects his rich legacy.

Several of Dr. Herring's former students contributed to this volume, but, owing to space limitations, numerous others could not. To this group of excellent historians, many good friends of mine, I apologize. Dr. Herring, both exacting and nurturing, was that wonderful blend of mentor and friend. By the late 1980s, he became America's leading Vietnam War scholar, and graduate students from across the country enrolled at the University of Kentucky to study with him. We wrote on differing aspects of the Vietnam conflict and routinely debated. Dr. Herring and his wife, Dottie, opened their home in an effort to bring us together. We enjoyed beers and bourbons with him, but he also expected high-quality work and put us through an academic boot camp of sorts. On the other side was his respect, something precious. He guided us through the publication process, attended our weddings and baby showers, and always went the extra mile to help us secure jobs. Today, Dr. Herring still makes himself available and, if we are lucky, takes us to a UK basketball game, where his typically mild, easygoing demeanor vanishes when the Wildcats struggle and the referees miss a call.

—John Ernst

Introduction

Why Vietnam Still Matters

Marilyn Young

> I told [Jordan's King Abdullah] I was sorry for the humiliation suffered by the Iraqi prisoners, and the humiliation suffered by their families. I told him I was equally sorry that people who have been seeing those pictures didn't understand the true nature and heart of America.
>
> —George W. Bush (May 2004)

> Jon, there's no question what took place in that prison was horrible, but the Arab world has to realize that the U.S. shouldn't be judged on the actions of a . . . well, that we shouldn't be judged on actions. It's our *principles* that matter; our inspiring, abstract notions. Remember, Jon, just because torturing prisoners is something we *did* doesn't mean it's something we *would* do.
>
> —Rob Corddry explaining Abu Ghraib to Jon Stewart,
The Daily Show (May 2004)

In 1965, the Pentagon released a documentary entitled *Why Vietnam,* a sequel to the World War II series *Why We Fight.*[1] James C. Thomson Jr., then on the staff of the National Security Council, wrote the script. "As I recall," Thomson told an interviewer many years later, "Mac Bundy told me the President wanted to put out something in the next couple of weeks that would put together what he had said, what Rusk had said, what Mc-Namara had said on three aspects of the war: the diplomatic, the mili-

Southeast Asia after Geneva

tary, and the sort of peace-making or international development aspect."
Thomson, "only partly facetiously," had tried to retitle the film "*Why Viet-nam?*" but he had "lost out on that and the question mark was dropped, because it was clearly an assertion and not a question."[2] Nevertheless, it has remained a question ever since.

Why Vietnam. This is a statement that insistently implies a question. One might suppose that *why Vietnam still matters* similarly harbors a question, but it does not. On the contrary, Vietnam seems always to matter, perhaps most especially when it is being actively denied. Each conflict in which the United States has engaged since 1975 begins with policymakers and generals stating, with confident emphasis: *This is not Vietnam.* By that they mean: *This time the United States will not lose, this time we were right to start a war, this time the American public will embrace our war utterly.* Then, if the war lasts longer than a month or two, Vietnam creeps back in, at first in the form of a question. *Is this Vietnam?* Sometimes, as in the case of Afghanistan, the question has been asked, answered, and then asked again. On October 31, 2001, R. W. Apple, who had reported on Vietnam for the *New York Times,* raised the issue directly in an article headlined "A Military Quagmire Remembered; Afghanistan as Vietnam." Apple's concerns were quickly buried as Afghanistan became a success story—at least as compared with Iraq. By the fall of 2006, however, as the war intensified, Afghanistan as Vietnam was back in the news.

More often the question *Another Vietnam?* takes the form of a denial. At the start of Operation Iraqi Freedom, for example, Gen. Tommy Franks announced, "We don't do body counts." Andrew Bacevich, who fought in Vietnam before he became a historian, explained that "Franks was speaking in code." Not doing body counts meant not doing what had been done in Vietnam, counting the bodies of the enemy dead as proof of U.S. progress in the war. "Franks was not going to be one of those generals re-fighting the last war," Bacevich wrote. "Unfortunately, Franks and other senior commanders had not so much learned from Vietnam as forgotten it."[3] Forgetting is a form of remembering.

Vietnam matters not only when it is denied but also when it is embraced. In the late summer of 2005, a group of men in surplus military gear moved out on patrol through the scrub of central Virginia hunting Viet Cong. Hiding somewhere out there, men and women in black pajamas (and, in one case, genuine North Vietnamese canvas boots) waited in ambush. "To get to Vietnam," Phuong Ly, a reporter for the *Washington Post,* explained, "follow Interstate 64 to Louisa, Va. . . . Signs show the way: 'To the Nam,' 'Phou Bai—2 km.'" The encampment, and the battles, took place on a fifty-acre clearing where some scorched forestland added a "nice touch." As one participant observed, "Looks like it's been napalmed." It had proved difficult to get anyone to play the enemy, though, in the interests of authenticity, a Vietnamese grocery store owner was asked whether the group could borrow his sons. One of the organizers worried about "turning the war into a game or parody" and about having fun when they were meant to feel "scared and somber."[4]

The Vietnam War had, thus, joined the roster of war reenactments—from the Civil War to World War II—that enliven the summers of thousands of Americans. Most of those involved, Phuong Ly wrote, think of playing war, including Vietnam War, as a "hobby, like golf or collecting model trains, but more educational." But some of those on that hot day in August in Virginia were there for more personal reasons: "It gives me a mental picture of what our dads did," one explained. "I was blessed. I never had to really do this." Another, who had volunteered to play a guerrilla, hoped to understand her father better, to find a way to "open up a conversation" with him. He, in turn, had initially expressed concern that the exercise would "trivialize" the war. Later, he said he was pleased that his war had "finally been treated like other wars." In this he was mistaken. As Phuong Ly observed, military reenactments of the Civil War or World War II were "staged to make history come alive for generations who know it only dimly from books." Vietnam, on the other hand, "isn't quite history. To many people, it's a painfully current event."[5] The reenactors hoped to lay it to rest.

In the interstices of war—between Gulf War I in 1991 and Afghanistan in 2001—Vietnam did begin to recede into the safe past. The relationship between Vietnam and the United States was normalized, and the presidency was in the hands of a young man who had himself protested the war while, like millions of his peers, managing to avoid both jail and military service. Vietnam became first an exotic and then an ordinary tourist destination, and five-star hotels dominated the beaches where the marines had landed. On June 6, 2006, Vietnam and the United States signed an agreement to "increase their military contacts and to discuss additional ways to broaden their defense cooperation." Donald Rumsfeld, on his first trip to Hanoi as secretary of defense, announced with "evident satisfaction" that the United States and Vietnam would increase "'exchanges at all levels of the military.'" The Vietnamese played the American national anthem, and, on a visit to the Temple of Literature, Rumsfeld praised Vietnam's economic success and cultural heritage, informing his perhaps puzzled hosts that, when the Temple of Literature was built in the eleventh century, "American Indians were still living in 'mud huts.'"[6] .

Of course, one way the Vietnam War matters has never had very much to do with Vietnam. The overwhelming majority of the books written about the war, and virtually all the movies made about it, are concerned solely with America and Americans: how the war divided the country, alienated a generation, destroyed public trust in authority; how the psychic injuries to those who had fought in Vietnam resisted healing; how the war had come close to destroying the American military.[7]

In the midst of a permanent war against "terrorists," Vietnam is recalled to the public by policymakers and the press mostly in tactical terms. This has been the burden of the endless stream of newspaper and journal articles about counterinsurgency, all of which one way or another regret the fact that the lessons painfully gathered and applied too late in Vietnam had been dropped from military curricula after the war and now must be relearned, painfully and perhaps too late, for application in Iraq.[8]

Vietnam is also recalled through the naming of things, an entire vocabulary of war and warfare that instantly brings it to mind: *Iraqification, search and destroy, triangles* (the Iron Triangle in Vietnam, the Sunni Triangle or the Triangle of Death in Iraq), *My Lai* (for war crimes of any origin or type), *credibility gap, hearts and minds, cut and run, quagmire.* There has also been a proliferation of new names to describe old practices: *kinetic,* or *kinetic kill,* and *nonkinetic warfare* (conventional and counterinsurgency), *netwar* and *fourth-generation warfare* (guerrilla warfare), *EBO* or *effects-based operations* (operations with clear objectives in view).[9]

Sometimes the connection between past and present is more direct. Two investigative reporters for the *Los Angeles Times* recently examined some nine thousand pages of testimony taken by a specially appointed military task force established in the immediate aftermath of the revelations about My Lai in the early 1970s. Declassified in 1994, the documents were reclassified shortly after the reporters used them. Except for the difference in the nationality of the victims, the stories recounted could have been written yesterday. A retired senior officer, Brig. Gen. John H. Johns, who had served on the task force, made the connection: "If we rationalize it as isolated acts, as we did in Vietnam and as we're doing with Abu Ghraib and similar atrocities, we'll never correct the problem."[10] Michael Sallah and Mitch Weiss's account of the sanctioned brutality of an elite unit of the 101st Airborne Division reinforced the sense of a bottomless pit of unknown war crimes.[11] It is likely that descriptions of unprosecuted war crimes in Vietnam will continue to emerge indefinitely, alongside similar stories about Iraq and Afghanistan.

Journalists and historians have written about the "defeat" of the United States in Vietnam. Some analysts, like Gen. William Westmoreland and Noam Chomsky, point out that, from many perspectives, the United States can be said to have won that war. It might be more accurate to say that, although the United States lost in Vietnam, it was not defeated. Defeat in a war in which criminal acts have taken place, or, because it was a war of aggression, constituted a violation of international law as such, has resulted in international trials, an acknowledgment of the crimes of war and crimes against humanity committed, even the payment of reparations to victims. Germany, Japan, and Serbia come to mind as examples. Other countries that have lost colonial or neocolonial wars—France in Indochina and Algeria, the Soviet Union in Afghanistan, for example—have gone through extended periods of national soul-searching.

It is impossible to imagine an international trial or an official national self-examination with respect to the widely recognized criminal behavior of the United States in Vietnam or Iraq. The closest the United States ever came to a formal acknowledgment of what it had done in Vietnam was when President Jimmy Carter deemed the destruction caused by the war to both the United States and Vietnam to have been "mutual."

In a recent exchange on Vietnam published by the *Journal of American History*, Patrick Hagopian observed that one result of the pardoning of Lieutenant Calley, and of the failure of the government to investigate and prosecute war crimes generally, has been a residue of "unallocated blame" that seemed for a time to stigmatize all Vietnam veterans. The result, Hagopian wrote, has been the disappearance of "public understanding of the Vietnam War into a moral void." The public reaction to the stories that appeared in the *Toledo Blade,* Hagopian noted, was tepid at best. Yet, he went on, every "month and year brings news of investigations into the truth of Japanese atrocities during the Asian wars of the 1930s and 1940s; Turkish admission into the European Union seems to hinge in part on that nation's acknowledgment of alleged crimes committed earlier in the twentieth century; investigators continue to hunt down the last surviving perpetrators of Nazi crimes against humanity. There is no shortage of international tribunals and truth commissions covering events on almost every continent in the 1980s and since. Yet about US-perpetrated crimes in Vietnam, there is still an embarrassed silence."[12]

Hagopian could have added that, after a small flurry of distress, embarrassed silence has been the general response to revelations of U.S. war crimes from the Korean War to Operation Iraqi Freedom. This seems to be the result of an inherent contradiction in the American self-understanding. By definition, the United States cannot wage aggressive war, commit war crimes or crimes against humanity, or require an international trial for crimes against humanity. When the evidence that these things have occurred is overwhelming, understanding has nowhere to go but the particular: this low-level guard, that misunderstood order, these soldiers grieving for comrades and under great stress.

Surprisingly, even open debate about the abrogation of the Geneva Convention on the treatment of prisoners does not move the discussion beyond the particular. Yet torture as an instrument of "counterterror" has a known history in the United States. None of those complaining that the military in Iraq has failed to learn the lessons of counterinsurgency note that some lessons had been fully learned: techniques of torture, assassination, and the use of indigenous death squads developed by the CIA in Vietnam and widely disseminated since. George W. Bush may not have fought in Vietnam, but he understands how that war was fought. "I don't care what the international lawyers say, we are going to kick some ass," he told his staff immediately after his public broadcast on September 11, 2001.[13]

Nicholas Fraser, reflecting on a current "softening of tone" among historians of French collaboration with the Nazis, suggested that it was as if "Vichy can now be studied dispassionately like anything else."[14] Something similar may be under way with respect to Vietnam. The excellent new scholarship being done on Vietnamese history, north and south, colonial and modern, on the international context of U.S. policy, on aspects of presidential policymaking that had gone unnoticed earlier, is striking. Yet it may also be the case that, rich and good as the scholarship has become, it runs the risk of skirting the reason Vietnam still matters.

Everyone now knows that, in Vietnam, the United States fought a war of great violence in a small country whose national choices could not have affected the safety and security of the United States in any way. Everyone now knows that terrible crimes were committed in the course of that war: the specific crimes of rape, torture, massacre; the more general crimes of unparalleled bombing of civilians. But this knowledge has had few long-run consequences.

In Iraq and Afghanistan too, the public knows without knowing and without consequence. To some degree this may be due to the way the press cushions its revelations of abuse. In February 2003, Carlotta Gall, a reporter for the *New York Times,* wrote a story about an Afghan prisoner being beaten to death at the Bagram air base in Afghanistan. The paper held on to it for almost a month before running it deep inside the paper. Roger Cohen, the newspaper's foreign editor, "pitched it . . . four times at page-one meetings, with increasing urgency and frustration." His inability to get the paper to run the story on the front page was, he said later, his "single greatest frustration as foreign editor." Howell Raines, then the executive editor, found it difficult to credit the story and demanded further confirmation. Even then he continued to delay, loathe, Gall thought, to "believe bad things of Americans." In addition, she said, there "was a sense of patriotism, and you felt it in every question from every editor and copy editor," she says. "I remember a foreign-desk editor telling me, 'Remember where we are—we can smell the debris from 9/11.'"[15]

A number of reporters filed stories about the abuse of prisoners and the policy of rendition (subcontracting torture to other countries), but it was not until pictures of systemic abuse taken by U.S. soldiers themselves involved in the abuses surfaced that the story gained traction. The silhouette of a hooded figure standing on a box with his arms out, his extremities apparently attached to electrodes, became as iconic of the war in Iraq as the picture of the execution of an unarmed National Liberation Front prisoner had been in Vietnam. Even then, as Eric Umansky wrote in the *Columbia Journalism Review,* the response was less domestic revulsion than international condemnation. Moreover, sharp investigative reporting was regularly "balanced" by policy stories that "passed along the administration's assertions that abuse was the work of a few bad apples, without offering key context—namely that the facts suggested those assertions were untrue."[16]

President Bush's effort to persuade the Congress to do an end run around the Supreme Court by passing legislation that explicitly exempts the United States from key provisions of the Geneva Convention has kept the story of prisoner abuse fitfully alive. Other aspects of U.S. military practice in Iraq regularly appear and as regularly disappear. In Mark Danner's telling phrase, they are "frozen scandals."[17]

I want to suggest that Vietnam still matters because the central issues it raised about the United States in the world over four decades ago remain the central issues today. Unresolved, they come back not as ghosts but as the still living. The Phoenix Program of targeted assassination, torture, and wholesale detention; the indiscriminate bombing of densely populated areas; the credibility of the United States as an explanation for an indefinite commitment to misguided military policies; the unchecked expansion of presidential power; the corruption and demoralization of the military; illegal domestic spying; dissent defined as treason; the insistence that fighting "them" over there protects "us" over here—all continue in daily practice.

I think that it is necessary for historians to continue to press for the necessity of a coming to terms with Vietnam. Else, when one day the war in Iraq ends, or maybe just simply stops, the United States will once again fail to come to terms with the damage done by this unprovoked war of aggression, laying the groundwork for the next war.

Notes

The epigraphs are taken from the following sources: George W. Bush quoted in Dan Froomkin, "About That Apology," *Washington Post,* May 7, 2004; Rob Corddry quoted in Mark Danner, "The Logic of Torture," *New York Review of Books* (posted on http://www.markdonner.com, June 24, 2004; reaccessed September 17, 2006).

1. In between, Twentieth-Century Fox, with Pentagon cooperation, had also produced the film *Why Korea* (1951), which, unlike its heroic predecessors, rapidly faded into obscurity.

2. Oral History, James C. Thomson Jr., July 22, 1981, LBJ Oral History, p. 31 (available online at www.millercenter.virginia.edu).

3. Andrew Bacevich Jr., "What's an Iraqi Life Worth?" *Washington Post,* July 9, 2006, B01.

4. Phuong Ly, "Vietnam Buffs Bring War to Va.," *Washington Post,* August 8, 2005, A01.

5. Ibid.

6. Michael R. Gordon, "Rumsfeld, Visiting Vietnam, Seals Accord to Deepen Military Cooperation," *New York Times,* June 6, 2006 (available online at www .newyorktimes.com; reaccessed September 15, 2006). Perhaps discomfited by all this goodwill, Gordon reminded his readers that the "Vietnam War still casts a long shadow." Over a thousand soldiers remained "unaccounted for," and a resident team continued to search for their remains, though their efforts had been "complicated by Vietnam's building boom and the dwindling ranks of witnesses from the war era." He also noted that the U.S. courtship of Vietnam was directly tied to the Bush administration's increasing "concern" about China.

7. In a perfect reflection of American solipsism, the battered hero of Oliver Stone's movie *Platoon* (1986) explains that the United States did not fight the enemy in Vietnam; it fought itself.

8. See David Elliott, "Parallel War?" and Marilyn B. Young, "Counterinsurgency Now and Forever," both in *Iraq and the Lessons of Vietnam,* ed. Marilyn B. Young and Lloyd Gardner (New York: New Press, 2007).

9. See, e.g., Robyn Read, "Effects-Based Airpower for Small Wars: Iraq after Major Combat," *Air and Space Power Journal* 19, no. 1 (Spring 2005), http://www .airpower.au.af.mil/airchronicles/apj/apj05/spr05/read.html (accessed June 5, 2007).

10. Nick Turse and Deborah Nelson, "A Tortured Past," *Los Angeles Times,* August 20, 2006. See also the second in their series, "Civilian Killings Went Unpunished," August 25, 2006. (Both are available online at www.latimes.com.)

11. See Michael D. Sallah and Mitch Weiss, *Tiger Force: A True Story of Men and War* (New York: Little, Brown, 2006). The book is based on their earlier stories for the *Toledo Blade,* the series "Buried Secrets, Brutal Truths—Tiger Force," which ran from October 22 to October 26, 2003.

12. Patrick Hagopian, "Interchange: Legacies of Vietnam," *Journal of American History* 93, no. 2 (September 2006): 456–57. The journal exchange, which involved scholars of different generations, was marked by a general avoidance of the issues that absorbed Hagopian. "Am I the last crank fighting the forgotten political battles of an earlier age against ghostly antagonists who have now sensibly moved on? If so, why? How did that happen?" Hagopian asked (457). His question was not answered.

13. George W. Bush quoted in Alfred McCoy, "Torture in the Crucible of Counterinsurgency," in Young and Gardner, eds., *Iraq and the Lessons of Vietnam,* 252, citing Richard A. Clarke, *Against All Enemies: Inside America's War on Terror* (New York: Free Press, 2004), 24. See also Alfred McCoy, *A Question of Torture: CIA Interrogation, from the Cold War to the War on Terror* (New York: Metropolitan, 2006).

14. Nicholas Fraser, "Toujour Vichy," *Harper's Magazine,* October 2006, 92.

15. Eric Umansky, "Failures of Imagination," *Columbia Journalism Review,* September/October 2006, http://cjrarchives.org/issues/2006/5/Umansky.asp. See also Carlotta Gall, "U.S. Military Investigating Death of Afghan in Custody," *New York Times,* March 4, 2003.

16. Umansky, "Failures of Imagination."

17. See the interview with Tom Engelhardt, "The Age of Frozen Scandal," posted on tomdispatch.com, February 26, 2006 (reaccessed September 17, 2006).

1

No More Vietnams

Historians Debate the Policy Lessons of the Vietnam War

David L. Anderson

It has been thirty years since the end of the Vietnam War, and historians of American foreign relations are still vigorously debating the historical questions of why the United States chose to persist in a major military campaign in Vietnam for so long and why, ultimately, that costly and controversial intervention failed to achieve Washington's stated objectives. Thousands of books and articles have been published on the American war in Vietnam, advancing knowledge and understanding of the conflict, yet the lessons learned and the meaning of the war for American diplomatic and military doctrine are still contested. What makes resolution of such important historical questions remain so elusive?

The war has left conflicting mythologies that continue to battle with each other. Boiled down to an extreme simplification, the debate is over the concept *no more Vietnams*. One interpretation of this term is that the United States must abjure from virtually all types of military intervention abroad. The term *Vietnam syndrome* came into use after the war to describe a pathological aversion among American policymakers to the use of force as an instrument of foreign policy. The other understanding of the term *no more Vietnams* is that the United States must never again "lose" in cases in which defense of the nation's security requires military intervention. Proponents of this view argue that the United States

National Security Adviser Walt W. Rostow briefs President Lyndon B. Johnson during the Battle for Khe Sanh in 1968. Y. R. Okamoto, courtesy of Lyndon Baines Johnson Presidential Library.

should get over the Vietnam syndrome and regain the political will to use America's massive power to achieve foreign policy objectives. In both cases, there is the implication that, because of its power and the global reach of its interests, the United States can choose where and when to engage its military force.

The Vietnam War was a war of choice. The Eisenhower, Kennedy, Johnson, and Nixon administrations chose to define the survival of South Vietnam as of vital strategic interest to the United States in the global policy of containment of Soviet and Chinese power. Official American rhetoric increasingly exaggerated the value of the objective as domestic opponents of the war questioned the choice and the cost of the intervention. There is a proclivity when policymakers choose war to exaggerate the results of the intervention and to understate the costs in order to justify continuing the intervention. One example of such an exaggeration is couching the reason for continuing the intervention in terms of preserving America's international *credibility*. Wars of choice, like the Vietnam

War, leave a gap between ends and means that almost invariably produces division, dissatisfaction, and domestic debilitation.[1]

The last American war that was not a war of choice was World War II. The danger to U.S. interests posed by the strength and ideology of the Axis powers left the United States no choice but to defend itself and its historical allies. World War II is often termed the *good war* and the Vietnam War the *bad war*. The Korean War in between the two gets obscured as a forgotten, stalemated war. The reasons for fighting the good war were much more self-evident to Americans than were the reasons for fighting the bad war. Moreover, the Unites States won the good war by the rational standard that the hostile power and oppressive ideology of the nation's enemies had been nullified. American forces came home to well-deserved victory celebrations and national self-congratulations. The reasons for fighting the bad war were much less evident, however. The small, rural country of Vietnam lacked the power to threaten the United States directly, and its internal politics were much too localized to be a crucial test of American ideology. In the end, there was no U.S. victory in Vietnam, and, thus, the questions were left open as to whether a victory was ever possible, how it could have been achieved, and, most challenging, what would have constituted victory.

At the end of Oliver Stone's *Platoon* (1986), about the realities of combat for American soldiers in Vietnam, the young GI who is the main character reflects, "I think now looking back that we did not fight the enemy, we fought ourselves and the enemy was within us."[2] In the context of the film, the line is a well-known literary allusion to works such as Joseph Conrad's *Heart of Darkness* (1902) that explore the presence of evil within the human psyche. The line could also be applied to what has become the historical exploration of the essence of American foreign policy as revealed by the Vietnam War. In much of the writing on the war, Vietnam and the Vietnamese are backdrops to what is more an examination of America and the Americans. Conflicting ideas of what Americans are as a people and of their values and beliefs become the points of analysis and argument.

Throughout its history, the United States has been shaped by both ambition and altruism. As a young nation, it was purposefully and consciously expansionist and idealist. It sought to build its own power and influence, and this ambition was, at times, at the expense of weaker nations, including Native American peoples, Mexico, and Spain. It sought also to share the benefits of liberty. The American self-perception forged in the Revolution was of a nation that was the freest, most democratic, most republican, and most progressive in history, and accompanying that perception was a sense of responsibility to share this ideal with others. This sense of mission combined with a sense of survival in a competitive world to form a potent prescription for an assertive and ambiguous U.S. role in international affairs. In World War II, for a brief historical moment, American might and right converged in a victory over tyrannical forces. In Vietnam, the United States experienced the limits of its power and its righteousness. Consequently, the Vietnam War has become not just the bad war but the endless war, a subject locked into a protracted debate over the responsibility for and the significance of the outcome.

This debate over the policy lessons of the war is not an abstract academic exercise in critical thinking. The United States failed to ensure the survival of its ally, the Republic of Vietnam (RVN), but its enemy, the Democratic Republic of Vietnam (DRV), did not defeat the United States as a nation. America remained a world power that was able, perhaps even expected, to apply its strength and influence in other international conflicts. Historians, policy analysts, and national leaders have offered numerous explanations of what the Vietnam War reveals as a guide to U.S. policies in the present. This process of reflection began even while the war was in progress and has continued ever since in some clearly discernible phases.

The official rationale for U.S. intervention in the affairs of Vietnam, as presented by American presidents from Truman through Ford, was the importance of the future of Vietnam in terms of the global Cold War that pitted the interests and ideology of the United States against those of the Soviet Union. When the French war with the Communist-led Viet Minh began in 1946, the Truman administration initially took a neutral position in a conflict that was manifestly an attempt by France to regain the colonial authority over Indochina that had slipped from its grasp during Japan's wartime occupation of the region. By 1950, however, the increasingly dangerous Cold War in Europe, the victory of the Chinese Communist Party in China's Civil War, the Soviet Union's successful test of an atomic bomb, and Senator Joseph McCarthy's reckless claims of Communist agents within the U.S. government had caused Washington to reexamine its perception of the Indochina conflict. When Truman ordered American troops to Korea in June 1950 to counter the threat of Communist North Korea to the U.S.-backed republic in South Korea, the Cold War went to Asia. In 1954, as the French grew weary of their eight-year war against the Viet Minh, President Eisenhower employed the metaphor of falling dominoes to declare the containment of the spread of Communist regimes in Southeast Asia to be a vital strategic imperative of the United States. By the early 1960s, the consensus view among American leaders was that the United States must contain Communist political power wherever it appeared—a consensus seemingly reconfirmed by a U.S.-Soviet arms race, Communist-led revolution in Cuba, military confrontation over Berlin, civil war in Laos, and a mounting armed insurgency organized by Communist Party cadre against the government in South Vietnam.

The idea that the containment of world communism somehow required the United States to be involved in Vietnam appeared in all the official explanations of the growing commitment of U.S. support for the survival of a South Vietnamese state independent of the Communist North Vietnamese regime that had grown out of the Viet Minh's successful resistance to the French. Although historical scholarship on Vietnam was woefully slim in the United States in the early 1960s, a body of American scholarship slowly developed as U.S. involvement in Vietnam grew. In the 1960s and 1970s, a first wave of historical analysis emerged.

Unlike the early historical studies of the Cold War that largely supported the validity of Washington's decision to seek to contain Soviet and, later, Chinese power, the initial American histories of the Vietnam War questioned the applicability of the Cold War paradigm to the internal conflict in Vietnam. Pioneering scholarship such as *The United States in Vietnam* by George McT. Kahin and John W. Lewis and *The Two Vietnams* by Bernard B. Fall criticized U.S. policymakers for overlooking the nationalism of Ho Chi Minh and the Vietnamese Communists and for failing to understand the internal politics of Vietnam. Departing from the Cold War model, in which the orthodox scholarship was sympathetic to official policy, the standard or orthodox interpretation of the Vietnam War was highly critical of the official rationales. Criticism did not always take the same form. Liberals such as Arthur M. Schlesinger Jr. and David Halberstam believed that American officials were often well-meaning but were too ignorant of Vietnam and arrogant about their own and America's abilities to understand the conflict. These writers characterized U.S. policy in Vietnam as a *quagmire* that had gradually trapped the United States in an unintended military commitment. Department of Defense analysts working in the late 1960s on a study that became known as the Pentagon Papers (after one of its authors—Daniel Ellsberg—leaked it to the press in 1971) disagreed with the quagmire thesis. These scholars, including Ellsberg and Leslie Gelb, developed the so-called stalemate argument, which maintained that U.S. leaders understood early on that there was no good American solution to the civil war in Vietnam but that they persisted in the war rather than admit a mistake and risk the loss of political power. Radical historians such as Gabriel Kolko went beyond the cynicism of the stalemate argument and contended that it was not lack of political courage that compelled U.S. policy but rather an American drive for hegemony and world order that made all revolutionary movements enemies to be defeated.[3]

By the late 1970s and early 1980s, the various criticisms of the government's strategic thinking about Vietnam began to coalesce into a prevailing historical interpretation that came to be labeled *flawed containment* or *liberal-realist*.[4] Relying on classified documents made public in the Pentagon Papers, journalists' accounts, and other evidence, many historians agreed that the containment policy originally conceived to counter Soviet political and military power in Europe after World War II had only limited utility, if any, as an American policy doctrine in Southeast Asia. The realist aspect of this critique noted that the Soviet army was not in the region, as it was in Eastern Europe, and that the postcolonial nations of Indochina were not closely connected economically and historically to the United States, as were the nations of Western Europe. Many U.S. strategists considered China to be America's enemy but also had been wary, since the Korean War, of the huge risks entailed in any military conflict with that country. Consequently, the strategic value of Vietnam to the United States was low, and the costs of intervention there were high. The liberal portion of the argument came from the recognition by many historians that the nationalist aspirations of Vietnamese leaders such as Ho Chi Minh, who had resisted French colonialism, were not unlike historic American values, despite the Vietnamese Communists' professions of Marxist ideology.

One of the first books to synthesize the flawed-containment thesis from then-available records and scholarship was George C. Herring's 1979 *America's Longest War*. Herring acknowledged that policy lessons from the war remained elusive, but on the central point he was direct: "That containment was misapplied in Vietnam, however, seems beyond debate." His book has gone through four editions. Although he has revised many sections on the basis of the outpouring of documents and monographs over the years, his conclusions have remained basically the same. His argument is that the external or global U.S. strategy of blocking Soviet and Chinese Communist influence wherever it spread led the United States to seriously misjudge the internal dynamics of Indochina. "By intervening in what was essentially a local struggle," Herring argued, "it placed itself at the mercy of local forces, a weak client, and a determined adversary." Despite the use of abundantly destructive military force, it was "beyond the ability of the United States" to settle the political questions of Vietnam.[5]

In addition to Herring, a number of other historians have penned studies with a similar argument, one that is sometimes termed *neo-orthodox* to distinguish it from the earlier quagmire thesis.[6] In the 1980s, the journalist-historian Stanley Karnow produced a sweeping narrative history of how the United States was "playing for global stakes" in Indochina, and George Kahin revived his earlier argument in a new book, *Intervention*: "Nearly all American officials . . . perceived Vietnamese communism as one of the fronts of contest with the Soviet Union and China—critically dependent on the two major Communist powers rather than drawing most of its strength from a fundamentally autonomous national foundation."[7] In a specific examination of the containment policy in Indochina, William J. Duiker, an acclaimed biographer of Ho Chi Minh, concluded that the Truman, Eisenhower, and Kennedy administrations "defined Vietnam as a 'test case' of U.S. capacity to stem the advance of communism into vulnerable areas throughout the Third World."[8] In another major study, Robert D. Schulzinger declared, "Had American leaders not thought that all international events were connected to the Cold War there would have been no American war in Vietnam."[9]

The liberal-realist explanations of why the United States intervened militarily in Vietnam in support of the RVN led to the proposition that the war was not winnable in any meaningful sense for the United States and, hence, should never have been undertaken. Historians of this school recall the assessment made by Gen. Matthew Ridgway when he contemplated the possibility of U.S. military involvement in Indochina during the French war. Ridgway contended that it would be the wrong war, in the wrong place, and against the wrong enemy. The orthodox historians argue that American intervention was a misapplication of containment, a failure to understand local conditions in Southeast Asia, and a product of arrogance or ideological obsession. These factors prevented a clear definition of objectives and a clear assessment of the means available to attain those objectives. In other words, there was no successful American strategy that is apparent to these authors.

As the liberal-realist interpretation was emerging in the late 1970s and early 1980s, a conservative revisionist school began to challenge what had become the orthodox view. These revisionist historians largely accepted the official reasoning that U.S. intervention in Vietnam was necessary to contain international Communist expansion. Just as the Vietnam War orthodoxy reversed the pattern of Cold War scholarship in its criticisms of U.S. strategy, the Vietnam War revisionists departed from the Cold War labels and became the defenders of American interventionism. One of the earliest revisionists was the political scientist Guenter Lewy, who wrote in 1978 that events since 1975 had demonstrated that the American failure to prevent a Communist triumph in Southeast Asia had weakened the faith in American commitments. "In the wake of the trauma of Vietnam," Lewy maintained, "America is in the grip of a 'No more Vietnams' psychology which stands in sharp contrast to the spirit of active involvement in global affairs prevailing in the years since World War II. . . . There is no reason to assume that the weakening of America's will to act will make for a better and more peaceful world."[10]

The failure of containment in Vietnam concerned the revisionists, and they concentrated their research, not on the origins of U.S. commitment, but on the way the United States fought the war and how it could have been successful. There were three types of revisionist arguments: (1) that the United States did not make sufficient use of its enormous conventional military power, (2) that the United States' military tactics were too conventional and failed to adapt to the challenges of guerrilla warfare, and (3) that, while military victory may not have been feasible, the effort still had moral and strategic value.

The first argument that a conventional military victory in Vietnam was available to the United States could be found in memoirs and histories written by high-ranking officers who had led U.S. forces in Vietnam. U.S. Army colonel Harry G. Summers Jr. wrote a particularly influential book, *On Strategy,* published in 1982, that began with the premise that the war was basically an assault by the DRV across an international boundary against the separate and sovereign RVN. Citing the classic military doctrines of Karl von Clausewitz, Summers reasoned that the United States should have positioned its forces to isolate the battlefield in the South in order to concentrate its superior firepower on enemy targets. Instead, he claimed, civilian strategists in the Department of Defense fashioned a dispersed and gradual deployment of U.S. forces against guerrilla forces that had little chance of stopping the DRV aggression against the RVN. Summers's book became a standard military history text for educating a new generation of U.S. officers. A number of general officers who had served in Vietnam, including Gen. William C. Westmoreland and Adm. Ulysses S. Grant Sharp, who held the highest-level command positions as the war escalated, agreed with this analysis. They insisted that higher levels of U.S. ground- and airpower and fewer restrictions from officials in Washington would have enabled them to force Hanoi into a negotiated settlement that would have preserved the RVN.[11]

The orthodox historians have challenged this argument, sometimes labeled the *win thesis,* on a number of points. They begin at the beginning—noting the lack of attention it gives to the political and social origins of the conflict. The demilitarized zone along the Seventeenth Parallel, rather than forming an international boundary between North and South Vietnam, delineated two "regroupment zones" for implementation of the cease-fire ending the French–Viet Minh war in 1954. Within South Vietnam, the government was corrupt and oppressive. It had little or no allegiance from many in the population, and no level of American military power could make it popular. In the view of some historians, American airpower and other high-technology and destructive warfare inflicted so much damage on the South Vietnamese population that this form of support for the RVN government served only to alienate the population from the Saigon regime. If the liberal-realists are correct that no amount of force could have produced an American victory in Vietnam, then was the United States incapable of winning the war?[12]

The advocates of the second version of revisionism maintain that the United States could have overcome the political insurgency against the Saigon government by following a pacification strategy. Rather than relying on massive force, the approach should have been to provide the population security and government services, such as health care and agricultural technology, to win its allegiance to the government's side. In actual practice, General Westmoreland and other commanders put more effort into attrition, killing the enemy, than into pacification, but some military historians and former aid officials have argued that, had counterinsurgency been made the primary approach, the result would have been better and certainly no worse than it was for the United States and its Saigon ally.[13]

The notion that there was an American solution to the contest for internal political power in Vietnam is dubious, however. The course and outcome of the Vietnam War were matters not only of American failure but also of Vietnamese success. Some studies of individual U.S. combat units that gave serious attention to village security and local improvements have found that these programs did not translate into loyalty to the Saigon regime after the Americans left the area. Other localized studies of particular villages or provinces have shown that the resistance to external interference—Chinese, French, American—has deep historical and cultural roots in Vietnam. Similarly, real economic and social inequities and injustices provided fertile ground for revolution. The Vietnamese Communists were not infallible and had their own internal divisions, but they also had advantages. They combined their disciplined and ruthless political tactics with appeals to patriotism and justice to create an effective strategy for withstanding the might of the powerful Americans.[14]

It is, in fact, because the Communist-led DRV and the National Liberation Front (NLF) were such formidable opponents that the third school of revisionists, labeled *legitimatists* by the historian Gary Hess, developed its analysis.[15] Like other revisionists, the legitimatists accept the premise that Washington's global credibility as a deterrent to Moscow and Beijing in the Cold War required the United States not to yield the future of Vietnam to the regime in Hanoi without a fight. The international strategic balance of power was at stake, in their view. They also point to the executions, reeducation camps, forced emigration, and other abuses of the Communist regime following its 1975 reunification of Vietnam as evidence of the brutality and immorality of Hanoi's leaders. Another variation on this revisionist theme can be found in those studies that contend that, for all its weaknesses, the Saigon regime was not so corrupt and venal as to be worse than its opponents. The legitimatists acknowledge, however, that the chance of American success in Vietnam was never very good. In effect, they borrow from both the orthodox and the revisionist schools to contend that the United States was correct to intervene in Vietnam and also correct to get out.[16]

The end of the Cold War in 1990 affected this debate among historians of the Vietnam War but did not end it. For revisionists, the dissolution of the Soviet Union confirmed the validity of containment as a strategy. The journalist Michael Lind wrote in 1999, for example, that "the sound and ultimately successful Cold War grand strategy of global military containment of the Communist bloc required Presidents Kennedy and Johnson to escalate U.S. involvement in Vietnam rather than withdraw without a major effort. . . . Once the Vietnam War is viewed in the context of the Cold War, it looks less like a tragic error than like a battle that could hardly be avoided."[17] A new, post–Cold War generation of liberal-realist scholars, however, reaffirms that containment was a flawed concept in Southeast Asia. These scholars, some of whom have made significant use of Vietnamese historical archives now open to research, go beyond the orthodox-revisionist debate to refocus study of the origins of the American intervention from the Cold War context to a postcolonial context. Mark Philip Bradley, for example, describes his research on American and Vietnamese images of each other at the end of World War II as an effort "to locate and analyze the relationship between Vietnam and the United States within the larger sweep of the international history of the twentieth century in which the global discourse and practices of colonialism, race, modernism, and postcolonial state making at once preceded, were profoundly implicated in, and ultimately transcended the dynamics of the Cold War."[18]

Another example of this new scholarship is Mark Atwood Lawrence's *Assuming the Burden,* which details how British, French, and American leaders came to identify Vietnam as a Cold War battleground in 1949–50. He considers it "a tragic moment when Western governments moved decisively toward forceful solutions that reduced complex social conflicts in many parts of the world to mere expressions of the confrontation between Western liberal capitalism and Soviet-led communism."[19] Elsewhere, Bradley provides a good summary of the current liberal-realist position: "Without question the Cold War provided the larger frame that shaped American involvement in Vietnam. . . . But if one accepts the premise that Vietnam was the wrong place to fight the larger Cold War battle (as I and I think many others do), you have to look elsewhere to understand the forces shaping American commitment and policy toward Vietnam."[20]

Not only has some form of the orthodox or critical view of the U.S. decision to intervene militarily in Vietnam in the name of containment persisted and been buttressed by new archival research; the American public's doubts about the war have also remained fairly consistent over the years. When presidents Kennedy and Johnson first increased the deployment of American ground- and airpower to Vietnam, members of the press, Congress, and the public generally accepted Washington's official Cold War explanations of the policy. By 1967, however, hundreds of thousands of Americans had served a tour of duty in Vietnam, thousands of tons of American bombs had rained down on Indochina, millions of dollars had been spent, and thousands of Americans and tens of thousands of Vietnamese had been killed or injured in the conflict. Americans grew increasingly skeptical of their government's explanation of how the survival of a weak and corrupt government in Saigon justified these high costs and the massive level of destruction. In early 1968, the DRV and the NLF surprised American military commanders with a military operation throughout South Vietnam known as the Tet Offensive. Although the attacks did not topple the Saigon government, as Hanoi had hoped, the ability of the Communists to launch the offensive after three years of pounding by American power persuaded many Americans that the drama in Vietnam was not worth the price of the ticket. Most historians of all types agree that the Tet Offensive was the point when American leaders began to respond to political pressure to find a way to end active U.S. participation in the war. The public sense that somehow the Vietnam War was "fundamentally wrong and immoral," which first gained broad acceptance following Tet, has continued to appear in public opinion polls. Although every president beginning with Nixon has asserted, as have the revisionist historians, that the American intervention in Vietnam was honorable and credible and was consistent

ARVN Radio repairmen at work. Courtesy of the Vietnam Archive, Texas Tech University, Douglas Pike Photograph Collection.

with American strategic and historic interests, one careful analysis of American public memory of the war has found that "a strong majority have long held, and continue to hold, that U.S. intervention represented not just an instrumental failure but a moral failure."[21]

Why and how the Nixon administration continued to wage the American war for four more years after the Tet Offensive before withdrawing the last U.S. forces have generated further historical debate over the meaning of the Vietnam experience and its meaning for present American policymaking. What has emerged is a curious dichotomy between the prevailing understanding among historians and the public, on one hand, and the revisionist historians and many policymakers, on the other, of the term *no more Vietnams*. The first group is instinctively wary of military intervention since the Vietnam War if the alignment of American interests and the local issues in a conflict are not perfectly clear, and the second group is determined to apply overwhelming American power in the name of American ideals in any case in which America decides its specific or general interests are at stake.

The historical debate over Nixon's actions that has continued the or-thodox/revisionist split over the policy lessons of the war comes from differing versions of what has come to be known as the *decent interval thesis:* the idea that the Nixon administration believed long before 1973 that the U.S. objective was not victory but the creation of a significant period between the U.S. military withdrawal and the inevitable collapse of the Saigon government. This decent interval presumably would pro-tect the credibility of U.S. foreign policy by separating American actions from the war's outcome. Nixon and Henry Kissinger, Nixon's national security adviser and principal foreign policy aide, have argued in their memoirs that they wore down the DRV through firm diplomacy backed by Vietnamization—the preparation of the RVN to defend itself—and the willingness to use American airpower and that they produced a "peace with honor" in Vietnam in 1973. Kissinger has insisted that the agree-ment signed in Paris "could have worked" and that "the agreement could have been maintained." "We sought not an interval before collapse," he declares in his account, "but lasting peace with honor." He concludes that, without Watergate, the congressional investigation that led to articles of impeachment against Nixon, and the resulting "collapse of executive au-thority," the United States "would have succeeded" in Vietnam.[22] Nixon and Kissinger charge that the DRV flagrantly violated the terms of the peace and that, in 1975, after Nixon had resigned his office, the blame is on Congress for not approving the financial aid that the RVN needed to survive the continuing aggression. "In the end, Vietnam was lost on the political front in the United States," Nixon wrote later, "not on the battle-field in Southeast Asia."[23] In concert with the revisionist historians, Nixon and Kissinger advanced the win thesis that the United States could have prevailed.

Other analysts view these claims of success differently. The intense secrecy of the Nixon White House makes it difficult for historians to know what Nixon and Kissinger really thought would be the outcome in Vietnam after America's departure, but it is clear that they began even as the treaty was being signed to try to avoid any appearance of American humiliation. They set out immediately "to make an American failure look like a success," in the words of Arnold Isaacs, "and thus preserve America's reputation elsewhere in the world."[24] More than a month before the sign-ing of the January 1973 agreement, Nixon ordered his chief of staff, H. R.

Haldeman, to begin an aggressive public relations campaign to portray the president as a peacemaker and the approaching diplomatic settlement as a success. In some tangible ways, the revisionist school of Vietnam War historiography was born in the Nixon White House.[25]

Despite claims by the president and his advisers that they had a strategy for victory in Vietnam, there is considerable evidence that, as early as the fall of 1969, the administration had an explicit decent interval strategy. After almost a year in office, Nixon and Kissinger were finding that they were getting no closer to a diplomatic and military victory than had Johnson and his aides and that the cost of the war in American lives and treasure continued to mount. They rejected out of hand the option of a unilateral U.S. withdrawal, which Kissinger said left two alternatives—escalation or Vietnamization. Planning began for a dramatic increase in U.S. bombing and other forms of military pressure on the DRV, coupled with a virtual ultimatum to Hanoi in an operation code-named Duck Hook. The administration gave up this escalation choice, however, because it understood that public and political opinion in the United States demanded lesser, not greater, American effort in Vietnam. In June, it had begun withdrawing U.S. troops from South Vietnam. It also knew that Saigon was not ready to assume its own defense and might never be. Nixon's policy had become, in Isaacs's words, "a sort of slow-motion defeat."[26]

On November 3, 1969, Nixon gave a major address—often referred to as his *silent majority speech* for its assertion that most Americans supported his policies—in which he heralded Vietnamization and did not issue a public threat or an ultimatum to the DRV. Jeffrey Kimball has argued that this speech began the decent interval strategy that defined American success in Vietnam as leaving a South Vietnamese government strong enough to defend itself. No longer was the U.S. objective to force Hanoi to recognize the southern regime and to cease its aggression against the RVN. Kissinger's notes in preparation for his 1971 secret meetings with Chinese leaders reveal that he would inform them that, "if the Vietnamese people themselves decide to change the present government, we shall accept it."[27] Larry Berman agrees that Nixon backed away from escalation in 1969 and touted Vietnamization for domestic political reasons, but he believes that the president would have reverted to escalation after the 1973 accords. Pierre Asselin finds that the Paris agreement served immediate political and strategic needs for both sides but that it was bound to fail and all the negotiators knew it.[28] Although Kimball, Berman, and Asselin present differing scenarios, all continue the liberal-realist thesis that there was no good solution for the United States in Vietnam. They reject Nixon's claim of peace with honor and his insistence that his policies would have been successful.

Despite evidence presented by Kimball and Berman that Nixon and Kissinger had little faith that Vietnamization was working and that the White House considered the concept a rhetorical device to justify to the American public continuing assistance to Saigon, Nixon and his successor, Gerald Ford, insisted that Vietnamization was producing a viable regime in South Vietnam. Asselin finds that Vietnamization was strengthening Saigon's forces, but not fast enough to accomplish its purposes. Nixon and Kissinger both blamed Congress for a lack of will to sustain Saigon financially after 1973 and for thereby contributing to the collapse of the RVN in 1975. Nixon's secretary of defense, Melvin Laird, an advocate of Vietnamization within the administration, reasserted the Congress-was-to-blame thesis in a 2005 article in *Foreign Affairs* that admonished the Bush administration to "stay the course" in Iraq and not lose the political will to continue. There is a preponderance of evidence, however, that in 1975 South Vietnam had a corrupt and poorly led government, rampant inflation, and a war-weary population and that U.S. support was all that had been giving the RVN life. T. Christopher Jespersen has described the Nixon and Ford administrations as having a "deliberate policy of denial" of the real conditions.[29]

As has long been the case, however, the revisionist rebuttal remains present, and not only in the memoirs of retired officials like Laird. The respected military historian Lewis Sorley has argued in his much-read book, *A Better War,* that the American leaders in Vietnam after 1968—Gen. Creighton Abrams, Ambassador Ellsworth Bunker, and the pacification director William Colby—made Vietnamization effective. They were approaching the Nixon goal of enabling the South Vietnamese to defend themselves, he contends, until the American political will to maintain the task in Vietnam finally ran out. Another equally reputable military historian, James H. Willbanks, has reviewed many of the same sources, however, and concluded that Vietnamization came too late and that the incredibly ineffective Thieu government in Saigon had no chance for victory and was able to survive only long enough to provide the decent interval that Washington had sought. Thus, the scholarly debate continues.[30]

If this dialogue were only some ivory-tower exchange among professors or confined to college seminar rooms, it would be interesting, but, in fact, it shaped national security policy in the real world in the first decade of the twenty-first century. The revisionist interpretations of the Vietnam War that lack of American success came from failed methods, not mistaken objectives, characterized the thinking of many U.S. leaders in the administration of George W. Bush. The president said that he had supported the containment rationale for U.S. policy and that "the essential lessons to be learned from the Vietnam War" were that "we had politicians making military decisions" and that presidents should set the goals and "allow the military to come up with the plans to achieve the objective."[31] Two of Bush's key advisers, Vice President Richard Cheney and Secretary of Defense Donald Rumsfeld, had been officials in the Nixon-Ford administrations. There is evidence from their careers in the three decades after the Vietnam War that the American defeat in Vietnam led them to a preoccupation with reestablishing and maintaining U.S. military power.[32] Faced with a global threat to U.S. security in the form of radical Islamic terrorism that recalled the Cold War–era threat from an armed and radical foe, these leaders led the United States into another military intervention in a regional political conflict to deter this global danger and defend American ideals.

Most historians, however, remain persuaded by the orthodox argument that American power failed in Vietnam because American purposes and interests were not accurately aligned with the historical conditions in Southeast Asia after World War II. As the historian Lloyd Gardner has written, in the Vietnam War "the victims were primarily the Vietnamese, and its victors were the Vietnamese. . . . The reality of Vietnam was as elusive to American policymakers as the enemy forces were to the men they sent to this hall of mirrors."[33] The logic of the liberal-realist view of the American war in Vietnam is that it could have and should have been avoided. Long before the American war in Iraq began, Herring reflected on the Vietnam War as an example of how intervention in the "poisonous tangle of local politics" can be complicated, costly, and not easily resolved. The policy history of the American experience in Vietnam offers no easy lessons, but it is a graphic caution. It stands, in Herring's view, "as an enduring testament to the pitfalls of interventionism and the limits of power."[34] Vietnam presented an instructive example of the tragic result when strategists fail to define the specific interests at stake, the real cost involved, and, thus, the reasonable form of any intervention in a violent regional conflict. There should be no more Vietnams.

Notes

1. "Interchange: Legacies of the Vietnam War," *Journal of American History* 93 (September 2006): 487–88.

2. Quoted in Katherine Kinney, *Friendly Fire: American Images of the Vietnam War* (New York: Oxford University Press, 2000), 3.

3. George McT. Kahin and John W. Lewis, *The United States in Vietnam*, rev. ed. (New York: Delta, 1969); Bernard B. Fall, *The Two Vietnams: A Political and Military Analysis*, 2nd ed. (New York: Praeger, 1967); Arthur M. Schlesinger Jr., *The Bitter Heritage: Vietnam and American Democracy, 1941–1966* (Boston: Houghton Mifflin, 1966); David Halberstam, *The Making of a Quagmire* (New York: Random House, 1964); Leslie Gelb and Richard K. Betts, *The Irony of Vietnam: The System Worked* (Washington, DC: Brookings Institution, 1979); Daniel Ellsberg, *Papers on the War* (New York: Simon & Schuster, 1972); Gabriel Kolko, *Anatomy of a War: Vietnam, the United States, and the Modern Historical Experience* (New York: Pantheon, 1985); Robert A. Divine, "Vietnam Reconsidered," *Diplomatic History* 12 (Winter 1988): 79–93.

4. Gary R. Hess, "The Unending Debate: Historians and the Vietnam War," *Diplomatic History* 18 (Spring 1994): 246; Robert J. McMahon, "U.S.-Vietnamese Relations: A Historiographical Survey," in *Pacific Passage: The Study of American–East Asian Relations on the Eve of the Twenty-First Century*, ed. Warren I. Cohen (New York: Columbia University Press, 1996), 316.

5. George C. Herring, *America's Longest War: The United States and Vietnam, 1950–1975*, 4th ed. (Boston: McGraw-Hill, 2002), 357–58. Compare George C. Herring, *America's Longest War: The United States and Vietnam, 1950–1975*, 1st ed. (New York: Wiley, 1979), 270–71.

6. Hess, "Unending Debate," 246.

7. Stanley Karnow, *Vietnam: A History* (New York: Penguin, 1983), 169; George McT. Kahin, *Intervention: How America Became Involved in Vietnam* (New York: Knopf, 1986), 126.

8. William J. Duiker, *U.S. Containment Policy and the Conflict in Indochina* (Stanford, CA: Stanford University Press, 1994), 2.

9. Robert D. Schulzinger, *A Time for War: The United States and Vietnam, 1941–1975* (New York: Oxford University Press, 1997), 329.

10. Guenter Lewy, *America in Vietnam* (New York: Oxford University Press, 1978), 426–28.

11. Harry G. Summers Jr., *On Strategy: A Critical Analysis of the Vietnam War* (Novato, CA: Presidio, 1982); Bruce Palmer Jr., *The 25-Year War: America's Military Role in Vietnam* (Lexington: University Press of Kentucky, 1984); Phillip B. Davidson, *Vietnam at War: The History, 1946–1975* (Novato, CA: Presidio, 1988); Shelby L. Stanton, *The Rise and Fall of an American Army: U.S. Ground Forces in Vietnam, 1965–1973* (San Rafael, CA: Presidio, 1985); Dave R. Palmer, *Summons of the Trumpet: US-Vietnam in Perspective* (San Rafael, CA: Presidio, 1978); William R. Westmoreland, *A Soldier Reports* (Garden City, NY: Doubleday, 1976); Ulysses S. Grant Sharp, *Strategy for Defeat* (San Rafael, CA: Presidio, 1978).

12. George C. Herring, "America and Vietnam: The Debate Continues," *American Historical Review* 92 (April 1987): 350–62; Gary R. Hess, "The Military Perspective on Strategy in Vietnam: Harry G. Summers's *On Strategy* and Bruce Palmer's *The 25-Year War*," *Diplomatic History* 10 (Winter 1986): 91–106; Jeffrey Kimball, "The Stab-in-the-Back Legend and the Vietnam War," *Armed Forces and Society* 14 (Spring 1988): 433–58.

13. Andrew F. Krepinevich Jr., *The Army and Vietnam* (Baltimore: Johns Hopkins University Press, 1986); Richard A. Hunt, *Pacification: The American Struggle for Vietnam's Hearts and Minds* (Boulder, CO: Westview, 1995); Robert W. Komer, *Bureaucracy at War: U.S. Performance in the Vietnam Conflict* (Boulder, CO: Westview, 1986); William E. Colby and James McCargar, *Lost Victory: A Firsthand Account of America's Sixteen-Year Involvement in Vietnam* (Chicago: Contemporary, 1989); Neil Sheehan, *A Bright Shining Lie: John Paul Vann and America in Vietnam* (New York: Random House, 1988).

14. Eric M. Bergerud, *The Dynamics of Defeat: The Vietnam War in Hau Nghia Province* (Boulder, CO: Westview, 1991); Frances FitzGerald, *Fire in the Lake: The Vietnamese and the Americans in Vietnam* (Boston: Little, Brown, 1972); Jeffrey Race, *War Comes to Long An: Revolutionary Conflict in a Vietnamese Province* (Berkeley: University of California Press, 1972); James W. Trullinger Jr., *Village at War: An Account of Revolution in Vietnam* (New York: Longman, 1980); Douglas Pike, *History of Vietnamese Communism, 1925–1976* (Stanford, CA: Stanford University Press, 1978); James P. Harrison, *The Endless War: Vietnam's Struggle for Independence* (New York: Free Press, 1982); David W. Elliott, *The Vietnamese War: Revolution and Social Change in the Mekong Delta, 1930–1975* (Armonk, NY: Sharpe, 2002); William J. Duiker, *Ho Chi Minh* (New York: Hyperion, 2000); Marc Jason Gilbert, introduction to *Why the North Won the Vietnam War*, ed. Marc Jason Gilbert (New York: Palgrave, 2002), 1–45.

15. Hess, "Unending Debate," 243–46.

16. Norman Podhoretz, *Why We Were in Vietnam* (New York: Simon & Schuster, 1983); Timothy J. Lomperis, *From People's War to People's Rule: Insurgency, Intervention, and the Lessons of Vietnam* (Chapel Hill: University of North Carolina Press, 1996); R. B. Smith, *An International History of the Vietnam War*, 3 vols. (New York: St. Martin's, 1984–90); Ellen J. Hammer, *A Death in November: America in Vietnam,*

1963 (New York: Dutton, 1987); Patrick L. Hatcher, *The Suicide of an Elite: American Internationalists and Vietnam* (Stanford, CA: Stanford University Press, 1990).

17. Michael Lind, *Vietnam, the Necessary War: A Reinterpretation of America's Most Disastrous Military Conflict* (New York: Free Press, 1999), 256.

18. Mark Philip Bradley, *Imagining Vietnam and America: The Making of Postcolonial Vietnam, 1919–1950* (Chapel Hill: University of North Carolina Press, 2000), 8.

19. Mark Atwood Lawrence, *Assuming the Burden: Europe and the American Commitment to War in Vietnam* (Berkeley and Los Angeles: University of California Press, 2005), 282.

20. "Interchange: Legacies of the Vietnam War," 472.

21. Robert McMahon, "Contested Memory: The Vietnam War and American Society, 1975–2001," *Diplomatic History* 26 (Spring 2002): 175.

22. Henry Kissinger, *White House Years* (Boston: Little, Brown, 1979), 1470.

23. Richard Nixon, *No More Vietnams* (New York: Arbor, 1985), 15.

24. Arnold Isaacs, *Without Honor: Defeat in Vietnam and Cambodia* (New York: Vintage, 1984), 498.

25. Jeffrey Kimball, *Nixon's Vietnam War* (Lawrence: University Press of Kansas, 1998), 368.

26. Isaacs, *Without Honor,* 491–92. See also Kissinger, *White House Years,* 288.

27. Jeffrey Kimball, *The Vietnam War Files: Uncovering the Secret History of Nixon-Era Strategy* (Lawrence: University Press of Kansas, 2004), 24–28, 106, 187.

28. Larry Berman, *No Peace, No Honor: Nixon, Kissinger, and Betrayal in Vietnam* (New York: Free Press, 2001), 57, 204; Pierre Asselin, *A Bitter Peace: Washington, Hanoi, and the Making of the Paris Agreement* (Chapel Hill: University of North Carolina Press, 2002), 178–80.

29. T. Christopher Jespersen, "Kissinger, Ford, and Congress: The Very Bitter End in Vietnam," *Pacific Historical Review* 71 (August 2002): 439. See also Gary R. Hess, *Vietnam and the United States: Origins and Legacy of War* (Boston: Twayne, 1990), 136–38; Marc Jason Gilbert, "The Cost of Losing the 'Other War' in Vietnam," in *Why the North Won the Vietnam War,* ed. Gilbert, 187–88; Melvin Laird, "Iraq: Learning the Lessons of Vietnam," *Foreign Affairs* (November/December 2005): 22–43; and Asselin, *A Bitter Peace,* 120, 169.

30. Lewis Sorley, *A Better War: The Unexamined Victories and Final Tragedy of America's Last Years in Vietnam* (San Diego, CA: Harcourt, 1999); James H. Willbanks, *Abandoning Vietnam: How America Left and South Vietnam Lost Its War* (Lawrence: University Press of Kansas, 2004). For comments by historians such as David Elliott and William Turley who are critical of the Sorley thesis, see Matt Steinglass, "Vietnam and Victory," *Boston Globe,* December 18, 2005.

31. Bush quoted in David L. Anderson, "One Vietnam War Should Be Enough and Other Reflections on Diplomatic History and the Making of Foreign Policy," *Diplomatic History* 30 (January 2006): 8.

32. James Mann, *Rise of the Vulcans: The History of Bush's War Cabinet* (New

York: Viking, 2004), 52; Marilyn B. Young, "Still Stuck in the Big Muddy," in *Cold War Triumphalism: The Misuse of History after the Fall of Communism,* ed. Ellen Schrecker (New York: New Press, 2004), 262–73.

33. Lloyd Gardner, "Hall of Mirrors," in *Why the North Won the Vietnam War,* ed. Gilbert, 240. See also David L. Anderson, *The Vietnam War* (Basingstoke: Palgrave Macmillan, 2005), 123–28.

34. Herring, *America's Longest War* (4th ed.), 358.

2

The United States and Vietnam

The Enemies

Walter LaFeber

In U.S. foreign relations, future deadly enemies have often initially appeared as people hoping to be friends. Japan was a valued informal American ally during the 1890s, but a half century later the two nations fought a bloody four-year war. At the end of World War II, the defeated Japanese withdrew from the empire they had seized by force in Southeast Asia. In 1944 and early 1945, President Franklin D. Roosevelt briefly believed that it was important to make friends with, and provide at least a modified independence for, Indochina—the French colonial possession in Southeast Asia that included Vietnam, along with Cambodia and Laos. Roosevelt thought the days of European colonial mastery were over. France, devastated by war, was too weak and the Vietnamese (inspired by the Japanese defeat of the French in 1940–41) overly ambitious to be independent. But between February and April 1945, the last three months of his life, Roosevelt bent both to French pressure and to his own growing belief that Indochina was in no way prepared for even a qualified independence. He finally allowed Great Britain and France, the two colonial powers, to invade Indochina so the French could replace the defeated Japanese.[1]

The pattern of beginning as a friend and ending as an enemy then began to play out in Vietnam. The leader of that country's anticolonial struggle, Ho Chi Minh, refused to take Roosevelt's no for an answer. In late 1945, Ho appealed directly to the United States for help. He quoted from Thomas Jefferson's Declaration of Independence, applauded the possibility of U.S.-Vietnamese cooperation, and later emphasized the need of his people for profitable commerce with and investment from Americans—an interesting emphasis given that he was widely thought to be a Communist. Roosevelt's successor, President Harry S Truman, nevertheless ignored Ho. During those rare moments when Truman and his advisers thought about Vietnam at all, they flatly rejected any idea about the country's independence. As George Herring has noted in his distinguished analysis of overall U.S.-Vietnam relations, Washington officials hoped that France, an ally in the budding Cold War, would be able to recover its colonial hold and milk Vietnam's wealth (notably in food products and rubber plantations). The French would then be in a position to help beat communism back from Western and Central Europe.[2]

The First Phase: 1945–1950

During 1945, Ho Chi Minh's Vietnam thus became an enemy in the eyes of U.S. leaders, not because it was affiliated with the Soviet Union (it was not), or because it was allied with China (which did not become Communist for another four years), but because these officials were willing to turn their eyes while the French tried to regain colonial control. Nor were Truman and his advisers at all interested in working with a Communist such as Ho. He might invite Americans to help rebuild his country, but Communists were known for their state-controlled economies, not U.S.-style capitalism. Truman and other U.S. leaders in government and business were convinced that attempts in the 1930s by states (notably Germany and the Soviet Union) to control their economies had worsened the Depression, led to economic warfare between nations, and, finally, climaxed in all-out war during 1939–41. The horrors of the 1930s, including the astronomical 25 percent unemployment rate in the United States, had stamped themselves on the minds of that generation of Americans much as the bloody terrorism of September 11, 2001, shaped later generations of Americans.

In late 1946, shooting erupted between Ho's soldiers and French military forces. A nearly thirty-year-long struggle began. Ho continued in 1947 to plead for U.S. help. In March 1947, Truman gave an answer without mentioning Indochina or even the Soviet Union. Speaking at Baylor

University, the president emphasized that "major decisions" about international trade and investment had to be "made, not by governments, but by private buyers and sellers, under conditions of active competition." Then he declared, "We must not go through the Thirties again." Truman told his university audience, "There is one thing that Americans value more than peace. It is freedom. Freedom of worship—freedom of speech—freedom of enterprise." "It must be true," he observed, "that the first two of these freedoms are related to the third." In other words, the enemy of freedom of worship and freedom of speech was any state-directed economy.[3]

The Baylor speech provided the economic side for the more famous Truman Doctrine address delivered to Congress six days later. In that landmark address of March 12, 1947, the president officially declared cold war on communism by saying that the world was divided simply between "free peoples" and governments resting on "terror and oppression." Americans, Truman believed, now had to spend vast amounts of money and make military commitments to defeat such oppressive governments—which, of course, had state-directed economies, as he had warned the Baylor audience the week before.[4]

Ho Chi Minh might be offering economic olive branches to gain Washington's support, but, in the eyes of U.S. officials, he was "Moscow-directed," as the State Department concluded. In truth, Ho was not "Moscow-directed." He had clashed with the Soviet dictator Josef Stalin as early as the 1920s and 1930s, and, since then, their relationship had not much improved. Ho's *Communist* label, however, was a sufficient reason to be wary in the minds of top Washington officials. They knew little about Ho and apparently less about his disputes with Stalin, but they knew enough that they were committed to supporting the French effort to regain colonial control over Vietnam.

Between 1945 and 1948, Stalin demonstrated little interest in Ho. The Soviet dictator mistrusted any Communist not under his direct control. He hoped most of all, moreover, to win victories in Europe, especially in France, where one of the largest Communist parties made a move for power. To support Ho just as he was beginning to kill Frenchmen in his anticolonial war would win few friends for Stalin in France. By 1948, however, the French Communist Party began to suffer defeats. That year, Stalin indicated his approval of Ho's battle against France. But, ever cautious, the Soviet dictator did not formally recognize the Vietnamese government until January 1950—that is, until he was forced to do so because Ho had begun a worldwide campaign to open diplomatic relations with any nation that would deal with him.

The Soviets, and now the Communist Chinese (who had seized power in the autumn of 1949 after their own thirty-year struggle), concluded that they had to recognize their comrade in Vietnam. They did so not only for the sake of supposed Communist solidarity but also for the real reason that the young Cold War was evolving into a new, highly dangerous adolescent phase in 1950, a phase that required increased cooperation and support. The first phase of American confrontation with enemies in Southeast Asia had run from 1945 to early 1950. It was marked by Vietnamese appeals for American help and, after February 1945, Washington's consistent refusals. The second stage of the confrontation began in 1950 and lasted until the mid-1960s.

The Second Phase: 1950–1966

This second phase was triggered by Truman's decision in 1950 to send, for the first time, U.S. military advisers to work with the faltering French effort in Vietnam. American soldiers would not leave for twenty-five years. The president's historic decision, however, emerged not primarily because of events in Vietnam but because of dangerous changes elsewhere.

During August 1949, the Soviets successfully tested their first atomic bomb. Surprised Americans no longer monopolized the ultimate weapon. At the same time, China fell to Mao Zedong's Communist forces. Much of Asia, including Vietnam, seemed threatened by a new, triumphant communism. In February 1950, the two Communist giants signed an alliance, although it emerged only after weeks of bitter bargaining between Stalin and Mao. On June 25, 1950, North Korean Communist forces invaded South Korea and nearly drove the southerners into the sea before Truman sent U.S. ground, sea, and air forces to stop the Communist advance. By late summer, the Americans and South Koreans made up most of a large force fighting under the UN banner. When they finally drove back the North Koreans and, in September–October, began to approach the Chinese boundary, Mao's government warned them that it would not tolerate their presence there. The U.S.-directed advance nevertheless continued.

North Vietnamese premier Pham Van Dong shakes hands with China's Mao Zedong. Courtesy of the Vietnam Archive, Texas Tech University, Douglas Pike Photograph Collection.

China then unleashed hundreds of thousands of troops, who in a late 1950 offensive killed thousands of American soldiers and their South Korean allies.

The Cold War had turned into a hot war between the United States and China. After somewhat cooling off with a Korean armistice in 1953, the conflict simmered down to a bitter cold war for more than a decade. It was a conflict in which the enemies of the United States were now well identified. Truman began a major military buildup to quadruple the U.S. defense budget (from $13 billion in early 1950 to over $50 billion in 1952). He also committed U.S. troops for the first time since 1945 to defend Europe and even moved to rearm the Germans.

As a part of this sudden buildup, Truman dispatched military advisers to help France in Vietnam. He also guaranteed Paris officials that he would send the needed dollars to help the nearly bankrupt French fight

Ho Chi Minh. By 1954, the United States was paying for about 80 percent of the French effort to recolonize Vietnam. U.S. leaders believed that they had little choice. Without American money, not just Ho but his allies in Beijing and Moscow would gain a triumph, while the French would suffer a historic defeat just as Truman needed their help to fight Soviet pressures in Europe. Vietnam had become not an isolated problem but a crisis that, Truman believed, he and the French had to win if they hoped to contain communism in Asia and Soviet expansion in Europe. American enemies in Vietnam were enemies elsewhere in Asia and Europe. In that sense, the war in the small country had global significance—and U.S. officials continued to believe that it did well into the 1960s.

The president committed the United States to the struggle in Vietnam for another reason of central importance. It was explained in October 1950 by John Foster Dulles, an influential international lawyer and diplomat whom Truman had appointed earlier that year to handle Asian problems. Dulles privately told an elite New York audience that the key U.S. ally in Asia was Japan. The Japanese might have been mortal enemies five years before, but now only they had the industrial capacity and military potential in Asia needed to counter and contain China. Japan, however, required both vast amounts of raw materials and large markets for its products. Historically, Dulles emphasized, the Japanese had found these materials and markets in two areas: Southeast Asia (where Japan had tried to establish control in the 1930s) and China, which was now Communist. If Japan and China became economically linked, then, Dulles implied, the United States could lose all of Asia. The obvious solution was for the Japanese to return to Southeast Asia for their raw materials and markets. This meant that the Vietnamese must not be allowed to turn Communist.[5]

Before 1950, Ho was, thus, viewed as an American enemy because he warred against a major U.S. ally, France, and because he headed a Communist, state-directed economy. After 1950, he was viewed as an enemy because—especially given his links to Communist China—if he triumphed, the Vietnamese and the Chinese could shut off most of Asia on which Japan (and the United States) depended for survival as capitalist nations.

All this was spelled out in President Dwight D. Eisenhower's remarkable press conference of April 1954. By then, the United States had sent hundreds of military advisers and billions of dollars to help the French, but Ho's forces nevertheless dealt France a devastating series of defeats. Paris officials, and some Americans, asked Eisenhower to intervene militarily—perhaps, they suggested, with nuclear weapons if necessary—to save the French. The president ruled out major U.S. military intervention, but he and John Foster Dulles, now Eisenhower's secretary of state, intended, once the French got out, to take over the anti-Ho war themselves. In the April press conference, Eisenhower for the first time elaborated on the soon-to-be-famous domino theory to explain why Ho and his supporters in Beijing and Moscow could not be allowed to capture Vietnam.

"You have a row of dominoes set up, you knock over the first one, and what will happen to the last one is a certainty that it will go over very rapidly," Eisenhower began. If the first domino were Vietnam, the dominoes of Taiwan and the Philippines would next topple over to communism. The fall of all these dominoes would, the president explained, take "away, in its economic aspects, the region that Japan must have as a trading area," leaving Japan with "only one place to go—that is, toward the Communist areas in order to live." So, if all the dominoes fell, down to the last one of Japan, Eisenhower concluded, the "possible consequences of the loss are just incalculable to the free world."[6]

A few months later in 1954, China, the Soviet Union, France, and the Vietnamese were the pivotal players at the Geneva Conference, which divided Vietnam between a Communist north and a capitalist south. The division, the participants understood, was to be only temporary, with elections to be held in the next two years. Eisenhower privately admitted that Ho would probably be triumphant in any election. For that reason, the United States never allowed the nationwide elections to be held. It instead brought in a Vietnamese leader who had been living in the United States, Ngo Dinh Diem. As a Roman Catholic, Diem represented only 10 percent of South Vietnam's people. The other 90 percent were mostly Buddhists, and, by the 1960s, they would be viewed as enemies by Diem and his U.S. supporters because Buddhist leaders were discussing stopping the military escalation and negotiating with Ho in the North.[7]

But that day lay in the distant future. Stalin had died in 1953. Nikita Khrushchev was now the Soviet leader. A tough, often primitive man, the new leader sensed a major, indeed, historic, turn in world affairs during the mid-1950s. It was a turn in which the so-called Third World (Asia,

Latin America, Africa) was emerging from decades of colonialism or, in Latin America, from a half century of Washington's control, control often exercised by the U.S. military. A Cold War competition between Communists and capitalists was emerging that centered on these newly emerging nations, many of which held considerable mineral wealth, including oil.

Khrushchev criticized Stalin (after, of course, the dictator was safely dead) for having little interest in the Third World. Even in Vietnam, where Ho was winning, Stalin had provided virtually no help between 1949 and 1953, except for some quiet cheering.[8] The new leader intended to pursue the emerging nations, use their trade to build the Soviet economy, and overtake the United States within a generation or two. At the 1954 Geneva Conference, however, the Soviets and the Chinese had both put tremendous pressure on Ho to stop fighting the French and accept a divided Vietnam, even though he now appeared the clear military victor. The Soviets certainly considered Vietnam less important than Europe, where they hoped to work with the French for the all-important purpose of stopping the U.S.-directed rearming of Germany. The Chinese, recovering from three decades of civil war and the Korean bloodbath, wanted Ho to do nothing that might lead to U.S. intervention and another Sino-American war (such as insisting on a united, Communist Vietnam). Essentially deserted by his two most important friends, Ho accepted the deal of a Vietnam divided between north and south in the hope that he could unify his country through the promised elections.

When the Americans blocked the elections, Ho backed off in the late 1950s to reconsider his position, while the Soviets and the Chinese, distracted by crises elsewhere, did little to help him. Khrushchev was making a major play for other newly emerging nations, especially in Africa and in Cuba, with its new revolutionary government led by Fidel Castro. Mao was immersed in trying to develop China while keeping it properly revolutionary.

Diem, the U.S. transplant in South Vietnam, then forced the issue. Using a series of repressive laws, he stopped most reform, notably the all-important land reform, and threatened dissenters, especially Communists who had remained in the South, with violence, even beheading. He created growing opposition to his own regime. For his part, Ho encouraged southerners to rebel against Diem, but he did so carefully. He rightly feared that the United States might intervene massively and possibly take the war from the South to the North. Because of this same fear, Russian and Chinese leaders urged Ho and Communist elements in the South to act with the greatest care.[9]

The anti-Diem (and anti-U.S.) rebellion spread in South Vietnam between 1959 and 1963 with little direct help from Russia or China. On January 6, 1961, Khrushchev did give a widely noted speech in which he fully supported so-called wars of liberation, that is, revolts such as those in Cuba, Africa, and Vietnam waged against Western powers. Whether he intended to send necessary aid and advisers to help advance these wars was left vague.

Two weeks later, John F. Kennedy took the oath to become president of the United States, and moments later, in his inaugural address, he issued an urgent call for Americans to fight the Cold War. Over the next thirty-four months, behind his charismatic good looks and Hollywood-style glamour, the president tried to intensify the U.S. military and economic commitments to Europe, Latin America, Africa, and South Vietnam far beyond anything Eisenhower had done. In South Vietnam, he quietly broke the 1954 Geneva Conference's limit of six hundred U.S. advisers. In the autumn of 1961, he sent his most trusted military adviser, Gen. Maxwell Taylor, to survey the Vietnamese situation. Taylor's recommendations of November 1 defined the enemies—and also the U.S. misconceptions. North Vietnam, the general reported, "is extremely vulnerable to conventional bombing," while "Chicoms [Chinese Communists] would face severe logistical difficulties" if they attempted to intervene to help Ho.[10]

By the time Kennedy was assassinated in November 1963, some sixteen thousand U.S. "advisers" were in South Vietnam, yet Diem's government had continued to weaken before the insurgency. Diem suffered a body blow in mid-1963 when several Buddhists gained worldwide attention by burning themselves to death before news photographers in protest against his policies. Kennedy decided to move. U.S. officials gave the green light to South Vietnamese military leaders who wanted to overthrow Diem. In early November, Diem and his brother were captured, then, to the surprise of some U.S. officials, shot. Three weeks later, Kennedy was killed in Dallas.

Throughout his presidency, Kennedy had understood that the South Vietnamese, with Ho's support from the North, were challenging Diem but that, especially in 1961–62, they had encouragement, although not much material help, from the Soviets and Chinese as well. When neighboring Laos began to wobble dangerously (largely because the North Vietnamese increasingly used the supposedly neutral country as a protected supply route into South Vietnam), Kennedy finally pushed for an agreement to reinforce its neutrality and have all sides pull back. The Soviets and Chinese agreed. Within months, the deal began to break down because of North Vietnamese and U.S. covert activities in Laos, but it seemed that Washington, Beijing, and Moscow were at least willing to try to limit the spreading Vietnamese conflagration.

In October 1962 came the ultimate test when Khrushchev and Castro tried secretly to place in Cuba a number of Soviet missiles capable of striking the eastern United States. In the most dangerous crisis of the Cold War, Kennedy and Khrushchev (not Castro) finally agreed that the Russian missiles would be removed and the United States would promise not to invade Cuba. Qualifications were attached by both sides, but world (and especially American) opinion concluded that the Soviets had lost in the confrontation and had decided to act more moderately, even in the newly emerging nations.[11]

Kennedy believed that the Soviet retreat had directly and dramatically defined who the enemy was in Vietnam and, indeed, in the new Cold War, which was increasingly focusing on the Third World. He spelled out his views in mid-1963 while talking with André Malraux, a distinguished author who served French president Charles de Gaulle as cultural affairs minister. Having learned the bitter lessons of his nation's defeat in Vietnam, de Gaulle was critical of Kennedy's military escalation. Now the American tried to win over the French leader by redefining the enemy. There was "no reason why there should be differences between us and France in Europe," Kennedy began, because, owing to the results of the Cuban missile crisis, "there was no longer a likely Soviet military threat." The great problem now was China, especially in the near future, when it would become a nuclear power. (China exploded its first nuclear weapon the next year, 1964.) "This was the great menace to the future, to humanity, the free world, and freedom on earth." Even the threat of taking military action might not deter China, the president continued, "because the Chinese would be perfectly prepared, because of the lower value they attach to human life, to sacrifice hundreds of millions of their own lives,

Vietnamese and Russian leaders sign the Vietnam-Soviet Friendship and Co-Operation Plan for 1971. Courtesy of the Vietnam Archive, Texas Tech University, Douglas Pike Photograph Collection.

if this were necessary in order to carry out their militant and aggressive policies."[12]

Kennedy's lecture did little good. Many Americans were now viewing de Gaulle as an enemy both in Europe, where he pulled France out of the U.S.-directed NATO alliance, and in Vietnam, a country with which he would have nothing to do. The French leader was determined to maintain his country's freedom of action, especially because he believed that the Americans wanted to drag France down a dead-end road. When in early 1964 he extended formal diplomatic recognition to the Chinese, Secretary of State Dean Rusk bitterly complained that it would give China the "idea that militancy pays dividends." Unmoved, de Gaulle was convinced that the United States had, indeed, hit a dead-end in Vietnam.[13]

Few U.S. presidents have viewed their foreign enemies as so dangerous and unrestrained as Kennedy viewed China. A year earlier, China and India had fought a brief but bloody battle over a boundary dispute. Much of the world believed that India had been the aggressor, but U.S. officials blamed the Chinese, who emerged victorious from the encounter. These officials also drew the false conclusion that China had finally retreated after the United States began to mobilize its forces in the Indian Ocean region. Now, in 1963, Kennedy, along with many of his top advisers, especially Secretary of State Rusk, feared that the Chinese, unlike the chastened Soviets, were willing to sacrifice hundreds of millions of their own people to achieve their "aggressive policies."[14] But, given the Indian experience, China might reconsider if faced again with American force.

With Diem's death in November 1963, the South Vietnamese government became dangerously unstable, and the military conflict escalated. By late 1964–early 1965, President Lyndon Johnson's administration believed that it had to increase U.S. involvement rapidly before the South either collapsed or sought peace talks with the North. LBJ dismissed as inconsequential antiwar movements, especially on American campuses. He was, instead, wary of right-wing, militaristic Cold Warriors who were powerful in Congress and the business community. Or, as he privately phrased it in defining his domestic enemies: "I don't give a damn about the pinkos on the campuses; they're just waving their diapers and bellyaching because they don't want to fight." Instead, he went on, "the great black beast for us is the right wing. If we don't get the war over soon they'll put enormous heat on us to turn it into an Armageddon and wreck all our other programs."[15] So in 1964–65 he spiraled the American troop numbers in Vietnam upward past 100,000, then the quarter-million mark, as China intensified its own involvement in the North.

The Chinese did so to support Ho's forces, but also to warn Johnson not to try to invade the North and move to the Chinese border—the grave error that Harry Truman had made in the Korean conflict. As Johnson escalated American involvement and landed more troops, Mao sent more of his soldiers to build highways and other infrastructure decimated by American bombing and to strengthen defensive positions in the North. By the end of 1965, China had increased delivery of guns and artillery to Ho's forces by nearly three times over the deliveries of 1964. The Chinese soon sent so much that the North's trade and transportation systems, as well as its warehouses, were swamped with military goods.[16]

Throughout these months, Beijing officials made clear that they wanted to avoid war with the United States. They funneled this message to Washington through European and African officials who talked with President Johnson. In mid-1965, Chinese foreign minister Chen Yi sent word that "China will not provoke war with the United States" but that "if the United States bombs China that would mean war and there would be no limits to the war."[17] As a U.S. senator during the Korean War, Johnson had learned the hard way that such Chinese warnings should be taken seriously. China's massive help to Ho, and its willingness to place initially more than fifty thousand of its own troops in North Vietnam, was a—probably *the*—major deterrent to U.S. officials who otherwise would have had little compunction about using maximum American pressure, even possibly an invasion, to destroy North Vietnam.

When, over the next forty years, critics condemned Johnson, and, later, President Richard Nixon, for not winning militarily in Vietnam, they too often overlooked that such an all-out victory could have required fighting the massive numbers of Chinese forces who were stationed in the North through most of the 1960s. The conflict in Korea, moreover, had led to an intense twenty-year cold war between the United States and China. A similar confrontation in North Vietnam not only would have been disastrously expensive in lives and money for both sides but also could have forced the ditching of the U.S.-Chinese diplomatic—and economic—relations, which took off in the 1970s.

The Soviets also gave North Vietnam massive aid; indeed, after the mid-1960s they became Ho's most important ally. But the Russians and the Chinese were increasingly competing against each other in North Vietnam. By the time Johnson became president, it was clear to all that the 1950 Soviet-Chinese alliance had disintegrated. Problems were apparent as early as the late 1950s, when Khrushchev pulled back from helping Mao develop nuclear weapons. His willingness to make deals in such pivotal areas as Germany and the Cuban missile crisis led Beijing officials to accuse him of selling out to what they termed the American *paper tiger*.

In late 1964, Khrushchev was overthrown by a group led by Alexei Kosygin and Leonid Brezhnev. The major reasons for his downfall were domestic issues (particularly early signs of the declines in food and industrial production that would help bring down the Soviet Union twenty-seven years later). Moscow leaders were also critical of some of Khrushchev's foreign policies, including the wide perception of his embarrassment in the Cuban missile crisis. The new leaders continued to negotiate with the United States, but they meanwhile intensified their aid program to North Vietnam—to help Ho Chi Minh while at the same time trying to neutralize China's influence. Vietnam became an arena not only for the great struggle between Ho Chi Minh and Lyndon Johnson but also for the less intense struggle between Mao and Brezhnev/Kosygin. The North Vietnamese exploited this growing animosity to demand the most help they could get from both the Chinese and the Russians. Lyndon Johnson and his advisers, however, could never figure out how to turn the growing Soviet-Chinese split to their advantage in Vietnam.

As Kennedy had told the French, the United States understood the divisions between the Communist powers, and Washington centered its attention on China's plans. In early 1965, however, Soviet premier Kosygin was visiting North Vietnam when U.S. officials decided to respond to a Communist attack on an American base in South Vietnam by bombing the North. Kosygin escaped, but he damned the attack as "a personal insult" and swore publicly that more Russian aid would reach Vietnam. At the same time, he moved to neutralize China's influence. A quick way to accomplish that would be to get the United States out of Vietnam as soon as possible.[18]

The Soviets took the initiative in 1965 to find a negotiated conclusion to the war. The problem was that the U.S. ally in the South was so weak, divided, and corrupt that Johnson knew a U.S. withdrawal would mean a Communist triumph. In the United States, such a result would both damn Johnson as a president who lost a war and, more immediately, cripple the chances for passing and implementing his domestic Great Society programs (which pledged massive help to minorities, the elderly, and education). Johnson rightly feared that, in the end, he might have to give up "the woman I really loved [the Great Society agenda]" for "that bitch of a war on the other side of the world." He continued to send troops, and the body bags of American dead increasingly came back, as the Russians and the Chinese poured in aid to help Communist Vietnamese forces.[19]

The Third Phase: 1965–1975

In the mid-1960s, the third and final phase of American involvement in Southeast Asia began as the United States tried to deal with its various enemies in Vietnam. Throughout the early years of this last phase, which ran from 1965 to 1975 (the year when, after nearly all the American soldiers had been brought home, the South Vietnamese government collapsed), China continued to help the North, sometimes massively. In

1967, Chinese troops in the North reached their peak numbers, 170,000. They helped rebuild bombed railroads and bridges. But, when they tried to help the Vietnamese more personally, such as offering medical aid, they were rejected. More than a thousand years of Vietnam's mistrust and hatred of the Chinese could not be shunted aside.[20] The growing mistrust combined with severe internal Chinese problems to produce a reduction in Chinese aid. Then, in 1968, Ho accepted Johnson's offer to begin negotiations in Paris. The Chinese bitterly objected; they wanted the war to continue to take American lives and soak up U.S. dollars. Beijing became sufficiently angry about the Paris talks that all Chinese troops were finally withdrawn from North Vietnam. The Soviets became the North's main ally and supplier.[21]

The American enemies thus had flip-flopped: the Soviets, whom Kennedy believed had learned their lesson and would be cooperative, now in the late 1960s fueled North Vietnam's military with large amounts of food and war materiel, while the Chinese, so despised by Americans since 1949–50, began pulling out of North Vietnam and vigorously opposed what Beijing liked to call Soviet *hegemonism,* that is, imperialism. The United States had gone into Vietnam in large part to prevent the expansion of Chinese Communist influence in Asia. By 1967–68, the U.S. commitment had to find a new purpose.

The United States, not China, tentatively opened this third phase. In late 1963, Johnson's new administration had publicly hinted at the possibility of coexisting with both China and Taiwan, where the pre-1949 Chinese leaders had taken over the government. Mao Zedong never bothered to pick up this initiative. In part, this was due to the refusal of any Chinese Communist leader even to consider the possibility that Taiwan was to be anything but a formal part of China; it certainly was not to remain as an independent nation tied to the United States. By 1965–66, moreover, Mao was consumed with a passion for reinvigorating his Chinese revolution. This passion resulted, for example, in sending important, and vitally needed, professionals and intellectuals to pull weeds and pick crops in fields while inexperienced, naive younger people, more revolutionary than knowledgeable, made crucial economic and political decisions. In this so-called Great Proletarian Cultural Revolution, China's development, especially its industrialization, was crippled and set back many years. The chaos was indicated years later when a young Chinese army officer revealed how he and several fellow officers decided to cap the Cultural Revolution by seizing Hong Kong, the rich, well-defended colony on China's coast controlled by the British for 125 years. After perhaps too much drinking, the young officers took off in several trucks to liberate the city. They were stopped only after one officer's father, a senior Chinese general, discovered the lunacy and dispatched a guard to stop the "invasion." Between 1966 and 1968, China was immersed in the Cultural Revolution, while the Soviets became more aggressive in the Third World.

The United States was trapped in one of those Soviet targets, Vietnam. By 1967, however, the U.S. effort seemed to be going better, if at great human cost. President Johnson planned to use this turn both to be reelected in 1968 and to resolve a range of problems with the Soviets at a summit conference with the new Brezhnev/Kosygin leadership. His hopes collapsed under two sudden blows in 1968.

The first occurred in late January when Ho launched a Tet (Lunar New Year) offensive. The North Vietnamese suffered enormous casualties, but they penetrated the U.S. embassy in South Vietnam and forced Johnson, along with many influential Americans, to conclude that the war was not being won despite the 500,000 U.S. troops. As the antiwar movement intensified and LBJ suffered a surprising setback in the New Hampshire Democratic primary, the worn-out president dramatically announced that he would not run for reelection. The second blow came in August. Faced with a Communist Czechoslovakia that seemed slowly to be freeing itself of Soviet-style government, the Russians suddenly invaded and reimposed strict controls. The Brezhnev Doctrine was announced: the Soviets had the right to use force to save another "socialist" nation from "world imperialism."[22] Trapped in the quicksand of Vietnam, Johnson could do little but cancel his summit with Brezhnev scheduled for later that year.

By then, Mao was calling a halt to the growing calamity of the Cultural Revolution and preparing for possible conflict with Russia. As blood was spilled along the Sino-Russian border in 1969, the world tensed for whatever was to occur next between the nuclear-armed Communist giants. Negotiations finally eased the crisis but did little to bridge the widening gap between the two. The Chinese continued to aid North Vietnam, but Ho, who had defied centuries of Vietnamese hatred of

China to work with and exploit the Chinese after 1954, died in 1969. With him went another strong link between Hanoi and Beijing.

As the two Communist powers approached the brink of war, Richard Nixon entered the White House. A California Republican who, like most Republicans and many Democrats, had become known for ardent anticommunism (especially his damnation of the Chinese while he was vice president from 1953 to 1961), Nixon seemed a highly unlikely person to devise a new, historic relationship with either China or the Soviet Union. In 1967, however, as he geared up for his presidential run, he indicated publicly, if cautiously, that it was time to rethink the twenty-year U.S.-China enmity. By 1969, he had decided to pull U.S. troops out of Vietnam slowly and to turn the conflict over to a newly armed South Vietnamese military. He hoped that a more cooperative China would help him escape the morass safely as well as perhaps work with him against the Soviets.

The president sent several signals indicating his desire to open a new relationship with China, including reducing the U.S. naval presence protecting Taiwan against possible Chinese invasion. Mao made little response until 1970, when he agreed to talks between the U.S. and Chinese ambassadors to Poland. The conversations did nothing to reduce the violence in Vietnam; Nixon even expanded the war by launching an attack into Cambodia to try to cut the North Vietnamese supply route into the South. His invasion did little good.

By the end of the year, Nixon said flatly, "We must have relations with Communist China." In 1971, he declared that China should be allowed to belong to the United Nations, although he wanted it seated alongside, and not replacing, Taiwan. Mao flatly rejected any "two-China" approach. Over the following months, Nixon retreated. He agreed to allow the People's Republic of China not only to replace the Republic of China (Taiwan) but also to assume its powerful veto power as one of the five permanent members of the UN Security Council. In 1972, the president took his historic trip to China.[23] He later made a similar visit to Moscow, a signal that he hoped to play the Chinese off against the Russians. In his talks with Brezhnev, progress was made to control the arms race and open some trade channels, but on Vietnam nothing could be agreed.

When the new North Vietnamese leadership launched a major offensive in 1972 on the eve of his trip to Moscow, Nixon launched the heaviest U.S. bombing of the war—and American planes had already released more tons of bombs on Vietnam than they had over Germany or Japan in World War II. The bombing directly threatened Chinese and Soviet ships using North Vietnamese harbors, but neither power retaliated, and the Russians continued to look forward to his visit. Nixon's response helped blunt the offensive, but the relief was only temporary. Behind the trips to China and Moscow, Nixon was pulling U.S. troops out of Vietnam. In 1973, he turned the war over to the South Vietnamese with the promise that the United States would provide them with everything (except soldiers) needed for their defense. The next year, Nixon resigned the presidency under the threat of impeachment for covering up crimes committed before the 1972 presidential election. In 1975, South Vietnam collapsed. The three-decade-long war was over.

During the next two decades, several events occurred that make students of history appreciate the role that irony plays in foreign affairs. In 1979, the Vietnamese attacked the brutal Pol Pot regime in neighboring Cambodia. Not only had Pol Pot murdered millions of his fellow Cambodians, but he also hated the Vietnamese and enjoyed protection from China. The Chinese invaded Vietnam. The war was inconclusive. For their part, U.S. officials were embarrassed that their new friends the Chinese, with whom they had just opened formal diplomatic relations, were so intent on saving a blood-soaked, anti-Vietnamese dictator. In 1995, the occasion was happier. The United States and Vietnam opened formal diplomatic relations. Amid the celebration and U.S.-Vietnamese commercial exchanges that followed, tens of thousands of American tourists noted not only that the Vietnamese Communist regime—which Harry Truman had mistrusted for its anticapitalist policies—welcomed their dollars, but also that, on the outskirts of the capital, Ho Chi Minh City (once the South Vietnamese capital of Saigon), the Communists had placed a large Coca-Cola advertisement on a billboard to welcome the tourists to Vietnam.

Notes

1. Roosevelt's reversal is traced, and documentation for his turnabout provided, in Walter LaFeber, "Roosevelt, Churchill, and Indochina: 1942–1945," *American Historical Review* 80 (December 1975): 1277–95.

2. George C. Herring, *America's Longest War: The United States and Vietnam, 1950–1975,* 4th ed. (Boston: McGraw-Hill, 2002), 3–14.

3. U.S. Government, *Public Papers of the Presidents: Harry S. Truman, 1947* (Washington, DC: U.S. Government Printing Office, 1963), 167–72.

4. Useful for understanding the context and implications of the Truman Doctrine is Richard M. Freeland, *The Truman Doctrine and the Origins of McCarthyism: Foreign Policy, Domestic Politics, and Internal Security, 1946–1948* (New York: Knopf, 1972), esp. chaps. 1–2.

5. Council on Foreign Relations, Study Group Reports, October 23, 1950, Conference Dossiers, John Foster Dulles Papers, Princeton University, Princeton, NJ.

6. U.S. Government, *Public Papers of the Presidents: Dwight D. Eisenhower, 1954* (Washington, DC: U.S. Government Printing Office, 1960), 382–83.

7. For a good overview of China's help to Vietnam in the last stages of the war against the French and the satisfaction with which the Chinese viewed the 1954 Geneva Conference, see Chen Jian, *Mao's China and the Cold War* (Chapel Hill: University of North Carolina Press, 2001), 134–43, 205.

8. George McT. Kahin, *Intervention: How America Became Involved in Vietnam* (New York: Knopf, 1986), 21–22.

9. Ibid., 107–14.

10. Taylor's report to Kennedy can be found in David L. Anderson, *The Columbia Guide to the Vietnam War* (New York: Columbia University Press, 2002), 262. Other important documents and background studies can be found there as well.

11. Especially useful for relating the missile crisis to larger, and future, foreign policy issues is James A. Nathan, ed., *The Cuban Missile Crisis Revisited* (New York: St. Martin's, 1992); see esp. the essays by Nathan and Raymond L. Garthoff.

12. Oral History Interview with William R. Tyler, March 7, 1964, John F. Kennedy Presidential Library, Boston.

13. Dean Rusk to Edwin O. Reischauer, March 4, 1964, in U.S. Department of State, *Foreign Relations of the United States, 1964–1968,* vol. 29, pt. 2, *Japan* (Washington, DC: U.S. Government Printing Office, 2006), 10.

14. For good background and emphasis on the U.S.-Indian connection, see Michael Brecher, "The Super Powers and the India-China War: Nonalignment at the Brink," in *Great Power Relations, World Order, and the Third World,* ed. M. S. Rajan and Shivaji Ganguly (New Delhi: Vikas, 1981), 111–30.

15. Johnson quoted in George Ball, "The Rationalist in Power," *New York Review of Books,* April 22, 1993, 34.

16. Qiang Zhai, *China and the Vietnam Wars, 1950–1975* (Chapel Hill: University of North Carolina Press, 2000), 130–34.

17. Ibid., 138–39.

18. Kahin, *Intervention,* 276–80.

19. George C. Herring, *LBJ and Vietnam: A Different Kind of War* (Austin: University of Texas Press, 1994), 130–31.

20. For a helpful overview of those centuries of Vietnamese-Chinese hatred and war, see Anderson, *Columbia Guide,* esp. 8.

21. Chen, *Mao's China,* 230–31.

22. A good study of the Brezhnev Doctrine and Soviet policy at this time is John Dornberg, *Brezhnev: The Masks of Power* (New York: Basic, 1974), esp. chaps. 15–17.

23. A useful summary of, and context for, these evolving policies is in Warren I. Cohen, *America's Response to China: A History of Sino-American Relations,* 4th ed. (New York: Columbia University Press, 2000), 191–99.

3

With Friends Like These

Waging War and Seeking "More Flags"

Gary R. Hess

In fighting regional wars since 1950, the United States has sought the support of other nations. Besides providing troops and other material benefits, allies are also significant diplomatically in that they lend international legitimacy to the war effort. That in turn helps sustain popular backing at home. In both the Korean War and the Persian Gulf War, presidents Harry S. Truman and George H. W. Bush gained the backing of the UN Security Council to oppose the aggression of North Korea and Iraq, respectively; Security Council resolutions of 1950 and 1990 provided the basis for substantial contributions of troops and (in the case of the Persian Gulf War) financial backing as well from other nations. These wars represented the United Nations fulfilling its mission as an agent of collective security. In the Vietnam War, as in the second war in Iraq, presidents Lyndon B. Johnson and George W. Bush were frustrated in their efforts at coalition building; neither war bore the imprint of the United Nations, and traditional allies generally distanced themselves from what much of the world saw as misguided "American" wars. Only a handful of nations responded to Johnson's call for "more flags" to join American and South Vietnamese troops on the ground, and those that did generally offered modest contributions. That limited support is comparable to the "coalition of the willing" in the Iraq War; while it included initially some thirty countries, there were, aside from Britain, no major power contributors, and most of the others provided nominal support.

The fact that Vietnam was an "American war" contributed to ultimate failure. Had Johnson been able to enlist the backing of all the other members of the Southeast Asia Treaty Organization (SEATO)—Great Britain, France, the Philippines, Thailand, Pakistan, Australia, and New Zealand—he could have presented the war as an expression of collective security. Had nations like Cambodia, Laos, Indonesia, Burma, and Malaysia—which were, presumably, most threatened by a Communist victory in Vietnam—been supportive, it would have enhanced Johnson's claim that the future of Asia was on the line. The lack of international consensus behind U.S. reliance on military means to achieve objectives in Vietnam weakened Johnson's leadership at home and abroad and undermined the credibility of American warfare.[1]

The failure of alliance building in Vietnam seems at odds with what historians now see as the most dangerous phase of the Cold War. During the late 1950s and early 1960s, Vietnam was part of a matrix of crises that focused also on Berlin, Cuba, the Congo, the Taiwan Strait, Laos, and other points, thus sharpening the division between the "free world" and the Communist powers. To American leaders, that international context magnified Vietnam's importance, leading to the escalation of the U.S. commitment and to the expectation that allies should join in the struggle.[2]

Yet the level of allied support was disappointing. Troop commitments were, with one exception, nominal, and nonmilitary assistance was mostly token. Moreover, Americans funded most of the allied military assistance, leading one scholar to characterize such support as that provided by "mercenaries."[3] Underlying the limited allied role were differences between the United States and most of its traditional allies over the strategic importance of Indochina, and these differences prevailed despite the intensification of the Cold War. Few countries outside the Communist bloc actually favored the unification of Vietnam under a Communist government. That did not mean, however, that allies and neutral countries viewed that outcome in the dire terms that underlay U.S. policy.

This cleavage between the United States and its European and Asian allies over Indochina's importance dated back to 1954 and the diplomacy marking the end of the First Indochina War between France and Vietnam and the establishment of SEATO. The Geneva and Manila conferences foreshadowed the American frustrations as it went to war in Vietnam a decade later. The Vietnamese siege of Dien Bien Phu, a French fortress near northern Laos, in early 1954 inflicted a decisive defeat on France's beleaguered army and ended a seven-and-one-half-year war to hold its empire in Indochina. As that battle raged, Secretary of State John Foster Dulles, reflecting the U.S. assumption that a victory by the Viet Minh, Communist-led Vietnamese nationalists, would enable the Soviet Union and the People's Republic of China to enhance their influence in Southeast Asia, made the first appeal for an anti-Communist coalition. In a speech of March 29, 1954, Dulles spoke ominously of the impending "imposition on Southeast Asia of the political system of Communist Russia and its Chinese Communist ally . . . [as] a grave threat to the whole free community . . . [that] should not be passively accepted, but should be met by united action." Warning that "united action" could entail "serious risks," Dulles implicitly sought allied backing to salvage the precarious French position.

At a press conference a few days later, President Dwight D. Eisenhower addressed Indochina's strategic significance and introduced the concept of "falling dominoes," which was to be a principal justification for U.S. involvement in Vietnam for the next two decades. The loss of the millions of people and the strategic resources of Southeast Asia to communism would result, Eisenhower warned, from countries one after another succumbing to the advance of communism. The loss of Indochina would lead eventually to Communist control of the region: "Finally, you have broader considerations that might follow what you would call the 'falling domino' principle. You have a row of dominoes set up, you knock down the first one, and what will happen to the last one is the certainty that it will go over very quickly. So you have the beginning of a disintegration that would have the most profound influences."[4] To this way of thinking, Indochina was the critical "first domino." Despite its importance, Eisenhower ruled out unilateral American military intervention and insisted that congressional leaders support any use of force. The United States naturally looked first to its strongest ally, but the British declined to join in any operation. Then, when congressional opposition to intervention also surfaced, "united action" to save France was shelved.

The concepts of falling dominoes and united action, however, shaped

U.S. planning for an expanded role in Southeast Asia as the diplomats at Geneva reached agreement to grant independence to Laos and Cambodia and to divide Vietnam temporarily into two "zones." The victorious Communist movement under Ho Chi Minh's leadership controlled the zone north of a demilitarized zone drawn at the Seventeenth Parallel, and the remnants of the French colonial regime controlled the southern zone. These two zones became commonly known as North Vietnam and South Vietnam, respectively. No one doubted that reunification elections, scheduled for 1956, would result in a Communist victory.

Regarding the Geneva Accords as a defeat for the West, Dulles stated that the "great problem from now on out is whether we could salvage what the Communists had ostensibly left out of their grasp in Indochina."[5] Indeed, during the deliberations at Geneva, the United States had begun planning for an alliance designed to deter aggression in Southeast Asia.

Six weeks after the Geneva Conference concluded, an American-led meeting in Manila established SEATO. A precarious arrangement from its founding, SEATO suffered from limited membership and vague procedures and responsibilities.[6] Despite American efforts to enlist the backing of leading nonaligned states like India, Indonesia, and Ceylon (Sri Lanka), SEATO's membership included only nations already linked to the American security system, and one of those was actually an unwelcome member. Most striking, only two members—the Philippines and Thailand—were Southeast Asian countries. Moreover, one of those—the Philippines—had little interest in the Asian mainland. Filipino leaders had long championed a Pacific security pact, which they regarded as a means of enhancing the Philippines's regional status at the expense of Japan and increasing its claims on U.S. military and economic assistance. SEATO was the next best thing to a Pacific pact, and membership served the purpose of demonstrating Philippine support of the United States, but not necessarily a commitment to act militarily on the mainland. Thailand, which bordered Indochina, was vitally concerned with regional stability and welcomed an enlarged U.S. role on the mainland. Thai leaders regarded increased American military assistance as essential to their country's security, and SEATO provided a means of moving toward an alliance with the United States.

Australia and New Zealand shared the U.S. objective of containing Communist influence in Asia and the Pacific. They were particularly concerned with the stability of Indonesia in the aftermath of the Communist victory in the Chinese Civil War. This had led already to the trilateral AN-ZUS (Australia–New Zealand–United States) Pact of 1951. While both Britain and France agreed to join SEATO, neither shared the American position that the results of the Geneva Conference were disastrous to the West, and both were resentful of what they considered American domination and manipulation. The British insisted that their Southeast Asian interests were limited to Malaya, and they saw an American-led alliance increasing U.S. influence over Australia and New Zealand; ANZUS had rankled London, and SEATO caused further aggravation. The demise of French power and influence foreshadowed not only a limited role for France in Southeast Asia but also a lingering bitterness over the American failure to come to the aid of the French at Dien Bien Phu. The French also resented the assumption of the Americans, as they took over South Vietnam while the French withdrew, that they would succeed where France had failed. To the French, American policy reflected more arrogance than understanding of the region.

SEATO's odd member was Pakistan. It was not located in Southeast Asia and had no significant interest in the region, but it viewed the alliance as a means of enhancing its security in its ongoing tensions with India. American officials attempted to dissuade Pakistan, with which it had recently signed a mutual assistance agreement, from pursuing SEATO membership. The United States did not want to antagonize further nonaligned India, which was openly hostile to a Western-led alliance system. In the end, the persistent Pakistanis could not be denied membership.

So the alliance went forward with its objective of deterring further Communist expansion. To make clear the U.S. determination to "draw a line," the pact's protocol area was extended beyond the member states to include Cambodia, Laos, and South Vietnam, described in the treaty as the "free territory of Vietnam under the jurisdiction of the State of Vietnam." This provision circumvented the provisions in the Geneva agreements that precluded Laos, Cambodia, and the two Vietnamese zones from joining military alliances.

Dulles, SEATO's chief architect, and other officials recognized the alliance's shortcomings, but they regarded it principally as a means of deterrence. Assuming that recent Communist gains in China and Vietnam foreshadowed further efforts at advancing in the region, Dulles and Eisen-hower saw SEATO as the only credible means of signaling the U.S. inten-tion to maintain the post-Geneva political balance. V. Adm. A. C. Davis, a member of the U.S. delegation, observed that SEATO served "more a psychological than a military purpose. The area is no better prepared than before to cope with communist aggression."[7] The historian Robert J. McMahon makes much the same point: "The alliance demonstrated the continuing U.S. interest in a non-communist Southeast Asia, drawing a clear line in the sand for China or any other potential aggressor."[8]

Yet, even in 1954, American officials recognized that outright aggres-sion was not the most immediate threat; Communist subversion and in-filtration were more likely to challenge established governments. Dulles acknowledged that there was "no simple and no single formula" that could counter such challenges to regional stability. In that light, SEATO offered at least a "buying-time" opportunity to build societies and govern-ments that could resist pressures from within. On this point, the scholar-diplomat Russell Fifield comments, "For the United States, the Manila Treaty of 1954 was designed to deter overt armed aggression from Com-munist China . . . and provide a shield to buy time for American and related programs of aid which might lead to the economic and social ad-vance of the people, to greater stability in their governments, and to the reduction of the communist appeal."[9]

Over the next decade, despite some early superficial success, the American effort to accomplish that mission in South Vietnam unraveled. At the same time, the United States tried to strengthen SEATO, but, by the 1960s, only Thailand, Australia, and New Zealand remained com-mitted to the organization's objectives; Leszek Buszynski, the historian of SEATO, writes that during its first decade "SEATO's efficacy had not been tested and its reputation was founded upon a good deal of bluff."[10]

Johnson's Americanization of the war in Vietnam with his open-ended military commitment in the summer of 1965 meant that SEATO had failed as an instrument of deterrence. The North Vietnamese and the Viet Cong, Communist insurgents in the South, pursued their campaign of overthrowing the South Vietnamese government by force. SEATO had also failed as a buying-time enterprise, for South Vietnam was un-der siege, not just because of the Communist insurgency, but because of the chronic inability of non-Communist leaders to work together and to

Republic of Korea soldiers recognized for their Vietnam service. Courtesy of the Vietnam Archive, Texas Tech University, Douglas Pike Photograph Collection.

build support among the peasantry. So now SEATO was to be tested as an instrument of collective security.

Had Johnson, like Eisenhower a decade earlier, made U.S. military involvement conditional on allied support, he would not have taken the country to war. As he moved toward a direct military role, the president was already frustrated by the lack of international support. As early as April 1964, he spoke of wanting to "see some other flags in there, other nations as a result of the SEATO meeting . . . [so] that we could all unite in an attempt to stop the spread of communism in that area of the world."[11] This marked the first reference to what became known as the More Flags Program, and, a few months later, in a message to the U.S. ambassador in South Vietnam, Johnson specifically mentioned seeking the "military and political cooperation of Thailand, the Philippines, Australia, New Zealand, and the United Kingdom."[12] He also "charged" the U.S. ambassadors to key governments to make certain that the leaders in their countries realized "how seriously we view the challenge to freedom in Vietnam and how heavily the burden of responsibility for defending that freedom falls on those Governments who possess freedom in their own right."[13] Yet these early entreaties underlined differences with allies, and it was evident to U.S. officials that military support would be limited. This international weakness might have been a restraining factor on the decision to go to war. Instead, Johnson plunged ahead, anticipating that he could still enlist meaningful international backing.[14]

From the beginning, SEATO dramatized not collective security but America's international isolation. The limitations of SEATO plagued the war effort. In addition to the differences over Vietnam's importance, other factors restrained allies. The ineptitude of the South Vietnamese government and the strong internal opposition to it—the factor that pulled Johnson into military intervention—left many other world leaders wondering whether it could, or should, be saved. Moreover, U.S. officials had to contend with the reluctance on the part of Asian allies to be seen as instruments of American power; they were all fiercely nationalistic and determined to assert their independence. This was reinforced by the fact that, in most Asian countries, the American war was not popular from the beginning; as it dragged on and the bombing of North Vietnam intensified, criticism mounted, thus making leaders ever more reluctant to support the United States.[15]

Although Johnson and other high-ranking officials frequently referred to SEATO membership as justifying U.S. military support of South Vietnam, the organization never took an official stand requesting members to act on behalf of South Vietnam. That reflected the lack of consensus among its members about Vietnam's strategic importance and, in particular, the opposition of Pakistan and France to any direct SEATO involvement.[16] So the United States pursued the individual members of SEATO, as well as other nations, to contribute to the war effort. American diplomacy used a number of tactics—persuasion, pressure, enticements—but with disappointing results. In the end, the Philippines, Thailand, Australia, New Zealand, and South Korea (the latter not a member of SEATO) sent troops to Vietnam, but Johnson always sought more than these nations provided and was frustrated by the inability to gain contributions from other allies. Moreover, the Philippines, Thailand, and South Korea took advantage of the president's desperation to gain important concessions as part of the arrangements for their troop contributions.

In the case of the Philippines, lengthy negotiations throughout 1965 concluded with an agreement that it would deploy a 2,300-man engineering task force.[17] Even that modest contribution—known formally as the Philippine Civic Action Group (PHILCAG)—proved controversial in Philippine politics, especially after Ferdinand Marcos was elected president in November 1965. As a candidate, Marcos had strongly opposed sending any military aid to Vietnam. Johnson applied the pressure. Over the course of several weeks in late 1965 and early 1966, he sent five diplomatic missions, including one headed by Vice President Hubert Humphrey and another by Secretary of State Dean Rusk, to persuade Marcos to go forward with PHILCAG. Marcos finally did so, explaining to his countrymen that his decision was based on the grounds that PHILCAG was not a combat unit. It was dispatched to Vietnam in late 1966. The United States paid considerably for this nominal show of allied support, not only increasing military assistance to the Philippines to cover the costs of PHILCAG, but also providing an additional $80 million in economic assistance. One of Johnson's advisers asked privately, "What is too high a cost for the presence of 2,500 Philippine fighting men in Vietnam?"[18] To Johnson PHILCAG was a first step toward a combat unit from the Philippines, while to Marcos it represented the extent of a politically risky contribution to the American war. Always mindful of domestic criticism, Marcos worked assiduously to minimize publicity about the levels of U.S. support that his government received, for he was determined not to be seen as dependent on America. That preoccupation also led him to reject several requests to expand the Philippine contribution, as Johnson pressed repeatedly for the dispatch of a combat unit. That was not to be, however, and Marcos in fact reduced the size of PHILCAG in 1968. Eventually, as the war became increasingly unpopular among the Filipinos, and as hearings in the U.S. Congress revealed the extent of American assistance to the Philippines, it became politically expedient for Marcos to order the withdrawal of PHILCAG, which he did in November 1969.

Thailand, as the sole SEATO member on the Southeast Asian mainland, was indispensable to the American war, both politically and militarily.[19] The unfolding crisis in Vietnam pulled the United States and Thailand into a closer relationship. A persistent concern of Thailand, even after SEATO was established, was that the Americans would not be a reliable, long-term partner. As the United States was being drawn more deeply into Vietnam, President John F. Kennedy reassured Thailand of America's support. This led to an agreement reached by Secretary of State Rusk and Thailand's foreign minister, Thanat Khoman, in March 1962 that committed the United States to the defense of Thailand. Thailand soon became critical to the American air war in Indochina, by permitting its bases to be used, first, in the covert bombing of the Communist Pathet Lao and North Vietnamese positions inside Laos and, later, in the bombing of North Vietnam. That support role dramatically increased in August 1966 when the United States opened the large Sattahip-U Thappao base complex. Its long runways permitted B-52 bombers to attack North Vietnam and Communist positions in South Vietnam (previously B-52 attacks had to be launched from Guam or Okinawa). The base complex included a deep harbor port and a large ammunition depot. By 1967, some thirty-seven thousand U.S. troops were serving in Thailand, nearly all stationed at the eight air bases that the United States had either expanded or constructed to wage war in Vietnam.[20]

Thailand's vital role in the air war, however, was not paralleled by a troop commitment. The United States did not push the issue until 1966, recognizing that Thailand's primary concern was in neighboring Laos and that political and military leaders in Bangkok opposed sending combat forces to Vietnam. Yet, when Johnson pressed the More Flags Program, the Thais relented. In early January 1967, they promised to dispatch "a reinforced Thai Battalion to fight in Vietnam," and, three days later, Prime Minister Thanam Kittikachorn publicly announced that Thailand would send a "ground force to take an active part in the fighting in South Vietnam."[21] What facilitated this change in Thailand's position was that the Vietnam force was to be an all-volunteer unit. The vast majority of the volunteers were, in fact, regular Thai soldiers. The deployment of this two-thousand-man force, known commonly as the Queen's Cobras, was delayed until September 1967, presumably because of the need for extensive training. Even before the Queen's Cobras arrived, Johnson was pressing for more troops. A special presidential mission headed by Clark Clifford and Maxwell Taylor in the fall of 1967 made its pilgrimage to Bangkok and other Asian capitals in search of more allied support.

In response to those entreaties, Thai officials put aside their misgivings and agreed to send a full division of twelve thousand men. Aware that the United States was in an increasingly isolated position in Vietnam and that it had paid generously for other allied troops, Thailand negotiated an agreement whereby the United States agreed to fund the training costs, equipment and supplies, and overseas allowances of Thai forces sent to Vietnam; in addition, the United States increased its military assistance to Thailand from $60 to $75 million per year.

Besides influencing the Thai troop increase, the Clifford-Taylor mission had its one other success in Australia, which agreed to increase its troop commitment to eight thousand.[22] Australia had, in fact, been an unequivocal supporter of U.S. policy in Southeast Asia, reflecting a disposition on the part of its leaders dating back to World War II to look to the United States as the principal guarantor of their country's security. This had led to the ANZUS Pact, the dispatch of troops to fight in the Korean War, and membership in SEATO. Underlying that collaboration was the Australian concept of "forward defense," which was similar to the U.S. policy of containment of the Soviet Union and People's Republic of China. Forward defense assumed that Australian security was enhanced by containing Communist influence on the Southeast Asian mainland, which was considered essential to preserving Indonesia as a non-Communist state. Also, the Australians believed that it was important to demonstrate support for the United States generally, as a means of assuring the preservation of a strong American position in Asia and the Pacific. Hence, the government of Sir Robert Menzies, who had served as prime minister since 1949, sent two battalions overseas in early 1965, one to work with the British in securing the border of Malaya against Indonesia, and the other to help the Americans in Vietnam. This marked the beginning of strong diplomatic and military support for the American war, which was succinctly expressed in 1966 by Menzies's successor, Harold Holt, when he reiterated the chant of Johnson's domestic supporters: "ALL THE WAY WITH LBJ."

The American-Australian solidarity was enhanced by events in Indonesia, where the army suppressed a Communist coup in late 1965. Prior to that unexpected and dramatic turning point in Indonesian history, American and Australian leaders feared that the nonaligned Indonesian government under Achmed Sukarno was drifting toward the Communist orbit and was susceptible to an internal Communist takeover. Such a change would have isolated Australia and New Zealand while increasing Chinese influence and risking the loss of resources valuable to the Western economy. The Indonesian army under General Suharto put down a coup led by junior army officers who were presumably working at the behest of the Indonesian Communist Party. Suharto's brutal suppression of his opponents ultimately claimed as many as half a million lives. However deplorable the tactics and the establishment of a military dictatorship, Americans and Australians welcomed the transformation of a vulnerable Indonesia into a strong anti-Communist state.[23]

Despite the sense of general solidarity with the United States among the Australian public, leaders faced increasing criticism at home, particularly from the opposition Labour Party. This opposition served to limit the dispatch of troops, for all increases, which were, in fact, modest, met with domestic criticism. Nonetheless, Australia committed about one-third of its available military forces to Vietnam. Accompanying the Australians were troops, numbering at their peak slightly more than five hundred, from New Zealand. Unlike the Asian contributors, Australia and New Zealand funded their own troops and provided financial assistance to the South Vietnamese government.

Much to Johnson's chagrin, the European members of SEATO remained distant from the war.[24] The response of France to the American-

A Republic of Korea soldier of the Tiger Division enters an underground Viet Cong bunker. Courtesy of the Vietnam Archive, Texas Tech University, Douglas Pike Collection.

ization of the war was predictable, for it had consistently regarded U.S. policy as misguided. Its leaders regarded the struggle in Vietnam as basically a civil war and saw the Americans engaged in a futile struggle. In 1964, President Charles de Gaulle proposed that an international conference be convened to bring about the "neutralization" of all Indochina. Such peace initiatives were not welcomed in Washington. Given the relative weakness of South Vietnam, American officials regarded any negotiated settlement as leading to the Communist takeover of Vietnam. The French government and media were critical of American warfare as it escalated from 1965 to 1968. This anti-Americanism undercut France's interest in mediating an end to the war.

The British response to the war was more complex and was influenced by what both American and British leaders regarded as their nations' "special relationship." That consideration, however, did not enable Johnson to obtain his overriding objective: a token British combat unit as part of the More Flags Program. The British fell back on two arguments to justify their nonmilitary role: first, as a coconvener (along with the Soviet Union) of the 1954 Geneva Conference, Britain was expected to use its influence to assure the realization of the Geneva agreements and an end to warfare; second, the primary British responsibility in Southeast Asia remained in Malaya.

In general, the government of Harold Wilson, who became prime minister in 1964, supported American objectives and warfare, including the bombing of North Vietnam, which was widely criticized in the British press. The British were interested in trying to promote an agreement to end the war, and they were sensitive to how the bombing campaign was an obstacle to peace, for North Vietnam insisted that the cessation of bombing had to precede any negotiations. At first, Wilson tolerated American warfare because he hoped that such support would enable his government to influence the United States to enter into negotiations.

By 1966, the intensified bombing campaign triggered widespread criticism within Britain and forced Wilson to criticize U.S. warfare. The British responded to reports that the U.S. bombing of North Vietnam was needlessly targeting the civilian population, a point on which the British were sensitive, having suffered from German bombing raids just twenty-five years earlier. When Wilson spoke out against the bombing, Johnson responded with a sharply worded message to the prime minister, defending the bombing, and castigating London's failure to provide combat troops: "I hope that you can give further thought to your own interests and commitments under the SEATO Treaty. . . . Five signatories of SEATO . . . are committing troops to repel an armed attack from the north. Nor do I believe that your role as co-chairman [of the Geneva Conference] means that Britain should stand aside; the other co-chairman [the Soviet Union] is furnishing large quantities of sophisticated arms and other assistance to North Vietnam and is, therefore, an active partner in the effort to take over South Vietnam by force."[25] Johnson's admonition failed to change British policy.[26]

The strongest allied support came, ironically, from South Korea—a nation that was not a member of SEATO.[27] One historian sees this distinction more as a matter of default than of Korean dedication; Kil J. Yi writes, "South Korea became America's largest third-country ally in the Vietnam War because of the Johnson administration's inability to mobilize allies in Southeast Asia who had more immediate interests in keeping

South Vietnam communist free."[28] The South Korean commitment, which reached about fifty thousand men, more than doubled the other allies' total contribution. In South Korean and American public statements, this support was presented as an expression of gratitude for the large-scale American military intervention of 1950–53 that assured the survival of South Korea. It was also characterized in terms of South Korea's understanding, derived from its enmity with Communist North Korea, of the nature of, and its solidarity with the United States in its determination to halt the spread of, communism. While such considerations may have influenced South Korean officials, it is also clear that they took advantage of the American desperation for "more flags" to obtain U.S. underwriting of the South Korean contingent, a substantial increase in economic and military assistance, and other concessions. Indeed, the demands of the South Koreans provided a model for the Philippines and Thailand in responding to U.S. pressure.

After two months of negotiation in early 1965, the South Koreans gained all that they wanted in return for sending a combat force, including U.S. financing of overseas allowances, training, equipment, logistic support, and transportation for troops sent to Vietnam; an increase in U.S. military assistance funds to the South Korean army, which would be upgraded in terms of firepower, mobility, and communications; assurances that the U.S. commitment in Vietnam would not lead to a reduction in the number of American troops stationed in South Korea; and the continuation of U.S. economic development programs in South Korea at least at current levels, accompanied by a promise to provide employment and welfare for needy people in South Korea. With this financial and security package, South Korea sent the twenty-thousand-man Tiger Division, which arrived in Vietnam in early 1966. Johnson, however, was already pressing for more South Korean troops. When the South Koreans initially balked, Johnson dispatched Vice President Humphrey to Seoul to negotiate, and he quickly met the essential demand that additional troops sent to Vietnam would be fully compensated and equipped by the United States. Accordingly, South Korea sent a second division to Vietnam. The Koreans believed that this military commitment would assure them of a larger role in American policy in Asia, in effect becoming a junior partner. Johnson may not have endorsed that ambitious agenda, but he did regard the increased assistance as vital to the long-term stability of South

Korea, which would certainly remain, regardless of the results of the war in Vietnam, a vital U.S. objective. So, to Johnson, the military and economic incentives were not "rewards for mercenaries" but were intended to "make South Korea indestructible from within so that it could serve as a partner in containment."[29] Indeed, the large-scale U.S. assistance contributed not just to South Korea's military stability but to the country's impressive economic growth and modernization.

Not surprisingly, Johnson sought more troops, but, by late 1967, President Park Chung Hee encountered substantial opposition to that proposal in the National Assembly. When the Clifford-Taylor mission visited Seoul in August 1967, Park rejected its plea. The internal criticism of Park's pro-American policy intensified in early 1968 when, within a matter of two weeks, a North Korean death squad attempted to assassinate Park and the North Koreans captured the U.S. spy ship *Pueblo*. These events escalated tensions on the Korean peninsula, and many South Korean opponents of Park's pro-American policy argued that the deployment of South Korean forces to Vietnam might have provoked the North Korean actions. In any event, those opposed to sending more troops now controlled the National Assembly, and the Americans stopped pressing the Park government on the issue.

Although the disappointing level of allied troop support could not be denied, the Johnson administration compensated by calling attention to the large number of nations that contributed nonmilitary assistance to South Vietnam. Under the Free World Assistance Program, thirty-nine nations provided economic, humanitarian, and technical assistance. These nations included all those that had sent troops; in addition, virtually all America's NATO allies, the pro-Western governments of Asia and the Middle East, and eight Latin American countries participated. As with the More Flags Program, much of this assistance resulted from U.S. pressure. Most of the nonmilitary assistance was token at best (ten thousand cans of sardines worth $2,000 from Morocco was the most modest contribution), but a few nations—notably Great Britain, West Germany, France, Australia, New Zealand, West Germany, Japan, and the Netherlands—established substantial programs.[30]

With the election of Richard Nixon to the presidency in 1968, America's relationship with its allies changed. Nixon, who sought a negotiated "peace with honor," began the gradual withdrawal of U.S. forces and the process of Vietnamization. Allied support was no longer central to American diplomacy, and, in a practical sense, the United States could hardly have asked allies for troops when it was itself disengaging. Nixon also moved toward détente with the Soviet Union and established diplomatic contacts with the People's Republic of China, in part because he believed that the major Communist powers could facilitate an agreement with North Vietnam. The Nixon Doctrine, announced in 1969, foreshadowed a lessening of U.S. military involvement in Asia and the expectation that allies would be responsible for their own security. More generally, Nixon's reorientation of U.S. foreign policy suggested that the time had come to reduce Cold War tensions and to work with the major Communist powers in constructing a new balance of power. To the Australians, the Thais, and the Koreans, these initiatives caused anxiety. Each felt let down by the country it had been supporting and resented that it had not been consulted about the redirection of U.S. policy.[31]

So, in the end, the deterioration of relations with its allies was one of America's Vietnam War casualties. Undertaken to stand by a beleaguered ally, the war resulted in that ally's demise. Assuming that SEATO and other free-world nations shared the U.S. determination to "hold the line" in Southeast Asia, Johnson pursued a futile campaign to enlist significant levels of military assistance. His pressures and occasional angry outbursts directed at longtime allies, combined with what much of the world saw as a cruel use of firepower against a small country, led to strained relationships. The lack of respect for the South Vietnamese government, and that government's chronic instability and unreliability, added to a sense that the leader of the free world was engaged in a losing cause. And, when Nixon began withdrawing, those nations that had contributed to the Many Flags Program felt ignored, even betrayed, and, most important, uncertain of America's postwar role in Asia and the Pacific. Finally, SEATO itself was a casualty of the war, the strains caused by the war underlining that the pact had outlived its usefulness. It was formally disbanded in 1977.[32] SEATO's historian Leszek Buszynski aptly summarizes its demise: "The most popular comment of the time was that SEATO, like an old soldier, had simply faded away. This old soldier, however, never fought."[33] So a war that was intended to strengthen America's stature concluded with its leaders facing the challenge of rebuilding confidence in its leadership.

Notes

1. George C. Herring, "Fighting without Allies: The International Dimensions of America's Failure in Vietnam," in *Why the North Won the Vietnam War,* ed. Marc Jason Gilbert (New York: Palgrave, 2002), 77–95.

2. For a discussion of the "most dangerous phase" of the Cold War, see Warren I. Cohen, *The Cambridge History of American Foreign Relations,* vol. 4, *America in the Age of Soviet Power* (New York: Cambridge University Press, 1993), 116–46.

3. Robert M. Blackburn, *Mercenaries and Lyndon Johnson's "More Flags": The Hiring of Korean, Filipino, and Thai Soldiers in the Vietnam War* (Jefferson, NC: McFarland, 1994).

4. *Public Papers of the Presidents: Dwight D. Eisenhower, 1954* (Washington, DC: U.S. Government Printing Office, 1960), 382–83 (see generally 381–90).

5. NSC Meeting, July 22, 1954, in U.S. Department of State, *Foreign Relations of the United States, 1952–54,* vol. 13, pt. 2, *Indochina* (Washington, DC: U.S. Government Printing Office, 1982), 1867–71.

6. On the establishment of SEATO, see Leszek Buszynski, *SEATO: The Failure of an Alliance Strategy* (Singapore: Singapore University Press, 1983), 1–43; Gary R. Hess, "The American Search for Stability in Southeast Asia: SEATO Structure of Containment," in *The Great Powers in East Asia, 1953–1960,* ed. Warren I. Cohen and Akira Iriye (New York: Columbia University Press, 1990), 272–95; and Robert J. McMahon, *The Limits of Empire: The United States and Southeast Asia since World War II* (New York: Columbia University Press, 1999), 63–68.

7. *U.S.-Vietnam Relations, 1945–67* (Washington, DC: U.S. Government Printing Office, 1971), bk. 10, p. 747.

8. McMahon, *Limits of Empire,* 67.

9. Russell Fifield, *Americans in Southeast Asia: The Roots of Commitment* (New York: Crowell, 1973), 236.

10. Buszynski, *SEATO,* 70.

11. *Public Papers of the Presidents: Lyndon Baines Johnson, 1963–64* (Washington, DC: U.S. Government Printing Office, 1965), 285.

12. Cited in Blackburn, *Johnson's "More Flags,"* 22.

13. Cited in Herring, "Fighting without Allies," 79.

14. Ibid., 78–80; Stanley Robert Larsen and James Lawton Collins Jr., *Vietnam Studies: Allied Participation in Vietnam* (Washington, DC: Department of the Army, 1975), 1–14.

15. McMahon, *Limits of Empire,* 141–44.

16. Buszynski, *SEATO,* 95–135.

17. On the Philippines's role, see Blackburn, *Johnson's "More Flags,"* 67–91; and Larsen and Collins, *Allied Participation,* 74–83.

18. Jack Valenti quoted in McMahon, *Limits of Empire,* 141.

19. On Thailand's role, see Blackburn, *Johnson's "More Flags,"* 95–116; and Larsen and Collins, *Allied Participation,* 25–45.

20. McMahon, *Limits of Empire,* 95–98, 137–40.

21. Blackburn, *Johnson's "More Flags,"* 106.

22. On Australia's role in Vietnam, see Peter Edwards, *A Nation at War: Australian Politics, Society, and Diplomacy during the Vietnam War, 1965-1975* (Sydney: Allen & Unwin, 1997), 1–176; Ronald Bruce Frankum Jr., *The United States and Australia in Vietnam, 1954-1968* (Lewiston, NY: Edwin Mellen, 2001), 201–91 and passim; Larsen and Collins, *Allied Participation,* 88–109; and Blackburn, *Johnson's "More Flags,"* 117–32.

23. McMahon, *Limits of Empire,* 119–24.

24. On the British and French responses to the war, see Caroline Page, "European SEATO Allies: British Diplomatic Support, French Opposition," in *New Perspectives on the Vietnam War: Our Allies' Views,* ed. William Schoenl (Lanham, MD: University Press of America, 2002), 43–66; Sylvia Ellis, *Britain, America, and the Vietnam War* (Westport, CT: Praeger, 2004); Frank Costigliola, "The Vietnam War and the Challenge to America Power in Europe," in *International Perspectives on the Vietnam War,* ed. Lloyd C. Gardner and Ted Gittinger (College Station: Texas A&M University Press, 2000), 143–53; Maurice Vaisse, "DeGaulle and the Vietnam War," in ibid., 162–65; and Wilfred Mausbach, "Triangle of Discord: The United States, Germany, and French Peace Initiatives for Vietnam," in ibid., 166–82.

25. Lyndon Johnson to Harold Wilson, June 14, 1966, quoted in Page, "European SEATO Allies," 60.

26. Two other important allies, Canada and Japan, generally provided diplomatic support, although the war in Vietnam became increasingly unpopular in both countries. Both were also active in trying to promote negotiations to end the war. Like the French and British efforts, theirs were for naught, but they did cause some annoyance within the Johnson administration. On Canada's role, see Douglas A. Ross, "Canada, Peacemaking, the Vietnam War," in *The Vietnam War as History,* ed. Elizabeth Jane Errington and B. J. C. McKercher (Westport, CT: Praeger, 1990), 133–61; and Andrew Preston, "Missions Impossible: Canadian Secret Diplomacy and the Quest for Peace in Vietnam," in *The Search for Peace in Vietnam, 1964-1968,* ed. Lloyd C. Gardner and Ted Gittinger (College Station: Texas A&M University Press, 2004), 117–43. On Japan's role, see Hideki Kan, "The Japanese Government's Peace Efforts in the Vietnam War," in ibid., 207–230; and Thomas R. Havens, *Fire across the Sea: The Vietnam War and Japan, 1965-1975* (Princeton, NJ: Princeton University Press, 1987).

27. On the South Korean commitment, see Blackburn, *Johnson's "More Flags,"* 31–66; Larsen and Collins, *Allied Participation,* 145–59; and Kil J. Yi, "The U.S.-Korean Alliance in the Vietnam War: The Years of Escalation, 1964-68," in *International Perspectives on the Vietnam War,* ed. Gardner and Gittinger, 154–75.

Besides South Korea, one other non-SEATO nation—Nationalist China (the

Republic of China, on the island of Taiwan)—offered to send a substantial military force to Vietnam. The United States rejected the offer because it feared that the use of Nationalist Chinese troops would trigger a military response from Communist China. The same consideration had led the United States to reject a similar National-ist Chinese offer during the Korean War. Also influencing the American decision in the case of Vietnam was the historic Vietnamese antagonism toward the Chinese. The Nationalist Chinese were permitted to send a political warfare advisory team and other forms of nonmilitary assistance. See Larsen and Collins, *Allied Participation,* 115–18, 161.

28. Yi, "The U.S.-Korean Alliance," 156.

29. Ibid., 163.

30. Larsen and Collins, *Allied Participation,* 160–69.

31. McMahon, *Limits of Empire,* 155–81.

32. Buszynski, *SEATO,* 182–226.

33. Ibid., 210.

4

The Perspective of a Vietnamese Witness

Luu Doan Huynh

I have often agonized over why Vietnam has, in the years since World War II, been perceived as a pariah state and, hence, the sufferings inflicted on it by both the West and the East. As far as relations with the United States in particular are concerned, many Vietnamese initially held out hope for friendship, but that hope turned first to disappointment, then to despair, and finally to anger. In hindsight, it is easy for us, the Vietnamese, to condemn you, the Americans. What is more difficult, and more necessary, is to understand the motives behind U.S. foreign policy in the past and how those motives might affect the direction that U.S. foreign policy is likely to take in the future. Therefore, what I wish to do here is present my frank perceptions on these issues, hoping thereby to elicit in response the critical views of my American colleagues and readers.

From World War II to Early 1950

President Franklin Roosevelt's assertion in the early 1940s that French colonial rule in Indochina would be replaced by a postwar UN trusteeship gave the Vietnamese people hope. But, in 1942 and 1943, in deference to the views of the Free French representatives, the U.S. embassy in Chungking did not reply to letters from Vietnamese patriotic organizations requesting that it intervene in order to secure the release of Ho Chi Minh, who had been jailed by the Chinese Nationalists (the Kuomintang).

Further, in 1944, when a Viet Minh representative met with the U.S. consul general, William Langdon, in Kunming and tried to secure American sympathy for the liberation struggle, Langdon responded that, if the Vietnamese had complaints against France, the normal course would be to deal directly with France. He also explained that the Vietnamese were "citizens of France," which was "fighting side by side with the USA . . . against the Axis," and that "it would not make sense if America, with one hand and at great expenditures of life and treasure, rescued and delivered France from German slavery and with the other hand undermined her Empire."[1] It was not until the March 9, 1945, Japanese coup d'état against the French colonial authorities had dried up the flow of American intelligence from Indochina and increased the fear of possible Japanese attacks in South China that assistance was given to Ho Chi Minh (who had been released by the Nationalists in 1943). This assistance, which started in July 1945, included the provision of military supplies and the training by the American Office of Strategic Services Deer Team of Viet Minh guerrillas for operations against Japan. This was a happy episode in Vietnamese-U.S. relations.

The new Democratic Republic of Vietnam (DRV) was naturally apprehensive about the consequences of Roosevelt's death on April 12, 1945. On November 23, 1945, at a regular meeting of the DRV provisional government, Ho Chi Minh told his colleagues, "The Americans do not like the French colonial policy, but they don't want to offend the latter." He also confided to his close colleague Hoang Minh Giam, "Truman is not anticolonial like Roosevelt."[2] His assessment was not very far off the mark, as the new U.S. policy document of October 5, 1945 (of which, presumably, Ho had no direct knowledge), stated: "US has no thought of opposing the re-establishment of French control in Indochina and no official statement by US government has questioned even by implication French sovereignty over Indochina. However, it is not the policy of this government to assist the French to reestablish their control over Indochina by force and the willingness of the US to see French control reestablished assumes that French claim to have the support of the population is borne out by future events."[3]

The first part of this statement, which completely undermined Roosevelt's anticolonial position, would, had it been known by the Vietnamese, naturally given cause for concern. But the last part still would have held out cause for hope. In fact, U.S. material assistance to the French war of reconquest was indirect, not very substantial, and coupled with the express desire to see peace maintained in Vietnam in accordance with the March 6, 1946, Franco-Vietnamese preliminary agreement. The DRV sought to encourage, through messages and contacts, this more or less de facto U.S. neutrality. In June 1946, Ho Chi Minh visited France and tried to reach a more comprehensive agreement with the French, hoping, among other things, to secure the continuance of American neutrality. But, in view of France's greater military power and its determination to recover all its former colonics,[4] a war was inevitable. When Abbot Low Moffat, the chief of the U.S. State Department's Division of Southeast Asian Affairs, visited Vietnam in early December 1946, Ho Chi Minh received him. But health problems forced Ho to ask Vice Foreign Minister Hoang Minh Giam to conduct concrete discussions with Moffat. The vice minister even went so far as to offer cooperation in developing Cam Ranh Bay as a U.S. naval base in return for U.S. efforts to discourage France from launching a war of reconquest, but Moffat replied that he "doubted if USA would be interested in such a base."[5]

When the French launched an all-out war of reconquest of Indochina in December 1946, the U.S. government brought little pressure to bear on them to come to terms with the DRV, mainly because, unlike the Netherlands, which still had a colony in the East Indies, France was regarded by the United States as a major power and an important ally. But it did make diplomatic maneuvers in Paris, deploring the "lack of French understanding of the other side," expressing its readiness to "assist in any appropriate way" to find a solution to the Indochina problem, and warning that, if the matter were to be brought before the UN Security Council, it would find it difficult to oppose an investigation "unless negotiations between parties were going on."[6] Of course, France paid no heed, presumably because it was certain that the Soviet Union (the only likely member nation) would not bring the matter to the Security Council.[7] Furthermore, it intended to exclude the DRV from any future negotiations and to destroy or subdue its armed forces and government, as evidenced, for example, in a meeting on March 11, 1947, between the French representative Paul Mus and Ho Chi Minh at which Mus put forward proposals that were, in fact, a demand for surrender, a demand that Ho firmly rejected.[8]

This was the situation that prevailed when the DRV launched a major diplomatic initiative, sending Deputy Minister Pham Ngoc Thach to Bangkok for talks with the U.S. embassy and American entrepreneurs from April to June 1947. During these talks, Pham stressed the fact that new appointments, including that of a representative of the Socialist Party as foreign minister, meant that the DRV government was now broadly representative. He admitted that it was not possible for the United States to take a position against France at this time, but he requested that it either undertake as a (relatively) neutral party mediation of the Indochina war or ask the Philippines to bring the matter before the United Nations. Also, in a memorandum submitted to representatives of the American International Engineering Group in Bangkok, he "offered a quid pro quo: guarantees of monopolistic economic concessions to American businesses in return for agricultural and industrial equipment as well as $10 to $20 million in American rehabilitation loans." He further promised "tax-free monopolies for American imports and for the rice export trade, potentially the largest in Asia," and called for the "establishment of small American manufacturing plants in Vietnam." Finally, he "proposed the establishment of joint scientific organizations, funding for a chair in American literature at the University of Hanoi, and scholarships for Vietnamese students at American universities to foster mutual understanding."[9]

On May 13, in the midst of the talks, the U.S. State Department informed its representatives in France and Vietnam that, as far as Southeast Asia was concerned, the United States was in essentially the same boat as France, Great Britain, and the Netherlands but, nevertheless, instructed them to approach the French government and the French high commissioner in Indochina and make certain points. First, the United States considered the war to have been caused by both sides, not by the DRV alone. Second, because the continuation of the conflict could jeopardize the position of all Western countries in Southeast Asia, the United States hoped that France would make a "generous attempt to find an early solution which, by recognizing the legitimate desire of Vietnam, will restore peace." Finally, the United States was concerned that French efforts to find the "true representatives of Vietnam" with whom to negotiate would result in the creation of an impotent puppet government along the lines of the Cochinchina regime or the attempted restoration of Bao Dai.[10] These views would seem to indicate that the U.S. government was sympathetic to the DRV cause, but it remains uncertain whether and to what extent they were influenced by the Bangkok talks.

Then, on July 17, 1947, the State Department instructed its consuls in Saigon and Hanoi to investigate a number of questions, including whether the outcome of a settlement between France and the DRV would be favorable to U.S. policy objectives (e.g., whether the result would be stability or chaos, whether Ho Chi Minh remained devoted to communism or felt that nationalist revolution must come before Communist revolution, whether the DRV would drift into the Soviet camp) and whether the United States could influence the future development of Vietnam.[11]

The consuls agreed that only negotiations with the Ho Chi Minh government could lead to a solution. But they were divided over the question of whether Ho remained dedicated to communism. And, while they feared the DRV becoming a police state, they were of the opinion that Soviet policy toward Vietnam favored "remote control" rather than "open support." Two U.S. ambassadors, Jefferson Caffery and William Bullitt, also weighed in on the issue. Their opinions were clearly influenced by Ho's past career, his close connections with Communist circles, and the extent of Soviet influence on the DRV and, thus, sympathetic to French perceptions, paralleling "French efforts to shift international opinion of the Indochina war from a colonial war to an anti-communist crusade," and revealing "how French views forcefully made their way into American policy discussions."[12]

Most likely, the DRV's bottom-line objective in the Bangkok talks was to ensure that the United States continue to give only limited support to the French colonial war, particularly because it suspected France of planning a major military operation in the near future. Whether it had a more important objective is a well-kept secret, and those few who were privy to that secret are now mostly in their graves. Yet, in retrospect, it seems to me that during the period 1945–49 there was in the DRV some degree of admiration for and deference to the United States because of the role it played in World War II and the establishment of the Atlantic Charter, and its willingness to grant independence to the Philippines. Therefore, any assistance that the United States would have been willing to supply would have been greatly appreciated. Even if such assistance had been tied to policy concessions, it is likely that the DRV would have been willing to negotiate. Certainly, assistance to the DRV would have been in the best interests of the United States since an independent DRV would have remained an underdeveloped, medium-size state with limited foreign policy goals, making it much easier to deal with than other, bigger countries. But, in the end, American foreign policy remained focused on the containment of communism in general and the power struggle in Europe in particular.

The following question is, thus, relevant: Did it occur to Washington that Moscow was not competing for influence in Indochina, that it was as anxious as Washington to ally itself with France, and, therefore, that it had little incentive to involve itself in Vietnam? If so, why did the United States not shift to a policy that was substantially different from that of France with respect to Vietnam? Need for French support in the power struggle in Europe, fear of Communist victory in France in particular, and a mood of anticommunism generally were three important reasons why it did not. Another, in my view, is the fact that it did not understand international politics—and, in particular, Asian politics. American leaders did not realize that colonialism was doomed and that more productive than pursuing colonialist policies would be trying to reach some kind of understanding with genuine Vietnamese nationalism, thus safeguarding U.S. strategic interests in Southeast Asia without having to make an open-ended military commitment.

Added to this was another American misperception: that a Communist cannot be a nationalist. Indeed, the U.S. government failed to understand that the emergence in the 1930s of the Indochina Communist Party as the leader of the revolution in Vietnam was the product of conservative and intransigent French colonial policies that, among other things, did not allow even bourgeois political parties to exist and engage in legal political struggle there. As a result, a real bourgeois nationalist alternative did not exist. Further, in the then-prevailing conditions of colonial-cum-feudal oppression, communism was rooted in nationalism from the start, and the fact that a majority of the middle class and the intellectuals joined and remained faithful to the Communist-led revolution from 1930 until 1975 is strong evidence of this. History has shown that the Vietnamese Communists were, in fact, genuine nationalists whose policies were not always tied to the objectives of the Soviet Union and Communist China. Examples of such policies include confiscating property owned by pro-Japanese and pro-French landlords, beginning in 1941; reducing rents by 25 percent, beginning in 1945; seizing power in August 1945; disbanding the Indochina Communist Party in November 1945; coming to terms with France in March 1946 and thereafter waging a war of resistance against French reconquest; and accepting the 1954 Geneva Accords but renewing the military-political struggle in 1959 when peaceful reunification proved a failure. The clearest example of the Vietnamese Communists' willingness to subordinate ideology to the national interest, however, was the introduction in 1986 of free market reforms.

The year 1949 witnessed the United States openly supporting France's colonial war and the Bao Dai expedient (which it had seemed to reject in 1947). Later, in his memoirs, former secretary of state Dean Acheson admitted that the United States had no choice if it was to secure the cooperation of the French in the creation of NATO (betraying, in the process, one of the limitations in the political thinking of U.S. policymakers at that time, in this case a reluctance to rework policies known to be less than efficient).[13] It was for this reason that he instructed U.S. consular representatives in Hanoi to dissuade those in power there from offering seats to DRV representatives in any future pro-French government in Vietnam. Further missteps on Acheson's part were that he considered the question of whether Ho Chi Minh was as much a nationalist as a Communist to be irrelevant and that he felt that the United States should consider intervening in Vietnam as it had in Yugoslavia only if every other avenue were closed.[14] Still, official DRV radio refrained from attacking U.S. policy. And, in September 1949, when two U.S. journalists, Andrew Roth and Sol Sander, asked Ho Chi Minh whether Vietnam could remain neutral, he replied, "Why not?" As a guerrilla establishment, the DRV had no more effective means of making its voice heard in U.S. policymaking circles.

In January 1950, when a number of socialist countries established diplomatic relations with the DRV, Acheson took the opportunity to attack Ho Chi Minh for not being a nationalist. I wish to throw some light on this episode. Liu Shao Chi, the secretary general of the Chinese Communist Party, visited the Soviet Union in July and August 1949, and among the proposals that he made to Joseph Stalin was that all socialist countries should establish diplomatic relations with the DRV. The DRV, however, had no knowledge of this diplomatic démarche. In fact, it seems to have had no contact with the Communists in China, at least as far as I have been able to discover, until December 5, 1949, when a message was sent by Ho Chi Minh to Chinese leaders congratulating them on the establishment in October of the People's Republic and expressing the hope that relations between the two nations would become closer (without suggesting that diplomatic relations be established). On January 2, 1950, Ho Chi Minh and Tran Dang Ninh, the director of the Logistics Department of the DRV Ministry of Defense, went to China seeking military and economic aid. Ho's statement of January 14, 1950, expressing DRV government readiness to establish diplomatic relations with any and all governments was made and broadcast at a time when he was holding discussions with Liu Shao Chi in Peking. In the early 1950s, I learned from high-ranking sources that Ho did not go to China intending to seek diplomatic relations because such a development held the potential to turn Vietnam's national struggle into a dispute between the two camps, placing additional obstacles in the way of victory. But he could not resist the Chinese proposal, partly because he was told that France had sounded out China about the establishment of diplomatic relations, an eventuality that had the potential to make it difficult for China to render aid to Vietnam, and also because it was implied that Chinese-Vietnamese diplomatic relations were related to Chinese aid. A small and not yet liberated country has few choices, and the world should understand that this was not the DRV's preferred course of action.

The Korean War: The Unfortunate Watershed

The Korean War, which broke out in June 1950, brought about a change for the worse in U.S.-Chinese relations and in U.S. policy toward East Asia, Indochina included, and China's deep disappointment with President Truman's decision of June 27 ordering the Seventh Fleet to prevent all attacks on Taiwan was evident. With the outbreak of war in Korea, France's efforts at colonial reconquest were transformed, in the U.S. estimation, into a part of the free world's efforts to stem Communist and particularly Chinese expansionism. Truman's July 27 order also stepped up military assistance to French forces in Indochina as well as called for the dispatch of a U.S. military mission there that was to work closely with the French High Command. U.S. military aid to the latter, which started at US$10 million in early 1950, rose to US$1.1 billion in 1954, accounting for 78 percent of France's war expenditures in Indochina.[15]

Following the massive intervention of Chinese troops in the Korean War beginning on October 25, 1950—which surprised the United States, and caused it substantial difficulties, but neither dislodged it from Korea nor changed its policy on Taiwan—the United States maneuvered the United Nations first into condemning China as the aggressor (February 1, 1951) and then imposing an embargo against it (May 18, 1951). More important, it concluded that the socialist countries constituted a monolithic bloc bent on aggression and that the People's Republic was the main danger in Asia and, consequently, adopted the policy of Communist containment there. It also came to see the Vietnamese struggle for independence as part of a Chinese Communist scheme to dominate Southeast Asia. To be fair, the U.S. government did not launch the Korean War, but indignation and alarm led it into making a wrong evaluation of the Communist world and, consequently, adopting wrong policies.[16]

That communism is monolithic is an erroneous conception, as is clearly borne out by the events of the 1960s and 1970s. Viewing Vietnam's national struggle for freedom as part of a general scheme of aggression directed by the Communist world and, in particular, China is a gross misreading of Vietnam's history, of the history of Vietnamese-Chinese relations, of the deep and nationwide nationalism that underlay the political movement led by the DRV government. That misassessment of communism was further compounded by the rising anti-Communist hysteria in the United States (which began in 1950 and lasted into the 1960s). The resulting policy distortions and errors would set the United States and Vietnam on a collision course and lead the United States into the quagmire of the Vietnam War.

As a small country still struggling for independence, having little leverage and few contacts, and facing mounting hostility from the West and, in particular, the United States, Vietnam had no other choice than to rely on its ideological compatriots, no matter how imperfect such an arrangement might be, an imperfection reflected in, among other things, the 1954 Geneva Conference and Accords, the latter being, indeed, the product of a compromise among the great powers, socialist and Western, at the expense of small and weak countries.

Vietnamese Communist leader Le Duan greets American Communist organizer Gus Hall. Courtesy of the Vietnam Archive, Texas Tech University, Douglas Pike Photograph Collection.

Post-Geneva Developments and the Second Vietnam War

In any case, the 1954 Geneva Accords gave the United States a good opportunity to come to terms with Vietnam's genuine nationalism by helping implement the clause on Vietnam's reunification through general elections. But Washington ignored the advice of Great Britain and instead took that of the South Vietnamese leader Ngo Dinh Diem in rejecting nationwide elections and in persecuting former resistance fighters.[17] This inevitably led to the Second Vietnam War, which, at least as far as Vietnam was concerned, was essentially a continuation of the struggle for independence that had been ongoing since French conquest in the nineteenth century, despite the fact that in some ways it resembled a civil war and created deep social and familial divisions. Still, just as in its own civil war the United States would allow no state to secede from the Union, Vietnam was unwilling to allow itself to be partitioned into two separate states. As for the United States, it saw the war as part of the ongoing struggle to contain communism.

Did Vietnam try to avoid war with the United States? Yes, it did. From 1954 to 1958, the DRV sought reunification by peaceful means. Only when that proved impossible did it switch to the pursuit of reunification by political and military means. The Party's published Fifteenth Resolution maintained, "We have basically favorable conditions to maintain peace, achieve victory for the socialist revolution in the North and the national democratic people's revolution in the South, achieve national reunification by peaceful means." It continued: "It is our policy to actively solve the national reunification issue by peaceful means, . . . [but] so long as the United States and Diem are present in South Vietnam national partition and the possibility of war still remain."[18] While the resolution spoke of the possibility of war, the hope was for a peaceful solution. Also, from 1960 to 1963, the Vietnamese leadership did not set up a military zone in the area immediately south of the Military Demarcation Line and did not intensify military activities there, in order not to provoke a large-scale U.S. military response.

In a July 1962 letter addressed to COSVN (the DRV's Central Office for South Vietnam) secretary Nguyen Van Linh, Le Duan, the Party leader, said, "There can be no doubt about U.S. defeat. But we must make careful and precise calculations about the extent of U.S. defeat and the extent of our victory. . . . If we make excessive efforts, particularly in armed struggle—something that the present balance of forces does not allow—the United States might have a reaction that we cannot fully foresee."[19]

Resolution 15 was a unanimous decision of the whole Vietnamese leadership and a turning point in the history of Vietnam's revolution, and Ho Chi Minh strongly supported Le Duan's candidacy for the post of general secretary for the sake of national reunification.

General Secretary Le Duan was elated at the 1962 Geneva Agreements on Laos because this was the first time the United States had agreed with the idea of neutrality and a coalition government, which gave the hope that something similar could be done in South Vietnam. Accordingly, on July 24, 1962, the *Nhan Dan Daily* published an editorial proclaiming that the success of the Geneva Conference on Laos showed that, in the present world situation, "the forces of peace can efficiently struggle against *limited war* waged by the imperialists and can successfully eliminate the hotbeds of such wars" (I interpret this as meaning that even a limited war could have been avoided in South Vietnam). The editorial continued:

"The peaceful solution of the Lao problem exerts an impact on the situation in Southeast Asia and the world and shows that *many other issues can be solved by peaceful negotiations*" (I interpret this as meaning that there is hope for a neutral solution in South Vietnam). It concluded: "The Vietnamese people thoroughly support Laos's struggle to build a peaceful, neutral, independent, unified, democratic, and prosperous Laos." In fact, while from 1959 to 1975 Vietnam built, with Pathet Lao permission, the western Ho Chi Minh Trail in Lao territory, neither the Vietnamese nor the Pathet Lao tried to take over the whole of Laos, despite the fact that the presence of Thai troops in Laos required an increase in the number of Vietnamese troops to maintain the balance.

Most likely no one in the United States read the *Daily*'s editorial, nor did the paper propose a similar scenario for South Vietnam. But it is regrettable that, during the meeting between Foreign Minister Ung Van Khiem and Ambassador Averell Harriman, the former (who, for unknown reasons, had not received instructions from Le Duan before going to Geneva for the signing of the Accords) failed to make clear Vietnam's peaceful intentions in Laos and did not propose direct talks, as and when necessary, between the two sides on the situation in Laos, an initiative that might have alleviated tension and promoted better understanding of the situation not only in Laos but also in Vietnam.

Vietnamese leaders apparently counted on the United States realistically assessing its position and on Diem's continued resistance to the entry of regular American troops. This position was reflected in, among other things, an appeal made by Ho Chi Minh to President John F. Kennedy in a May 8, 1963, speech before the National Assembly in which he referred to Kennedy's opposition as a senator in 1954 to U.S. intervention in Vietnam and called on him, as president, to live up to the promise of his earlier position. It was also reflected in repeated calls by the National Liberation Front (NLF) in 1963–64 for a policy of peace and neutrality and for a coalition government in South Vietnam as well as in the positive attitude on the part of the DRV and the NLF in 1962–63 toward Diem and Nhu.

Following the anti-Diem coup in 1963, the situation in South Vietnam was both favorable (because of confusion and infighting in the Saigon administration and lowered morale among the southern troops) and unfavorable (because of the increasing likelihood of direct U.S. military intervention) for reunification. And it was in the context of this situation that the Communist Party of Vietnam (CPV) issued its Ninth Resolution. The resolution stated that the establishment of "a neutral government in Laos" shows that "before launching a limited war the United States would have to ponder over the specific balance of forces in Southeast Asia and the serious consequences" of such a decision. It continued: "By opposing U.S. aggression, for national independence, democracy and peace and neutrality, the revolution in South Vietnam has been trying to contain the enemy in the special [i.e., counterinsurgent] war." "We must and can," it declared, "contain and defeat the enemy in the special war." At the same time, however, "we must always enhance our vigilance and make active preparations to stand ready in case U.S. imperialism runs the risk of expanding the war in South Vietnam into a limited war." In order to achieve victory in the "special war," however, it would be necessary to "rapidly achieve a basic change in the military balance of force" by "wiping out and fully disintegrating the puppet troops" and, "most importantly, by strengthening our forces in all fields, and particularly our military forces," objectives that were deemed possible. The resolution also stated, "While having a full grasp of the principle of long-term struggle, we must make the most of the opportunity to achieve victory in not too long a period of time."[20]

While Resolution 9 misread U.S. intentions and involved big risks, it was a positive approach, marked by an "offensive" and "proactive spirit." Indeed, in 1964 and 1965, the DRV leadership tried to make the most of certain favorable conditions. That is, it attempted to destroy the bulk of the Saigon army, thereby hoping to discourage U.S. intervention. At that particular time, maintaining a protracted and small-scale guerrilla war meant missing a historic opportunity to shorten the war, but even that course of action risked U.S. intervention, the United States looking to win decisively in Vietnam. Still, even if U.S. intervention did come, it could only delay, not prevent, Saigon's ultimate defeat. So, in the end, Resolution 9 did not involve risking everything.

While full consensus prevailed on the component of Resolution 9 outlining military strategy, the component advocating opposition to Soviet revisionism did not receive the concurrence of Ho Chi Minh and a number of other leaders. Ho refrained from taking part in the vote. In 1964, all Politburo members, including Le Duan, agreed with the president that it was essential to restore friendship with the Soviet Union, and a series of corrective measures were taken in this regard. Following the ouster of Khrushchev in October 1964, Vietnam and the Soviet Union succeeded in normalizing and improving relations, thus making it possible for Vietnam to obtain assistance from both the Soviet Union and China while maintaining its independence with respect to the conduct of the revolution in South Vietnam. Important international conditions for the success of the revolution were, thus, ensured.

Yet Vietnam continued to abide by the strategy outlined in Resolution 9: trying to achieve victory while avoiding a direct confrontation with the United States. On June 18, 1964, when the Canadian ambassador, J. B. Seaborn, conveyed to him a threatening message from the United States, Prime Minister Pham Van Dong responded, "We want peaceful national reunification, without outside pressure. We want sincere negotiations in a conference." Pham affirmed that a "just solution" involved, among other things, the establishment of a neutral regime in South Vietnam and added that "how long South Vietnam would remain neutral would be decided by its people."[21] Receiving Seaborn again on August 13, 1964, a week after U.S. air attacks against North Vietnam, the prime minister stressed the gravity of the situation and said that it was necessary to return to the Geneva Accords of 1954.[22]

But, as it turned out, Vietnam could not prevent massive U.S. military intervention, not only because it did not or could not engage in direct talks with the United States, but also, and more important, because U.S. policymaking was then governed mainly by Cold War considerations and anticommunism, meaning that American withdrawal from the South and the creation of a neutral South Vietnam were not options. The only relevant issue was how to win the war. The DRV leadership had been wrong in 1964–65; U.S. military intervention was, indeed, inevitable.

Vietnam found itself faced with the difficult decision of whether to fight back. The power and the wealth of the United States were obvious. But its position was also characterized by serious weaknesses: among other things, little unity or dedication, as well as the lack of a strong nationalist sentiment, in South Vietnam; the difficult tropical climate and a topography conducive to guerrilla activity; the drain on the U.S. military position of an extended concentration of troops in one place; the necessity to escalate the air war only gradually; and the necessity to refrain

Le Duan (white shirt) and General Vo Nguyen Giap at a meeting of Vietnamese Communist leaders. Courtesy of the Vietnam Archive, Texas Tech University, Douglas Pike Photograph Collection.

from a ground invasion of North Vietnam in order to avoid a military confrontation with the Soviet Union and China. When the Saigon troops were obviously heading for defeat in 1965, the U.S. decision to resort to large-scale military intervention was motivated not so much by staunchness and determination as by a sense of impasse and the absence of a realistic alternative. The United States first launched an air war against North Vietnam and later launched a limited (i.e., land) war in the South, despite the fact that various simulations showed that an air war would not achieve success. Many U.S. officials were apprehensive that direct U.S. military intervention in Vietnam would in the long run involve mostly negative consequences for U.S. strategy worldwide, expose the administration to increasing domestic and world condemnation, and end in failure. The one thing that did make Washington optimistic was the absolute military superiority of the United States.[23] Added to this was, perhaps, the notion of American exceptionalism, although such terminology did not have a dominant place in the literature at the time.

Noting that nearly 180,000 U.S. troops had been sent to South Vietnam, that that number might climb as high as 400,000 in the future, and that the bombing of North Vietnam would likely be intensified, the December 27, 1965, resolution of the Central Committee of the CPV said that the enemy's military strategy had changed and had gone beyond the limits of a "special war." But it acknowledged that the United States was "afraid of a long, drawn-out war with prospects of heavier defeats" and that, in fact, over the last several months it "had to scatter its forces in various battlefields, had suffered heavy defeats, with concomitant confusion and passivity." Further, direct intervention in the war had exposed the United States as the aggressor and the puppet administration and its troops as traitors, thus aggravating further a most basic U.S. political weakness and resulting in ever greater opposition at home and abroad. The resolution set the following objectives: "to wipe out an important portion of U.S. troops," "to wipe out and disintegrate a majority of the Saigon troops," "to crush the U.S. will of aggression," and "to fully grasp and apply the line of long, drawn-out war" while "seizing the opportunity to achieve a decisive victory in South Vietnam within a relatively short time."[24]

It was also decided to conduct negotiations with the United States as and when possible for a settlement of the war. To this end, in 1965 the Politburo member Nguyen Duy Trinh was appointed foreign minister, and, ten days after the start of the U.S. bombing of North Vietnam in February 1965, a group of senior foreign affairs officials, under the leadership of Ho Chi Minh, Le Duan, and Pham Van Dong, began to draft the four-point policy that was formally announced on April 8, 1965. It is noteworthy that, unlike the 1954 Geneva Accords, the four points did not provide for the holding of general elections with the aim of national reunification. The third point (that South Vietnamese affairs were to be dealt with in accordance with the NLF program), which was viewed by U.S. officials as a hard-line proposal, was something that could be reworded in the course of negotiations. In fact, the main components of the four points were subsequently included to varying degrees in the January 27, 1973, Paris Agreement. When for the first time Washington stopped bombing (the Mayflower Project, which lasted from May 12 to May 18, 1965) and sounded out Hanoi about conditions for peace, the move was officially attacked by Vietnam, but, on May 18, Vietnam's representative in Paris visited the Quai d'Orsay to convey to the United States that the four-point position was not a precondition but simply the best basis on which to enter direct talks, subject to certain conditions. At that time, Vietnam also began receiving emissaries, whether American or foreign, in order to ascertain whether the United States was really ready for negotiations on acceptable terms. In 1966, Vietnam detected a certain war weariness among the American people, troops, and statesmen, but through 1967 the hawks still clamored for, and in fact obtained, an escalation of the war effort.

It was under these conditions that the thirteenth Central Committee meeting adopted on January 27, 1967, a new strategy, according to which: "Along with the military and political struggle in South Vietnam, we must launch attacks on the enemy in the diplomatic field." The diplomatic struggle was seen as "compelling the enemy to end unconditionally and for good all bombings and other acts of war against the DRV, to recognize the NLF as the sole genuine representative of the people of South Vietnam and negotiate with it, to withdraw all troops of the United States and its satellites from South Vietnam, and to let the people of Vietnam solve by themselves the Vietnam problem." The immediate efforts, however, must, it was stated, be focused on the first demand (as reflected in Foreign Minister Nguyen Duy Trinh's statements of January 27 and December 29, 1967).[25] In essence, the Thirteenth Resolution meant switching to a policy of fighting while talking. In view of the bellicose posture of a number of U.S. political and military figures and their persistent demand for the conditional cessation of bombing and unconditional talks, on the one hand, and the growing antiwar movement, on the other, the fourteenth Central Committee meeting, after intense deliberations, adopted in January 1968 the Fourteen Resolution, which called for "staging a series of general attacks and uprisings in South Vietnam," starting from the Lunar (Tet) New Year, in order to "wipe out and disintegrate an overwhelming majority of the Saigon troops, overthrow the Saigon administration at various levels, seize full power, . . . [and] wipe out an important portion of U.S. troops and means of war, thus making it impossible for U.S. troops to carry out their political and military tasks in Vietnam." It was "on that basis" that the DRV sought "to break the U.S. will of aggression, to compel it to accept defeat in South Vietnam, to stop all acts of war against North Vietnam, . . . [and] to negotiate in order to end the war in accordance with our objectives and demands."[26]

At that point, General Vo Nguyen Giap, who did not agree with certain major points in the Lunar New Year military plan, was convalescing abroad. Ho Chi Minh, who attended the fourteenth Central Committee meeting, refrained from voting on Resolution 14: by doing so, he warned Le Duan to refrain from acting rashly but did not forbid him from carrying out the project. He expressed an important reservation while striving to maintain unity inside the leadership.

The general attacks did not achieve all their objectives and were later criticized as involving "subjectivism and voluntarism, a poor grasp of the law on uprising and revolutionary war,"[27] but they did help break the U.S. will of aggression (by revealing the pursuit of military victory to be futile), impel the United States to deescalate the war and proceed toward disengagement, cease air bombardment and other acts of war against North Vietnam (at first in areas north of the Twentieth Parallel), and start negotiations. While banking on the United States realistically assessing its position did not pay off in 1964–65, it did in 1968. Common to Resolutions 12–14 was a desire to end the war within a relatively short period of time, presumably to minimize the sacrifices of the people, and also to deny the great powers the opportunity to collude and impose a solution similar to the 1954 Accords.

Negotiations from May 1968 to January 1973

Negotiations aimed at ending the bombing of North Vietnam started on May 13, 1968, and lasted for about five and a half months, an agreement being reached on October 27, and a suspension of bombing enforced as of October 31, 1968. Thereafter, with the coming to power of President Nixon, the four-party talks began in Paris on January 25, 1969, but remained deadlocked until the second half of 1972.

During these six years of simultaneous fighting and talking, Vietnam remained unpersuaded by the Nixon administration's madman theory and its other threats and successfully exploited domestic pressure in the United States in order to compel the steady withdrawal of American troops from South Vietnam, but it failed to get Washington to agree to the replacement of the Saigon regime by a coalition government. Furthermore, it feared collusion among the great powers when Kissinger and Nixon visited Beijing and Moscow in 1971 and 1972. While the March 1972 offensive failed to achieve substantial results, it did warn the United

States not to seek a solution in Beijing or Moscow. But it was not until October 8, 1972, that Vietnam could offer a proposal—not involving the often-repeated demand for removal of the Thieu government—that was instrumental in accelerating the movement toward an agreement. In hindsight, one could see that the October 8, 1972, proposal was prompted by no prior knowledge of or speculation about the administration's "decent interval" strategy, being based instead on other considerations, among which were those mentioned in a message sent by the Politburo to the delegation in Paris on October 4, 1972: "We must shelve some other demands on the internal affairs of South Vietnam. Even if we continue to negotiate until after the U.S. elections we would not be able to reach an agreement on these issues. But, if we put an end to the U.S. military involvement in South Vietnam, then in the subsequent struggle against the puppet regime we would be able to achieve a solution to the issues and win even greater victories."[28] One can intuit certain other reasons behind these new instructions: the failure of the March 1972 offensive to achieve substantial results; the firm U.S. refusal to replace the Saigon government with a coalition government; the recognition that Nixon would likely win reelection; the fear that drawn-out and inconclusive negotiations might open the way for great-power collusion. The instructions of October 4 were wise, but they should have come earlier.

The Paris Agreement and After

I will not rehash the details of the last stage of the negotiations, the new U.S. demands following Thieu's negative reactions, the Christmas bombing, the resumed negotiations, the signing of the Paris Agreement in January 1973 and its provisions, and the military situation from 1973 to April 1975, which are well-known. I will simply emphasize the following points:

- When President Ho Chi Minh received the Italian professor Georgio La Pira on November 11, 1965, he stated, "We are ready to roll out the red carpet with flowers for U.S. withdrawal from Vietnam."[29] Accordingly, the DRV/NLF leadership did consciously strive to bring about an agreement that could meet the U.S. demand for "peace with honor."
- In spite of the conclusion of the Paris Agreement in January 1973,

Le Duan was less than optimistic because, in his view, the situation in South Vietnam was very complicated and there was vacillation in the ranks of the revolution. As he saw it, it was not a foregone conclusion that the full potential of the 1973 victory would be realized. He was also "worried lest the praise of the foreign press give rise to euphoria among the people, which might cause them to forget about the difficulties and prevent them from fully grasping the situation."[30]

- Owing to its focus on U.S. military action in Indochina and a concomitant lack of understanding of the true aims of U.S. foreign policy, the Vietnamese leadership was of the view that the Nixon doctrine showed that "the United States had not completely abandoned its neocolonialist plan against our entire country and the whole of Indochina"[31] and that Washington's basic scheme was to continue to "implement U.S. neocolonial policy in South Vietnam and to divide Vietnam on a long-term basis."[32]

- There was a continued fear of great-power collusion, and, in particular, U.S.-Chinese collusion, as well as of the potential of that collusion to cause renewed bombing and hinder the reunification of Vietnam.

- The twenty-first Central Committee plenum, held in October 1973, criticized the defensive posture of Provisional Revolutionary Government of South Vietnam/North Vietnamese troops over the previous eight months and concluded that Thieu did not intend and could not be made to implement the Paris Agreement, and, therefore, "the revolutionary path in South Vietnam is revolutionary violence." Since the situation in South Vietnam was still uncertain, the plenum could only lay down a tentative strategy based on two different conceptions of future developments: (*a*) The first conception was formulated as follows: "It is possible [because of the enemy's basic weaknesses] to gradually compel it to implement the Paris Agreement on Vietnam and really restore peace, and the struggle of the South Vietnamese people for independence and democracy, which still remains long, difficult, and complicated, will increasingly develop and advance vigorously." (*b*) The second conception was more pessimistic: "The Paris Agreement continues to be violated and undermined by the enemy, military conflicts may grow, the war may increase in intensity and scope, and we must wage an arduous and fierce revolutionary war in order to defeat the enemy and achieve full victory." While "endeavor[ing] as best we can to make the first possibility prevail," that is, gradually compelling the implementation of the Paris Agreement, Vietnam "must stand ready to cope with the second possibility," that is, "the renewal of a big war."[33]

- One year later, at a September 30–October 8, 1974, meeting, that is, nearly two months after Nixon's resignation, the Vietnamese leadership unanimously agreed that in South Vietnam the revolutionary forces were now stronger than the enemy forces; that it would be most difficult for the United States to intervene militarily once again since its ability to provide military assistance to Saigon was decreasing daily; that a unique opportunity for liberating the country had, therefore, arisen and should be seized; and that it was essential to combine vigorous and rapid attacks with shrewd planning in order to achieve a neat and thorough victory in 1974–75. In particular, the resolution stated: "If the opportunity comes at the beginning or at the end of 1975, we must immediately liberate South Vietnam in 1975."[34] Consequently, the deadline for the full liberation of South Vietnam was set for 1975, then for the early months of 1975, prior to the onset of the monsoon, that is, by the end of April 1975.

The start of the offensive was repeatedly moved up so as not to miss a historic opportunity, one believed to be available only once in a thousand years, so as not to allow the Saigon forces any breathing room, and so as not to allow a great-power collusion to frustrate the country's reunification.

An exclusive focus on the war effort meant that the offensive was prepared and carried out without any detailed plan being made for dealing with the basic political and economic realities of South Vietnam. This lack of planning, coupled with the ideological rigidity and the physical and intellectual exhaustion of the leadership and the officials, meant that no postwar foreign policy could be worked out. Therefore, a unified Vietnam was unprepared for developments in both domestic and foreign affairs.

Vietnam had achieved a great victory and fulfilled its sacred national objectives—the liberation of South Vietnam and the reunification of the country—against heavy odds, at a time when the bipolar world was still intact. But, owing to its shortsightedness, it soon found itself in the grip of a serious postwar crisis that dragged on for about a decade.

In foreign affairs, Vietnam bungled the normalization of relations with the United States because of its poor understanding of post-1975 U.S. politics (including the bad loser mentality) and its insistence on war reparations. It also bungled the normalization of relations with the ASEAN (Association of Southeast Asian Nations) countries because of hubris and certain prejudices left over from the Second Vietnam War. And blind ideological commitment and a serious lack of vigilance caused it to underestimate the criminal schemes of the Khmer Rouge.

More important, Vietnam failed to understand that China viewed the partitioning between North and South as necessary if Vietnam were to remain its obedient satellite and would, therefore, inevitably view Vietnamese unification as a hostile move requiring retaliation. Faced with the terrible attack by the Khmer Rouge on September 24, 1977, against Tay Ninh and other provinces of Vietnam as well as the news of China's increased military aid to Pol Pot's forces, Hanoi concluded that the top leadership of the Khmer Rouge, encouraged by China, was behind all armed attacks against it since 1975. Hanoi became deeply concerned about the great danger of two-pronged attacks from the southwest and from the north. Following nearly a year of negotiations coupled with investigations, a July 27, 1978, Central Committee meeting decided to destroy the Khmer Rouge leadership and armed forces in order to ensure the security of southern Vietnam, end the Cambodian genocide, and cope with subsequent military attacks from China.

The decision was correct because history has shown that, when China wants a war, diplomatic negotiations cannot secure the peace and that the first priority must, therefore, be the country's security and survival. But Vietnam committed two grave mistakes: concluding a treaty of friendship and cooperation with the Soviet Union (which provoked a negative reaction from many countries, including the United States, but did not result in Soviet intervention when China invaded Vietnam) and failing to hold frank and exhaustive discussions with the ASEAN countries prior to the military action against the Khmer Rouge, antagonizing them (particularly Thailand) and resulting in strained relations for years to come.

Hanoi at first intended to withdraw from Cambodia after a few years, but this proved impossible: while the Khmer Rouge troops were initially decimated, they subsequently received substantial aid from certain countries and international organizations. Therefore, a hasty Vietnamese withdrawal before the government and armed forces of the new Cambodia could be sufficiently strengthened would allow the Khmer Rouge to return and massacre the people, and the blame would again be laid at the door of Vietnam. Persistence in fighting the Khmer Rouge and rebuilding Cambodia was a must, although Vietnam respected world opinion and abided by its demands when possible.

From 1986, the CPV leadership decided to carry out comprehensive reforms, including a peaceful settlement of the Cambodian problem and normalization of relations with the ASEAN countries, the United States, China, and other countries. This was done by holding negotiations on Cambodia in various forums, negotiations that resulted in the withdrawal in 1989 of all remaining Vietnamese troops from Cambodia and the signing of the Paris Agreement on Cambodia in 1991. As a result, by 1995 Vietnam had normalized its international relations and joined ASEAN, which from that point was truly representative of the whole of Southeast Asia. Meanwhile, the process of implementation of the Paris Agreement finally resulted in the outlawing and subsequent disintegration of the Khmer Rouge.

Some Final Reflections

Since 1945, Vietnam has had to make three most difficult decisions: the French war, the American war, and the Cambodian war. The last one involved not only a war on two fronts but also world condemnation and isolation. Yet, of all the three foreign military interventions in Southeast Asia and South Asia, the Cambodian was clearly humanitarian and successful in spite of certain mistakes and shortcomings.

However, the period 1945–95, including the years of crisis from 1975 to 1995, shows that Vietnam suffered from serious problems in the handling of political and diplomatic issues, problems due to, among other things, poor training, poor research, ideological blindness, and ignorance about the strength—both positive and negative—of nationalist sentiment. Since 1945 Vietnam has continuously learned things the hard way, but it is high time for it to review seriously and exhaustively, and learn from, its past mistakes if it is to be successful in nation building, statecraft, and foreign relations in a modern world marked by globalization and integration.

It is noteworthy that from 1965 the American people did generously and effectively seek peace in Vietnam. That political movement was unprecedented in terms of its scope, composition, moral content, vision, and courage. In spite of the decades-long anti-Communist hysteria, the American people had come to agree that national liberation was the substance and just cause of the war waged by the Vietnamese people. While the heroism and sacrifices of the Vietnamese mainly account for the victory, important credit should go to the staunch U.S. antiwar movement for bringing about the withdrawal of all U.S. troops from Vietnam—with no "peacekeeping" force left behind, as has happened elsewhere—and an end to U.S. bombing and all other military activities in Vietnam, Laos, and Cambodia.

Another point that strikes me is that, many years after the end of the war, the debate over it continues to rage, with over seven thousand books published to date on the war itself and on Vietnam as a country. Such self-examination is not characteristic of all nations. This shows that the Americans are a responsible people who are serious about learning from the past. The U.S. war veterans have also contributed substantially, both as private citizens and in their capacity as political representatives, to the normalization of relations. I must do justice as well to those American statesmen we condemned for their role in the war. Once they recognized the futility, and the harmful consequences, of their policies, they were willing to change course. Why such positive developments could not prevent a new adventure in Iraq is a matter of deep regret. There is a common point between the Vietnam and the Iraq wars: a president who allowed his policy to be shaped exclusively by a coterie of like-minded advisers. Is that one of the basic causes of costly errors of policy? From 1949 to 1961, most Americans supported U.S. policy toward Vietnam, but from 1965, and particularly from 1968, things became quite different. The same can be said about the congressional elections of November 2006. This should give us hope that the American people will be able to steer their country toward a saner and more realistic course.

I also owe a personal debt to the American people and their scholars. From 1978 to 1983, in addition to my main duties at the Vietnamese embassy in Bangkok, I was asked to deal with American officials and citizens. I was surprised to find that many of them were honest and frank, and it was quite a pleasure to work with them. Thus, a question arose in my mind: Why did we have a war with them? Therefore, in addition to day-to-day issues, I discussed with them the war and its effects and did additional reading. In 1988, I attended the first conference on the Vietnam War in Hanoi with a number of U.S. scholars, and from then on I was engaged in research on the diplomatic history of the Vietnam wars. I enjoyed, in that connection, the cooperation of, and candid and informed discussions with, many American scholars, in particular professors George C. Herring and George McT. Kahin, whose works *America's Longest War* and *Intervention* have been my reference books for several years, helping elucidate many issues. Because of space constraints, I cannot mention many other books that have also been helpful to me. In my view, American scholars were instrumental in promoting the antiwar movement and in contributing substantially to the current good understanding that exists between our two peoples.

There are at present two important and positive factors in Vietnamese-U.S. relations. First, since 1995, both governments, their officials and citizens, can talk directly and regularly to one another, unlike the period 1945–94, with its numerous and sometimes tragic misunderstandings. Second, Vietnam is an ASEAN member. Vietnamese-U.S. relations—political, economic, cultural, and others—have been normalized, and friendship is being promoted, some important milestones being the conclusion of the Bilateral Trade Agreement and the recent agreement on Vietnam's entry into the World Trade Organization. Year by year, the United States is acting less like a bad loser and Vietnam less like a bad winner. I have talked with many common people, and I am happy to say that there are no anti-American feelings among the majority of my fellow countrymen, who have firmly left the war behind and now hope and trust that there will be no new military conflict with the United States. There are, in international relations, no permanent friends, no permanent enemies, only permanent national interests: this view is becoming more attractive to many Vietnamese. Some of them even cautiously look forward to seeing the United States function as a stabilizing factor in the Asian Pacific region, although others still have reservations about what they consider the irrational U.S. policy toward Asia and Vietnam. Even after normalization, Vietnamese-U.S. relations still involve certain irritants, old and new, with the U.S. great-power mentality and U.S. policies toward Vietnam being, to a great extent, shaped by U.S. relations with other great powers, issues of human rights and religious freedom, and trade disputes. These difficulties, which arise against the backdrop of rapid change in Vietnam and vigorous growth in trade and other relations with the United States, should not erode our optimism and hinder friendship as both nations, and, in particular, their younger generations, try to develop the positive aspects of U.S.-Vietnamese relations with vision, goodwill, and hard and imaginative work. Cynics often say that it was not until 1995, that is, five hundred years after Christopher Columbus, that Vietnam started to "discover" America, meaning that a lack of knowledge about the United States will, among other things, seriously hinder U.S.-Vietnamese relations. One can counter optimistically that younger generations, free of old prejudices, can be fast learners and effective doers.

The Vietnamese who from 1945 put down their pens and took up weapons have fulfilled their national liberation tasks and are now leaving the national stage. As one of them, may I offer my best wishes to the younger generations of both countries in their endeavor to engage in a frank and constructive dialogue and to build up friendly and cooperative relations in a new and more complex world. I offer no specific advice, not simply out of modesty, but mainly because the younger generations are operating in circumstances that are different from those that obtained in the past and have different values and, therefore, would and should have their own approaches. Similarly, the Vietnamese who lost the country to foreign invaders in the late nineteenth century could not tell us how to recover it, although many of them had strong patriotic feelings.

Notes

The views expressed in this essay are the author's own and do not represent the views of the Government of Vietnam and the Institute of International Relations, Hanoi.

1. Archimede L. A. Patti, *Why Vietnam? Prelude to America's Albatross* (Berkeley and Los Angeles: University of California Press, 1980), 54 (see generally 50–54).

2. Oral briefings given to the author by Foreign Minister Hoang Minh Giam in 1951 at the Ministry of Foreign Affairs in the Viet Bac military zone, seat of the Ho Chi Minh government from 1947 to 1954.

3. Gareth Porter, ed., *Vietnam: A History in Documents* (New York: New American Library, 1981), 38.

4. The French mood was best illustrated by what Max Andre, chief French representative at the Franco-DRV talks in Fontainebleau, told his counterpart, Pham Van Dong, in June 1946: "Vous, Vietnamiens, ne vous faites pas trop d'illusions. Si vous n'etes pas sages, il nous suffira d'une simple operation de police. En huit jours, on vous aura" (Alain Ruscio, *Les Communistes français et la guerre d'Indochine, 1944–1954* [The French Communists and the Indochina War, 1944–1954] [Paris: L'Harmatta, 1985], 148; "You, Vietnamese, don't harbor any illusions. If you don't behave, we would need just a simple police operation. In eight days, we will finish you.").

5. Porter, ed., *Vietnam,* 56.

6. Ibid., 60–61.

7. Bernard Fall (*The Two Viet-Nams: A Political and Military Analysis* [New York: Praeger, 1964], 196) quoted the French prime minister Paul Ramadier praising, in March 1947, "the correct attitude of the Soviet Government" on the Indochina question.

8. Meeting President Ho Chi Minh near Thai Nguyen town, Professor Paul Mus, the representative of the French high commissioner Emile Bollaert, put forward the following nonnegotiable conditions:

- The Vietnamese troops will surrender all their arms and munitions to the French army.
- The French army has the right to circulate throughout and occupy freely the territory of Vietnam. The Vietnamese troops will assemble in places designated by the French army.
- The Vietnamese government will hand over French troops and/or legionnaires who defected.
- The Vietnamese government will release French and pro-French detainees being held by it.

Diplomatic Struggle during the National and Democratic Revolution, 1945–1954 (in Vietnamese) (Hanoi: Institute of International Relations, 2002), 381–82.

9. Mark Bradley, "An Improbable Opportunity: America and the Democratic Republic of Vietnam's 1947 Initiative," in *The Vietnam War: Vietnamese and American Perspectives,* ed. Jayne S. Werner and Luu Doan Huynh (New York: Sharpe, 1992), 6–7.

10. Porter, ed., *Vietnam,* 64.

11. Ibid., 66.

12. Bradley, "An Improbable Opportunity," 13–14.

13. As Dean Acheson (*Present at the Creation* [New York: Norton, 1971], 673–74) wrote, "The result of withholding help to France would, at most, have removed the colonial power. It could not have made the resulting situation a beneficial one either for Indochina or Southeast Asia, or in the more important effort of furthering the

stability and defense of Europe. So while we may have tried to muddle through and were certainly not successful, I could not think then or later of a better course." He continued: "I decided, however, that having put our hand to the plow we would not look back." The consequences of this decision for both Vietnam and the United States were particularly unfortunate.

14. Ibid., 79.

15. William S. Turley, *The Second Indochina War: A Short Political and Military History, 1954–1975* (Boulder, CO: Westview, 1986), 4–5.

16. In commenting on U.S. reactions to the Korean War, I find my mind turning also to the reactions of the current U.S. administration to the events of September 11, 2001. How similar certain aspects of these reactions are is, of course, a matter of opinion. Certainly, Vietnam faced similar challenges following the 1975 Khmer Rouge takeover in Cambodia.

17. In these post-Geneva years, only one U.S. action was useful to the national cause of Vietnam. On January 23, 1957, the United States proposed to the UN Security Council that South Vietnam and South Korea be allowed to join the United Nations. The next day, the Soviet Union offered a counterproposal that would have allowed both Vietnams and both Koreas to join the United Nations. The United States, moved by Cold War considerations, rejected the Soviet proposal, which, had it been accepted, would have obstructed efforts to reunify Vietnam.

18. Fifteenth Resolution, January 12–22, 1959, in *Full Documents of the CPV* (in Vietnamese), vol. 20 (Hanoi: National Political Publishing House, 2002), 61–69.

19. Le Duan, *La thu vao Nam* [Letters to the South] (Hanoi: Su That, 1985), 139.

20. Ninth Resolution, December 1963, in *Full Documents of the CPV,* vol. 24 (Hanoi: National Political Publishing House, 2003), 819–39.

21. Luu Van Loi and Nguyen Anh Vu, *Secret Contacts between Vietnam and the USA prior to the Paris Conference* (in Vietnamese) (Hanoi: Institute of International Relations, 1990), 22–23.

22. Ibid., 29.

23. William S. Turley wrote that, in the mid-1960s, many Americans "believed that the revolution (read: Vietnamese revolution) would dissolve before the mere display of US power. If it did not, the USA was confident it could crush the revolution with its overwhelming armed might. That had always been the American way, and it had always prevailed" (Turley, *Second Indochina War,* 65).

24. Twelfth Resolution, December 27, 1965, in *Full Documents of the CPV,* vol. 26 (Hanoi: National Political Publishing House, 2003), 623–38.

25. Thirteenth Resolution, January 27, 1967, in *Full Documents of the CPV,* vol. 28 (Hanoi: National Political Publishing House, 2003), 175–76.

26. Fourteenth Resolution, January 1968, in *Full Documents of the CPV,* vol. 29 (Hanoi: National Political Publishing House, 2004), 50–56.

27. General Vo Nguyen Giap wrote two articles that, among other things, provided comments on the Tet Offensive. In "Great Victory of the Anti-U.S. War of Re-

sistance: Historical Lessons" ([in Vietnamese] *Xua va Nay* [Past and Present], no. 234 [April 2005]: 10, 12), he wrote:

> The Tet general attacks are a military move marked by creativity and originality that produced a basic turning point in the war situation and started the process of U.S. deescalation of the war. We took a step in breaking the U.S. will of aggression at a time when the United States had the biggest number of troops in Vietnam, was at the peak of its strength and its war efforts. As its limited war strategy had gone bankrupt, the U.S. administration had to de-Americanize and Vietnamize the war.
>
> Because of subjectivism and voluntarism, a poor grasp of the law on uprising and revolutionary war, it was decided to stage general uprisings that exposed all the revolutionary bases and assets during the war, at a time when over 1 million U.S., puppet, and satellite troops were operating in South Vietnam. The continued attacks on urban centers and the slowness in shifting the operations to the rural areas in 1968 did cause many losses to the revolution in terms of strategic posture and forces.

See also his "Comrade Le Duan, the Firm and Loyal Communist, the Outstanding Leader of Vietnam's Revolution" (in Vietnamese), *Tien Phong Sunday Paper* (Hanoi), no. 19 (May 12, 2002): 11.

28. *The Diplomatic Front and the Paris Negotiations on Vietnam* (in Vietnamese) (Hanoi: National Political Publishing House, 2004), 442.

29. Luu Van Loi and Nguyen Anh Vu, *Secret Contacts*, 103.

30. Informal talk given by Le Duan to the staff of the *Nhan Dan Daily* on February 24, 1973.

31. Hoang Tung, "Our Very Great Victory and Our New Tasks" (in Vietnamese), *Hoc Tap Journal*, April 19, 1973, 11–18.

32. General Van Tien Dung, *Spring Great Victory* (in Vietnamese) (Hanoi: People's Army Publishing House, July 1976), 13.

33. Twenty-first Resolution, October 13, 1973, in *Full Documents of the CPV*, vol. 34 (Hanoi: National Political Publishing House, 1973), 231–32.

34. Vo Nguyen Giap et al., *The General Headquarters during the Spring of Full Victory* (in Vietnamese) (Hanoi: National Political Publishing House, 2000), 138.

5

Ho Chi Minh, Confucianism, and Marxism

Robert K. Brigham

The Vietnam War ended thirty years ago, yet a number of important questions remain unanswered. Not the least of these is how Vietnam's Communist Party won peasants to its cause. To many Western observers, the
war was all about winning the hearts and minds of Vietnam's rural poor.[1]
These same scholars and journalists claim that Vietnamese traditions dictated that whoever had the mandate of heaven—legitimacy in the eyes
of the people—would win the contest for political control of Vietnam.
This mandate could not be demanded; leaders earned it through practice
of the great Confucian virtues—honesty, simplicity, obedience, and duty.
Some Western scholars suggest that the Party used the personality of Ho
Chi Minh, the president of Vietnam's Communist Party, to cement the
bond between peasants and the revolution.[2] They argue that Ho embodied many of the traditional Confucian virtues and that this led peasants
to follow his revolutionary movement. Since Vietnam had a hierarchi-
cal, patriarchal political tradition, peasants looked for a political leader
who behaved in the proper way and who took the correct position. This
theory of the Party's success utilizes a cultural explanation for the war: the
Communists won because they understood the essence of Vietnamese
national character better than their adversaries in Saigon did. The Party
earned the right to claim the loyalty of Vietnam's peasants through proper
conduct and a natural understanding of what it truly meant to be Viet-

Ho Chi Minh at
Communist Party
Congress, 1954.
Courtesy of the
Vietnam Archive,
Texas Tech University,
Douglas Pike
Photograph Collection.

namese. Following this logic, the mandate of heaven belonged to Ho Chi
Minh and his followers.

The French sociologist Paul Mus perhaps best explains the mandate
of heaven. He concludes that this idea is a Sino-Vietnamese concept with
strong ties to Confucianism. According to Mus, *chinh nghia* [the just
cause] was the collective view of what was right and proper. It was the
body of public opinion that determined whether your cause had merit.
A government that followed *chinh nghia*—and, thus, gained acceptance

by collective will—could legitimately claim the devotion of the people and govern their behavior. It was impossible, for instance, to simply claim the mandate of heaven. The will of the people was not something that could be demanded or forced. It had to come from the alchemy of social, supernatural, and psychological factors that had helped shape collective opinion in Vietnam's countryside for hundreds of years. Mus wrote, "The major premise presents itself neither as a circle of things nor of persons but as the balanced total of opinions professed on the things that matter by the persons who count in the eyes of the community as a whole."[3] In other words, confirmation of *chinh nghia* brought moral and ideological power that transcended all individual power. For Mus and others, because Ho Chi Minh embodied the correct way, peasants willingly followed him. Through his own actions, Ho brought to the Party the power to claim the peasants' loyalty. As the prizewinning journalist Frances FitzGerald, a follower of Mus, writes, "To many Vietnamese . . . Ho Chi Minh was perfectly sincere, since he always acted in the *correct* manner, no matter what it cost him. And it was the very consistency of his performance that gave them confidence that he would carry the revolution out in the manner he indicated."[4] According to Mus, Ho used Vietnam's long-standing Confucian practices to condition peasants to accept the Party's discipline, much like a son accepted his father's rule.[5]

This view is also shared by one of the leading Vietnamese intellectuals of the twentieth century, Nguyen Khac Vien. In one of his most important works, an essay titled "Confucianism and Marxism," Vien suggests: "For ten centuries Confucianism was the intellectual and ideological backbone of Vietnam." He also argues that Confucianism was even more influential in shaping Vietnam's modern revolution than Marxism's "law of historical development."[6] He consistently maintains that the similarities between Confucianism and Marxism were profound. Both stressed social order, both believed that there were laws governing historical forces, and both emphasized duty and obligation to a society over individual rights. Vien concludes that these similarities made it easy for the vanguard of the anticolonial movement to accept Marxism. In his view, once the revolution focused squarely on Vietnamese political traditions, there was no stopping it. He therefore stresses continuity with Vietnam's past and unity within the revolutionary movement. For Vien and others who believe that the Communist Party's success was tied to its ability to capture the essence of Vietnamese national culture and identity, Ho Chi Minh clearly stands as the most important link between Vietnam's Confucian past and its socialist future.

Ho is often portrayed as a revolutionary mandarin with strong ties to Confucianism and Marxism. For example, the journalist David Halberstam refers to him as "pure, uncorrupted in a corrupting world, a man of the land and its simple virtues."[7] In other words, Halberstam sees Ho as the perfect Confucian. He was an uncle to the people of Vietnam and a father to the nation. The anthropologist Neil Jamieson argues that Ho and his South Vietnamese counterpart, Ngo Dinh Diem, were both Confucians. He writes, "Both spent large portions of their adult life in obscure, self-imposed exile. Each tried, in his own way, to be the father of his country. Both were strong authoritarian leaders and stern disciplinarians; neither was very nurturant or forgiving." But, according to Jamieson, Ho—unlike Diem—also understood that Vietnam's peasants needed to belong to a tradition-bound community. In Vietnam's modern revolution, individualism had no place. Peasants were freed from tradition-bound family practices only "because they had become totally immersed in a larger, stronger, and more enlightened social group: the supervillage of the insurgency, which was so organized as to become a surrogate family, a replacement for the family, a superfamily."[8] The revolution replaced the family and won the hearts and minds of the peasants by simultaneously adhering to strict Confucian principles and appealing to their need to belong to a larger community, and this, Jamieson argues, was why the Communists won the war. He suggests that Vietnam's peasants were willing to make enormous sacrifices for the revolution because they had been properly conditioned along Confucian lines to do so. In short, the cosmology of Marxism and Confucianism was responsible for the Party's victory.

Ho's most important biographer, William Duiker, accepts some of the culturalists' argument for the revolution's success. He believes that Ho's revolutionary ethics developed slowly and deliberately. In the early political writings, according to Duiker, it is clear that Ho had little understanding of Marxist theory. Following the Second Comintern Congress in the summer of 1920, however, he began to appreciate Lenin's message. He wrote of Lenin's famous "Theses": "There were political terms difficult to understand in this thesis. But by dint of reading it again and again, finally

I could grasp the main part of it. What emotion, what enthusiasm, clear-sightedness, and confidence it instilled in me! I was overjoyed to tears. Though sitting alone in my room, I shouted aloud as if addressing large crowds. Dear martyrs, compatriots! This is what we need, this is the path to our liberation."[9]

With Lenin's words ringing in his ears, Ho, who was at that time living in Paris, became a more outspoken anticolonialist within the French socialist community. He called for all oppressed people to unite against the imperialists, fully embracing Lenin's thesis. In the summer of 1923, the Comintern invited him to Moscow. Buoyed by Moscow's faith in his revolutionary activities in Paris, he hoped that he would be able to have an impact on the growing anticolonial movement in Vietnam. Occasionally, he would travel to Canton, China, to teach at the Special Political Institute for the Vietnamese Revolution, a Marxist training school for future Vietnamese revolutionaries. It is at this stage in his life that he began to write seriously about revolution. In his now famous *The Revolutionary Path* (1926), he introduced Marxist-Leninist doctrine to his countrymen. In simple and straightforward language, he outlined a two-stage revolutionary process. First would come the nationalist stage, followed by the second stage of world revolution. Simply put, Vietnam would achieve its independence from France through a nationalist struggle, and then it would be part of a global socialist movement that would lead to the second stage, social transformation.

Most important for this discussion, however, is the emphasis placed in *The Revolutionary Path* on revolutionary behavior. Duiker points to this document as a point of departure between Ho and Lenin. While Lenin "assumed that contemporary standards of morality had little relevance to the revolutionary code of conduct," the ethical core of Ho's list of behavioral norms "was strongly reminiscent of traditional Confucian morality." Ho argued that cadres must "be thrifty, be friendly but impartial, resolutely correct errors, be prudent, respect learning, study and observe, avoid arrogance and conceit, and be generous." Duiker concludes that this list of revolutionary commandments "could easily be accepted as behavioral norms in any devout Confucian home."[10] Most Western scholars agree, believing that it was Ho's personality, his simplicity, his goodness, his sense of honor and duty, that led peasants to embrace his revolutionary ethics and cause.

But are those scholars who emphasize a cultural approach to the Party's success right? Was a cosmology compounded of Marxism and Confucianism responsible for the Party's victory? Did Vietnam's peasants follow Ho Chi Minh willingly because they found in his revolutionary movement strains of tradition-bound rural life? Did Ho Chi Minh use Vietnam's long-standing Confucian practices to condition peasants to accept the Party's discipline, much like a son accepted his father's rule? Did the Communists win the war in Vietnam because they understood this important cultural link with Vietnam's past better than the government in Saigon did? Was the war really about winning the hearts and minds of the peasants, and was this connected to the Confucian idea of the mandate of heaven? As compelling as the argument for Confucian primacy is, it may not go far enough in explaining the appeal of Ho Chi Minh and his revolution. It now seems clear that Confucianism had very little impact on modern Vietnam and that peasants were responding not to Ho's use of Confucianism but rather to his use of the concept of proletarian virtue. Furthermore, the purely cultural explanation for Ho's success denies the modern Vietnamese revolution any social basis. In the end, peasants turned to the Party because of its land-to-tiller program and because they believed that Ho and his revolutionary followers could replace a corrupt and outdated social system with a better one.

The Impact of Confucianism

Despite popular views to the contrary, Ho Chi Minh had a very limited traditional Confucian education. Born in the village of Hoang Tru, Nghe An Province, on May 19, 1890, Ho Chi Minh (then known as Nguyen Sinh Cung) was the second son of Nguyen Sinh Sac, a Confucian scholar and teacher. Young Ho attended Confucian school under the guidance of his father's friend Vuong Thuc Qui, who, Duiker writes, emphasized the "humanitarian inner core of Confucian classical writings while simultaneously instilling in [his students'] minds a fierce patriotic spirit for the survival of an independent Vietnam." When Ho was fifteen, his father enrolled him in a Franco-Vietnamese preparatory school at Vinh, a coastal city in Nghe An Province. According to Duiker, Ho's father had become convinced that his sons must adapt "to the new reality and learn from the country's new masters."[11] That new reality was French colonialism. The

French had come to Vietnam in the 1850s seeking an Asian jewel to add to their imperial crown. The weak Nguyen dynasty (1802–1945) in Hue had provided token resistance to French rule, and, by the early twentieth century, many of Vietnam's elites believed that the only way for Vietnam to be free and independent was by following Western ways. Apparently, this is what Ho's father believed in 1905 when he sent his second son to study at the Franco-Vietnamese school. He also believed that the old Confucian system existed to serve French colonial interests at the expense of the Vietnamese. Those who passed the Confucian exams simply became administrators for the French in Vietnam. This was in line with the thinking of one of Vietnam's leading nationalists, Phan Chu Trinh. Like Nguyen Sinh Sac, Phan Chu Trinh believed that Vietnamese nationalists should cooperate with the French to convince them to launch Western reforms that would alter Vietnam's weak institutions, including the Confucian system. Over the next several years, Ho would study at three Franco-Vietnamese schools, including the Quoc Hoc [National Academy] in Hue, the Nguyen dynasty's imperial capital.

From an early age, therefore, Ho had been exposed to a nontraditional education. Furthermore, the most profound impact on his revolutionary thinking was not his formal education inside Vietnam but his travels to France, the Soviet Union, and China in the early twentieth century. In May 1910, Ho was expelled from the Quoc Hoc for his revolutionary activities. He had served as an interpreter for peasants protesting French tax policies in the village of Cong Luong, near Hue, and French authorities placed him on a list of troublemakers at the school. In 1911, he left Vietnam aboard the small ocean liner *Admiral Latouche-Treville*. He spent two years at sea as a cook's helper, traveling between Saigon and Marseilles, and eventually making his way to the United States. In 1913, he traveled to Great Britain, where he worked as a boiler operator in a boy's school and as a chef's assistant in the kitchen at the Carlton Hotel. In December 1917, he settled in Paris, where he worked in a photography shop and taught Chinese. While in Paris, he also came into contact with the overseas Vietnamese community and many influential French socialists. He regularly attended meetings of various socialist groups and contributed essays to Marxist publications. These first stabs at political activity show no signs of a sophisticated understanding of Marxist-Leninist philosophy or any lingering belief in Confucianism. In fact, by 1919, when the anticolonial community in Paris first knew Ho, it had been fourteen years since he had had any contact with traditional, Confucian teachings. Half his life had been spent outside Vietnam, and he had been drawn to Lenin and his anticolonial thesis without making any connections to Vietnam's culture and traditions.

Furthermore, there is significant evidence today that, as the historian Shawn McHale puts it, "Confucianism's impact on Vietnam has been exaggerated and misconceived." In his recent *Print and Power*, McHale uses Vietnamese-language sources to argue that Confucianism had a deep impact on certain areas of human thought and behavior but that the "vast majority of Vietnamese did not understand Confucianism as a coherent and structured doctrine, sharply distinguishable from other teachings and of such power that it fundamentally transformed daily practices and beliefs." According to McHale, modern Vietnamese understood a few Confucian notions like *tu doc* [Four Virtues] and *tam tong* [Three Submissions], and they commonly spoke of virtues like filial piety and loyalty, but these were no more than a "loose sense . . . of a cluster of practices and ideas that seem to have some recognizable coherence."[12] McHale is also leery of any attempt to depict a Vietnamese national character and even more reluctant to say that culture and tradition played much of a role in the war. He is no doubt right about the limited influence of Confucianism on modern Vietnamese peasants. Vietnamese sources attest to the fact that few twentieth-century Confucian scholars even understood classical Confucianism.[13] Their writings and teachings merely told modern Vietnamese a simplified version of a few Confucian tenets. Vietnamese scholars rarely engaged texts from before the nineteenth century, and few ever consulted Confucian scholarship produced in China during the previous five hundred years. Even the Confucian exam system had fallen into a state of disrepair by the late nineteenth century. Students simply memorized questions and answers without any real appreciation for the lessons. As the historian Hue-tam Ho Tai has written, by the twentieth century, Confucianism had "become a set of behavioral principles and had lost its potency as a personal philosophy or method of government."[14]

Perhaps most striking, however, was the Nguyen dynasty's inability or unwillingness to promote Confucianism. What we see by the mid-nineteenth century is a weak dynasty that has been overrun by a colonial power, France, and its interests. Because of the nature of French colonialism, many imperial officials promoted a version of the Vietnamese past that celebrated watered-down Confucianism. The goal was to re-Confucianize the past in order to strip modern Vietnamese life of any subversive teachings. The French closed traditional Confucian schools by 1920 in order to promote their own schools, which taught obedience and subservience. By stressing the orderly and passive side of Confucianism (and Buddhism, for that matter), the French hoped to quell any rebellion. By exaggerating the significance and coherence of a Confucian tradition, they were preparing Vietnamese intellectuals to accept imperial rule. It now seems clear that Ho Chi Minh understood that Confucianism served French imperial interests.

For many of Ho's followers, Confucianism was "irrevocably linked with feudalism, and thus those who argued for its retention anywhere in the twentieth century were either idealistic or reactionary, or both."[15] In most Party publications in the early twentieth century, Confucianism is a target of the revolution. Just as his father had grown to see Confucianism as a mechanism to promote and sustain colonialism, Ho Chi Minh himself saw the link between Confucianism and imperialism. Furthermore, he believed that Confucianism had become the enemy of the masses, for several important social reasons. One was that it trapped women inside the oppressive *che do gia dinh* [family system]. Ho was particularly interested in drawing women to the revolutionary cause, promising to do away with many Confucian traditions that kept women inside a master's house. For example, he wrote: "In order to work, one must be educated or strong. But women are ignorant, weak, and often immobilized by pregnancy. They will never be able to earn their living like men, whose slaves they are, so long as proletarians must work for capitalists. If we wish men and women to enjoy the same rights and advantages, we must totally reform customs, education, and the method of distributing wealth."[16] The mixture of proletarian socialism and the reform impulse was pure Ho Chi Minh. He often wrote and lectured on the dangers of Confucianism and the capitalist system. For Ho, the two went hand in hand.

Proletarian Virtue

In the absence of classical Confucianism, what many Western scholars see as Ho's tradition-based revolutionary ethics were really the Party's pur-

Photograph of
President Ho Chi
Minh. Courtesy
of the Vietnam
Archive, Texas
Tech University,
Anonymous
Collection.

poseful appeal to Vietnamese peasants utilizing the concept of proletarian virtue. When writing *The Revolutionary Path* and other essays, Ho had
tried to distance himself from one aspect of Leninism that he knew would
not translate well to contemporary Vietnam. Lenin had little interest in
contemporary standards of morality and even thought that they might be
in conflict with his revolutionary ideas. Lenin believed that cadres had to
be courageous, bold, and willing to subordinate their own needs to that
of the revolution, but he did not believe that integrity, honor, simplicity, and humility were of much use to a revolutionary. In sharp contrast,
Ho understood that modern Vietnamese needed to be organized around
these ethical characteristics because the revolutionary vanguard would
be made up of people from different classes. He had to replace the exist-

ing social order with one that recognized that capitalism and all that had helped it take root in Vietnam must be replaced with an alternative set of values. Imperialism and Confucianism were part of an old, corrupt order and were the primary targets of the revolution. Accordingly, Ho stressed what he considered to be revolutionary characteristics that were the antithesis of the existing social order.

Ho made no attempt to link himself with Vietnam's Confucian past. On the contrary, it was his attempt to distance himself from that past and create a new social order that attracted so many followers. As the historian David Marr has correctly noted, using symbols for and rhetoric about duty, honor, simplicity, and virtue did not make Ho a Confucian. Ho became a national leader "because he knew how to take old symbols and use them creatively according to the political needs of the moment."[17] By stressing a new set of values that stood in sharp contrast to imperial ones, he was giving modern Vietnamese a clear social choice. Jeffrey Race, an expert on the revolution, believes that it was the Party's ability to communicate this difference to the mass of Vietnamese peasants that won them to the cause. In his classic study of the village war, *War Comes to Long An,* Race argues: "Victory of the revolutionary movement . . . could be stated as the communist [*sic*] leadership's comprehensive view of revolution as a stage-by-stage social process." At the heart of that process, Race contends, was the understanding that the revolution was about replacing one social system with another. Once that idea was communicated properly, the Party's success came about "through the development of social policies that led to superior motivation."[18] That motivation, according to U.S. Army general Hamilton Howze, "decisively defeated a South Vietnamese Army . . . numerically stronger and equipped with billions of dollars in U.S. arms."[19]

Through the creation of the public Ho Chi Minh, the Party promoted the revolution as a clear alternative to the French- and then the American-backed Saigon regime. Some intellectuals may have recognized Confucian characteristics in the code of revolutionary behavior, but it now seems clear that it was the Party's intention to destroy any links between its revolutionary movement and the traditions that had made Vietnam weak. Ho's public behavior and the code of revolutionary ethics were not tied to Confucianism; instead, the Party presented them as part of a new social movement. As part of that movement, cadres were constantly asked by Ho to be loyal [*trung*] to the fatherland and pious [*hieu*] toward the masses. He mixed these familial attitudes with the revolution's most important ethical component, what Marr has called *revolutionary heroism*.[20] By *revolutionary heroism,* Marr and others mean the promotion of the Party as the vanguard in the struggle against foreign invaders through the purposeful manipulation of images of sacrifice for the fatherland. The Party created national heroes out of those who sacrificed for the revolution. Celebration of this sacrifice gave the Party preponderant power to assemble a pantheon of champions, such as Ho Chi Minh, tied to Vietnam's glorious past. It was not Ho Chi Minh's Confucian background that the Party celebrated but rather his ties to an ethical warrior past. The code of ethics was part of the proletarian code, but it was also tied to this warrior tradition, which had just as much influence as Confucianism on modern Vietnam, if not more.[21]

Land to Tiller

Whatever debates might arise about the nature of the modern Vietnamese revolution and the influence of Confucianism on that movement, we must remember that at the heart of the Party's effort to win peasants to its cause was its land-to-tiller programs. Even though cadres were, indeed, instructed on revolutionary ethics, it was the Party's decision to reduce rents and redistribute land that caught the attention of Vietnam's rural poor. From the origins of the modern revolution in the 1920s until the fall of Saigon in 1975, the Party's social program resonated most loudly with Vietnamese peasants. From his first political stirrings, Ho believed that socialism provided the only remedy to "the tyranny of capitalism."[22] At the heart of his revolutionary program was land reform. Ho argued that, in land reform, the Party had found its key to success: "Land reform is a class struggle against the feudalists; an earth-shaking, fierce, and hard revolution."[23] He instructed cadres that they had to help "build up a completely new society unknown in our history. We have to radically change thousand-year-old customs and habits, ways of thinking and prejudices. We have to change old relationships in production, abolish the exploiting classes, and establish new relationships without exploitation and oppression.... Step-by-step collectivization of agriculture has to be implemented." He concluded that the "socialist revolution demands of the Party members and cadres a firm proletarian stand and high socialist consciousness."[24] In these passages, we see Ho combine his views on proletarian virtue and his views on land reform.

Ho's socialist beliefs became the cornerstone for Party policy from 1920 until 1986. During the Vietnam War, the Party's united front in South Vietnam, the National Liberation Front (NLF), supported local farm labor exchanges that made up the difference in labor shortages caused by the war. Beginning in 1961, the NLF openly formed work-exchange teams to help peasants plant and harvest crops. Poor families could pool their resources to come to the mutual aid of all those in a farming association, or they could hire NLF-controlled labor at reduced prices. The NLF supported this program by charging large landholders high association membership fees and demanding that they pay up to 60 percent more in labor costs for work on their own lands. NLF cadres enforced these rules vigorously, hoping in the end to scare large landowners away from the village. If successful, the NLF divided large tracts of land into smaller agricultural plots and reallocated them to local peasants. Smaller plots meant less stress on labor and families. The NLF also reduced rents from 25 to 10 percent of annual tenant crop yields, further reducing the need for larger fields and more labor.

According to the political scientist David Elliott, who served five years in Vietnam with the U.S. Army and the Rand Corporation, the Party's land-to-tiller policies were what had attracted large numbers of peasants to the revolution. Elliott writes, "The epic independence struggle of the revolution and the concrete benefits of ending the worst excesses of landlordism and the petty tyranny of local officials had attracted the peasants to the revolution and provided political capital for the long struggle." At the village level, the support for the Party and Ho Chi Minh's message was widespread. For example, by 1962 in Vinh Kim, a village in the Mekong Delta, "about 90 percent of the villagers began to support the Front [NLF] energetically," according to the head of the Party's propaganda unit in the region. "Their former fear had disappeared because they realized that the Front had really taken care of the poor by giving them land."[25] Other village sources confirm this view. In James Trullinger's study of My Thuy Phuong, a village near Hue in central Vietnam, peasants often reported that they had been attracted to the revolution because of its land-to-tiller policies. "The Liberation [NLF] had answers for all of the most important problems that we all knew. They had an answer about land reform, which was that they would give land to the poor people. They had an answer about high taxes. They said that the Liberation would spend the taxes only for the people, and would collect them without corruption. They also said that they would help the poor, and this was something else that made them popular, because many people in the village were poor."[26]

In Dinh Tuong Province, located in the Mekong Delta, peasants routinely joined the Party because of its position on land tenure and taxes. According to one important study of the province, William Andrews's *The Village War,* Dinh Tuong's land policy became the prime political instrument and was the "means by which the Party gained dominance over the rural population." One captured Party document from Dinh Tuong stated, "The main interest of the farmer is in land. Before, during, and after the elimination of our enemy's influence, the Party . . . always used the subject of land as a means of propagandizing the masses."[27] Jeffrey Race reports similar evidence from Long An Province, one of the most contested during the entire war. He argues that the Party's land policies captured the attention of the peasants in Long An more than any other aspect of the revolutionary movement. He believes that the Party went to great lengths to make its land policies appear more attractive to peasants than those of the Saigon government. For Race, this was the crucial difference in the war.[28] Even Nguyen Khac Vien, who supports the Confucian explanation for the Party's success, concedes that it was the land-to-tiller policies that won most villagers to the revolutionary cause.[29]

Over time, of course, the Party became a victim of its own success. While its land reform campaigns and threats reduced the numbers of large landholders in the Mekong Delta, the NLF had also reduced its ability to extort money. Financial demands on the NLF thus grew at a time when the Vietnam War was expanding rapidly. The consequence was the institution of a special tax, which the NLF eventually applied throughout South Vietnam. The tax was at times collected at gunpoint, undoing much of the work that earlier cadres had done to win peasants over to the Party's cause. In addition, the war had taken its toll on many villagers, and by 1967, with the war stalemated in the countryside, terror and fear were the primary motivators for Party membership and loyalty. Villagers were caught in the spiral of escalation and thought they had limited options. Many divided their loyalties between the Party and the government in Saigon, hoping not to get caught in the cross fire. Furthermore, following the war, the Party launched a full-scale program of collectivization. From 1975 until 1986, the socialist policies followed by Party leaders in Hanoi plunged Vietnam into the depths of a huge economic depression. Despite these enormous setbacks, there is no denying that Ho Chi Minh's initial promotion of proletarian virtue and his land-to-tiller ideas brought hundreds of thousands of peasants to the revolutionary movement.

Although the cultural explanation for Ho Chi Minh's revolutionary success has dominated Western scholarship for decades, there are a growing number of scholars who are using Vietnamese-language sources to complicate the picture. What emerges from this new scholarship is a more comprehensive view of the revolutionary process inside Vietnam. It suggests that Ho was not a Confucian, that peasants were not drawn to the Party because it had replaced the Confucianized state, and that Ho never promoted himself as a Confucian. Instead, he made appeals to proletarian virtue and land reform, two aspects of the revolution that resonated loudly with Vietnam's peasants. A more nuanced reading of Vietnam's revolutionary past also helps explain why so many peasants who had no contact with Confucianism were drawn to Ho's movement. It was not a romanticized view of Vietnam's Confucian past that attracted them but rather the promise that the revolution would rid Vietnam of an outdated and corrupt social system. The enemies of feudalism and imperialism were revolutionary virtue and socialism, Ho argued, and peasants from all over Vietnam believed him. Some scholars would suggest that Ho was more believable than his political rivals because he understood the essence of Vietnamese life. However, Ho argued that his cause won the day because socialism was the wave of the future for all societies. The social basis for the modern Vietnamese revolution simply cannot be ignored, even if socialism proved to be a false god.

Notes

1. See, e.g., Frances FitzGerald, *Fire in the Lake: The Vietnamese and the Americans in Vietnam* (New York: Vintage, 1972). *Fire in the Lake* won the Pulitzer Prize, the National Book Award, and the Bancroft Prize for History.

2. William Duiker, *Vietnam: Revolution in Transition,* 2d ed. (Boulder, CO: Westview, 1995), 123.

3. Paul Mus, foreword to *Village in Vietnam,* by Gerald Hickey (New Haven, CT: Yale University Press, 1964), xxi.

4. FitzGerald, *Fire in the Lake,* 39.

5. Paul Mus, *Vietnam: Sociologie d'une guerre* (Paris: Seuil, 1952).

6. Nguyen Khac Vien, "Confucianism and Marxism," in *Tradition and Revolution in Vietnam* (Berkeley, CA: Indochina Resource Center, 1974), 17, 50.

7. David Halberstam, *Ho* (New York: Vintage, 1971), 14.

8. Neil Jamieson, *Understanding Vietnam* (Berkeley and Los Angeles: University of California Press, 1993), 235, 256.

9. Ho quoted in William Duiker, *Ho Chi Minh: A Life* (New York: Hyperion, 2000), 65.

10. Ibid., 135.

11. Ibid., 23, 27.

12. Shawn McHale, *Print and Power: Confucianism, Communism, and Buddhism in the Making of Modern Vietnam* (Honolulu: University of Hawaii Press, 2004), 67, 76.

13. Ngo Tat To, *Phe binh Nho giao Tran Trong Kim* [A criticism of Tran Trong Kim's Confucianism] (Hanoi: Mai Linh, 1940), 11.

14. Hue-tam Ho Tai, *Radicalism and the Origins of the Vietnamese Revolution* (Cambridge, MA: Harvard University Press, 1992), 50.

15. David Marr, *Vietnamese Traditions on Trial* (Berkeley and Los Angeles: University of California Press, 1981), 275.

16. Ho quoted in Tai, *Origins of the Vietnamese Revolution,* 201.

17. Marr, *Vietnamese Traditions on Trial,* 134.

18. Jeffrey Race, *War Comes to Long An: Revolutionary Conflict in a Vietnamese Province* (Berkeley: University of California Press, 1972), 141, 165.

19. Gen. Hamilton Howze, "Vietnam: An Epilogue," *Association of the United States Army* 25 (July 1975): 2.

20. Marr, *Vietnamese Traditions on Trial,* 135.

21. McHale, *Print and Power,* 71.

22. Ho quoted in Duiker, *Ho Chi Minh,* 74.

23. Ho Chi Minh, "Letter to the Peasants and Cadres on the Successful Completion of Land Reform in the North (August 18, 1956)," in *Ho Chi Minh on Revolution, 1920–1966: Selected Writings,* ed. Bernard Fall (New York: Praeger, 1967), 275.

24. Ho Chi Minh, "Speech Opening the First Theoretical Course of Nguyen Ai Quoc School (September 7, 1957)," in *Ho Chi Minh on Revolution,* ed. Fall, 285, 286.

25. David Elliott, *The Vietnamese War: Revolution and Social Change in the Mekong Delta, 1930–1975* (Armonk, NY: Sharpe, 2003), 853, 620.

26. James Trullinger, *Village at War: An Account of Revolution in Vietnam* (New York: Longman, 1980), 99.

27. William Andrews, *The Village War: Vietnamese Communist Revolutionary Activities in Dinh Tuong Province, 1960–1964* (Columbia: University of Missouri Press, 1973), 65–66.

28. Race, *War Comes to Long An.*

29. Nguyen Khac Vien, *Vietnam: A Long History* (Hanoi: Gioi, 1999), 289–301.

6

Vietnam during the Rule of Ngo Dinh Diem, 1954–63

Ronald B. Frankum Jr.

Diem, like Sukarno, Rhee, and Chiang, is cast in the mold of an oriental despot, and cannot be "brought around" by threats, or insistence on adoption of purely Western concepts. To be successful, the approaches must be made on the plane of advisors, not as adversaries, with emphasis on Diem's primary responsibility and control.
—Sterling Cottrell, Director, Interdepartmental Task Force on Vietnam, October 27, 1961

There is little that escapes historical controversy or intrigue during the American experience in Vietnam. This should not be surprising, as America's longest war pushed the boundaries of political discourse, military strategy and tactics, cultural norms, and the fabric of American society, which appeared to unravel as the war progressed. It should also not be a surprise that the first ally of the United States in the struggle for Vietnam and the containment of communism in Southeast Asia is at the center of this lingering debate. Ngo Dinh Diem led the government of the Republic of Vietnam, first as the president of the Council of Ministers of the State of Vietnam, and then, after a national referendum on October 23, 1955, until his assassination in November 1963, as president and chief of state. In creating the Republic of Vietnam from the ashes of nearly one hundred years of French colonialism in the region, Diem faced numerous chal-

Ngo Dinh Diem enters the presidential palace on Dedication Day. Courtesy of the Vietnam Archive, Texas Tech University, Douglas Pike Photograph Collection.

lenges and obstacles that shaped his policy and determined his fate. He inherited a country, new to the international community of nations, that was without infrastructure and divided along social, cultural, religious, and ideological lines. At the same time, his supporting cast included few with administrative experience and many who harbored deep-seated suspicion of one another. It was Diem whom the United States entrusted to guide the Republic of Vietnam as a bulwark against communism in Southeast Asia and to serve as a leader of the free world in the region. Ultimately, it was Diem's failure to consolidate the support of his countrymen and reform his democratic experiment to the liking of the Americans that led to his death.

For those who remember Ngo Dinh Diem from 1954–55, such as Adm. Lorenzo Sabin, who was in command of Task Force 90 during Operation Passage to Freedom, which saw the removal of over 810,000 Vietnamese from the Democratic Republic of Vietnam to the South, he was Vietnam's only real hope as a leader who could bring that nation into the international community as a responsible member. Sabin made his acquaintance with Diem immediately after the July 1954 Geneva Agreements, which temporarily divided the former French colony of Vietnam into two halves, near the Seventeenth Parallel. He admired Diem's ability to consolidate his power despite numerous obstacles, and he witnessed Diem's administration as it tried to cope with the addition of the 810,000 refugees who had fled communism with only what they could carry. From this experience grew an admiration for the Vietnamese leader, who, in the face of so many obstacles, worked to consolidate his control over his fledgling country racked by the internal conflict of the three sects—Hoa Hao, Cao Dai, and the criminal organization Binh Xuyen—that vied for control during the early days of Diem's rule. Sabin witnessed Diem at his finest, as did many Americans involved in the early days of reorganization and rehabilitation. For Sabin, the November 1, 1963, assassination and coup d'état were disturbing indications of an American foreign policy gone wrong. "The little nation of freedom for which Diem had labored so courageously to establish now hangs precariously on the Communist ledge," he wrote in the early days of November 1963. "Ngo Dinh Diem has been destroyed. The most indomitable foe of Communism in all Southeast Asia was betrayed in a coup d'état with the connivance of our own government and for which some day we shall have to account before the bar of human justice. It will require a lot of explaining to justify our part in the overthrow of a duly constituted government which we were assisting in a war against a common enemy."[1] For many in the United States who had supported Diem in his rise to power, the events of November 1963 were confusing. They questioned what had gone wrong as all had looked to a future with Diem as one with promise for a Vietnamese peace and an American diplomatic victory.

More is known about the Diem regime as it collapsed in 1963, but what is often neglected is the beginning point in the United States–Diem relationship and the transition of Ngo Dinh Diem from this one true hope for Vietnam's future, as the then vice president Lyndon Baines Johnson remarked after his visit to the Republic of Vietnam in May 1961, to one of the most despised leaders the Kennedy administration had ever had to deal with during its tenure in office. There is little doubt that Diem contributed to his own self-destruction, but what must be considered, at least, is that the United States also shares responsibility for his tragedy. For Admiral Sabin, this tragedy was more than one of a person. "It is the tragedy of a nation," he concluded, "but even more than that it is the tragedy of another Communist triumph; a triumph which, if allowed to proceed to its grim conclusion, will bring the Hammer and Sickle over an entire area as vital to the free world in the East as is Europe in the West."[2]

Diem's rule in Vietnam was intertwined with the growing American participation in the region as first President Dwight D. Eisenhower and then President John F. Kennedy sought to contain Communist influence in Asia and build up a country to serve as a model for others to emulate. From his rise to power to his downfall, a series of events tested Diem and his relationship with the West. These events serve as a window on his political philosophy as well as on his attempt to reconcile Vietnamese tradition with growing American influence. From the beginning of his life, Diem learned to combine East and West in his attempt to govern. This complementary, if not often conflicting, approach to rule over the nine years of his tenure are seen in his consolidation of power after the 1954 Geneva Convention, his decision to reject the scheduled July 1956 elections, the fight for the countryside and the failed Agroville experiment, the November 1960 coup d'état attempt and American tunnel vision during the crisis, the Strategic Hamlet Program, the attempt at neutralizing Laos, and the Buddhist Crisis. Throughout his presidency, Diem held fast to his conviction that only the Vietnamese could provide the means for Vietnam's independence. He reconciled this belief with the necessity of American support in the early years of his administration as he attempted to rebuild the nation and provide for the Vietnamese people who had suffered from French colonial rule and the Communist insurgency. He eventually failed in his attempt when he became too reliant on American aid without acceding to American demands at democratic reform. He moved his country further away from the model government, and himself further away from the model leader, that Eisenhower had originally envisioned. By the time Kennedy entered the White House, the Diem experiment was yielding diminishing returns. Six years of nation building had failed to create the model state to showcase as an alternative to Communist rule in Asia, and Diem became increasingly resistant to American advice and calls for reform, as Kennedy's "best and brightest" offered solutions to a problem for which they had very little understanding. In many ways, those Kennedy officials directly responsible for American foreign policy in Vietnam clashed with Diem and his brother Ngo Dinh Nhu because they never made a concerted attempt to understand the nature of Vietnamese rule or the dynamics of leadership. Diem viewed this American ignorance as one of the main obstacles to the continued relationship with the United States, though he worked, in his own way, to educate American officials who went on fact-finding missions to Vietnam; the Kennedy officials, unwilling to be educated by Diem, began to see the limits of his usefulness. This attitude would culminate in Diem's assassination in November 1963 and add twelve years of war and untold suffering for the Vietnamese people who continued to fight against the Communist insurgency.

Born the third son of Ngo Dinh Kha on January 3, 1901, Ngo Dinh Diem was deeply influenced by his father, who had served as the minister of rites and counselor to the Nguyen dynasty emperor Thanh Thai (1889–1907). Kha was one of the leaders conducting passive resistance to French colonial rule. His resistance eventually resulted in his resignation from the government.[3] This estrangement from the French and the Vietnamese officials who supported colonialism influenced Diem just as Ho Chi Minh's father's dismissal from office in 1911 helped guide Ho toward a path of resistance to French and Vietnamese collaborative rule.[4] A strong sense of Vietnamese nationalism, embedded within the nearly two thousand years of Vietnamese resistance to foreign influence, was passed from Kha to Diem. Also passed from father to son was the value of both a Western and a Vietnamese education, which Diem received at the National School in Hue, a school founded and directed by Kha. Diem's early education and subsequent international experience gave him a worldview that transcended traditional Vietnamese notions of government and a level of sophistication beyond that of the contemporary Vietnamese leadership; this would later result in increased friction between Diem and Vietnamese leaders, who often disagreed on the best course for Vietnam. While Diem escaped the notice of the French during his formative years, he progressed rapidly within the Vietnamese civil service, reaching the rank of minister of the interior in 1933. Like his father before him, he protested against French involvement in Vietnamese affairs and the consequences of French colonial rule. He too resigned his position and spent the next decade in contact with Vietnamese leaders who were engaged in various levels of Vietnamese nationalism. Like Ho Chi Minh, he needed allies to assist in the struggle against French colonialism. Where Ho eventually turned to communism and revolution, Diem sought to blend East and West to achieve this goal.

During the Second World War, Diem remained out of Vietnamese government, though Emperor Bao Dai twice offered him the opportunity to form a government during the Japanese occupation of Vietnam. Diem refused to participate in a government that replaced one form of oppression (French colonial rule) with another (Japanese imperial rule) as it would mean continued subjugation under a foreign power. At the war's end, he also refused to participate in the Viet Nam Doc Lap Dong Minh Hoi [Viet Minh] government and declined participation in Ho Chi Minh's government in January 1946. One of the reasons for this refusal was that Diem's brother Ngo Dinh Khoi had been assassinated by the Viet Minh, and Diem never forgave the incident. At the time, Diem still believed in the role and value of the emperor in Vietnamese society. It was the prerogative and duty of the emperor to lead his people toward a better future. Diem was willing to wait and see if Bao Dai would take

Ngo Dinh Diem at the Holy Family Hospital at Qui Nhon. Courtesy of the Vietnam Archive, Texas Tech University, Douglas Pike Photograph Collection.

the initiative to bring about Vietnamese independence before he would consider supporting another type of government in Vietnam. He did not believe that the Viet Minh had the authority to take over the role played by the emperor.

As the First Indochina War (1945–54) intensified, a war pitting the French Union forces against the Viet Minh, Bao Dai again requested Diem's aid in uniting Vietnam, but Diem refused the Bao Dai solution of forming a provisional central government and advocated, instead, a preliminary national committee that would serve as a representative of the Vietnamese to address with the French the serious and continued difference between the two peoples. He rejected the March 8, 1949, agreement between Bao Dai and the French that brought French recognition of Vietnamese independence and the establishment of Bao Dai as the head of state and refused to serve as premier of the country when asked by Bao Dai in May 1949. He believed that the agreement fell well short of providing the Vietnamese with the independence he desired and maintained that the agreements only tied Bao Dai more closely to the French colonial regime. The years immediately following the end of Japanese occupation of French Indochina during the Second World War forced Diem to reconsider his support for the emperor, but his dedication to this tradition had not waned enough to seek action on his own or to support Ho Chi Minh.

By 1950, Diem had made enemies of the French colonial officials, members of the Bao Dai government, and the Viet Minh, who had put a price on his head. He left Vietnam to visit several countries, including the United States, where he took up residency in a self-imposed exile at the Maryknoll Seminary in Ossining, New York, and the Maryknoll Junior Seminary in Lakewood, New Jersey, from 1951 to 1953 and at the Saint Andrew Abbey, in Bruges, Belgium, from 1953 to 1954. It was during this time that Diem made the acquaintance of a number of influential Americans, including Cardinal Francis Joseph Spellman and the then senator John F. Kennedy, who would later serve as the core cadre of the American Friends of Vietnam and remain his staunchest supporters through the Eisenhower years. Diem, already an opponent of Communist rule in his country, realized that he had a staunch ally in the United States as the Cold War mentality of the 1950s became entrenched. Later, after the French defeat at Dien Bien Phu, Diem agreed to form a government at the request of Bao Dai, which he did on July 7, 1954, serving as the president of the Council of Ministers. Diem still had confidence in the role of the emperor and in Bao Dai's ability to lead his people toward independence. For the next year, he governed a Vietnam that underwent tremendous strain as the French began their withdrawal of troops while continuing political intrigue designed to damage the new Vietnamese government. Although he was prime minister of the Republic of Vietnam, Diem was not a signatory to the July 1954 Geneva Agreements that partitioned Vietnam near the Seventeenth Parallel and began the end of nearly one hundred years of French colonial rule. This put him in a difficult position as he had to recognize an agreement that was not of his own making and certainly not one that he favored. He also had to contend with the introduction of the over 810,000 refugees from the Democratic Republic of Vietnam who had fled that country under Articles 8, 14, and 15 of the agreement, which allowed for unobstructed movement to either zone until the country was reunited along the old French boundaries. At the same time, he began working with both French and American personnel to begin the process of constructing a bureaucracy that could handle the new population while assisting in the building up of an infrastructure to lead Vietnam toward prosperity. These significant problems were intensified by the continued obstruction of the Diem-led government and the plethora of problems that threatened to destabilize South Vietnam.

Although Diem had always been committed to the emperor system, a notion reinforced by his father and a part of his early education, he also believed that the role of the emperor was to protect his people. When the emperor failed to do this, he was no longer immune from criticism or entitled to his place at the head of government. Between the time Diem formed his government, which brought him back to Vietnam and allowed him to experience firsthand Bao Dai's mismanagement of Vietnamese relations with the French, and October 1955, when he had consolidated his power and eliminated the internal threats to the regime posed by the three existing sects—Hoa Hao, Cao Dai, and Binh Xuyen—his faith in the emperor waned. In a national referendum on October 23, 1955, the Vietnamese people called for the removal of Bao Dai from power. While Diem certainly had a hand in orchestrating this move and his followers engaged in very undemocratic practices, at least as seen by Western standards, Diem's purpose was clear. He believed the emperor incapable of achieving Vietnamese independence or assisting the Vietnamese people toward a better future. When Diem proclaimed himself president and chief of state of the Republic of Vietnam on October 26, 1955, replacing Bao Dai, he ushered in a new era for Vietnam, one that promised peace and prosperity but delivered only tragedy to a Vietnamese people who had suffered so long.

Diem faced his next significant test when he had to decide whether the Republic of Vietnam would participate in the scheduled July 1956 elections as outlined in Article 7 of the 1954 Geneva Agreements. No representative of the Republic of Vietnam or the United States signed the declaration, though the American representative at the conference, Undersecretary of State Walter Bedell-Smith, agreed that the United States would adhere to the document and refrain from using force to disrupt it. Diem's decision not to participate in the July 1956 election was, in part, due to the reality of the two Vietnams. There was a greater population in the North, and the likelihood of a fair election was diminished by a combination of the Communist Party apparatus in the Democratic Republic of Vietnam and the failure to educate all Vietnamese people on the nature and value of the democratic process. Most likely, Diem would have been defeated, and he was not willing to forsake his people in this premature attempt at democracy. His failure to see the election through did cost him international support and added to the North Vietnamese propaganda against his regime. While American representatives in Vietnam realized that no pressure could have forced Diem to change his mind, there were few who really wanted the elections to occur. The ease with which Diem rejected this pillar of democratic institutions would become a cornerstone for the anti-Diem faction within American circles. They would exploit this decision during the Kennedy administration.

After the time period for the July 1956 election passed, Diem concentrated on building the infrastructure of his country. With American economic aid and technical assistance, the Vietnamese people made inroads at improving their daily lives. The Michigan State University Group, headed by Wesley Fishel, brought to Vietnam the expertise of a cadre of academicians who worked toward the improvement of Vietnam's education system, economy, government, and related institutions.[5] Diem's Vietnam improved during the late 1950s, but it was still under threat from southern insurgents who wished nothing less than Diem's overthrow and the unification of the two Vietnams. At the same time, the pressure in the countryside increased as those battling the government practiced the policy of *tru gian* [extermination of traitors], which was the targeted assassination of Republic of Vietnam officials who were loyal to Diem and had proved themselves efficient in their positions of power.

In mid-1959, Diem introduced the Agroville Campaign to combat insurgent violence in the countryside.[6] Agrovilles, the first of which opened on March 12, 1960, at Vi Thanh, were self-contained, extended villages with schools, medical facilities, agricultural and industrial centers, and relative safety. They were designed to isolate the insurgents from the peasants while, at the same time, enhancing the lives of the people through an infusion of capital and technical improvements, such as sanitary facilities and electricity. The Agrovilles would also serve as a barrier to the insurgents, who would be denied recruits, intelligence, and support from the people. While the Agroville concept was sound, its implementation caused much grief for the Diem regime. Peasants were forced from their land, and their ancestral homes, without choice. Diem made the decision to proceed because he believed that his people needed government protection. When the government failed to produce the desired results as envisioned by the Agroville Campaign, the people began to resent the government interference. Agrovilles did improve from the first one developed to the time the plan was discontinued a little more than one year later, but not enough to offset the initial stigma attached to them. Diem was forced to abandon the effort before the April 1961 Vietnamese national elections. He was also persuaded of the need to change by the events of November 1960, which served as a major turning point in the Diem–United States relationship.

The November 11, 1960, coup d'état attempt by some dissatisfied Vietnamese paratroopers and other Army of the Republic of Vietnam (ARVN) personnel played a significant role in Diem's turning away from American support and advice, especially when coupled with the change of government that had brought John F. Kennedy into the White House a week earlier. While the coup d'état failed, the American reaction, on the part of both the officials on the ground and the press that had been covering the country, must certainly have caused Diem to pause and reconsider the American attitude toward his government. In the first real exchange on November 12, the chief of the Military Assistant Advisory Group, Vietnam, Lt. Gen. Lionel C. McGarr, and Ambassador Elbridge

Edward Lansdale and Ngo Dinh Diem. Courtesy of the Vietnam Archive, Texas Tech University, Douglas Pike Photograph Collection.

Durbrow used the attempted coup d'état to press Diem on reforms within the Vietnamese government that the United States had been urging for some time, rather than reaffirming American support for Diem and his government.[7]

Whether or not American pressure to hasten reforms at a time when rebel forces still held positions within Saigon was appropriate, it is clear that there was a difference in primary objectives between Diem and his American allies. The situation most likely became more confused when it was learned that a Vietnamese air force C-47 took off from Tan Son Nhut airfield at 2:00 P.M. on November 13 with the failed coup d'état leaders aboard, headed toward Phnom Penh.[8] Whether the United States had a role in the transport of these individuals is less significant than Diem's perception that such might have been the case. Perception and reality—sometimes complementary, sometimes conflicting—would drive the post–coup d'état analysis and lead to a fission between the two allies.

After the attempted coup d'état, Secretary of Defense Thomas A.

Gates ordered Brig. Gen. Edward Lansdale to visit Vietnam from January 2 to 14, 1961, to assess the situation and reestablish a rapport with Diem, whose confidence in Durbrow and the Americans had been clearly shaken as a result of the November 1960 event. Lansdale, who had known Diem since 1954, argued that the United States needed to support Diem until he was legally replaced. American action before, and during, the coup d'état attempt had only caused Diem to feel as if American officials attacked him as much as did the Communist insurgency.[9] Lansdale argued that the United States needed to show Diem that it was with him. Action, not just words, was necessary to prove American friendship. For Lansdale, the issue really became whether American officials could talk *with* Diem rather than talk *to* him. Given his personality and the actions taken in his rise to power, Diem certainly considered himself an equal to the American representatives in Vietnam; that these same Americans, especially Ambassador Durbrow, viewed the relationship differently helps explain the growing divide between the American officials and Diem. It was from the November 1960 coup d'état attempt that Diem's relationship with American officials began to noticeably diminish. By a matter of fate, rather than contrivance, the Kennedy administration brought new Americans to Vietnam with clear ideas of how to conduct the war against the Communist insurgency. With the exception of Ambassador Frederick Nolting, these individuals continued to talk *to*, rather than *with*, Diem. The conflict that ensued, as Diem moved further away from American advice, relying more on his own judgment and the counsel of his family, would eventually lead the United States down that slippery slope to its inevitable and disadvantageous conclusion: the assassination of Diem and a new, more intense American involvement in Vietnam.

One of the immediate sources of contention for Diem was his call for an increase in the size of the ARVN by twenty thousand. Durbrow did not believe the increase necessary and, when queried by Diem, chose to focus on reforms to liberalize Vietnamese society and its government. There is no question that Diem became annoyed with this exchange. For Diem, Vietnam was at war, and, as such, certain conditions needed to be understood. He saw little difference between his actions and those of Franklin Roosevelt during the Second World War. That Durbrow failed to make this connection, at least to Diem's satisfaction, when other world leaders acknowledged it resulted in increased tension between the president and the lead representative of the United States in Vietnam.[10] For Diem, the American leaders did not understand the situation in Vietnam. Conversely, his growing insistence on demanding that his strategies and tactics be employed led to skepticism by American decisionmakers as to whether he should continue in office.

The tension mounted in the days leading up to the April 1961 election in Vietnam, for which there were three slates of candidates. Even after the election results came in—Diem won 89 percent of the vote—there were accusations of election fraud. American officials heard rumors of Vietnamese government employees who had been instructed to "adopt" ten families, teach them about the electoral process, and encourage them to vote for the Diem–Nguyen Ngoc Tho slate. The employees were then instructed to indicate on a list which families agreed to vote for the slate and hand the list over to the government.[11] While early rhetoric from the Kennedy administration and the May 1961 visit of Vice President Lyndon Baines Johnson negated immediate concerns about the undemocratic nature of the Diem regime, there remained lingering doubt as to the validity of Vietnam's version of democracy as compared to how Americans wished that country to evolve.

Central to Diem's strategy was control of the Vietnamese peasantry, who made up a majority of the population and dwelled in the villages and hamlets in the countryside. Diem's Agroville Campaign recognized the importance of isolating this population from the Communist insurgency, even though that program failed to achieve its desired results. A central criticism of Diem's government in the summer of 1961 was his insistence on using military chiefs of provinces rather than civilian chiefs. For Diem, military control helped ensure a more rigid chain of command and increased the likelihood of obedience in the war against the insurgents. As the situation continued to deteriorate, Vietnamese opposition to this strategy increased. Not only did Diem bear the brunt of criticism for the seeming inflexibility of his position, but so did his brother Ngo Dinh Nhu, who served as a counselor to the president.[12] Indeed, as 1961 closed, there was a refocusing of attention toward Nhu and other members of Diem's entourage who, Vietnamese critics claimed, were exerting a bad influence on the president. Nhu played an important role in Diem's government, organizing the Can Lao Nhan Vi Cach Mang Dang [Revolutionary Personalist Labor Party], which served as the political base for

Diem's support and led the special police force that acted against internal dissenters during the later part of Diem's rule. Also an influential member of the Ngo family was Madame Ngo Dinh Nhu, who used her position as the wife of Ngo Dinh Nhu to serve as spokesperson for the Diem government, often criticizing Vietnamese opponents to his rule and Americans who failed to support Diem and Nhu.

While the political atmosphere in Saigon deteriorated, there were indications that the war against the Communist insurgency was improving. The ARVN had increased to nearly 200,000 as a result of government action and American support, while the Civil Guard and the Self-Defense Corps of the Republic of Vietnam each numbered approximately 70,000–80,000. These three forces, all of which had also received additional training and more modern weapons, were used to supplement Diem's next attempt at securing the countryside.[13] After the failed Agroville Program, Diem and Nhu devised another plan aimed at denying the Viet Cong the ability to interact with the Vietnamese people. The Strategic Hamlet Program, a plan similar to Sir Robert Thompson's experiments in protecting the people from a Communist insurgency in Malaya, was put forth by Diem and Nhu, who were interested in keeping the Americans involved in the defense of South Vietnam as well as preserving government control in the countryside. Similar to the Agroville Program, the purpose of the Strategic Hamlet Program was to deny the Viet Cong access to the people in the countryside. By isolating the people, the Strategic Hamlet Program would deny the Viet Cong access to resources such as food, shelter, and intelligence on government troop movements as well as revenue and recruits to fill the Viet Cong coffers and ranks, which had begun to show signs of strain through 1961.[14] Diem and Nhu also believed that the program would serve as a vehicle for their attempt to unite the countryside under their rule and eliminate the Communist alternative.[15] Unlike the old Agrovilles, the new strategic hamlets were initially designed not to force the people off their ancestral lands unless it was absolutely necessary.

Diem also created the Strategic Hamlet Program to ensure the continuance of American financial assistance and counter the increasingly vocal minority within the Kennedy administration that had begun to grow impatient with the failure of the South Vietnamese government to achieve positive effects against the insurgency. Nhu, who was put in charge of the program, became too zealous in the creation of the strategic hamlets in order to impress on the Americans that something positive was being done. The haphazard way in which the program developed led to its eventual demise. Where Thompson had envisioned a slow process that saw the addition of strategic hamlets only after previous ones had been established and fortified, Nhu wanted to accelerate the construction of the hamlets to secure the countryside by the end of 1963. As a result, the interdependence of the strategic hamlets, a necessary requirement if the program was to succeed, was sacrificed for a quick fix to satisfy American officials who were observing the war in South Vietnam with increasing interest and anxiety. Diem failed to rein in his brother and did not respond well to American criticism of Nhu's flawed plan. The seed of distrust between Diem and the Americans that had been planted during the November 1960 coup d'état attempt continued to grow, and Diem found himself between an American contingent that criticized South Vietnamese government action via the Strategic Hamlet Program and a brother whose actions were sanctioned but failed to stabilize the countryside or appease the United States.

In addition to the internal struggles to consolidate his power, build the infrastructure of the new Vietnamese state, and fight the Communist insurgency, Diem also had to contend with the development of a foreign policy to offset the growing Communist threat within Southeast Asia. South Vietnam's two neighboring countries, Cambodia and Laos, presented a delicate situation for Diem as both were utilized by the People's Army of North Vietnam and the Viet Cong, the southern insurgents who were supported by North Vietnam to wage war against Diem and destabilize the royal governments that opposed their own Communist insurgencies. For the Kennedy administration, the neutralization of Laos was a priority of its Southeast Asian diplomacy, and one of the architects of this approach was the elder statesman and diplomat Averell Harriman, who served as an ambassador-at-large from February 13 to December 3, 1961, and then as the assistant secretary of state for Far Eastern affairs during the 1962 Geneva Conference that decided the Laotian future. Diem was adamant in his opposition to the 1962 Geneva Accords on Laos that promised neutralization, arguing instead that they "would result in the communization of Laos by legal means."[16] Diem's opposition did nothing more than earn the animosity of Harriman, who increased his public and private rhetoric against Diem in the months that followed. In many respects, Harriman, who had the ear of the president, helped orchestrate the growing anti-Diem atmosphere in Washington, specifically with regard to the role of Nhu in formulating Vietnamese domestic and foreign policy.[17]

On the heels of the Strategic Hamlet Program and the Laotian settlement came a division within South Vietnam that those in the United States who had opposed Diem's rule could utilize to push forward their case for a change in South Vietnamese leadership. The 1963 Buddhist Crisis evolved into one of the most significant chapters, and, ultimately, the final one, in the life of Ngo Dinh Diem. Diem is often remembered for his role in the incident, though he was reacting to events that had spiraled out of control. His belief in the importance of family, coupled with the traditions of Vietnamese leadership and the ongoing Communist insurgency, pushed him past the point of no return in the eyes of many Americans and, ultimately, led to his assassination. The crisis resulted from two coincidental events. The first was the display of the white and gold Catholic flag as a part of the episcopal silver jubilee for Ngo Dinh Thuc, the archbishop of Hue and Diem's older brother; the second was the 2,507th anniversary of the birth of the Buddha on May 7, 1963. Diem's government allowed the former to occur without incident but forbade the latter unless the Vietnamese national flag was also displayed in a prominent place.[18] Many of the Buddhists protested the discrepancy and the government's canceling of events associated with their celebration. Because Diem was Catholic, the inconsistency in the government handling of the two situations fueled a growing consensus among Buddhists that the president practiced discrimination and was not sympathetic to the predominant religion of Vietnam. They used the event to display their anger over Diem's inability to accede to their demands of including greater Buddhist representation in the government and relaxing laws and decrees that were seen as a direct threat to the religion.

In the course of the protest, a confrontation occurred between the Buddhists and local security forces, resulting in several casualties thought to have been inflicted by a grenade. Each side claimed that the other had started the violence, and neither was willing to back down from the affront. The tension continued to escalate, pushed forward by the self-immolation of the Buddhist monk Thich Quang Duc on June 11, and culminating in a series of pagoda raids on August 21, led by the special forces of Ngo Dinh Nhu, who claimed that his actions were designed as a countercoup against Communist insurgents who had infiltrated the Vietnam General Association of Buddhists.[19]

Diem and the Americans mishandled the crisis. For Diem, family loyalties called for the support of Thuc and Nhu, even though he later disapproved of Thuc's actions. As the crisis progressed and American officials and the American media became hostile to Nhu, Diem moved to support him against this foreign criticism. Additionally, he had made some efforts at reconciliation with the Buddhist leaders during the early weeks of the crisis but failed to satisfy their demands. When the Buddhists called for his removal from power, he responded by claiming that the Buddhist movement had been co-opted by the Communists—even though he was not able to provide any evidence that convinced the growing anti-Diem contingency in Washington. Diem believed that opposition to Vietnamese rule was justified so long as the leader no longer had the best interests of his people in mind. But he also believed that he still had the winning strategy for Vietnamese independence either with or without American support. For officials within the Kennedy administration, Diem's reaction to the crisis and his inability to rein in his family members was a clear indication that he had reached the end of his usefulness in Vietnam.

Early in the crisis, the American position became one of identifying actions that hurt Diem but not the war effort. That position was initially prompted by an interview between Nhu and Warren Unna that appeared on the front page of the *Washington Post* on May 12, in which Nhu called for a decrease in American forces in Vietnam.[20] The "hurt Diem" strategy progressed as the Buddhist Crisis deepened in an effort to force him into social, cultural, political, economic, and religious reforms. That Diem had become isolated from his people and resistant to American advice seems reasonable given the nature and speed of the crisis, but that disconnect was also intensified by an American desire to reform through punishment rather than to refine through advice. This subtlety was not lost on Diem as he moved further away from his American advisers and closer to Nhu, further deteriorating an already bad situation.

By the fall of 1963, there were few left in Washington who supported the continuation of the Diem regime as long as the United States continued to contribute its resources to Vietnam's survival. On August 26, Henry

Cabot Lodge Jr. replaced Frederick E. Nolting Jr. as the American ambassador to Vietnam. Nolting had finished his assignment on August 15 and had been out of Vietnam on a scheduled trip when the Buddhist Crisis erupted. The replacement, though scheduled, came at a difficult time as Nolting was known to have the confidence of Diem while Lodge represented that element within the Kennedy administration that believed that it was time for a change. Diem continued to feel the American pressure to reform his administration and alleviate the Buddhist complaints. Nhu's August countercoup helped intensify that pressure as Lodge and his cadre took the position that they could no longer reason with Diem and that negotiations could not proceed until there was a change in the Vietnamese leadership. At an August 28 conference at the White House, Harriman offered the assessment that the war could not be won with Nhu: "We put Diem in power and he has doublecrossed us. Diem and his followers have betrayed us."[21] As a result, Lodge began to entertain suggestions of a Vietnamese coup d'etat and met informally with a number of generals and opposition politicians who put forth strategies for change. Diem did show increasing concern for the shift in the American attitude toward Vietnam, but, at the same time, he continued to resist what he saw as American attempts to take over his government. He continued to believe that those American officials who served in Vietnam in the fall of 1963, not to mention the Washington decisionmakers isolated from Vietnam, did not truly understand the nature of rule in Vietnam; he also believed that the United States alone could not solve Vietnam's problems. He continued to believe that he understood how to consolidate his country in 1963, as he had in 1955, even if he knew that would result in a failure in American confidence in his leadership.

Diem's intransigence, coupled with the failed Strategic Hamlet Program, the Buddhist Crisis, and an increasingly vocal minority in Washington that called for a change in the Vietnamese government, made a coup d'etat a real possibility. At the October 2, 1963, meeting of the National Security Council, President Kennedy, supported by those in attendance, called for continued criticism of Diem, though the participants were divided on whether they should focus on how Diem's actions were losing the fight against the Viet Cong or highlight America's moral opposition to the direction of the Diem government.[22] Kennedy authorized Lodge to unite the American position in Saigon toward reform of the Diem government and called for a series of economic sanctions against the Republic of Vietnam to remain in place as long as Diem refused to change. The October decision pushed the Vietnamese coup planners forward; they had previously been checked only by Lodge's refusal to sanction a coup attempt. When, at the end of the month, Lodge did not refuse—nor did he approve—a proposed coup attempt, the Vietnamese, led by Major General Duong Van Minh (a military adviser to Diem), Major General Ton That Dinh (the military governor of Saigon), and Major General Tran Van Don (the commander of the ARVN and the acting chief of the Joint General Staff), proceeded at approximately 12:30 A.M. on November 1, 1963. Diem and Nhu escaped the presidential palace and made their way to the Chinese suburb of Cho Lon, where they continued to try to rally troops still loyal to the government. When these troops failed to materialize, Diem offered to reorganize the government but was told that it was too late. This had been a strategy employed during the November 1960 coup attempt to buy time; it was not successful in 1963. Diem then agreed to surrender if he and his brother received assurances that they would not be harmed and that they would be allowed to leave the country. The two were taken into custody on November 2 and executed in the back of an armored personnel carrier rather than given the safe passage that they had been promised. The immediate reaction from Kennedy was one of shock that Diem had been assassinated, though his administration welcomed the change of government and the chance to reestablish the battle against the Viet Cong. That the United States, with Lodge as the principal agent in Vietnam, knew of the coup d'état seems clear from the available evidence, and it seems surprising that the officials in Washington would be shocked by its bloody outcome.[23] Hindsight alone does not explain away the understanding that any change of government required the elimination of Diem. That American officials believed that they could help orchestrate a coup d'état without Diem's death seems a poignant example of how naive American officials still were when it came to Vietnamese history, culture, and society. The most significant difference after November 1 was that the one leader who had guided his country since its artificial creation in 1954 had been killed—because he either could not or would not conform to the American sense of what was appropriate for the Vietnamese people.

In 1954, Bao Dai offered Ngo Dinh Diem the opportunity to form a government in Vietnam, believing that he could control the new president of the Council of Ministers. The emperor underestimated Diem. The Americans, however, would continue to underestimate him, and, over the next year, he would survive the turbulence of consolidating the Republic of Vietnam and defusing the remnants of French colonialism, religious and political faction influence, and the Viet Minh. When Diem emerged as the only legitimate leader after the October 1955 national referendum, the Americans undervalued his vision and leadership in the Vietnam that was to serve as a model state for democracy. Despite some successes, as well as a few setbacks, Diem led his country in the best manner possible given the circumstances of war and revolution with which he had to deal daily. He never achieved the desired results of serving as the democratic leader of this bulwark against communism that the Americans had envisioned; he never instituted the reforms expected of him by the Americans, and, in many respects, he moved away from the type of leadership those within the Kennedy administration demanded. He had the singular vision of freeing Vietnam from foreigners and opposing the Communist form of government, even though the two objectives were conflicting as the latter required the assistance of a foreign power, the United States. Diem's Vietnam was not dissimilar to Washington's Vietnam, though the methods required to achieve the end results were very different. At some point after the November 1960 coup attempt and the election of John F. Kennedy to the White House, the two sides began to separate, leading to the eventual dissolution of the partnership forged in the common purpose of democracy and Cold War struggle. Ultimately, it was the Kennedy administration's final underestimation of Diem's importance to Vietnam that led to his assassination and ushered in a period of war and destruction that would intensify over the next twelve years and leave Vietnam devastated, if not finally reunited, after a long and arduous struggle.

Notes

1. Adm. Lorenzo S. Sabin, "The Tragedy of Ngo Dinh Diem," Folder 9, Box 1, Papers of VADM Lorenzo S. Sabin, USN, 1954–1967, Operational Archives, Naval Historical Center, Washington, DC.

2. Ibid.

3. See Bernard Fall, *The Two Vietnams: A Political and Military Analysis* (1963; reprint, New York: Praeger, 1967), 234–57; "Short Biography of Mr. Ngo Dinh Diem

President of the Republic of Viet-Nam," Folder 14, Box 3, John Donnell Collection, Vietnam Archive, Texas Tech University; and Phuc Thien, "President Ngo-Dinh-Diem's Political Philosphy," Folder 17, Box 8, Douglas Pike Collection, Vietnam Archive, Texas Tech University.

4. William Duiker, *Ho Chi Minh* (New York: Hyperion, 2000), 27–41.

5. For more information on the role of the Michigan State University Group, see John Ernst, *Forging a Fateful Alliance: Michigan State University and the Vietnam War* (East Lansing: Michigan State University Press, 1998).

6. Welsey R. Fishel, "Political Realities in Vietnam," *Asian Survey* 1, no. 2 (April 1961): 15–23; Joseph Zasloff, "Rural Resettlement in South Viet Nam: The Agroville Program," *Pacific Affairs* 35, no. 4 (Winter 1962–63): 327–40.

7. CHMAAG, Saigon, to CINCPAC #1439, November 12, 1960, in Record Group 59, General Records of the Department of State, Bureau of East Asian Affairs, Vietnam Desk, Subject Files, 1955–1962, Entry 5155, Box 1, Folder 83, "VN 1960—Attempted Coup d'Etat."

8. CHMAAG, Saigon, to CINCPAC #1445, November 13, 1960, in ibid.

9. Lansdale Memorandum for Secretary and Deputy Secretary of Defense, stamped January 17, 1961, Record Group 59, General Records of the Department of State, Bureau of East Asian Affairs, Vietnam Desk, Subject Files, 1955–1962, Entry 5155, Box 3, Folder 20, "GVN 1961—General Lansdale."

10. Diem's annoyance is expressed in various conversations with American leaders. See Memorandum for File, Interview with the President of the Republic of Vietnam, G. P. Case and S. M. Strasburger, December 30, 1960, Record Group 59, General Records of the Department of State, Bureau of East Asian Affairs, Vietnam Desk, Subject Files, 1955–1962, Entry 5155, Box 1, Folder 91, "VN 1960—Chief of Executive Ngo Dinh Diem." Statements by international leaders include Australian Minister for External Affairs, Sir Robert G. Menzies, Remarks to the Australian House of Representatives, December 6, 1960, Record Group 59, General Records of the Department of State, Bureau of East Asian Affairs, Vietnam Desk, Subject Files, 1955–1962, Entry 5155, Box 1, Folder 30, "VN 1960 GVN Australian Relations."

11. Memorandum of Conversation between Hoang Huy, Directorate General of Customs, and John J. Helble, American Embassy, Saigon, April 1, 1961, Record Group 59, General Records of the Department of State, Bureau of East Asian Affairs, Vietnam Desk, Subject Files, 1955–1962, Entry 5155, Box 2, Folder 14-c, "GVN—Elections."

12. Memorandum for the File, "Account of an Interview between Mr. Nguyen Don Duyen and General Lawton Collins," August 23, 1961, and Under Secretary of State for Political Affairs, U. Alexis Johnson, to Assistant Secretary of State for Far Eastern Affairs, Walter P. McConaughy, "Call of Le Van An, Former Viet-Namese Ambassador in Bangkok," August 2, 1961, both in Record Group 59, General Records of the Department of State, Bureau of East Asian Affairs, Vietnam Desk, Subject Files, 1955–1962, Entry 5155, Box 2, Folder 14, "GVN 1961—Political Situation—General."

13. Robert Scigliano, "Vietnam: A Country at War," *Asian Survey* 3, no. 1 (January 1963): 48.

14. Ibid., 49.

15. For a detailed account of Diem and Nhu's goals for the Strategic Hamlet Program as well as the Vietnamese and American clash over the strategic role of the program, see Philip Catton, *Diem's Final Failure: Prelude to America's War in Vietnam* (Lawrence: University Press of Kansas, 2002).

16. U.S. Department of State, *Foreign Relations of the United States* (hereafter *FRUS*), *1961–1963* (Washington, DC: U.S. Government Printing Office [USGPO], 1991), 3:514. For more on the legal aspects of the Laotian conference, see John J. Czyzak and Carl F. Salans, "The International Conference on the Settlement of the Laotian Question and the Geneva Agreements of 1962," *American Journal of International Law* 57, no. 2 (1963): 300–317.

17. See Frederick Nolting, *From Trust to Tragedy: The Political Memoirs of Frederick Nolting, Kennedy's Ambassador to Diem's Vietnam,* with a foreword by William Colby (New York: Praeger, 1988), 81–84; and Geoffrey D. T. Shaw, "Laotian 'Neutrality': A Fresh Look at a Key Vietnam War Blunder," *Small Wars and Insurgencies* 13, no. 1 (Spring 2002): 25–56. Examples of Harriman's approach are located throughout the first four volumes of *FRUS, 1961–1963* (Washington, DC: USGPO, 1988–91), which cover Vietnam.

18. Charles S. Joiner, "South Vietnam's Buddhist Crisis: Organization for Charity, Dissidence, and Unity," *Asian Survey* 4, no. 7 (July 1964): 915–28. See also Robert Scigliano, "Vietnam: Politics and Religion," *Asian Survey* 4, no. 1 (January 1964): 666–69. Documents related to the crisis and the evolution of American perceptions of Diem and Nhu are located in vols. 3 and 4 of *FRUS, 1961–1963.*

19. Telegram from the Embassy in Vietnam (William Trueheart) to the Department of State, August 21, 1963, *FRUS, 1961–1963,* 3:595–97.

20. Memorandum from the Deputy Director of the Vietnam Working Group (Theodore Heavner) to the Assistant Secretary of State for Far Eastern Affairs (Roger Hilsman), May 15, 1963, *FRUS, 1961–1963,* 3:303–6.

21. Memorandum of a Conference with the President, August 28, 1963, *FRUS, 1961–1963,* 4:1–6. See also Joiner, "South Vietnam's Buddhist Crisis," 923.

22. Summary Record of the 519th Meeting of the National Security Council, White House, Washington, DC, October 2, 1963, *FRUS, 1961–1963,* 4:350–53.

23. See *FRUS, 1961–1963,* 4:427–537.

7

The Buddhist Antiwar Movement

Robert Topmiller

In May 1963, a group of students marched through Vietnam's old capital, Hue, carrying Buddhist flags in defiance of a recent order by South Vietnamese president Ngo Dinh Diem. Security forces fired on the demonstrators and killed eight young people, leading Buddhists throughout the nation to take to the streets in protest.[1] As antigovernment demonstrations grew larger and more unwieldy throughout the summer, the government of South Vietnam (GVN) responded with increased repression. By August, the Buddhist rebellion had exposed widespread dissatisfaction with Diem, leading to the fateful American decision to back his overthrow. Finally, rebellious South Vietnamese troops toppled the government and murdered Diem during a military coup that November.[2]

Yet the Buddhist Crisis of 1963 represented much more than just an argument over flags. Led by their charismatic leader, Thich Tri Quang, Buddhists had dreamed for decades of launching a social revolution that would eradicate poverty and injustice while relieving the distress of the masses of Vietnamese whose lives of extreme privation rendered them susceptible to National Liberation Front (NLF, better known as the Viet Cong) promises of a future egalitarian society under its tutelage.[3] The growing war in the countryside particularly concerned Buddhists because of the human suffering involved and its potential to derail their long-planned societal transformation.[4]

Buddhist monks march for fair treatment. Courtesy of the Vietnam Archive, Texas Tech University, Douglas Pike Photograph Collection.

As a result of their impressive victory over Diem, Buddhist antiwar activists emerged as a powerful political, religious, and social force and the only significant non-Communist opposition group in South Vietnam from 1963 to 1966. Their message of nationalism, peace, and neutralism carried so much weight that, for a short time, they gained the ability to bring down governments, veto appointments to high office, and call thousands of followers into the streets.[5] Nevertheless, a great irony lies within the antiwar faction's victory over Diem. Buddhists opposed Diem because of his association with the Americans and his desire to find a military solution in South Vietnam. Little did they realize that he had restrained the United States and that Washington had supported the coup to gain a more malleable regime. Diem's demise produced a situation that Buddhists sought to avoid at all costs: increased American involvement and escalation of the fighting.

By bringing Diem down, Buddhists produced a political vacuum filled by the United States. Subsequent Buddhist-inspired agitation created even more instability, again strengthening the American position in South Vietnam. This situation perpetuated itself throughout the years of the Buddhist struggle: every effort to find a government not under Washington's domination led to increased American control, with the result that the South Vietnamese exerted less and less influence over the direction their country's affairs took as the war expanded.

Moreover, vital differences underscored the 1963 agitation and later relations between Buddhists and the GVN. Most Buddhists viewed 1963 as a battle to preserve their way of life and assert their religious freedom. From 1964 on, the conflict became more politically and emotionally charged, given that Buddhist clerics believed that nothing less than the fate of Vietnam and their own centuries-old relationship with the people remained at stake.[6] They asserted that they must rescue their country from a war driven by foreign ideologies that had swept aside traditional Buddhist attitudes of love and brotherhood. Hence, political action evolved from their commitment to two of the fundamental tenets of Buddhism: compassion and nonviolence.

The GVN's fragile political legitimacy had called forth the Buddhist peace movement, most South Vietnamese having no legal way to confront their government. Indeed, only two groups challenged the GVN internally: the NLF and the Buddhists. By emphasizing Buddhism, opponents of the regime highlighted its association with foreign elements and its alienation from the people. Thus, when Buddhists demonstrated against the GVN while claiming to represent the people, they emphasized their dedication to Vietnamese history and tradition. They stood in stark contrast to the GVN, which had allowed the introduction of American forces into the country, turning it into a battleground between the United States and communism.

While some Buddhists, particularly Thich Tri Quang's followers, wanted to establish a middle way between the violence of the United States and that of the NLF, their peace movement suffered from a fatal flaw. Because they had no weapons or areas of refuge and had to operate within the territory of one of the two main forces, they could be destroyed at any time and had to maneuver between two more powerful adversaries. In a democratic system, the Buddhists could have had a decisive impact owing to the popularity of their antiwar position, but their vulnerability remained the most significant aspect of their movement. As a result, they exerted great efforts to establish a civilian government free of dictatorial elements.

At the same time, internal disputes weakened their labors to end the conflict as the Buddhist peace movement fragmented badly after 1964. While serious arguments arose over the political activism of some clerics, a large degree of dissent revolved around the issue of war and peace.[7] Many Buddhist leaders recognized that an American-dominated GVN could never muster the people's support while the war's tremendous financial costs worked against launching a social revolution. Afraid of a GVN that spurned negotiations with the NLF and a U.S. government dedicated to pressing the contest in South Vietnam, Buddhists demanded democracy as a way of masking their real goal: "restoration of peace and negotiations with the NLF. " Not surprisingly, Buddhist leaders seldom made such statements publicly for fear of arrest or assassination by GVN authorities.[8]

No one can say for sure how the majority of the Vietnamese felt about the fighting. Certainly, the United States never tried to find out. But the ability of the Buddhist hierarchy to call thousands of protesters into the streets and topple a number of American-backed regimes indicates its ability to articulate a message that resonated deeply with the Vietnamese. In fact, even though in 1966 the Unified Buddhist Church (UBC) represented only about 1 million of the estimated 16 million Buddhists in South Vietnam, it constituted the foremost interest group in the country.[9] Thus, the largest non-Communist group in the nation contested the hostilities and the American-controlled government prosecuting them. When the NLF, which assuredly opposed U.S. intervention in the country, is considered along with the UBC and the other religious sects that silently supported the Buddhists, it seems probable that a majority of South Vietnamese objected to American interference in their country.[10]

This essay examines the Buddhist peace movement in the context of its antiwar activities, the expanded role of women, self-immolation, and its relationship to nonviolence and possible links between the Buddhists and the Communist insurgency.

Buddhist Protests, 1964–66

By 1964, Buddhist leaders recognized that most Vietnamese did not want war and worked assiduously to end the conflict and expel the Americans.

Thus, they made representative government the hallmark of their struggle since they knew that no regime calling for expanded war could survive in a democratic South Vietnam. Without U.S. interference, the Buddhist leadership likely would have placed a neutralist government in office and parleyed an end to the fighting. Understanding this, U.S. officials resolved to halt Buddhist attempts to remove the dictatorial regimes established by Washington to perpetuate its hegemony. Indeed, a succession of South Vietnamese governments tried to bring peace to the country from 1963 to 1965, but every effort to collaborate with the NLF and create a neutral government brought a violent reaction and ejection from office by the U.S.-backed Army of the Republic of Vietnam (ARVN).[11]

After Diem's removal, the Buddhist peace movement appeared triumphant with the installation of the new government of Gen. Duong Van Minh in November 1963. South Vietnam's future seemed bright. Newspapers sprang up, political parties proliferated, and, for the first time in the country's brief history, open discussion began on its direction. A widespread feeling that the United States had agreed to the Diem coup to bring freedom to South Vietnam contributed to the rising tide of democracy—and the later disillusionment when it failed. Soon after Minh formed a government intent on seeking talks with the NLF, Gen. Nguyen Khanh overthrew the GVN in January 1964, temporarily ending any opportunity to stop the war through dialogue. Concerned mainly with winning the war, the United States squandered the immense political capital it had gained with the Diem coup by moving away from its often-stated commitment to representative government in favor of stability by embracing the brand-new Khanh regime.[12]

Nevertheless, the replacement of one dictator with another left many South Vietnamese seething with anger and ready to strike back at Khanh. He provided them an opportunity when he promulgated a new constitution and declared himself president of South Vietnam in August 1964.[13] Suddenly, the burst of liberty that had been the fruit of the hard-fought victory against Diem seemed endangered, leading the country to erupt into frenzied anarchy—known as the First Buddhist Crisis of 1964—as students carried out ferocious demonstrations similar to those of the preceding year.[14] Adding to the chaos in the streets, simmering tensions between Catholics and Buddhists burst into religious warfare as the country descended into anarchy.[15] Disregarding appalling violence and disorder,

Khanh refused to restore order because he feared that a strong move against the rioters and more instability might turn the Americans against him, as with Diem.

Desperate to find a solution, Khanh reached out to Buddhist leaders, who demanded an immediate cessation of his dictatorial powers, called for a purge of Catholics in the GVN, and insisted on a government that followed the popular will.[16] With virtually no support left besides the United States, Khanh quickly embraced the opportunity to gain the Buddhists' backing when they presented their demands to him on August 25. To the Buddhists' utter astonishment, their power had increased dramatically in less than two weeks, and they had paid an incredibly small price for their victory. No sweeping arrests of monks, no raids on pagodas, no repression, and, most significantly, no self-immolations had accompanied their struggle.[17]

Unfortunately, Buddhist success persuaded U.S. ambassador Maxwell Taylor that the growing instability and weakness of the GVN could, in time, force the United States "to take the major responsibility for prying the Viet Cong and the North Vietnamese off the backs of the South Vietnamese population." Tragically for the United States and Vietnam, Taylor advocated "escalating pressure on the DRV [Democratic Republic of Vietnam, North Vietnam] for the purpose of holding [the] GVN together." Ironically, Buddhist efforts to bring peace and neutralism to South Vietnam had convinced Taylor and other U.S. officials that only an American expansion of the fighting could forestall GVN moves to settle the conflict through negotiations.[18]

The appointment of Tran Van Huong as the successor to Khanh in November 1964 soon incited renewed opposition to the GVN and ignited the Second Buddhist Crisis of 1964. Saigon again exploded in antigovernment fury as Buddhists joined students in demanding Huong's ouster, leading exasperated government officials to tap regular army units to quell the disturbances.[19] Nevertheless, the Huong regime disintegrated in January 1965, sparking more instability, the eventual ascension to power of Air Marshal Nguyen Cao Ky, and the introduction of U.S. ground forces into South Vietnam in March 1965 in a desperate attempt to keep the GVN afloat.

In February 1966, GVN and American leaders met in Hawaii to strengthen ties and plan ways to defeat the Communist insurgency. While the conferees saw this meeting as a milestone in their relationship, Buddhists viewed it with horror because it would mean increased fighting in South Vietnam. Thus, they decided to risk everything in a desperate challenge to end the conflict before it grew even more difficult to control.

On his return from Honolulu, Prime Minister Nguyen Cao Ky dismissed his main rival in the GVN, Gen. Nguyen Chanh Thi, providing Buddhists a pretext for launching a new antiwar campaign.[20] To Ky's great surprise and Washington's consternation, Thi's firing ignited antigovernment demonstrations throughout South Vietnam, reinforcing Buddhist beliefs that the time had arrived to challenge directly the GVN and end the conflict.[21] Civil disorder spread quickly throughout South Vietnam; most of Danang, for example, shut down in a general strike.[22] By the end of the month, massive protests with heavy anti-American overtones reached Nha Trang and Dalat. In Hue, students seized the radio station, the site of the original Buddhist protest against Diem, turning it into the voice of their message.[23]

It was no coincidence that open rebellion by Buddhists and their allies first occurred in Danang and Hue. The initial elements of the American ground forces had landed at Danang a year earlier, and the area around the city had witnessed the initial interactions between Vietnamese and Americans. The appearance of alien troops waging war against Vietnamese inflamed the community, leading to greater recruitment for the NLF, strong anti-American sentiment, and enhanced support for Buddhist antiwar efforts.[24]

The result was the Buddhist Crisis of 1966, the culmination of Buddhist peace efforts and an event that best typified America's frustration over its inability to influence events in South Vietnam and the ambiguity felt by many Vietnamese over the American crusade to defend them from their countrymen. Indeed, as a result of Buddhist-inspired upheaval in 1966, the critical northern provinces of South Vietnam plunged into what the historian George C. Herring referred to as a "civil war within an insurrection."[25] This internal ferment witnessed an alliance between rebellious ARVN troops and the Buddhist-dominated peace movement, on one hand, and the GVN and the United States, on the other, in the most serious non-Communist threat to South Vietnam in its short, tumultuous history.

Adding to the "hallucinatory" quality of the agitation, a number of

Buddhist monks appeal for international assistance. Courtesy of the Vietnam Archive, Texas Tech University, Douglas Pike Photograph Collection.

factors converged during the spring of 1966 to generate widespread support for the Buddhists. A local desire for autonomy and a political uprising blended into an emerging peace movement, student demonstrations against government corruption, a dramatic increase in anti-Americanism, and an intellectual and trade union revolt over cultural and economic upheaval in the country, leading the nation to the verge of collapse similar to the situation in August 1964.[26] More seriously for the GVN, large numbers of ARVN soldiers participated in the Hue and Danang protests. No greater indication of Ky's impotence and the widespread resistance to his war aims seemed possible than the wholesale defection of troops retained by the state to combat the Communists.[27]

After weeks of open rebellion by the Buddhists, Ky flew to Danang in early April to resolve the impasse. When he arrived, he found himself confronted by peace activists, their numbers augmented by rebellious

ARVN who made it clear that they would fight GVN efforts to liberate the city. Following a tense confrontation between his troops and the rebels, Ky wisely negotiated a political solution and fled back to Saigon.[28] Ky's retreat sparked consternation and severe discomfort in Washington and led to a painful reconsideration of the U.S. role in South Vietnam. Although the Americans eventually decided to continue fighting, few retained any illusions about the legitimacy of the GVN.[29]

More ominously for the peace activists, antiwar advocates suffered a steady erosion of support among the Buddhist population because of their involvement in politics and the ongoing factionalism within the UBC. Buddhist leaders stumbled when they lost touch with large segments of the UBC and the society they wanted to save. In the ideological split that fatally weakened the Buddhists, many supported the conservatives because Thich Tri Quang's radicalism seemed dangerous and had brought the GVN down on all Buddhists. The militants, on the other hand, saw the war as the greater hazard since they believed that the U.S. presence would eventually lead to a Communist victory and the end of the UBC, while the conservatives wanted to confront the insurgency on the battlefield. Thus, all factions viewed communism as the greatest danger, but they disagreed on the best way to halt it. Moreover, while Buddhist leaders exhibited high levels of scholarship in terms of philosophy and textual criticism, they remained political neophytes and immature in their thinking. Unprepared for the rough-and-tumble world of politics, their capacity to solve the problems of South Vietnam did not match their ability to understand the inherent dilemma of U.S. intervention in their country.[30]

Realizing that he had to act forcefully to survive politically, Ky launched a surprise attack against Danang in May. In the process, possibly the strangest series of events in the history of the Vietnam War unfolded when the prime minister of one of America's closest allies launched an attack against the main operational and logistics base of the U.S. III Marine Amphibious Force (III MAF) without notifying its commander or any of his subordinates. Eventually, a triangular conflict arose between the Buddhists and their ARVN allies, ARVN units loyal to the GVN, and U.S. Marines, leading to casualties on all sides. By May 23, the dissidents had collapsed, and the city fell to the GVN.[31]

Hue, the beautiful, peaceful, graceful city along the Perfume River, next emerged as the Buddhists' last bastion, its pastoral quality now marred by the mobs of students who surged through its streets in waves of anti-U.S./GVN outbursts. Realizing that the GVN would soon invade the city, Buddhist students "sacked and burned" the American cultural center and library on May 26, destroying close to ten thousand books.[32] On June 1, an enraged crowd smashed the American consulate in the city.[33] By June 19, government troops had occupied the city with little resistance and placed Thich Tri Quang under house arrest, effectively bringing the three-year Buddhist rebellion to an end.[34] In one of the greatest ironies of the whole conflict, by destroying the Buddhist peace movement and effectively blocking calls for representative government, the GVN doomed itself by failing to broaden its political base, leaving opponents of the regime little choice but to join the insurgency.

NLF-Buddhist Relations

Given that Buddhist leaders remained reluctant to espouse anticommunism publicly, American and GVN commentators seized on this silence to label Buddhists, particularly Thich Tri Quang, as Communist sympathizers.[35] Certainly, one of the most hotly debated issues concerning the Buddhist peace movement centered on its relationship with the insurgency. Despite numerous U.S. government and press assertions to the contrary, little evidence exists of NLF involvement with the Buddhist hierarchy at any time during the Vietnam War. Indeed, many Buddhists expressed contempt for communism, which they viewed as a retarded form of Buddhism and a Western concept unsuited to Vietnam. Realizing that many non-Communists had joined the NLF, some Buddhists saw their peace movement as a way to lure these elements into a coalition government designed to end the war.[36] Buddhists believed that hastening an American exit and creating a coalition government remained the only ways to deny the NLF victory because GVN/U.S. actions served as potent recruiting tools for the NLF. Thus, the Buddhist peace movement could be viewed as a last, desperate effort to prevent a complete Communist victory in Vietnam.

The NLF did benefit tremendously from Buddhist-inspired disorder and certainly hoped for its continuation. The appearance of widespread resistance to the GVN gave great strength to the revolutionaries' claims that they had the support of the population and that the GVN constituted little more than an American creation. Moreover, the positioning of major ARVN elements around Saigon to guard against possible coups and put down Buddhist-led demonstrations granted the insurgency relative impunity in the countryside.

In some ways, the NLF and the Buddhist clerics had much in common. Both sought to end the war and expel the Americans, appealed to and drew their main support from the people, emphasized nationalism, and saw neutralism, for different reasons, as the answer to South Vietnam's problem. Abhorrence at the idea of Americans killing Vietnamese, moreover, gave a huge boost to the nationalism that continued to be a critical component of both movements.

Although less apparent, differences between the insurgents and the Buddhists remained quite real. While the Communists succeeded in winning the battle for the people in the countryside, Buddhist leaders demonstrated an ability to stimulate mass action in metropolitan areas that had eluded the revolution. Remembering the enormous triumph of the Viet Minh in provoking an urban uprising in August 1945, the NLF dreamed of replicating that event in South Vietnam.[37]

Nevertheless, the insurgency faced a real dilemma: Buddhists helped it tremendously by stimulating mass action, but they also appealed to a group the Communists considered absolutely critical to their success.[38] Both Buddhists and the NLF recognized the revolutionary potential in the urban proletariat, but the antiwar movement appeared more effective at tapping it, a source of increasing concern for the insurgency.[39] The NLF found itself in the uncomfortable position of wanting the Buddhists to take on the government, but not to the extent that they could deny the Communists access to the disaffected elements of the urban population. This developed into a larger issue when the war caused a massive influx of peasants into the cities. Thus, the insurgency saw more of its supporters fall under the sway of the Buddhists, whose plan for a coalition government seemed designed to deny the NLF victory on the battlefield.[40]

Buddhists, for their part, remained mindful of the danger of an alliance with the NLF. The bitter experience of Buddhism in Tibet, China, and North Vietnam convinced them that they had no future under a Communist regime. In many ways, they feared more the establishment of a puppet organization, which had occurred in North Vietnam and China, over outright repression, the model in Tibet, because a Communist-controlled organization could confuse the people and lure them away from the Buddhists' leadership. Moreover, alliance with the NLF would have forced the GVN, the Americans, and non-Communist Buddhists to oppose the peace movement. In the end, neither Buddhists nor the NLF desired an alliance; each wanted to use the other to attain its goals.

Self-Immolation

Buddhists never successfully resolved the problem of confronting a brutal government with passivity. The emotions unleashed by Buddhist protests often contributed to outbursts of dreadful savagery and destruction when the leadership lost control of its followers, particularly students, who had much to lose in a country constantly expanding draft calls to fight an increasingly futile and senseless war. Buddhists responded to this challenge by confronting adversaries with various forms of nonviolence, including addressing social problems, publishing antiwar literature, aligning with peace organizations outside Vietnam, launching hunger protests, and encouraging noncooperation with the GVN.[41] Yet the most dramatic demonstration of Buddhist peacefulness occurred on June 11, 1963, when an elderly monk, Thich Quang Duc, sat on a busy Saigon street and set himself afire. This first and most spectacular self-destruction stamped an indelible image on the Vietnam War that never faded.[42]

During the course of the war, some seventy Buddhists sacrificed themselves to protest the fighting. Indeed, self-immolation went to the very heart of Buddhist antiwar efforts because it represented the highest manifestation of Buddhist nonviolence, given that those committing the act harmed themselves rather than another being. In addition, the Buddha's injunction always to act with compassion could be fulfilled by people willing to sacrifice themselves to call the world's attention to the plight of South Vietnamese Buddhism.[43] The willingness of monks, nuns, and lay people to die for peace in the most horrible manner serves as a poignant and lasting testament to the feelings of some Vietnamese toward the hostilities.[44]

Vietnamese Buddhists argued vigorously that self-immolation did not represent suicide. Rather than the act of a despondent person fleeing the problems of the world, it was an act that sought to liberate the people from a ruinous war.[45] Indeed, the destruction of the physical self by fire had a long tradition in Buddhism. When Alexander the Great invaded India in the fourth century B.C., for instance, a Buddhist monk immolated himself before the Macedonian forces.[46] As the historian Douglas Pike points out, setting oneself afire constituted "an ancient gesture . . . against actions by the state seen as against religion." Buddhists also utilized it against the French and the Chinese during their occupations of Vietnam.[47]

While some historians point to the Chinese roots of self-immolation, which predated the introduction of Buddhism, Vietnamese history contained numerous stories of Buddhists who sacrificed themselves by fire. On occasion, clerics continued the old practice of burning off a finger to "aid their liberation from the world," while, before the development of gasoline, "monks who decided to immolate themselves would eat fatty foods for a couple of years so they would burn better."[48] Certainly, the Buddhist belief in self-negation and nonattachment to the physical self, combined with the relation between concepts of fire and of purity, could evolve into a belief in achieving a state of physical nonself through self-immolation, particularly after achieving enlightenment.

But self-destruction was not confined to elderly monks. At least twenty women, mostly young, set themselves on fire during the conflict as well. Thus, the peace movement became an outlet for an idealism that for some turned into self-sacrifice when they failed to stop the killing.[49] Furthermore, the women who annihilated their bodies may also have been motivated by the possibility of release from the endless round of death to rebirth to death by escaping the bonds of both karma and patriarchy. Although most nuns accepted that they would be reborn as men on their path to enlightenment, many also believed that a person who obliterated her body became a bodhisattva because of the exquisite purity of her perfect action. Thus, if she had an untainted spirit and had been motivated to die for her people, her self-sacrifice enabled her to avoid rebirth as a man, forever escaping gender identification and the endless process of reincarnation.[50] Ultimately, by immolating themselves, many Buddhist women declared their complete liberation from patriarchy and the world.[51]

Buddhist Women in the Peace Movement

While self-immolation constituted the most dramatic form of resistance by women, a combination of religious ethics and resistance to patriarchy led many women to embrace the Buddhist peace movement. Their pacifism grew out of traditional Buddhist beliefs in compassion and nonviolence, a desire to save the nation from a ruinous war, and the increased sense of empowerment felt by Vietnamese women in the twentieth century. For Buddhist women, in particular, popular attitudes linking womanhood and compassion infused them with a fervent desire to assist their people through a socially active application of Buddhist teaching.

Vietnamese Buddhism had long been considered the religion of women, while the Vietnamese Bodhisattva of Compassion, Quan The Am, is a female deity. In many ways, Quan The Am epitomizes empathy in that she remains intensely interested in ending human suffering, reinforcing the image of women as sympathetic liberators of the nation.[52] Vietnamese particularly expected women to serve humanity. However, this did not represent biological determinism. Instead, Vietnamese had been primed to believe that women remained more compassionate than men both by a society that subscribed to the view and by the ubiquitous representations of Quan The Am reminding them of the benevolent nature of women. Women may have internalized this universal belief and viewed themselves as agents of Buddhist empathy.

Alfred Hassler, an American pacifist who contacted Buddhist antiwar activists in 1969, maintained that many South Vietnamese supported the notion of a "third force" to end the conflict.[53] Third force advocates claimed that they were neither anti-NLF nor anti–United States but, rather, pro-peace because they wanted to halt the misery caused by the fighting.[54] Rejecting the idea that the conflict had to be settled on the battlefield, many saw the "third solution"[55] as a way for the United States to withdraw honorably from Vietnam.

Women performed an essential role in the third force despite the fact that many felt great ambivalence about entering the political arena. But the Buddha's injunction to practice compassion convinced them that they could not remain silent and apolitical. Many believed that their history, religious and cultural orientation, and obligation to their people left them no choice but to act.[56] Hence, Buddhist women participated in demonstrations, placed family altars in the streets, led students out of classes to protest against the war, made efforts to ease the human impact of the conflict, and immolated themselves to call attention to the plight of their people.[57]

Police forcibly disperse Buddhist monks during a Saigon demonstration. Courtesy of the Vietnam Archive, Texas Tech University, Burch Collection of the National Vietnam Veterans Coalition Collection.

Some women objected to Buddhist clerics engaging in political activity and found an outlet for their idealism in the new School of Youth for Social Service (SYSS).[58] They wanted the SYSS to act as an internal third force neither supporting nor opposing either side. In the early 1960s, the well-known Vietnamese Buddhist philosopher Thich Nhat Hanh had reintroduced the concept of engaged Buddhism, a militant social activism that ignored both sides of the war and concentrated on ministering to its victims.[59] However, he spent much of his time outside South Vietnam, leaving the leadership and the dangerous work to a Buddhist woman named Cao Ngoc Phuong, who became the organization's inspirational leader and the person most responsible for its successes.

In her memoir of the SYSS, Cao Ngoc Phuong placed particular emphasis on *Engaged Buddhism,* a tract written by Thich Nhat Hanh in 1964 calling for radical activism to cure the suffering of the Vietnamese people. Despite the fact that the government outlawed this work, Buddhists smuggled over four thousand copies out of Saigon and spread them all over the country. The document electrified Buddhists in particular and a significant portion of the urban population in general with the hope that the Buddhists could relieve the agony caused by the fighting.[60] Established in 1965, the SYSS represented the culmination of Thich Nhat Hanh's and Cao Ngoc Phuong's belief in socially engaged Buddhism.[61]

Women constituted around 25 percent of the program's students, while SYSS leaders located the first school building in the women's section of the Tu Nghiem Pagoda in Saigon. Thich Nhat Hanh specifically called for "religious youth, young monks and nuns to be present in the movement" and never expressed reservations about admitting women. Instead, he seemed eager to enlist them as equals. The SYSS espoused a radically egalitarian approach to the social crisis in South Vietnam while anticipating a large measure of agency on the part of its volunteers, irrespective of gender.[62]

By employing a spirit of love and volunteerism to attack the acute social crisis in South Vietnam, Cao Ngoc Phuong sought to instill hope in a society increasingly resigned to never-ending hostilities. In time, as more students graduated from the training program, despite the war going on around them, SYSS members opened schools, built hospitals, fed the hungry, housed the homeless, cared for refugees, arranged local truces during natural disasters, worked for peace, and tried to end the suffering of the innocent victims of the war. Despite extreme GVN repression after 1966, Buddhist women continued to work to alleviate the suffering brought on by the fighting.

Conclusion

In the end, the UBC saw its three-year campaign to end the fighting and protect the politically powerless citizenry of South Vietnam turned back by GVN/U.S. police and military power. Despite a brief period of self-doubt on their part, U.S. leaders soon increased American troop levels, resulting in more violence and greater distress for Vietnamese and Americans. Thus, Buddhist-inspired instability led to greater U.S. hegemony over the GVN and to an escalation of the fighting that resulted in one of the great human tragedies of the twentieth century.

Notwithstanding their enormous sacrifices, Buddhist leaders failed in their quest to topple the GVN and end the war. Ironically, at a time when the United States claimed it wanted to deliver the Vietnamese from the dangers of communism, Buddhists sought to liberate their country from U.S. dominance and a conflict imposed on them by outsiders: the United States, northerners, and southerners. They simply sought the right to live their lives in peace and ameliorate suffering in a country not controlled by foreigners.

Buddhists suffered imprisonment without trial, persecution, and political annihilation for the remainder of the war as casualties increased and the people endured unimaginable horrors at the hands of the NLF, the GVN, and the United States. Entry into the political realm eventually undid the peace movement, but Buddhists came amazingly close to victory: bringing the GVN to the brink of extinction, leading central Vietnam out of the GVN orbit from March to mid-May 1966, and forcing Washington into a painful reconsideration of its role in South Vietnam.

As the hostilities and GVN repression of peace advocates increased, the UBC exerted greater efforts to end the fighting. In February 1969, Buddhists who had been advising Vietnamese to avoid the draft received extended prison terms for their efforts. In 1970, GVN security forces ruthlessly attacked a UBC peace campaign. A few months later, the Buddhist-supported Lotus Blossom political party received the highest vote total in an election, the result of the Buddhists' call for a U.S. departure and the formation of a regime dedicated to peace. In 1971, some 150,000 Vietnamese rallied at the An Quang Pagoda to demand an immediate cease-fire with no preconditions. In 1974, the UBC inaugurated a "DO NOT SHOOT YOUR BROTHER" campaign that encouraged combatants on both sides to refrain from killing each other. All the while, Buddhists immolated themselves to call the world's attention to their people's suffering. Finally, Thich Tri Quang helped arrange for Duong Van Minh to take power in the conflict's waning days, ensuring that "a long and hideous war was finished."[63]

The United States had exited Vietnam in 1973 under conditions that seemed remarkably similar to the Buddhists' position in 1966. After nine long years of war, the country laid waste by American firepower and the chemical defoliant Agent Orange, the population ravaged, and the people in the grasp of hatred and bitterness, Buddhists had the right to ask what the previous nine years had accomplished. If the fighting had ended in 1964 or 1966 with a negotiated settlement, would anything have been different from the way they were in 1973 except for the enormous human cost?

The United States paid a heavy price for its determination to continue the war despite evidence that many Vietnamese wanted it to end. Yet, compared to the cost incurred by the Vietnamese, American losses seem inconsequential. This was the Buddhists' point all along. Their people and country bore the burden of America's determination to stop communism. Ironically, in trying to rescue their country, Buddhist leaders almost saved the United States from pursuing its self-destructive course in Vietnam.

Notes

1. Robert L. Mole, *Vietnamese Buddhism,* Navy Personal Response Project Study (Washington, DC, 1967), 57–65; "Buddhism in Vietnam: 1968," in *Buddhism and the Buddhist Programming of the Asia Foundation in Asia,* vol. 4, *Vietnam* (San Francisco: Asia Foundation, January 1968), 17–20, 110–20. When I refer to *Buddhists* in this study, I mean the group who followed the lead of Thich Tri Quang and the Vien Hoa Dao [Institute for the Execution of the Dharma]. Buddhists in South Vietnam split into a number of major groupings, the Buddhist peace movement representing about 1 million. Internal divisions between conservatives, led by Thich Tam Chau, and radicals, led by Thich Tri Quang, also weakened the peace movement. The movement had a regional component as well; Thich Tri Quang remained most powerful in central Vietnam, while Thich Tam Chau retained an edge in Saigon. Neither side had much influence with the Hoa Hao or the large number of Buddhists who lived in the Mekong Delta.

One of the great challenges in studying the Buddhist movement lies in estimating the exact number of Buddhists in South Vietnam. According to "Buddhism in Vietnam: 1968," a 1961 survey conducted in Saigon concluded that over 80 percent of the city's population considered themselves to be Buddhists, while Catholics constituted 13 percent and Confucians 3 percent. The Asia Foundation estimated that the same percentages would apply to South Vietnam in general, although probably only about 40 percent of the populace actively practiced Buddhism.

2. "Telegram from the Department of State to the Embassy in Vietnam," July 2, 1963, in U.S. Department of State, *Foreign Relations of the United States, 1961–1963* (hereafter *FRUS, 1961–1963*), vol. 4, *Vietnam, August–December 1963* (hereafter *Vietnam, 1963*) (Washington, DC: U.S. Government Printing Office, 1991), 443–44; David Halberstam, "Diem Regime under Fire," *New York Times,* July 7, 1963, sec. 4, p. 5; "Telegram from the Embassy in Vietnam to the Department of State," August 14, 1963, in *FRUS, 1961–1963,* vol. 4, *Vietnam, 1963,* 565–67; "Memorandum of a Conversation, White House, Washington," September 11, 1963, in ibid., 188–90. For more on the Buddhist Crisis of 1963, see Robert Topmiller, "The 1963 Buddhist Crisis in South Vietnam" (M.A. thesis, Central Washington University, 1994).

3. During the war, most American correspondents incorrectly reported that

Thich, adopted by all Buddhist monks in Vietnam on ordination, meant "reverend" or "venerable." Actually, it comes from the Vietnamese translation of the Buddha's name, Thich-Ca or Shakyamuni. *Thich Nu* indicates that the individual is a nun. Thich Nhat Hanh, *Zen Keys,* trans. Albert Low and Jean Low, with an introduction by Philip Kapleau (Garden City, NY: Anchor, 1974), 1.

4. For more on the Buddhist peace movement, see Robert Topmiller, *The Lotus Unleashed: The Buddhist Peace Movement in South Vietnam, 1964–1966* (Lexington: University Press of Kentucky, 2002).

5. "Telegram from the Embassy in Vietnam to the Department of State," November 3, 1963, in *FRUS, 1961–1963,* vol. 4, *Vietnam, 1963,* 548; and Stanley Karnow, *Vietnam: A History* (New York: Viking, 1983), 339, 379, 380, 445–50.

6. For an excellent explanation of the importance that Buddhist monks and nuns attach to their relationship to the people, see Minh Chi, Ha Van Tan, and Nguyen Tai Thu, *Buddhism in Vietnam: From Its Origins to the Nineteenth Century* (Hanoi: Gioi, 1993); and Minh Chi, "A Survey of Vietnamese Buddhism: Past and Present," in *Buddhist Institute of High Studies* (n.p., n.d.). I discussed this during interviews with Professor Minh Chi in Vietnam in 1996, 1999, and 2000. Notes from this and all the interviews conducted for this work remain on file in my office at Eastern Kentucky University.

7. CIA memo, "The Political Situation in South Vietnam: The Current Crisis, Possible Future Developments, US Options," April 2, 1966, Vietnam Volume 50, Vietnam Country File, National Security File (hereafter NSF), Lyndon Baines Johnson Presidential Library (hereafter LBJ Library), Austin, TX.

8. Vo Van Ai, e-mail message to author, May 23, 1996; and George McT. Kahin, *Intervention: How America Became Involved in Vietnam* (New York: Knopf, 1996), 414.

9. Charles Mohr, "Buddhists Insist Ky Junta Must Go," *New York Times,* May 28, 1966, 1.

10. After conducting over one hundred interviews with Vietnamese associated with the Buddhist peace movement, I remain convinced that most South Vietnamese did not want to fight the war. Almost every person interviewed made it clear that the Buddhists were convinced of this also and were deeply concerned with the impact of the war on their people and took extraordinary risks to end the conflict. I received further confirmation of this in my interviews with Gen. Nguyen Khanh and Gen. Nguyen Chanh Thi, both of whom concluded that the war had to end while they held power, and George Kahin, who heard the same thing from Buddhist activists during his trip to South Vietnam in 1966. See Nguyen Khanh, interview with the author, Fremont, CA, July 1996; Nguyen Chanh Thi, interview with the author, Lancaster, PA, April 1997; and George Kahin, interview with the author, Ithaca, NY, September 1996.

11. George Kahin, interview with the author (n. 10 above).

12. Bui Diem, with David Chanoff, *In the Jaws of History* (Boston: Houghton Mifflin, 1987), 106–12.

13. "General Khanh, President of the Republic," *Saigon Post,* August 17, 1964, 1.

14. "Saigon Students Score Army Rule," *New York Times,* August 22, 1964, 2; "Students Burn Charter Copy," *New York Times,* August 23, 1964, 3; Peter Grose, "Khanh Responds to Young Critics," *New York Times,* August 23, 1964, 3; "Students Attack National Radio Station," *Saigon Post,* August 24, 1963, 1; "Ministry Office Sacked," *New York Times,* August 24, 1964, 3; "US Army Billet Stoned," *New York Times,* August 24, 1964, 3; "Struggle Continues, Buddhists Told," *Saigon Daily News,* August 19, 1964, 2; "Students Honor Youthful Martyr," *Saigon Post,* August 26, 1964, 1.

15. Peter Grose, "Violence Widespread," *New York Times,* August 25, 1964, 10; Peter Grose, "Riots Continuing," *New York Times,* August 26, 1964, 1; "Anarchy and Agony," *Time,* September 4, 1964, 33; Peter Grose, "Rulers in Saigon Unable to Agree on a New Regime," *New York Times,* August 27, 1964, 1; "Danang Rioters Hit US Run Hospital," *New York Times,* August 27, 1964, 3.

16. Peter Grose, "Khanh Quitting but May Return under Code," *New York Times,* August 26, 1964, 1; "Drastic Changes Urged by Buddhist Leaders," *Saigon Post,* August 26, 1964, 1; "General Khanh Resigns as President," *Saigon Daily News,* August 26, 1964, 1.

17. James Forest, *The Unified Buddhist Church of Vietnam: Fifteen Years for Reconciliation* (Alkmaar: International Fellowship of Reconciliation, 1978), 6, 31.

18. "Telegram from the Embassy in Vietnam to the Department of State," September 6, 1964, in U.S. Department of State, *Foreign Relations of the United States, 1964,* vol. 1, *Vietnam* (Washington, DC: U.S. Government Printing Office, 1992), 733–35.

19. "Huong Blames Riots on 'Politicians,'" *Saigon Post,* November 24, 1964, 1; "Troops Disperse Demonstrations," *Saigon Post,* November 23, 1964, 1; and "Huong Government Faces Crucial Test," *Saigon Post,* November 25, 1964, 1.

20. Kahin, *Intervention,* 417; Vo Van Ai, e-mail message to author, May 23, 1996; Charles Mohr, "Behind Saigon's Purge: Honolulu Talks with Johnson Gave Ky Confidence to Move against His Rival," *New York Times,* March 14, 1966, 2.

21. Charles Mohr, "Ky Rival's Ouster Sets off Protest," *New York Times,* March 12, 1966, 3; Embtel 3288 (Saigon) Lodge to Rusk, April 10, 1966, Vietnam Volume 48, Vietnam Country File, NSF, LBJ Library; Robert Shaplen, "Letter from South Vietnam," *New Yorker,* June 4, 1966, 148; Diem, *Jaws of History,* 166.

22. Charles Mohr, "Buddhist Criticize Ky Regime; Protests on Ouster of Thi Grow," *New York Times,* March 13, 1966, 1.

23. Charles Mohr, "Anti-Ky Protests by Saigon Monk Draws Thousands," *New York Times,* March 17, 1966, 1; "Anti-Ky Rallies Erupt in Saigon," *New York Times,* March 27, 1966, 1; R. W. Apple Jr., "Protest March in Nha Trang," *New York Times,* March 26, 1966, 2; Frances FitzGerald, *Fire in the Lake: The Vietnamese and the Americans in Vietnam* (Boston: Little, Brown, 1972), 374.

24. Nor were these conditions confined to central Vietnam. In 1997, two Cambodian Theravada monks assured me that most of their fellow monks opposed U.S. intervention in the country because of the heavy civilian casualties caused by American

operations. Even though they were not part of the UBC, they claimed that Buddhist compassion led them to oppose the war and protect the people. In addition, they argued that most Vietnamese opposed the presence of the Americans in South Vietnam. Phala Suvanna and Eka Suvanna, interview with the author, Candransi Pagoda, Ho Chi Minh City, Vietnam, March 1997.

25. George C. Herring, *America's Longest War: The United States and Vietnam, 1950-1975,* 2nd ed. (New York: Knopf, 1986), 157.

26. FitzGerald, *Fire in the Lake,* 374-75; Herring, *America's Longest War,* 156-57.

27. Charles Mohr, "3000 Troops Lead Vietnam Protest against Regime," *New York Times,* April 3, 1966, 1.

28. *Saigon Daily News,* April 7, 1966, 1. (The title of this article was blanked out by Vietnamese censors.)

29. For more on this, see Robert Topmiller, "1966—a Missed Opportunity for Peace in Vietnam," *Peace and Change* 27, no. 1 (January 2002): 59-96.

30. Karnow, *Vietnam,* 449.

31. For a detailed explanation of the fighting in Danang, see Robert Topmiller, "Confrontation in Danang: III MAF and the Buddhist Struggle Movement in South Vietnam, 1966," *Journal of American-East Asian Relations* 6, nos. 2-3 (Summer-Fall 1997): 207-34. Some Vietnamese claim that the tanks that participated in the attack on Danang, M-41s, were new to the area, having been landed the night before. They also argue that Americans drove the tanks and participated in the suppression of the Buddhists. This assertion receives support from Gen. Edward Lansdale, who reported in 1981 that he had a conversation with the U.S. ambassador, Henry Cabot Lodge Jr., during the crisis. Lodge told him, "Well, Westy [William Westmoreland, the U.S. commander in South Vietnam] and I have sent some troops and armor up to . . . the area." Unfortunately, Lansdale could not remember exactly where the troops were sent. He did point out, however, that "both [Westmoreland and Lodge] were very proud" of the actions they had taken in Danang. Edward G. Lansdale, Oral History, September 15, 1981, pp. 55-57, LBJ Library.

32. R. W. Apple Jr., "Buddhist Students Wreck American Center in Hue," *New York Times,* May 27, 1966, 1, 4.

33. Memo for the President, June 1, 1966, Vietnam Volume 55, Vietnam Country File, NSF, LBJ Library; Jerold Schecter, *The New Face of Buddha: Buddhism and Political Power in Southeast Asia* (New York: Coward-McCann, 1967), 232-33; "Student Mob in Hue Burns American Consular Office," *New York Times,* June 1, 1966, 1; R. W. Apple Jr., "Students End Broadcasts," *New York Times,* June 1, 1966, 1.

34. Schecter, *New Face of Buddha,* 241-50.

35. Robert Shaplen, *The Lost Revolution: The Story of Twenty Years of Neglected Opportunities in Vietnam and of America's Failure to Foster Democracy There* (New York: Harper & Row, 1965), 248. Douglas Pike, who served as a U.S. foreign service officer in South Vietnam from 1960 to 1975, told me that he spent eighteen months

after the Buddhist Crisis of 1963 questioning NLF prisoners in a failed attempt to prove Communist complicity in the overthrow of Diem. Douglas Pike, interview with the author, Berkeley, CA, July 1996.

36. Pike, interview with the author (n. 35 above). Pike believes that this contemptuous attitude may have contributed to the NLF decision to slaughter over two thousand mainly Buddhist civilians during the occupation of Hue in 1968. See also Topmiller, "1963 Buddhist Crisis," 14; E. Benz, *Buddhism or Communism: Which Holds the Future of Asia?* trans. Richard Winston and Clara Winston (Garden City, NY: Doubleday, 1965), 97, 229; and Kahin, interview with the author (n. 10 above).

37. Gabriel Kolko, *Anatomy of a War: Vietnam, the United States, and the Modern Historical Experience* (New York: Pantheon, 1985), 205. I was able to find a number of NLF documents confirming this point at the Indochina Archive, University of California, Berkeley, including "The Processes of Revolution and the General Uprising," *Vietnam Documents and Research Notes,* October 1968, 11–13; "COSVN Resolution on Mission in the South" (January 1965), 4–9; and "Le Duan Letter to the Saigon Party Committee—Issued between Mid-1966 and Mid-1967," 6–10.

38. Shaplen, *Lost Revolution,* 272–73.

39. Kolko, *Anatomy of a War,* 205. The Indochina Archive (n. 37 above) reveals that, at times, local NLF cadres received criticism from higher authorities for failing to tap into the Buddhist movement. See "COSVN Resolution 2, Late 1963 or Early 1964," 4–12.

40. Schecter, *New Face of Buddha,* 157.

41. Thich Nhat Hanh, *Love in Action: The Non Violent Struggle for Peace in Vietnam* (n.p., n.d.), 1–13.

42. Thich Thien-An, *Buddhism and Zen in Vietnam in Relation to the Development of Buddhism in Asia* (Rutland, VT: Tuttle, 1975), 172–91; David Halberstam, "Diem Asks Peace in Religious Crisis," *New York Times,* June 12, 1963, 7.

43. Thich Nhat Hanh, "Please Call Me by My True Names," in *The Path of Compassion: Writings on Socially Engaged Buddhism,* ed. Fred Eppsteiner (Berkeley, CA: Buddhist Peace Fellowship, 1985), 38; Thich Thien Chieu, interview with the author, Ho Chi Minh City, March 1997.

44. Christopher S. Queen and Sallie B. King, eds., *Engaged Buddhism: Buddhist Liberation Movements in Asia* (Albany: State University of New York Press, 1996), 336.

45. Mole, *Vietnamese Buddhism,* A-4.

46. Elmar Gruber and Holger Kersten, *The Original Jesus: The Buddhist Sources of Christianity* (Rockport, MA: Element, 1995), 62.

47. Douglas Pike, Oral History, June 4, 1981, p. 26, LBJ Library.

48. Topmiller, "1963 Buddhist Crisis," 37–40.

49. Cheney Ryan, "The One Who Burns Herself for Peace," *Hypatia* 9, no. 2 (Spring 1994): 21–39.

50. Su Gia Thich Nu Nhu Phuoc, Thich Nu Dieu Bach, and Thich Nu Chuc Hoa, interviews with the author, Duc Vien Pagoda, San Jose, California, August 2003; Schecter, *New Face of Buddha,* 233–34; Thich Nu Dieu Tam, interview with the author, Dieu Duc Pagoda, Hue, Vietnam, December 2002; Thich Nu Minh Tanh, interview with the author, School of the Beloved, Hue, Vietnam, December 2002; Thich Tu Phong, interview with the author, Hue, Vietnam, December 2002; Thich Nu Bao Nghieu, interview with the author, Hue, Vietnam, December 2002; grave inscription, To Dinh Tay Thien, Hue, Vietnam, transcribed December 2002; Queen and King, eds., *Engaged Buddhism,* 337; Forest, *Unified Buddhist Church of Vietnam,* 8–14.

51. Su Gia Thich Nu Nhu Phuoc, interview with the author (n. 50 above). In recent years, I have noted an increased willingness on the part of Buddhists to discuss self-immolation in the context of their peace work. Perhaps, on one level, Vietnamese honor the women who burned themselves because they defied the government, an almost unthinkable action in Communist Vietnam. Ironically, peace advocates have fared better in the minds of many Vietnamese than the women who fought on the winning side. As Vietnamese writers and novelists have increasingly questioned the cost of the war, the role of women has become even more important in a society that realizes that many sacrificed their lives and futures to rescue Vietnam.

52. For more on the critical role of women in the Buddhist peace movement, see Robert Topmiller, "Struggling for Peace: South Vietnamese Buddhist Women and Resistance to the Vietnam War," *Journal of Women's History* 17, no. 3 (Fall 2005): 133–57.

53. Alfred Hassler, *Saigon, U.S.A.,* with an introduction by George McGovern (New York: Baron, 1970), 16.

54. Queen and King, eds., *Engaged Buddhism,* 332.

55. Hassler, *Saigon, U.S.A.,* 13.

56. Ni Su Nhu Hai, interview with the author, Tu Nghiem Nunnery, Ho Chi Minh City, Vietnam, December 2000.

57. Queen and King, eds., *Engaged Buddhism,* 335; Kahin, *Intervention,* 430; Memo for the President, June 9, 1966, Vietnam Volume 55, Vietnam Country File, NSF, LBJ Library; Schecter, *New Face of Buddha,* 240; Richard Stevenson, interview with the author, Lexington, KY, May 2001.

58. Queen and King, eds., *Engaged Buddhism,* 323–26.

59. Stephen Batchelor, *The Awakening of the West: The Encounter of Buddhism and Western Culture* (Berkeley, CA: Parallex, 1994), 360–61.

60. Chan Khong, *Learning True Love: How I Learned and Practiced Social Change in Vietnam* (Berkeley, CA: Parallax, 1993).

61. John T. Bennett, "Political Implications of Economic Change: South Vietnam," *Asian Survey* 7, no. 8 (August 1967): 581–91; Kahin, *Intervention,* 410–11; "South Vietnam: Pilot with a Mission," *Time,* February 18, 1964, 26; (Thich) Nhat Hanh, "Policy and Method: Basic Concepts of Movement of Youth for Social Services" (Saigon: University of Van-Hanh School of Youth for Social Service, 1966), 16–21.

62. Nhat Hanh, "Policy and Method," 16–21.

63. Forest, *Unified Buddhist Church of Vietnam,* 8–13; "South Vietnam: Victory to the Buddhists," *Time,* September 14, 1970, 22; James Forest, *Only the Rice Loves You: A Month with the Vietnamese Peace Delegation in Paris* (New York: Hoa Binh, 1972); Steven Denny, "Human Rights in Vietnam," *The Mindfulness Bell,* Summer 1994, 30–31. The UBC had little time to celebrate at the end of the conflict. Its new Communist overlords, fearing the UBC's broad appeal, gradually attacked the church and other religious organizations with the same vigor they had utilized against the GVN and the United States. In time, security forces raided pagodas, closed down orphanages, disbanded religious organizations and placed prominent Buddhist leaders like Thich Tri Quang under house arrest or imprisonment in remote locations. Worst of all from the UBC standpoint, the new regime eventually established a government-sponsored and -controlled Buddhist church that became the only recognized Buddhist religious association in the country. For more on this issue, see Robert Topmiller, "Tu do ton giao tai Viet Nam?" [Religious freedom in Vietnam?], *Que Me* [Homeland] (Winter 1997): 75–80, and "Vietnamese Buddhism in the 1990s," *Cross Currents* 50, nos. 1–2 (Spring/Summer 2000): 232–39.

8

The Long-Haired Warriors

Women and Revolution in Vietnam

Sandra C. Taylor

"When the invaders come, even women have to fight." This traditional Vietnamese aphorism is repeated by Communist women while at the same time they stress their love of peace. Yet, as inhabitants of a small country adjacent to a large and powerful neighbor, the Vietnamese have been warriors many times.[1] Since 1930 they have scarcely known peace, fighting French colonialists, the Japanese, then the Americans, then Pol Pot's Cambodian Khmer Rouge and their supporters, and then the People's Republic of China. Vietnamese women have been deeply involved in the struggles, particularly during the wars against France and the United States. If they did not "win" the war, they nonetheless proved to be a significant and often overlooked component of the forces arrayed against Americans.

Women were committed revolutionaries who knew Communist doctrine and could win supporters to it. They were warriors; they did liaison work; they were propagandists who taught, recruited, and handed out leaflets. They excelled at intelligence work, and they were nurses, administering first aid and other health care. They farmed and supplied soldiers with food as well as clothing. A few women were able spokeswomen for their cause abroad, and at least one was a well-known diplomat. Asking why they did such things raises some important issues.

Reprinted by permission of Texas Western Press, from *The Vietnam War: Its History, Literature, and Music,* ed. Kenton Clymer (1998).

Vietnam, China's vassal for a thousand years, absorbed its written language, social structure, literature, and concept of the universe. China's Confucian belief system specified that women were virtually valueless. Such sayings as "To have a son is to have something, to have ten daughters is to have nothing," and "Man is noble, woman is base," merely suggest women's inferior status. A woman was first subservient to her father, then to her husband, and, after his death, to her oldest son. She also had to serve and please her mother-in-law, virtually as her slave. This could be the hardest task of all. The Confucian "three obediences" limited her to the family, which was, and still remains, the center of the Vietnamese universe. Ancestor worship ensured the perpetuation of the husband's family name, but not hers. Fidelity was an iron law, but a husband might cast out an unsatisfactory wife or take secondary wives or concubines. As patriarch, he owned them and their children, arranged their marriages, and, in extreme circumstances, even decided whether children should live or die.[2] Even after the expulsion of the Chinese in the tenth century, these family patterns persisted.[3]

Nonetheless, certain Vietnamese women became legendary warriors. The Trung sisters led an uprising against Chinese invaders in the year A.D. 40 and ruled for three years; during their rebellion, forty-four other women also led uprisings or fought against the enemy.[4] The Trungs committed suicide when the Chinese returned. Despite their ultimate defeat, Vietnamese even today know their story; they are cult figures, revered as the earliest heroines of the land. A few centuries later, Lady Trieu Thi Trinh, a giant with breasts three feet long, led another uprising against China. She supposedly threw her breasts over her shoulders and bound them down, leading the men into battle. Her defeat came when her adversary learned that she hated filth and crudeness. The opposing Chinese general sent his men into action filthy and naked and then put symbols of penises over the huts. She abandoned the battlefield in shame and horror.[5]

These semilegendary women exerted no impact on the reality of everyday life, especially that of the vast majority of illiterate peasants. Vietnamese women did have more freedom than Chinese women, as studies of the Nguyen and Le legal codes have shown.[6] Even after the imposition of Confucianism, women did the marketing and handled finances for the family. Although merchants had low status in Confucian society, market women exchanged information as well as wealth and moved outside the confines of the family compound. During the war, their gossiping was a useful adjunct to revolutionary activity; even American intelligence learned to be wary of the *market mouth*—a term the Vietnamese themselves used to refer to the exchange of information in the market.[7]

After the expulsion of the Chinese, Vietnamese dynasties continued enforcing Confucian restrictions on women, even increasing them. Forced marriages were allowed, as were polygamy and the burning of the emperor's wives on his death.[8] By the Le dynasty in the eleventh century, male domination had been embedded into law, and women's inferiority was firmly established by the time the French arrived in the nineteenth century.[9] Women were to be modest, speak in a quiet voice, dress in a simple manner, and, above all, be virtuous and faithful.

This harsh treatment of women extended to all classes. The historian David Marr recounts the story of a schoolteacher who went out for the evening and did not return home until 2 A.M. His wife dutifully waited, then fed her hungry children about 11 p.m. When the husband returned home, he berated her for "forgetting the three submissions" and "four virtues," having been polluted by Western ideas acquired at school. He did not drop the issue there but continued to tell everyone in the village and ordered her to stay at home (after he had severely beaten her). All the villagers, even the "sharp-tongued women in the marketplace," supported the husband.[10] No matter how unreasonable the man's behavior, the wife's place was to obey him, as Confucian strictures made clear.

However, by the early twentieth century, the status of women became part of widespread intellectual ferment. The revolutionary Phan Boi Chau recognized that women were useful as radicals because they were less likely to arouse the suspicion of the French Sûreté. The drive for sexual equality was linked to the movement for independence. By the 1920s, intellectuals debated the "question of women" among themselves as they speculated whether Vietnam needed reform or independence. Writers and scholars mused about women's capacity for education, colonialism's particular harshness toward them, and their place in the increasing radicalization of society. Indeed, the metaphor of woman-as-victim became a mode in which political discourse, forbidden by the French, might occur. But the French prohibited the education of women, and, in the late 1920s, the revolutionaries concluded that education should precede their emancipation and inclusion in the revolution. A few reform newspapers called for an end to arranged and early marriages as well as polygamy, but no one questioned the idea of fidelity throughout marriage and even into widowhood or the concepts of obedience and submissiveness.[11]

Ho Chi Minh recognized the role that women might play in what became not merely a struggle for freedom from French colonial oppression but a Marxist-Leninist revolution. Freeing women from feudal restraints provided for many a natural link to communism, but many revolutionaries accustomed to submissive and passive women worried about their inclusion in the Communist Party on an equal basis with men. Party members had to put aside duties to parents, and women would have to postpone or abandon the notion of marriage and family. They would also be unable to care for their aged parents and tend the family altar. Serving in the jungle with men could open the door to sexual liaisons and might cause de facto sexual equality. This shift in gender roles was a particularly difficult transition for uneducated peasants to make. However, Ho Chi Minh stated in the new marriage code enacted in 1946: "Women are half the people. If women are not free, then the people are not free."[12]

Young women from revolutionary families who had moved north in 1954 or who were sent north for safety and education by their parents when the war widened in 1965 were told that they occupied a "special place" in Uncle Ho's heart, and many women venerate him now and cherish personal memories of his life. Some met Ho in southern China when he was in exile and they were students.[13] As Ho became "uncle" [*bac*, literally "father's elder brother"] to his people, he took the place of father in many young women's hearts, which made the transition to revolutionary much easier. The revolution itself drew on the strong ties to family that Vietnamese all shared, and *Bac Ho* became a term of special reverence for a figure who had mythic proportions, even for many nonradical southerners.

The Indochinese Communist Party was founded in 1930 at the time of the Nghe An and Ha Tinh peasant uprisings in central Vietnam. Following the model of the Soviet Union, its membership included women. The Women's Liberation Association, founded at the same time, was part of Ho's plan to teach the people about the need for independence, freedom, and resistance to French colonialism. He intended that each segment of society form organizations to foster hatred of imperialism and teach

Two female antiaircraft gunners in North Vietnam. Courtesy of the Vietnam Archive, Texas Tech University, Douglas Pike Photograph Collection.

the need for revolution. The women's organization went through several name changes during the war[14] and today is know as the Women's Union. The associations's primary purpose was to promote women's emancipation and liberation, cultivate sexual equality, promote literacy, educate women in the domestic arts, improve medical care, and teach the writings of Marx and Lenin, Ho Chi Minh, and other Party leaders. In 1946, the Vietnamese constitution, promulgated at the end of World War II, proclaimed the political and economic equality of women and men and extended the franchise to women.[15]

When war began against the French, women were as important as men in what was termed the *people's war.* Communist theory taught that there were two types of struggle, political and military, that would lead to a mass uprising and victory. The military struggle should take place only when conditions for victory were optimum, while the political struggle should be continuous. If, as in the early stages of the war, there was a shortage of weapons and women were unarmed, they served as porters, constructed trails and set ambushes, and aroused the people through "political struggle" to support the revolution.[16] Mary Ann Tetreault, citing two Vietnamese women authorities, states that 840,000 female guerrillas served in the North and 140,000 in the South during the French war. Women from nearby villages carried weapons and provisions for the Viet Minh on their backs or bicycles during the battle of Dien Bien Phu—apparently they were more reliable than men.[17]

After the Geneva Accords, Americans slowly replaced the French, and, for the Vietnamese revolutionaries, the "French war" soon became the "American war," with a new set of invaders and imperialists. The North, the Democratic Republic of Vietnam, began to assist the guerrillas of the South, the Republic of Vietnam, as early as 1957. Northern women were given what became known as the *three responsibilities:* to continue production when men went into the army so that the people would be fed, to run family affairs and care for their children, and to fight the enemy when necessary. Women helped construct the Ho Chi Minh Trail and kept it in repair, and they cared for men injured or disabled by disease while traveling south. After the frequent bombing attacks, girls helped fill the holes on the trails. They nursed the soldiers who were injured along the trail and also those who fell ill from malaria. Some dressed in white shirts so that truck drivers, traveling at night without lights, could find their way. The Women's Museum in Hanoi honors the memory of eleven young women who stood at a crossroads at Dong-Loc to guide soldiers and repair the roads; after some two hundred days and nights they all were killed in a nighttime bombing.[18] Some women used artillery themselves, shooting at low-flying planes. The number of American planes shot down by women in the North varies between eight and thirty-five, depending on whose figures one uses.

Professor Le Thi Nham Tuyet, a philosopher and women's studies specialist at Hanoi University, described northern women in the following terms: "One hand harvests, one hand with gun." These were women farmers. The second group, she said, had "one hand with hammer, one hand with gun." These were women who worked in industry. Those who had "one hand with pen, one hand with gun" were the intellectuals.[19] Women were also part of the home guard—camouflaging antiaircraft guns, supplying clothing, food, and drink to the battlefield—ready to defend the village when the bombers came. They also picked up unexploded ordnance after an attack, which they used to make mines and hand grenades.[20]

Women's actions fueled wonderful propaganda. A photograph of a small Vietnamese woman taking prisoner a large American pilot during the Christmas bombing of 1972–73 became famous worldwide.[21] That image made a striking contrast to the more common "women-as-victim" photographs from the South; since they had always had to guard their villages, northern women may have been more truly "long-haired warriors" than their southern sisters.[22]

Organized in 1960, before widespread fighting began in the South, the National Liberation Front (NLF, or Viet Cong) trained many female cadres to recruit forces for the insurgency. Propagandists from the Women's Liberation Association spent months with villagers, teaching politics and conjuring up hatred of foreign oppressors, tax collectors, and the police of the Saigon regime. They organized meetings and, using tactics as simple as the beating of drums or screaming at the enemy, gained converts and raised morale for the forthcoming battles against the hated regime of Ngo Dinh Diem and, subsequently, the Americans.[23] When Americans took captives, among the questions they asked prisoners was, "Who . . . is the head of the women's organization?" Silence or refusal to answer brought a round of torture.[24] The women "motivated the people" by stressing several themes. They told their sisters that they would be liberated from three oppressions: the system of daughter-in-law (whereby the wife was the virtual slave of the husband's family), the traditional contempt accorded them, and male oppression.

The NLF promoted sexual purity—a difficult restriction for young men and women thrown together away from their families and the eyes of the villagers. It punished polygamy and criticized promiscuity. Such activities, both the Women's Liberation Association and the NLF agreed, demeaned women, who should remain pure for the cause. Uncle Ho's supposed celibacy was to be an example for all to emulate. The Communists ended the old Viet Minh custom of posing women as prostitutes to gain access to government military posts. Documents and even postwar stories tell of penalties enacted against men and women who violated this dictum. The NLF was not puritanical; it just wanted its members to keep their attention on the task at hand. Single people made the best fighters. Young people were urged not to date members of the opposite sex. If they had to date, they should postpone marriage. If they married, they should postpone having children.

Interviews conducted by the Rand Corporation from the early 1960s to 1971 to determine NLF motivation indicate that, by 1967, main force units of the People's Liberation Armed Forces inducted more women than men by a proportion of two to one.[25] Figures vary on the number of women in the NLF: one author contends that in some areas of the South women made up 29 percent of the units, while another says that in one area the figure approached 50 percent. Some units, it was said, were entirely female—these were primarily support troops. Statistics on this subject are as unreliable as the so-called body count figures of the Americans.[26] Clearly, in their propaganda the Communists sought to exaggerate the number of women in the war, but Americans fighting in some areas also believed that the number of women in the enemy forces was very large.

Proselytizing for the NLF required persistence. People feared for their lives, from the NLF activities as well as from the government of Vietnam and the Americans. They did not want to leave their land and families for the harsh life of the jungle. Female cadres also encountered resistance from men, who disliked women presuming to be their equals in making revolution—fighting instead of farming and tending to the family. Elderly Vietnamese were appalled at young women who behaved like men, acting "without caution or care" and not as traditional girls did.[27] But, for the most part, villagers—men, women, and children—aided the revolution by acting as lookouts and providing food and hiding places under the floors of their huts. In one village near Hue, guerrillas rarely tried to recruit women; only after 1965, as the need for fighters increased, were women allowed into the self-defense forces—and then only on a limited basis.[28] But this was uncommon, especially in this area, which was strongly committed to revolution.

Converts to communism assumed responsibilities according to their age and experience. In the American war, girls in their early teens might be recruited into the Youth Brigade—groups of young boys and girls who transported goods on rivers and into the jungle. They would be promoted to messengers, perhaps then becoming nurses' aides, feeding or washing clothes for the fighters. Some—girls as well as boys—went out at night to set up roadblocks, demolish roads, and set booby traps, while others constructed *punji* stakes (boards with nails set in them) and primitive grenades. Some were skilled terrorists and assassins. Old women made useful spies; some even faked insanity to gain access to American bases and gather information.[29] The Women's Liberation Association promised to care for its members in widowhood and old age. The NLF's message, transmitted through the women's organizations, inspired women to send their sons and husbands—and occasionally their daughters—to join the NLF forces in the jungle and to spy on their neighbors and the soldiers of the hated Saigon regime. In so doing, the NLF strengthened the hatred for foreign occupation that had colored Vietnamese life since the thousand-year-long Chinese domination. Proselytizers taught the peasants that a Communist victory would mean owning their own land, that factories would be run by the workers, that Vietnam would be liberated from American imperialism, and that exploitation by the foreigners and their elite accomplices would end. Of course, not all the persuasion came from the Communists. The American bombing, the destruction of crops and livestock, and the defoliation and destruction of the land, as well as the indiscriminate killing of civilians, also proved potent recruiting devices. Indoctrination sessions taught women the necessity of obedience to the Party's wishes and absolute loyalty to their comrades—male or female. The reward—freedom and independence—would be worth the sacrifices of the present.

Some southern women, especially Catholics, supported the national government, which, under president Ngo Dinh Diem, had its own Women's Solidarity Movement, organized by Madame Ngo Dinh Nhu, Diem's sister-in-law, as a counterpart to the Women's Liberation Association. Madame Nhu had her "girls" in uniform, and they were taught to march and parade, even to fire pistols. But this short-lived experiment, lasting from 1955 to 1963, never rivaled the Communist women's associations; it did not concede to women true equality; rather, it served as an extension of Madame Nhu's egoism.[30] Ngo Dinh Diem did not abolish polygamy, for example, until 1958.

The devotion with which the women in the NLF served the Communist cause was intense. For example, two sisters from Cu Chi, Nguyen Thi Bao and Nguyen Thi Hanh, were recruited from a village in the Iron Triangle when they were young. Living in a heavily bombed area no doubt influenced their decisions, as did Communist ideology. The sisters carried messages from Saigon to guerrillas in the jungle. Since women traditionally did the marketing, always following the same routes to town, they were known to the police along the way. They could memorize short messages and hide longer ones in the bottoms of baskets, in hollow bamboo sticks, even between layers of dried fish. The smelly fish were rarely searched.[31] One sister, Bao, was apprehended but released for lack of evidence. The sisters were fortunate. One courier from Danang who hid messages in a hollow tree to be retrieved later by someone she never saw was betrayed, captured, tortured, and killed, according to women in the Women's Union of Danang.[32]

Captives were routinely tortured for the names of their contacts. Generally, they knew few names, and those were code names or aliases. In 1969, one woman, Nguyen Thi Hi, was betrayed by her comrades. She carried messages in bolts of cloth she took to market; when she resisted arrest, fought with the guards, and refused to reveal the names of her comrades, she was sent to Con Dao, built by the French in 1868 on an island that the French called Poulo Condore and the South Vietnamese Con Dao, some 180 miles off the coast. This maximum-security prison was feared most by the prisoners, for it held the so-called tiger cages, where up to eight prisoners, both men and women, their legs shackled to the floor, were held in cells five feet by eight feet, open at the top so that the guards could drop lime on them. Hi had joined the resistance out of hatred for Saigon's oppressive taxes, and her treatment made her a more determined Communist.[33]

Starting as young teenagers, women also worked in the jungles as nurses and cooks. Mrs. Hoang Thi Khanh, at one time the vice president of Vietnam's General Confederation of Labor, came from a poor family of rubber workers living on a plantation in Cambodia. When they moved to Vietnam, Khanh realized that conditions were equally bad and that the Americans were as cruel as the French. As a teenager, she became a cook for American and Australian soldiers. By 1967, she had been recruited by the Communists and transferred to Saigon as part of a special force of undercover agents. She served as a liaison between the city and the countryside, transported arms into the city before the Tet Offensive of 1968, and recruited workers for the revolution. After the defeat of the NLF in the Tet Offensive, she helped rally the survivors and formed a guerrilla unit that was 80 percent women. Their task was to kill Saigonese who might betray surviving members of the NLF to the forces of President Thieu. Khanh was eventually captured and imprisoned in a series of jails, like Hi ending up in the infamous Con Dao.[34]

Mrs. Khanh exemplified perfectly the dual methods of the revolutionary, what Douglas Pike has identified as *dau tranh*—struggle both political and military, protracted conflict leading to a general uprising when victory seemed near.[35] She was a committed Communist who could use arms when necessary and could also serve as a liaison agent or propagandist, recruiting others to join the revolution. Although women were very effective at the latter task, Khanh said that recruitment was difficult, that most people preferred to stay out of harm's way.[36]

Douglas Pike refers to these women revolutionaries as the "water buffalo of the revolution."[37] They dug tunnels and hiding places, carefully removing all the soil; they hauled heavy loads up and down mountains and forded rivers; and they did all the agricultural labor when the men were away. Some traditional gender roles remained unchanged, despite the overlay of communism. Women in Dinh Thuy and Thuy Phuong villages (one is near Ben Tre, the other near Phu Bai) related that several of their number had been engaged to be married when their fiancés went to war. When the men were killed, the women never married, out of respect for their memory. Women whose husbands died also rarely remarried. Their own parents strongly disapproved, and the parents of the dead spouse objected. And, as one woman said, caring for one mother-in-law was sufficient. Others cited their fear that a second husband might not love the children of the first spouse as much as his own. And, if women did remarry, the Party itself might punish them later, as, indeed, it did. A widow, for example, could not achieve "heroic mother" status if she married a second time.[38]

Frequently, women who became Communists came from families who had resisted the French and were, thus, conditioned to the tradition of revolution. Some came from families in which the parents had regrouped in the North in 1954, leaving a daughter as a stay-behind. Some had returned to the South after 1954 and then joined the revolutionaries. Peasant families were generally large, and children joined the Youth Brigade and then the NLF as soon as they were old enough. Since this was a people's war, there were tasks for all ages. Children could lure soldiers into an ambush or a minefield, adolescents made ideal assassins and saboteurs, and older women could become "mothers of soldiers." When NLF soldiers remained in one area for a time, widows might "adopt" one, becoming his foster mother and providing food, shelter, and clothing as well as a cover. The soldier would be identified to government authorities as a nephew or some more distant relative returning home and, as his "mother" might explain, lacking identification papers for that reason.[39]

Ho Chi Minh preached equal rights for women in a way no other Vietnamese revolutionary did. Under Ho, the Party ordered its men to respect women and punished them for unauthorized sex. Ho's constitution of 1946 outlawed polygamy and concubinage, promoted the education of women, extended the franchise to women, called for equal pay for equal work, and advocated equal work opportunities. These were good devices for recruiting women. The Party maintained strict rules on sexual conduct. Cadres were to have no sexual relations with each other, nor were they to sexually abuse the peasantry. The Party preferred as members single people over married couples since the former could give it their undivided loyalty.[40] One disaffected Party member told an interviewer from the Rand Corporation that she had quit because she was accused of having a love affair, which she strongly denied, as did the man supposedly involved with her.[41]

One tale of individual heroism will suffice for many women's experiences. Nguyen Thi Hong Phau, the members of whose family were all revolutionaries, joined when she was seventeen. From 1964 to 1966, she was assigned to study the enemy situation and report to the Party's Central Committee. Since she was from a village near Hue, she saw much violence. She did not understand Party theory at this time, but she knew that she wanted revenge. She participated in the heavy fighting of the Tet Offensive and thought that her side had won, only to come under heavy fire when American and South Vietnamese forces counterattacked. She then joined a guerrilla division of eleven young women. After the Communists won a temporary victory, her division was sent to Hue to arrest the "Saigon regime spies" and also to fight the enemy. She claimed that, together with other forces, they killed 120 Americans and destroyed two tanks, at the cost of the lives of two of the women. The women were then sent to the jungle since their identities were known and they would have been killed. In the jungle, they had very little food or clothing, and many fell ill from malaria. Whenever there was rice, it went to the regular soldiers. They were under constant enemy harassment, and half the remainder were killed. When the women were finally relieved, they were sent to the North for a rest and retraining. There they learned, to their great sorrow, of the death of Ho Chi Minh. Hong Phau fully expected to return to the fighting, but, when she relocated to Hue in 1971, she was kept in the rear as a typist. She did not marry until 1982, and her husband died a year later as a result, she said, of Agent Orange poisoning. Fortunately, she had a normal child, so she is not alone. One woman told me that Vietnamese women fear nothing so much as being alone. Hong Phau's hostility toward Americans was still evident more than twenty years later.[42]

More may be said about imprisoned women. There were many prisons in the South, located in virtually every provincial capital. The largest prison—and one entirely for women—was Chi Hoa near Saigon, but Tan Hep was large and well-known too. The worst prison was undoubtedly Con Dao. The heat was intense in the dry season, and it was damp and chilly in the rainy season. Women and men were kept in cells and large cell blocks, but the worst, as we have seen, were the infamous tiger cages. Women, like men, were tortured to divulge information or as punishment, and the standard methods were used—nails under fingernails, soft bamboo poles for beatings, lime on raw skin, electricity placed on vulnerable extremities and genitals, and charges shot through their bodies. Women had soapy water forced down their throats, then guards jumped on their distended stomachs. Prisoners were given just enough food to stay alive, but many died of malnutrition or disease. They ate mainly moldy rice and, occasionally, decayed, dried fish. Clever prisoners caught geckos on the walls and dumped them in their thin gruel or supplemented their diet with a dead bird. Former prisoners reported that the Americans did not participate in the torture at Con Dao, although they were there and knew that it took place. For the women, perhaps the worst torture was not having more than three cups of water a day, so they were unable to wash themselves during menstruation.[43] They also lacked rags, so they had to tear pieces of their clothing for sanitary needs. Since they received only one set of clothing per year, by the end of the year they were virtually naked.

The American public was not aware that women were prisoners in Con Dao until 1970, when an International Voluntary Service worker, Don Luce, took several congressmen there, including Augustus Hawkins and William Anderson, and later Senator Tom Harkin. Their description of the women prisoners was particularly appalling: five to a cage, lying on the floors of the cages almost immobile, their faces covered with sores, and their eyes full of pus. When the results of the trip were publicized, the resulting uproar caused the women to be moved back to the mainland, at least for a while; it also resulted in Luce's expulsion from Vietnam.[44]

The women interviewed for this study remain committed Communists today, proud of their work in the wars. However, not every man or woman endured hardships or remained a believer in the ultimate victory of communism. One defector, a person who "rallied" to the government's cause, said that no one had ever told him that life with the NLF would be so hard and that he wanted to defect and return to the Saigon regime before he was killed. A woman defected from the NLF because she was very poor and wanted to go home to help her aged mother. A female guerrilla who cooked for the NLF contracted malaria and liver trouble; she asked her commander for permission to go home, but he refused. Shortly after that, she was captured.[45] Fear of death, exhaustion, and intimations of the NLF's demise caused many defections, but people also switched according to which side they thought was winning at any given time. Some women did well with the NLF. A fishmonger joined in 1959 while living in Cambodia; at first, she crossed the Vietnamese border to proselytize, but, later, the NLF let her join a military unit. Soon she acquired a liking for fighting and refused any attempt at political indoctrination. The Americans and the supporters of President Diem were the enemy, and the NLF was the advocate of the people, she felt. As a successful soldier, she rose in the ranks to become an assistant company commander. She defected when her husband, who had led a sapper company, was killed and she was not told, only accidentally learning of his death. Before this, fighting was exciting and even offered the possibility of profit; her skills had attracted the attention of the famed military leader Mrs. Nguyen Thi Dinh, who awarded her the gift of a special Colt. However, the former fishmonger had several grievances. The withholding of news of her husband's death was painful and humiliating. News that she had been promoted to company commander had not been told her by her superior, who wanted the position for his brother. (She retaliated by shooting him in the legs.) She became dispirited and resolved to contact relatives in the Saigon government to get an identity card so that she could safely rally, and, ultimately, she did so.[46]

What is one to conclude about these women of the Vietnamese revolution? Certainly not that all women were Communists—to maintain loyalty required putting ideology above family and rejecting family and religious ties. Many Communist women were convinced Marxist-Leninists who adored Ho Chi Minh, and these women recount with great emotion the times they actually met him.[47] They joined the resistance because they hated foreign oppression and wanted independence and freedom, as they understood it. But many were buffeted about by both sides, changing loyalties with the fortunes of war, and desiring only to be left in peace. One such woman was Le Ly Hayslip, the author of *When Heaven and Earth Changed Places,* who recalled a song her mother sang to her during childhood. It included the lines:

> In our village today, a big battle was fought.
> Old ladies and children were sent straight to hell.
> Our eyes fill with tears while we watch and ask God:
> Why is the enemy so cruel?[48]

Many in her family were killed in the war. She was abused by both sides and finally married an American and came to the United States. However, he soon died, and her second husband was abusive. Although she rose above her hardships to succeed, she was an exceptional person. Her story was made into a movie—the 1993 *Heaven and Earth*—by the filmmaker Oliver Stone.[49]

Most women were closer to the model of Le Ly than the few who were well-known leaders. The majority desired only to raise their children in peace but were caught in the tides of war. For many, the choice of which side to support was quite arbitrary—a function of time and place. However, three women achieved special prominence.

Nguyen Thi Dinh came from a small village near Ben Tre, the poorest part of South Vietnam, in the Mekong Delta. The province was one of the six most Communist provinces in Vietnam. Dinh's elder brothers were revolutionaries, as was the man she married. But, shortly after their marriage in 1938, he was arrested and taken to Poulo Condore, where he soon died. She gave birth to a son soon after her husband's arrest but left the infant with her mother in order to fight with the revolutionaries. Dinh was imprisoned herself in 1940, but after her release (owing to ill health), she continued her activities, working with the Women's Liberation Association. She was elected to the executive committee of the association in the province and became its representative to the Viet Minh

Three female gunners preparing to fire on a target. Courtesy of the Vietnam Archive, Texas Tech University, Douglas Pike Photograph Collection.

NLF province committee.[50] In 1946, she traveled north to Hanoi and successfully obtained weapons from Ho Chi Minh for the southern insurgency. In January 1960, she organized a group of village women in Ben Tre to surround the Saigon soldiers, taking up hand-carved wooden guns. Children then crept up behind the men and set off firecrackers, which so frightened them that they dropped their weapons and fled. Uncle Ho was so impressed that he called her force the *long-haired warriors* (women in this area customarily wore their hair long). The term became one of honor applied later to all fighting women of the NLF and even of North Vietnam.[51]

Dinh's military and political career flourished, and she intimidated men of both sides. She helped found the NLF and became a member of its Presidium Central Committee, then chairman of the South Vietnam Women's Liberation Association. In 1965, she became deputy commander of the People's Liberation Armed Forces—the highest-ranking woman of the war.[52] After the war, she became president of the national Women's

Union. She was modest about her achievements, later stating that there was "no other road to take" to honor her husband's memory and to obtain justice for her people. Memories of her abound, and the women's museums in Ho Chi Minh City and Hanoi feature numerous exhibits honoring her.

The women Dinh organized subsequently led demonstrations and recruited other women to join the Women's Liberation Association and support the NLF. The usual target of demonstrations was the Saigon troops, to whom they might appeal in their own language, berating them for their cruelty. They beat large bamboo drums and screamed at the approaching men. They demanded compensation when one of the villagers was killed or injured, and they urged the soldiers to quit harming them and to go home to their own villages. They had clever tactics of camouflage, such as wearing three or four shirts so that they could take one off and not be recognized at the next demonstration. They were at most a nuisance and at best effective propagandists who caused war-weary soldiers to become disaffected and, occasionally, to desert. Some did learn to fight. The long-haired warriors formed a hard core of seasoned Communists whose offspring still dominate local women's unions and the police force.[53] Many are recipients of the heroic mother medal.

Mrs. Dinh, Dr. Duong Quynh Hoa, and Madame Nguyen Thi Binh were probably the best-known women revolutionaries in the South. Dr. Hoa, a very wealthy Chinese-Vietnamese woman born in Saigon and educated in Paris, met Ho Chi Minh (then Nguyen Ai Quoc) and became a Communist convert as an idealistic schoolgirl. She returned to Vietnam radicalized and helped found the NLF in 1960; she later became minister of health in the People's Revolutionary Government. Her money, she said proudly, protected her from arrest by the Diem regime, but, as the situation became more dangerous for Communist revolutionaries in the late 1960s, she fled to the jungle with her husband and the other members of the government. The bombing was intense, and they had to move constantly. She gave birth prematurely to a son, who died seven months later from malaria. Dr. Hoa remained an active Party member until 1976, when, disillusioned with Communist corruption and the betrayal of her youthful idealism, she resigned. When I knew her, she was still well-known to government leaders and was free to travel whenever she wanted. She had family in Paris and was well-known abroad. But she still spent much of her time in Ho Chi Minh City, where she ran a pediatric clinic before her retirement.[54]

Madame Nguyen Thi Binh, also a Saigon native, joined the revolution as a schoolgirl, leading demonstrations against the presence of American ships in the Saigon River in 1954. She was imprisoned several times over the next few years and, on her release, joined the revolutionaries and helped found the NLF, later becoming its foreign minister.[55] Binh kept a low profile as far as her family was concerned; even the CIA could find out little about them. But it was known that she was a descendant of the famed revolutionary Pham Chau Trinh. Binh traveled extensively to Third World countries representing her "peace-loving" country during the war and afterward. She was a junior member of the negotiating team later headed by Le Duc Tho, and she incurred the wrath of Henry Kissinger, who accused her of changing the negotiating terms in Tho's absence.[56] In this capacity, she became the most well-known revolutionary woman of Vietnam. The French called her the "Queen of the Viet Cong," although, in fact, she never fought. She was minister of education in the 1980s and later served as vice president of the country.

Vietnamese women endured the horrors of war as women have since time began. They were victims—at My Lai and elsewhere—their bodies violated, their children killed. From 1954 to 1965, according to one source, women suffered 250,000 deaths, 40,000 disabilities caused by torture, and 36,000 imprisonments.[57] They were also fierce combatants, many as effective with weapons as men. For those who survived the conflict, the price of war could mean spinsterhood, life as a widow, or being the spouse of a war cripple. Many in the Mekong Delta suffered from the effects of defoliants, which produced an abnormally high number of deformed and stillborn children. What is surprising is that so many Vietnamese women did fight, an action that grew out of their belief that revolution might bring improvement to their lives. Others fought for revenge, out of anger at those who bombed their villages and killed their husbands and children. They considered Americans invaders and the Saigon regimes American puppets. For many, Nguyen Thi Dinh's statement that there was no other road to take was true. Whatever their motivation, they represented a positive asset for the Communists because they added to the force of the opposition and cared for themselves. The republican women of the South, on the other hand, were a liability. Many of them and their children followed the army to care for and be protected by their husbands. When the retreat of the Army of the Republic of Vietnam from the central highlands began in March 1975, they had to be evacuated and fled with their husbands, who then turned the retreat into a rout. The long-haired army was an asset, not a liability, and one more reason why the NLF and the People's Army of North Vietnam, which included women in its ranks, won the war.

Notes

I thank Professor Mary Ann Tetreault for her insightful comments on an earlier version of this work.

1. The Vietnamese pride themselves on having a culture more ancient than China's. Bronze drums found in the Red River Delta are dated to 2000 B.C., and a recent work by Nguyen Khac Vien, *Vietnam: A Long History* (Hanoi: Foreign Languages Publishing House, 1987), 9, states that rice agriculture probably has existed in Vietnam for five or six thousand years.

2. Mai Thi Tu and Le Thi Nham Tuyet, *Women in Vietnam* (Hanoi: Foreign Languages Publishing House, 1978); Nguyen Khac Vien, *Vietnam: A Long History*, 34; caption on display of the Trung sisters at the Women's Museum, Ho Chi Minh City.

3. Ta Van Tai, *The Vietnamese Tradition of Human Rights* (Berkeley and Los Angeles: University of California Press, 1988), 110–24.

4. Nguyen Khac Vien, *Vietnam: A Long History*, 27; David G. Marr, *Vietnamese Tradition on Trial* (Berkeley: University of California Press, 1981), 194, 198.

5. Vietnam Women's Union, *Vietnamese Women in the Eighties* (Hanoi: Foreign Languages Publishing House, 1989), 14–15. In *Vietnam: A Long History*, Nguyen Khac Vien credits Trieu Thi Trinh with saying, "I'd like to ride storms, kill the sharks in the open sea, drive out the aggressors, reconquer the country, undo the ties of serfdom, and never bend my back to be the concubine of whatever man." David Marr embellished Trieu Thi Trinh's story further. Not only did she have three-foot-long breasts, but she also had a voice like a temple bell; she could eat several pecks of rice a day and walk five hundred leagues in a day. In addition, she was a renowned beauty. She was repelled, however, by anything smelly, impure, or dirty, and, when the Chinese commander ordered his troops to charge her naked, yelling like wild animals, she rode away and abandoned her troops, who were surrounded. She then committed suicide. But the Chinese leader still saw her in his dreams, so he got rid of her by ordering his woodcarvers to make images of penises and hang them over his doors. She remained in public memory and succored Vietnamese who would oppose the Chinese as much as three centuries later. Marr, *Vietnamese Tradition*, 198–99.

6. Nguyen Khac Vien, *Vietnam: A Long History*.

7. Douglas Pike, discussion with the author, April 20, 1996, Indochina Archive, Texas Tech University, at the conference "After the Cold War: Reassessing Vietnam."

8. Mary Ann Tetreault, "Women and Revolution in Vietnam," in *Women and Revolution in Africa, Asia, and the New World,* ed. Mary Ann Tetreault (Columbia: University of South Carolina Press, 1994), 112, citing Mai Thi Tu and Le Thi Nham Tuyet, *Women in Vietnam,* 30–31. The Vietnamese refer to this period as the *feudal period.* Although the Vietnamese hated Chinese domination, the ruling class emulated the Chinese in their usage of Confucian ethics and a writing system based on Chinese characters.

9. Tetreault, "Women and Revolution in Vietnam," 111–13.

10. Marr, *Vietnamese Tradition,* 190–92. See also Hue-Tam Ho Tai, *Radicalism and the Origins of the Vietnamese Revolution* (Cambridge, MA: Harvard University Press, 1991), chap. 3.

11. Tai, *Radicalism,* 90, 97–98, 104–5, 198–201.

12. Ho quoted in Tetreault, "Women and Revolution in Vietnam," 114. Tetreault states that this familiar remark has a variety of phrasings, as does the statement: "When the enemy comes, even women have to fight."

13. Mrs. Nguyen Thi Sau, interviews and conversations with the author, Ho Chi Minh City and Ben Tre City, Vietnam, November 6–19, 1995. Other conversations took place in the summer of 1995, when Mrs. Sau lived with the author in Salt Lake City, Utah.

14. For example, Frances FitzGerald (in *Fire in the Lake: The Vietnamese and the Americans in Vietnam* [New York: Vintage, 1972], 284–85) refers to the group as the Women's Association. Eric M. Bergerud (in *Dynamics of Defeat: The Vietnam War in Hau Nghia Province* [Boulder, CO: Westview, 1991], 55, 60) refers to the women as members of the Women's Liberation Association and emphasizes their importance in radicalizing the peasantry. Tetreault ("Women and Revolution in Vietnam") refers to the organization as the Women's Union throughout her essay.

15. Tetreault, "Women and Revolution in Vietnam," 114–15.

16. Douglas Pike, *Viet Cong* (Cambridge, MA: MIT Press, 1966), 85–92.

17. Tetreault, "Women and Revolution in Vietnam," 115, citing Mai Thi Tu and Le Thi Nham Tuyet, *Women in Vietnam,* 30–31; William J. Duiker, *Sacred War: Nationalism and Revolution in a Divided Vietnam* (New York: McGraw-Hill, 1995), 87. Duiker states that the porters came from nearby villages and were drafted when the Viet Minh discovered that they were more effective than the men.

18. Le Thi Nham Tuyet, "Vietnamese Women Soldiers during and after the War" (typescript, University of Hanoi, Department of Anthropology, n.d.; a copy is in my possession). Displays in the Women's Museum, Hanoi, illustrate these activities. See also Robert Stevens, *The Trail: A History of the Ho Chi Minh Trail and the Role of Nature in the War in Viet Nam* (New York: Garland, 1993), 68.

19. Le Thi Nham Tuyet, "Vietnamese Women Soldiers," 3.

20. Mai Thi Tu and Le Thi Nham Tuyet, *Women in Vietnam,* 16; Le Thi Nham

Tuyet, "Vietnamese Women Soldiers," 3; Lady Borton, conversations with the author, Hanoi, November 24, 1995; information at Women's Museum, Hanoi, described by translator, November 29–30, 1995.

21. The picture is on display in the Women's Museum, Hanoi. It was even reproduced on postage stamps.

22. The term *long-haired army* was originally applied to Madame Nguyen Thi Dinh and her female guerrilla unit at Ben Tre, who were credited with having begun the widespread uprising in the South in January 1960. Ho Chi Minh called the women this to honor their bravery, and soon it was also extended to all southern women. Whether it was also extended to northern women is a subject of some debate. William Duiker states that the women porters of Dien Bien Phu were called the *long-haired army* (*Sacred War*, 87; conversations with the author, El Paso, TX, March 28, 1996). Douglas Pike contends that the phrase was used only in the South (conversation with the author, Lubbock, TX, April 18, 1996). Tetreault states that the term was first applied to the Ben Tre women and was gradually extended to all women fighting for the NLF ("Women and Revolution in Vietnam," 121).

23. David Hunt, "Organizing for Revolution in Vietnam," *Radical America* 8 (1974): 35–38.

24. Mark Baker, *Nam: The Vietnam War in the Words of the Men and Women Who Fought There* (New York: Morrow, 1981), 214–15.

25. Hunt, "Organizing for Revolution," 143. Hunt utilized Rand Corp. interviews from the "DT" series to analyze the revolutionary situation in the province around My Tho. His assessment was based on a small sample from one province only.

26. For problems with the body counts, see James William Gibson, *The Perfect War: Technowar in Vietnam* (Boston: Atlantic Monthly Press, 1986), 155–59 and passim.

27. Hunt, "Organizing for Revolution," 147–51.

28. James Walker Trullinger Jr., *Village at War: An Account of Revolution in Vietnam* (New York: Longmans, 1980), 121, 131.

29. Women's Union, interviews with the author, Hue, November 20, 1996.

30. FitzGerald, *Fire in the Lake*, 96–97.

31. Miss Bao and Miss Hanh, interview with the author, Ho Chi Minh City, February 9, 1994.

32. This information was part of anecdotal material collected in Danang on November 18, 1995.

33. Mrs. Nguyen Thi Hi, interview with the author, Con Dao, February 19, 1994.

34. Mrs. Hoang Thi Khanh, interview with the author, Ho Chi Minh City, November 5, 1995.

35. Pike, *Viet Cong*, 178. See also Duiker, *Sacred War*, 131.

36. Khanh interview (n. 34 above).

37. Pike, *Viet Cong*, 167.

38. Dinh Thuy Village, interviews with the author, November 8, 1995; Thuy Phu-

ong Village, interviews with the author, November 22, 1995.

39. William Andrews, *The Village War: Vietnamese Communist Revolutionary Activities in Dinh Tuang Province, 1960–1964* (Columbia: University of Missouri Press, 1973), 77, as cited in Tetreault, "Women and Revolution in Vietnam," 120.

40. For a good account of the discipline of Ho's disciples and their willingness to follow his example in living a monogamous life, see Tran Tu Binh, *The Red Earth: A Vietnamese Memoir of Life on a Colonial Rubber Plantation,* trans. John Spragens Jr., ed. David G. Marr, Monographs in International Studies, Southeast Asia Series, no. 66 (Athens: Ohio University, Center for International Studies, Center for Southeast Asian Studies, 1985).

41. Rand Corp. Series of Interviews with Chieu Hoi and Defectors, AG 243, July 1965, Special Collections, Marriott Library, University of Utah, Salt Lake City.

42. Nguyen Thi Hong Phau, interview with the author, Hue City, November 17, 1995. The story of another young woman fighter who also hated Americans with a passion until one incident where she observed them in a more human setting is recounted in Tom Mangold and John Penycate, *The Tunnels of Cu Chi* (New York: Random House, 1985), chap. 19.

43. Women who had been prisoners said they were given enough to eat so that their menses did not stop and they did not starve to death (former prisoners on Con Dao Island, interviews with the author, February 18, 1994).

44. Former prisoners interviews (n. 43 above); Gloria Emerson, *Winners and Losers: Battles, Retreats, Gains, Losses, and Ruins from a Long War* (New York: Random House, 1972), 343–46; Holmes Brown and Don Luce, *Hostages of War: Saigon's Political Prisoners* (Washington, DC: Indochina Mobile Education Project, 1974), 14–15.

45. Rand interviews, AG 486.

46. Rand interviews, AG 581. According to this informant, Mrs. Dinh admired her because she had commanded male troops, whereas Mrs. Dinh, although of higher rank, had commanded only female troops.

The woman first moved her family out of the area controlled by the NLF, then moved herself to get identity papers. As it happened, the government forces moved into her village, and she followed them out and rallied, which allowed her to avoid trouble with the NLF. She had an aged mother to support. According to her file, she had commanded three hundred men, and, had the government succeeded in capturing her prior to her defection, she surely would have been killed.

47. Many southern women went north for indoctrination, treatment of injuries or illness, or education, and women such as Nguyen Thi Dinh and Ho Thi Bi met Ho several times and are pictured with him in the women's museums in Ho Chi Minh City and Hanoi. Col. Ho Thi Bi, now eighty years old, is his "adopted" daughter.

48. Le Ly Hayslip with Jay Wurts, *When Heaven and Earth Changed Places* (New York: Doubleday, 1989).

49. Le Ly Hayslip, *Child of War, Woman of Peace* (New York: Doubleday, 1993).

50. Nguyen Thi Dinh, *No Other Road to Take: Memoir of Mrs. Nguyen Thi Dinh,*

trans. Mai V. Elliott (Ithaca, NY: Cornell University, Southeast Asia Program, Department of Asian Studies, 1976), v.

51. See n. 22 above.

52. See Nguyen Thi Dinh, *No Other Road to Take.*

53. Women in Dinh Thuy Village, interviews with the author, Mo Cay District, Ben Tre Province, November 9, 1995.

54. Dr. Duong Quynh Hoa, interviews with the author, Ho Chi Minh City, February 20, 1994, and November 11, 1996.

55. Truong Nhu Tang, *Viet Cong Memoir* (New York: Harcourt Brace Jovanovich, 1985), 149, 206, 227, 234, 237, 244, 255.

56. Henry Kissinger, *The White House Years* (Boston: Little, Brown, 1979), 1024–25.

57. Le Hanh Danh, "The Long-Haired Army," *Vietnamese Studies* 10 (1966): 61–62, as cited in Tetreault, "Women and Revolution in Vietnam," 121.

9

Military Dissent and the Legacy of the Vietnam War

Robert Buzzanco

The U.S. war in Vietnam that George Herring and others have described so well is being rewritten in politically motivated and disturbing ways, with a number of scholars now claiming that the American intervention was justified and appropriate; that the southern state that the United States created in Vietnam was legitimate and its early leader, Ngo Dinh Diem, was making progress toward building a viable government; and that the Americans abandoned the South because of political constraints at home even though they were winning the war.

This work is suspect on many levels, not the least of which being that many American officials, especially military officers, were often candid, bleak, and pessimistic about U.S. prospects in Vietnam *while the war was being fought.* Far from describing a noble purpose, a viable state, a representative government, or successful operations, American military leaders, from the aftermath of World War II, when the United States began its commitment to keep Ho Chi Minh and his nationalist and Communist followers from taking power in Vietnam, into the 1960s, when the American commitment grew to over a half million troops and cost hundreds of billions of dollars, consistently reported that the war was not going well, that the ally, the "South" Vietnamese, had serious problems, and that the enemy, the National Liberation Front and its armed units, was formidable and maintained the initiative. Looking back over three decades from the end of the war, it is difficult to see how one can vindicate the American experience in Vietnam in the face of such widespread dissent from within the military while the war was in progress.

Roots of Involvement, Roots of Dissent

Scholars trying to rehabilitate the war often write of the 1950s and early 1960s in positive terms, arguing that the southern regime and its leaders, the Ngo family, were developing a stable, effective, and representative state. Such views, however, amount to intellectual alchemy. As Herring observed in *America's Longest War,* democratic political reform "would have been lost on Diem, for whom democracy was alien in terms of experience and temperament." Diem used his political philosophy, "personalism," as a "rationalization for absolute state power, distrust of popular rule, and a belief that a small elite was responsible for defining the general welfare." To Diem, compromise and criticism were subversive and had to be suppressed. While, to please his American patrons, Diem "paid lip service to democracy, . . . in practice he assumed absolute powers."[1]

More to the point, U.S. military officials, who had some direct knowledge of Southeast Asia and would be responsible for any warfare in that area, offered candid and usually negative appraisals of possible interventions into Vietnam. During and after World War II, American officers attached to the Office of Strategic Services (OSS) worked with Ho Chi Minh and the Communist-led Viet Minh resistance to the Japanese and French and took away positive impressions, with Major Allison Thomas of the OSS lobbying for more contacts with Ho and sympathizing with his nationalist ambitions, and Gen. Philip Gallagher, the U.S. adviser to Chinese occupation forces in northern Vietnam, wishing that the Viet Minh "could be given their independence."[2] Gen. George Marshall, who served as secretary of both state and defense, lamented that the Indochina war "will remain a grievously costly enterprise, weakening France economically and all the West generally in its relations with Oriental peoples."[3] In July 1949, the Joint Chiefs of Staff (JCS) produced, in policy paper JCS 1992/4, their most striking summation of the perils of interference in Indochina. The "widening political consciousness and the rise of militant nationalism among the subject people," they understood, "cannot be reversed." To attempt to do so, they presciently argued, would be "an anti-historical act likely in the long run to create more problems than it solves and cause more damage than benefit." The army's Plans and Operations Division added, likewise pessimistically, that the Viet Minh would drive the French out of Indochina on the strength of popular support alone, not Chinese assistance. Ho enjoyed the support of 80 percent of the Vietnamese people, army planners reported, yet 80 percent of his followers were not Communists. Such indigenous appeal, as well as limited support from Communist China, virtually assured Viet Minh success.[4]

Despite such warnings, the Truman administration began to increasingly support the French suppression of Vietnamese nationalism, especially after 1950. But, still, the military balked, with the Joint Strategic Plans Committee seeing no reason for the United States to consider committing its forces to a "series of inconclusive peripheral actions which would drain our military strength and weaken . . . our global position." Army chief of staff J. Lawton Collins was more blunt. "France will be driven out of Indochina," he prophesied, and was "wasting men and equipment trying to remain there."[5] When JCS chair Omar Bradley expressed his doubts that "we could get our public to go along with the idea of our going into Indochina in a military way," Collins agreed and concluded: "We must face the probability that Indochina will be lost."[6] Still, Harry S Truman and his successor, Dwight Eisenhower, continued to pour funding into French Indochina—$785 million in 1953 alone. And Collins continued his warnings, pointing out that a campaign in Indochina would be worse than the one in Korea. Any U.S. forces could expect a "major and protracted war. . . . Militarily and politically we would be in up to our necks." But he also understood that he spoke "from a military point of view" and that the JCS's judgment was not decisive, that "if our political leaders want to put troops in there we will of course do it."[7]

Collins was, of course, an experienced and intelligent official and, thus, was conceding the obvious in acknowledging the primacy of politics in decisionmaking, and this is a point that cannot be overemphasized. Already in the 1950s one could observe the dialectic of military reluctance and civilian enthusiasm for war in Indochina. Collins and others, taking into account "a military point of view," understood that Vietnam was not vital to American interests, was not an area conducive to military success, was engaged in a revolution-cum-civil war brought on by centuries of outside aggression and colonialism, and was likely to be hostile to a U.S.

presence. The Viet Minh, as the JCS recognized, held the military initiative and had successfully identified itself with the struggle for "freedom from the colonial yoke and with the improvement of the general welfare of the people."[8] Civilian policymakers, however, had larger visions, seeing Vietnam as an important piece in the larger reconstruction of capitalism and Japanese economic health in Asia.[9] Consequently, the United States would fight in Vietnam for well over a decade at odds with itself—with military leaders always aware of the serious barriers to success and civilian political leaders escalating the war owing to larger concerns about global politics and economics.

Looking back, the early 1950s presented the best opportunity for the United States to avoid what would become such a great tragedy in Vietnam. Rarely does a nation engage in armed conflict with its military leadership so wary of intervention, but that is precisely what happened in Indochina. In 1954 and 1955, when the Eisenhower administration took over the French role in Vietnam, General Collins, as well as Gens. Matthew Ridgway, James Gavin, and others, forcefully pointed out the perils of war there. In the early months of 1954, as the Viet Minh laid siege to a French outpost at Dien Bien Phu, the White House began contemplating intervention, but Ridgway led the battle against American involvement. Bolstered by the report of a technical survey team, he noted that Vietnam lacked adequate port and bridge facilities, that monsoons would limit military operations, and that the local communications system was too primitive to support an American presence there. Even if engineers could build up ports and airfields to handle the influx of U.S. troops, standard army units were "too ponderous" for combat in Vietnam, a land "particularly adapted to the guerrilla-type war" at which the Viet Minh had been so successful. The army chief stressed, moreover, that China, not Ho Chi Minh, represented the more viable threat to U.S. interests in Asia. Accordingly, a combat commitment in Vietnam would amount to a "dangerous strategic diversion" of limited U.S. military power to a "non-decisive theater to the attainment of non-decisive local objectives." Ridgway reported such findings to the president in a late-May briefing, and he believed that "to a man of [Eisenhower's] military experience its implications were immediately clear."[10]

The JCS agreed with Ridgway, warning that intervention at Dien Bien Phu would not be a "'one-shot' affair" but, rather, a "continuing logistic supply requirement" for America's Far East forces and that it would, ultimately, involve U.S. troops in direct military operations, create increasing demands for reinforcement, risk American casualties, and possibly provoke Chinese intervention. Thus, the "real question" attending the debate over Dien Bien Phu was whether the United States would "commence active participation by [American] forces in the Indochina war." But other concerns, such as rearming the Federal Republic of Germany, were of principal interest to service officials, and the French garrison at Dien Bien Phu was doomed, so nonintervention in Vietnam was a reasonably easy recommendation for the brass.[11]

Throughout the first months of 1954 the military had coordinated a strong campaign against intervention. Though concerned with the ramifications of Communist success in Vietnam, most officers understood that the political and military environment in both America and Indochina militated against U.S. prospects in Southeast Asia. Gen. Thomas Trapnell, past commander of the American advisory group in Saigon, typified the American military dilemma regarding Vietnam. Though an advocate of holding the line against the Viet Minh, Trapnell recognized that the enemy had developed effective regional militia, possessed a "tremendous capability" for mobility and endurance, and was skilled in political and psychological indoctrination. Believing that time—and U.S. and French public opinion—was on their side, the Vietnamese Communists were conducting "a clever war of attrition." Though Trapnell believed that the United States should resist the Left in Asia, he insisted that a "military solution to the war in Indochina is not possible."[12]

The army's assistant chief for planning, Gen. James Gavin, corroborated that assessment in a hundred-page report on Vietnam commissioned by Ridgway. The army, Gavin found, would also need to extend its terms of service for active personnel, activate reservists, increase draft calls, reopen military bases, and increase material production for Indochina, all of which ran contrary to the president's attempt, in the "New Look," to limit military budgets in the interest of reducing the national debt. Worse, he estimated that American troops would suffer about twenty-eight thousand casualties monthly. And of course, he reminded his superiors, the Viet Minh remained a formidable military force.[13]

Even into mid-1954, Eisenhower and Dulles still sought multilateral action to stem the Communist advance in Vietnam and had not yet dismissed a combat role there. The JCS again moved to scotch any plans for intervention, limited or otherwise. Any involvement, the chiefs explained, "would continue and expand considerably even though initial efforts were indecisive." In time, the United States would have to commit additional naval and air units "and extensive ground forces to prevent the loss of Indochina," an area "devoid" of vital resources and "not a decisive theater" in Asia. Defense Secretary Charles Wilson, presumably putting forth the JCS's views, argued that the most desirable course of action in Vietnam was to "get completely out of the area. The chances of saving any part of Southeast Asia were . . . nothing." Gavin was more succinct as he echoed Gen. Omar Bradley's analysis of Korea in asserting that an American military commitment to Vietnam "involves the risk of embroiling the U.S. in [the] wrong war, in the wrong place, at the wrong time."[14]

Such views held sway. U.S. forces did not intervene in Indochina, although neither did the United States dissociate itself from Vietnamese affairs. Despite such overwhelming reluctance, the White House moved ahead with its plans for Vietnam, essentially inventing a country below the Seventeenth Parallel, the Republic of Vietnam (RVN), putting a regime in place led by the U.S. client Ngo Dinh Diem, and pumping billions of dollars into the fictive nation to enable it to survive. Still, military officials sounded the alarms about such a commitment. Service officials were quick to point out that there was a crisis of political legitimacy in the South. Diem and his family ran the RVN as a personal fiefdom and had little tolerance for even the trappings of democracy. Even prior to the Geneva armistice in 1954, which partitioned Vietnam and called for unifying elections in 1956, the JCS conceded that any settlement of the French-Vietnamese conflict "based upon free elections would be attended by the almost certain loss of [Indochina] to Communist control." Diem, as JCS intelligence officials reported, had "no intention of tolerating an election he cannot win."[15]

Gen. J. Lawton Collins, sent to Vietnam as Eisenhower's special representative in November 1954, also understood that internal turmoil, not outside aggression, was destroying southern Vietnam. Appalled by Diem's authoritarian ways and failure to challenge the various sects involved in southern political and economic affairs, Collins recognized as well that the Viet Minh "have and will retain the capability to overrun Free Vietnam if they wish." He even suggested that U.S. withdrawal, although the "least desirable" option, "may be the only sound solution."[16] Diem, however, rescued his position in April 1955 by beating back the factions' challenge to his leadership, at which point Eisenhower and Dulles decided to stick with him over the long haul.[17] By October 1955, when Diem became president in an election that would have embarrassed a Chicago alderman, the RVN was officially established, and the United States was heading toward war in Vietnam.[18]

Despite Diem's successes, the military remained critical of plans to establish a training mission in Indochina.[19] Communist troops were "laying the groundwork for a strong, armed dissident movement" in the South, Gavin and Gen. Paul Adams concluded, and it would be dangerous to put American trainers in the middle of an imminent "civil war," which might well provoke greater intervention by the Soviets and the Chinese.[20] Still, the White House did establish a military training program through the Military Assistance Advisory Group, or MAAG, headed by the hawkish Gen. Samuel Williams. But even Williams presented a bleak view of the situation in Vietnam in mid-1956. While he agreed that the southern Vietnamese would have to be responsible for their own security, Williams worried that the Viet Minh outnumbered the VNA (the [southern] Vietnamese National Army) by a two-to-one ratio and lamented that "large-scale Asiatic support would not appear to be forthcoming." In the event of hostilities, he estimated that VNA forces north of Da Nang would "unquestionably be badly mauled" but that, if Diem reinforced that area, the Communists would simply bypass it. Moreover, the usually sanguine MAAG leader also provided a laundry list of VNA disadvantages in any war against the Viet Minh: Ho and Vo Nguyen Giap, military commander of the Viet Minh, could not be expected to attack without thorough planning and infiltration along protected routes; enemy morale would be bolstered by claims that Diem was a "puppet" of "Western colonialists"; the VNA command would be unable to communicate with field units; and the rainy season would thwart established plans to attack northward via Laos. In effect, then, the VNA's lack of skill and experience put it at an even greater disadvantage than its numerical inferiority. At least two U.S. divisions would be needed to contain the Viet Minh, Williams assumed, but the development of a much larger and stronger indigenous ground force remained the key to successful warfare in Vietnam.[21] Accordingly, the U.S. presence should be limited to "absolute needs," while "discretion and circumspect behavior is [sic] a *must.*" Despite his apparent satisfaction with the situation, even Williams hoped to "resist pressure to increase American personnel" in Vietnam, in part by employing foreign nationals instead of U.S. representatives where possible.[22]

And so it went. By the mid-1950s, the pattern was clear. Military officials would either defend involvement in Vietnam but recognize the serious obstacles to an effective deployment there or, more likely, recommend against intervention altogether. Even when officials like General Williams tried to prevent a sanguine view of the war, military officials in Washington tended to be doubters and critics. Naval commander Arleigh Burke, a hawk in the 1960s, believed that neither Eisenhower nor anybody else "had any intention of committing troops to either South Vietnam or Laos."[23] Gen. Lyman Lemnitzer, the army chief and later JCS chair, observed that the military always expected to limit its role in Vietnam to military assistance and advisory groups because military leaders such as Eisenhower and Douglas MacArthur insisted "that we should not get engaged in a land battle on the continent of Asia."[24] J. Lawton Collins agreed, adding that he did not "know of a single senior commander that [sic] was in favor of fighting on the land mass of Asia."[25]

Despite such sentiments, American leaders turned Vietnam into a symbol of the Cold War and progressively increased the U.S. stake there. Although military leaders in Saigon and Washington presented an ambivalent view of their prospects in Indochina, American aid continued to flow to a country that was led by the authoritarian Ngo family and that had an ill-prepared army without a credible mission. The antidemocratic stance of Diem's brother Ngo Dinh Nhu and his outspoken wife, Madame Nhu, particularly troubled U.S. officials. Although American leaders saw problems with the RVN, 78 percent of U.S. aid to Diem from 1956 to 1960 went into the military budget, while only 2 percent was allocated to health, housing, and welfare programs.[26]

Though claiming to want to avoid American intervention in Indochina, U.S. leaders made it inevitable by feeding Diem's and Nhu's addiction to power, guns, and money. As the Ngos received more resources from the United States, they became even more arbitrary and authoritarian and, in turn, unpopular. Ultimately, American "advisers" would enter Vietnam to prop them up. Despite reports from Saigon that stressed the confusion and contradiction inherent in the American policy in Vietnam, military and political leaders never advocated the type of "agonizing reappraisal" that might have led to a different policy. U.S. military officials consistently recognized the enemy's strength as an indigenous force in the South, the fatal weaknesses of Diem and the ARVN (the Army of the Republic of Vietnam), and the questionable priority of Indochina in national security considerations, yet they continued to accentuate whatever positive characteristics they could detect or invent in the RVN. By late 1960, John Kennedy of Massachusetts was awaiting inauguration as president, and the American role in Vietnam was about to expand markedly.

Occupying an Essentially Hostile Foreign Country

What had begun as a limited effort to placate the French in the aftermath of World War II had become a major endeavor to prevent Ho Chi Minh and his nationalist-Communist followers from achieving democratic leadership of Vietnam by the later 1950s and early 1960s. The Eisenhower and Kennedy administrations sent billions of dollars, thousands of advis-

President Lyndon Johnson confers with Secretary of Defense Robert McNamara, Gen. Earle Wheeler, and Gen. William Westmoreland. Courtesy of the Vietnam Archive, Texas Tech University, Larry Berman Collection.

ers, and advanced weaponry to southern Vietnam to try to preserve the "nation" that they had invented below the Seventeenth Parallel, but, by the mid-1960s, to little avail. Hanoi finally yielded to southern insurgent pressure to help form the National Liberation Front and begin armed struggle in the South, the Diem regime remained corrupt and repressive (both attacking opposition Buddhists and talking to representatives about the possibility of a negotiated, neutralist settlement), the southern army was passive, the enemy held the initiative, and the United States moved closer to full-scale intervention. Kennedy, despite posthumous revisionism attributing "dove" status to him and claiming that he would have pulled out of Vietnam, was a committed warrior who sought victory. In fact, his advisers complained that the military was insufficiently bellicose. Roger Hilsman charged that armed forces' leaders were tying the president's hands on Indochina policy. In mid-1962, amid continued turmoil in Laos and Vietnam, Kennedy and his chiefs considered possible military responses. Although the president and the secretary of state, Dean Rusk, among others, wanted to deploy U.S. troops to the area—in Rusk's case into the DRV (Democratic Republic of Vietman)—Hilsman and NSC (National Security Council) staff member Michael Forrestal worried "that the military was going to go soft" in its approach to Indochina. The chiefs, Hilsman complained, "beat their chests until it comes time to do some fighting and then [they] start backing down." Gen. George Decker, acting JCS chair at the time, had drawn up a list of possible courses of action—including negotiations, diplomatic approaches to the Soviet Union, and committing SEATO (Southeast Asia Treaty Organization) defense forces—that Hilsman called "the damndest collection of mush and softness I have seen in a long time."[27]

Just a few years later, there were about eighty thousand American troops in Vietnam, and, in the aftermath of the Gulf of Tonkin incident in August 1964, the air force began flying reprisal air strikes, yet the situation in the South remained grave, with the National Liberation Front and Viet Cong (VC) guerrilla forces retaining the initiative, the ARVN remaining ineffective, and the political situation still chaotic, with about a dozen governments in the aftermath of the November 1963 assassination of Diem. By January 1965, National Security Adviser McGeorge Bundy and Defense Secretary Robert McNamara feared the worst and met with President Lyndon Johnson to tell him "that both of us are now pretty well convinced that *our current policy can lead only to disastrous defeat.*" The United States could no longer "wait and hope for a stable government" while the VC expanded its control over the South, and Bundy and Mc-Namara urged Johnson to "use our military power . . . to force a change of Communist policy."[28] Gen. Maxwell D. Taylor, the ambassador to Saigon, was, however, "caught by surprise" when the administration began to press for combat troop deployments to the RVN. "The President was thinking much bigger in this field," he recalled, "than the tenor in Washington" had indicated.[29] Clearly, then, America's civilian leadership favored introducing combat troops into Vietnam in early 1965. At the same time, as McGeorge Bundy admitted, "we had no recommendations from the military for major ground deployments."[30] There was, in fact, no military imperative to intervene. After the VC had bombed an officers' billet in Saigon on Christmas Eve, the White House had encouraged Taylor to ask for ground troops, but the ambassador, the commander of the MACV (Military Assistance Command, Vietnam), Gen. William Westmoreland, and Taylor's deputy, U. Alexis Johnson, quickly moved to scotch such measures.[31]

In a prescient analysis of U.S. policy, Westmoreland and his staff explained their resistance to employing combat forces and recommended that the United States continue on its flawed path of providing operational support and improving the advisory system. As the MACV staff saw it, the United States had already spent a great deal of time trying to develop the ARVN, and, "if that effort has not succeeded, there is even less reason to think that U.S. combat forces would have the desired effect." The Vietnamese, Westmoreland assumed, would either let Americans carry the burden of war or actively turn against the U.S. presence in their country. Given such circumstances, MACV officers concluded that the involvement of American ground forces in the RVN "would at best buy time and would lead to ever increasing commitments until, like the French, we would be occupying an essentially hostile foreign country."[32]

Army chief of staff Harold K. Johnson was not unduly optimistic either, telling an audience in Los Angeles that he expected U.S. military involvement in Indochina to last a minimum of five years and possibly as long as twenty.[33] Johnson, as well as other officers, would overcome his reservations about sending ground troops to Vietnam only two months later. Maxwell Taylor, however, continued to virulently oppose such steps.

In a series of memorandums to the president and others throughout the winter months of 1965, the ambassador detailed the risks of U.S. intervention and the bleak prospects facing American soldiers in southern Vietnam. Above all, he still insisted that political turmoil in the RVN was the major obstacle to success, and one that American troops could not remove. In early January, as Gen. Nguyen Khanh maneuvered to return to power in the South, Taylor called for "hard soul searching" to decide whether U.S. officials ought to tolerate another coup or instead reject Khanh altogether and accept the consequences, "which might entail ultimate withdrawal."[34] In fact, after Khanh had staged another coup on January 27, Taylor advised against recognizing the new government, telling Bundy that the United States should prepare to "reduce [its] advisory effort to policy guidance [or] disengage and let the [RVN] stand alone."[35]

Taylor, however, continued to see airpower as a virtual panacea to America's problems. Graduated air strikes against the DRV, he believed, would signal to Ho the cost of supporting the insurgency, provide leverage in any negotiations, and improve RVN morale. While Taylor, and most other military and political officials, did not expect an air campaign to decisively alter the situation in Vietnam, he did see it as a way of "producing maximum stresses in Hanoi minds."[36] With the war going so badly, the president had little choice but to finally accept Taylor's strategy. Thus, by mid-February, the United States was beginning a full-scale air campaign in Vietnam.

The immediate cause of the air war came on February 7, when the VC mortared an army barracks in Pleiku, killing 9 and wounding 109 Americans, and destroying or damaging 22 aircraft. U.S. officials then cited the attack at Pleiku to justify American retaliation, but any provocation would have satisfied the administration's desire to expand the war. Indeed, Bundy was in Vietnam at the time and, looking to justify stronger military measures, saw the incident as the vehicle by which the president could authorize an air campaign against the North, even sarcastically observing that "Pleikus are like streetcars."[37] Thus, Johnson authorized Operation Rolling Thunder, which in three years would unleash more tonnage of bombs than all previous air wars combined.[38] As the historian Mark Clodfelter has shown, Johnson's decisions did not satisfy everyone. While Taylor, McNamara, McGeorge Bundy, and John McNaughton thought that the president had demonstrated American resolve, William Bundy and Rusk doubted that air strikes would deter Ho.[39] The JCS, although satisfied that Johnson had finally acted, continued to press for intensified air operations against the North.[40] Harold K. Johnson continued to decry the emphasis on the air war over the DRV since the United States, he believed, still had to focus on defeating the insurgency in the South and did not have to destroy the North to force a settlement in the RVN.[41] Westmoreland, also taking the army line, "doubted that the bombing would have any effect on the North Vietnamese," although he did hope that it might boost morale in the South.[42]

The bombing, however, did not appreciably change conditions inside southern Vietnam, so in March, President Johnson deployed the first ground troops, a Marine brigade, to guard the U.S. base at Da Nang. Westmoreland remained wary, cautioning that it was "most important . . . to avoid the impression by friends and enemies that [the] U.S. has taken over responsibility for war from the Vietnamese."[43]

American officers had not recommended the use of combat troops before February 1965 and, in Westmoreland's case, had firmly rejected such proposals earlier. But, with civilian authorities in Washington rushing in that direction, Wheeler, the MACV commander, and others fell in line, as concerned with the political impact of decisionmaking as with the war in Vietnam itself. The deployment to Da Nang resulted from civilian pressure, not military factors, and was in the cards even prior to the events of early 1965. As Gen. William DePuy later observed, the commitment of combat forces was not the "product of a Westmoreland concept for fighting the war." The MACV staff, he explained, still expected U.S. troops to advise and assist the ARVN, not fight the war themselves.[44]

So did Maxwell Taylor. Although he had to acquiesce in the troop commitment, the ambassador persisted in warning about a wider war. Expressing his "grave reservations" about committing ground forces to Vietnam, the soldier-cum-diplomat warned that, "once this policy is breached, it will be very difficult to hold [the] line" on future troop moves. As soon as RVN leaders saw that the United States was willing to assume new responsibilities, they would certainly "seek to unload other ground force tasks upon us," which would inevitably lead to increased political tension with the local population and friction with the armed forces of the Republic of Vietnam over command arrangements. Taylor recognized the need to defend U.S. airfields at sites such as Da Nang or

Bien Hoa but thought that accepting a combat role against the VC was just not feasible. The "white-faced soldier armed, equipped, and trained as he is" was "not [a] suitable guerrilla fighter for Asian forests and jungles," he explained. Pointing to the French failure in the First Indochina War, Taylor had to "doubt that US forces could do much better."[45] By mid-March, Westmoreland's request for more troops to protect an American radio unit in Phu Bai, about fifty miles below the demilitarized zone, reinforced Taylor's fear that such proposals would continue unabated and might induce the ARVN to perform even "worse in a mood of relaxation at passing the Viet Cong burden to the US."[46]

In March 1965, however, U.S. officials were concerned with getting more ground forces into Vietnam amid the continued deterioration there. Military officials, however, held forthright reservations. The commitment to Da Nang had alienated various marine generals, who pointed out to their commandant, Gen. Wallace M. Greene, that the Corps "was overcommitted . . . and unable to meet any kind of challenge in the Atlantic area."[47] Gen. Arthur Collins, an army planning officer who believed that the United States was going to "nibble away at this Vietnamese problem" and that the southern Vietnamese had no will to fight, urged the MACV official Bruce Palmer to oppose the commitment of ground troops to the RVN in early 1965.[48] Collins and the marines both got nowhere with their complaints. The United States had already passed the point of no return in Vietnam, and, in March and April 1965, American policymakers seemed solely concerned with sending more troops to the RVN, not in debating whether they should be there. Within months, by July 1965, the commitment to Vietnam would become irreversible, with Johnson approving a major reinforcement of about fifty thousand troops, with more to be deployed "as requested," and increasing draft calls to thirty-five thousand monthly. The war had been "Americanized" despite over a decade of military misgivings, and within a few years, by Tet 1968, the fears and bleak predictions of so many officers had been borne out.

Who's to Blame?

Not surprisingly, with White House and service officials at odds over Vietnam, civil-military relations were at a low point. Indeed, the military, sensing early on that conditions in Vietnam were not conducive to

Adm. U. S. Grant Sharp, the Pacific commander in chief, meets the Korean ambassador to Vietnam, Shin Sang Chul, in central Vietnam. Courtesy of the Vietnam Archive, Texas Tech University, Douglas Pike Photograph Collection.

American success, looked for ways to avoid responsibility for what they saw as a likely disaster there. So, in addition to fighting a war in Vietnam, U.S. officials found themselves involved in political conflict at home over who would bear the blame for failure in Southeast Asia.

Such concerns were evident in 1961 in a thorough and candid analysis of the political and military factors that were conditioning U.S. policy in Indochina. The MAAG commander, Lionel McGarr, feared that the civilian establishment would try an end run around the military in Saigon, so, "for the protection of the Armed Forces of the United States and specifically the Army which runs MAAG Vietnam," he wanted Lemnitzer to see his unfiltered judgment of the "presently worsening situation here." State Department officials, McGarr believed, were overlooking past mistakes and "basic differences of opinion between them and the military" in Vietnam. Both the State Department and the embassy, he added, had ignored or opposed the need to build up the ARVN and develop counterinsurgency capabilities, and it was only "Kennedy's pronouncements on Vietnam as well as Vice President Johnson's visit here, not to mention increasing Viet Cong pressure, [that] made [the ARVN increase] imperative." Worse, the RVN's leaders, also bypassing reluctant U.S. military officials, now "feel they can get anything they want, regardless of MAAG recommendations, by going through the Ambassador to top American levels." McGarr thus saw a "slimmer and slimmer" chance to "pull this one out of the fire." Aware of the political factors involved in developing Vietnam policy, the MAAG chief concluded with striking honesty, "As I am jealous of the professional good name of our Army, I do not wish it to be placed in the position of fighting a losing battle and being charged with the loss."[49]

McGarr's views may be as close as one comes to finding a smoking gun as far as the politics of Vietnam in the Kennedy years are concerned. In his report, the MAAG chief had crystallized the major factors that were dooming the U.S. experience in Vietnam. Not only clearly recognizable battlefield deterioration—caused principally by an imposing enemy as well as a deficient ally—but also, and just as important, domestic political brawls would make it virtually impossible for America to meet its objectives in Vietnam. Civilian officials apparently felt the same way. In a bluntly honest memorandum to Lyndon Johnson in 1964, Jack Valenti, the president's closest adviser, advised him to "sign on" the JCS before making any "final decisions" about Vietnam. Fearing the "future aftermath" of such decisions, and invoking Omar Bradley's support of Harry Truman at the MacArthur hearings during the Korean War, Valenti wanted the JCS's support of the president's policy to be made public so as to avoid future recriminations. In that way, the chiefs "will have been heard, they will have been part of the consensus, and our flank will have been covered in the event of some kind of flap or investigation later."[50]

By mid-1965, service leaders were obviously suspicious of their civilian counterparts and worried about their conduct of the war. Adm. David McDonald, the naval commander, likewise was concerned that Johnson's graduated bombing campaign would fail, but he was also concerned that the president would eventually leave office and "the only group left answerable for the war would be the military."[51] Admiral Sharp explicitly addressed such political considerations in his instructions to Westmo reland. Although the ambassador had already told MACV commanders that they could commit their forces to battle against the VC and Sharp had reiterated that authorization, the commander in chief of Pacific forces (CINCPAC) also urged that Westmoreland "realize that there would be grave political implications involved if sizable U.S. forces are committed for the first time and suffer a defeat." The commander should, thus, "notify CINCPAC and JCS prior to [the] commitment of any U.S. ground combat force."[52]

Indeed, such political maneuvering would be an implicit yet critical element in Vietnam policymaking from that point on because military men were aware that civil-military relations as well as battlefield conditions would determine the nature of U.S. involvement in the war. American officers—although not usually as candid as Sharp in discussing the "grave political implications" of their decisions—did recognize that the president and the defense secretary would never authorize unlimited resources or operations in Vietnam. Military policy was not made in a vacuum; public opposition to the war, Johnson's domestic agenda, and international political considerations, as well as the situation on the ground in the RVN, would always be significant elements in the formulation of strategy. The president himself made this clear at a mid-June 1965 NSC meeting on Vietnam. To Johnson, dissent at home, trouble in the field, and the threat of Chinese intervention meant that the United States had to limit both its means and its ends in Vietnam. It thus had to contain the enemy "as much as we can, and as simply as we can, without going all out." By approving Westmoreland's reinforcement request in midyear, he explained, "we get in deeper and it is harder to get out. . . . We must determine which course gives us the maximum protection at the least cost."[53]

The president's concern about a deeper commitment was revealing, indicating that he would not authorize unlimited resources being given to or wholly unrestrained operations being conducted in Vietnam. Johnson would, however, escalate the war to levels not imagined just years earlier. Military leaders, despite recognizing the risks of intervention in Vietnam and having arrived at no consensus on how to conduct the war, nonetheless continually pressed the White House to expand the U.S. commitment. Unable either to develop any new ideas to alter conditions in the RVN or to admit that they were not likely to reverse the situation there, American officers asked for more of the same. The president in turn would both "get in deeper" and not fully satisfy the military's requests. Either way, Lyndon Johnson would be responsible for what happened in Vietnam.

As the war continued on, without appreciable improvement, in 1967 and thereafter, civil-military jockeying to avoid blame for the war intensified. Military leaders, in fact, began to plant the idea that they had to fight with "one hand tied behind their backs," a staple of postwar conservative revisionism regarding the war, while the conflict was in progress. Time and again, though they recognized that the Johnson administration was not going to escalate the war without restraint, take the battle to the North, or activate reserves, the military would request those very measures to make the civilians responsible for fighting shorthanded, as it were.

Admiral Sharp, in another of his candid political evaluations, virtually admitted as much. The reinforcements that the JCS requested "are simply not going to be provided," he understood. "The country is not going to call up the Reserves and we had best accept that." On the other hand, Sharp, like marine leaders, saw Westmoreland's plans, a war of attrition, as a "blueprint for defeat." The Pacific commander, as unimaginative as ever, urged Westmoreland to keep the pressure on the White House. "Continue to state your requirement for forces," he told the commander, "even though you are not going to get them."[54] Sharp later alleged in his memoirs that politicians in Washington stabbed the military in the back, but the admiral must have seen the knife headed his way well before the war had ended. Westmoreland too understood the political considerations involved in developing strategy.[55]

In the end, of course, Westmoreland would develop no new approach to the war. Instead, he continued to request more troops and resources, despite Sharp's blunt awareness that they would not be forthcoming, and despite similar warnings from Harold K. Johnson. "You are painfully aware of the problems ahead of us," the army chief cabled Westmoreland, "if we cannot find some way to bring our authorized and operating strengths into line." Calling for "personnel economy" and greater "discipline" in requisitioning resources, Johnson asked for the commander's support to stem the problem before the Defense Department began to investigate the army's handling of manpower issues.[56]

Everything, of course, would come to a boil in early 1968, as the enemy staged its countrywide Tet Offensive. In the aftermath of Tet, which had undermined Westmoreland's recent claims that there was "light at the end of the tunnel," Wheeler traveled to Saigon, where he offered a gloomy appraisal of conditions in Vietnam—his famous "it was a very near thing" report. But he and Westmoreland also requested 206,000 more troops and the activation of about 200,000 reservists. It was clear, however, that major reinforcement was not forthcoming in February and March 1968. Wheeler recognized the pervading gloom in the White House, admitting that "Tet had a tremendous effect on the American public . . . on leaders of Congress . . . on President Johnson." As a result, while Wheeler was in Vietnam, Bruce Palmer, now a MACV commander, informed Westmoreland that Gen. Dwight Beach, the army's Pacific commander, had been aware of the new reinforcement request and "had commented that it would shock them [Washington officials]."[57] As Westmoreland himself admitted, he and Wheeler "both knew the grave political and economic implications of a major call-up of reserves." Westmoreland tried to be upbeat but conceded that the JCS chair "saw no possibility at the moment of selling reinforcements" unless he adopted an alarmist tone to exploit the sense of crisis. "Having read the newspapers," Westmoreland wondered, "who among them [civilian leaders] would even believe there had been success?" Wheeler's approach to the issue notwithstanding, Westmoreland suspected that "the request may have been doomed from the first in any event" owing to long-standing political pressure to deescalate.[58]

Harold K. Johnson suspected as much. In their initial meetings after the Tet attacks began, the chiefs decided to wait for the dust to settle before making recommendations for future strategy. Within days, however, it was clear that the JCS and the MACV did not have that luxury and would have to make a prompt policy statement. Instead of deliberating over the proper course for the future, Johnson observed, the chiefs just endorsed a program for major reinforcements. "I think this was wrong," the army chief later asserted. "There should have been better assessment" of the situation before forwarding military plans to the White House. The chiefs, despite their misconceptions, approved the reinforcement request anyway, essentially because they did not want to reject the chair's suggestion. "If you want it bad," Johnson sardonically remarked, "you get it bad."[59]

And the brass did get it bad. Political leaders had also made it clear that substantive reinforcements would not be forthcoming. Johnson, with his advisers, was upset, charging, "All of you have counseled, advised, consulted and then—as usual—placed the monkey on my back again. . . . I do not like what I am smelling from those cables from Vietnam."[60] During his first post-Tet press conference, the president asserted that he had already added the men that Westmoreland thought were necessary. "We have something under 500,000," Johnson told reporters. "Our objective is 525,000. Most of the combat battalions already have been supplied. There is not anything in any of the developments that would justify the press in leaving the impression that any great new overall moves are going to be made that would involve substantial movements in that direction." By the following week, with more advisers expressing their concern about Tet and the war in general, it was clear to the president that the military could exploit White House division over Vietnam. "I don't want them [military leaders] to ask for something," Johnson worried aloud, "not get it, and have all the blame placed on me."[61]

That, to a large degree, was precisely what happened. In the aftermath of Tet and the reinforcement request, Johnson found himself in an untenable position, unable to send more troops to Vietnam, given the shocking nature of the enemy offensive, and unwilling to admit defeat and move on. Politically, he was weakened beyond repair, with the Democratic senators Eugene McCarthy and Robert Kennedy opting to challenge for the party's nomination for president, thereby forcing the president to withdraw from the race and, thus, opening the door for Richard Nixon's triumph, which was based on his pledge to get out of Vietnam. Subsequently, conservatives and military officials began to attack Johnson for his tentative approach to Vietnam, for not activating reserves, for not conducting operations north of the Seventeenth Parallel, for not giving the military the resources it needed to win, for making American soldiers fight "with one hand tied behind their back."

Today, with American soldiers in another deadly and futile war in a faraway place, journalists, politicians, and everyday people wonder whether Iraq is another Vietnam. Though it has been more than three decades since American troops left Indochina and the nationalist-Communist forces won their long struggle for independence and revolution there, the war remains with us, which we saw with chilling clarity in the 2004 elections, as John Kerry, a three-time Purple Heart winner, was smeared, accused of lying about his service, by the representatives of a political campaign headed by two draft dodgers. So looking back at the work of George Herring and others is vital to our role, not just as scholars, but as citizens. And, today, as ranking military leaders such as Anthony Zinni, Wesley Clark, Eric Shinseki, and others have expressed their fears about the war, the lies and delusive reasons given for fighting, the likely dismal outcomes, and the incompetent leadership, we would do well to look back at the brass in the 1960s, who sounded the alarms about Vietnam but were drowned out in a cacophony of political wrangling. When the men charged with fighting a war speak out and warn against it, they ought to be heard. If, as George Orwell suggested, those who control the past can control the present, and, thus, the future, then the legacy of military dissent has to be remembered, and it has to be discussed today, with regard to both Vietnam and Iraq. To do less is to guarantee, not just more "very near things," but more "sure things" like casualties, terrorism, wars, and global insecurity.

Notes

1. George C. Herring, *America's Longest War: The United States and Vietnam, 1950–1975*, 4th ed. (Boston: McGraw-Hill, 2002), 75–78.

2. Commanding General (hereafter CG), U.S. Forces, India-Burma Theatre, Memorandum to War Department, CG, U.S. Forces, China Theatre, and CG, U.S. Army Liaison Section in Kandy, Ceylon, September 11, 1945, CRAX 27516, Records of the Joint Chiefs of Staff, Record Group 218, Chairman's File, Admiral Leahy, 1942–1948, National Archives, Washington, DC (hereafter RG 218, with appropriate filing information); Gallagher, Hanoi, to Gen. R. B. McClure, Kunming, September 20, 1945, in *Vietnam: The Definitive Documentation of Human Decisions*, ed. Gareth Porter, 2 vols. (Stanfordville, NY: Coleman, 1979), 1:77–78, document 41. See also Report on Office of Strategic Services' "Deer Mission" by Major Allison Thomas, September 17, 1945, in *Vietnam*, ed. Porter, 1:74–77, document 40; Memorandum for the Record: General Gallagher's Meeting with Ho Chi Minh, September 29, 1945, in ibid., 1:80–81, document 44; and U.S. Congress, House Committee on Armed Services, *United States–Vietnam Relations, 1945–1967: Study Prepared by the Department of Defense* (hereafter *USVN Relations*), 12 vols. (Washington, DC: U.S. Government Printing Office, 1971), bk. 1, I.C.3., pp. C-66–C-104.

3. Marshall Telegram to Caffery in Paris, May 13, 1947, in *Vietnam*, ed. Porter, 1:145–46, document 101; Marshall Telegram to Caffery, July 3, 1948, in ibid., 1:176–77, document 118. See also Marshall Telegram to Reed, July 17, 1947, in ibid., 1:156–57, document 104. It became standard practice for the military to question any large commitment to Vietnam. In Joint Chiefs of Staff studies of national security

priorities in 1947, Southeast Asia was consistently ranked at the bottom, while officials in the Navy and War Departments more specifically recognized Ho Chi Minh's overtures to the United States and realized that he was not a puppet of Stalin. Melvyn P. Leffler, *Preponderance of Power: National Security, the Truman Administration, and the Cold War* (Stanford, CA: Stanford University Press, 1992), 148, 166.

4. JCS 1992/4, "U.S. Policy toward Southeast Asia," July 9, 1949, 092 Asia to Europe, case 40, Records of the U.S. Army Staff, Record Group 319 (hereafter RG 319, with appropriate filing information); Plans and Operations Position Paper, "U.S. Position with Respect to Indochina, 25 February 1950," RG 319, G-3 091 Indochina, TS.

5. JSPC 958/5, "U.S. Military Measures in Southeast Asia," RG 218, CCS 092 Asia (6-25-48), sec. 9; U.S. Minutes of U.S.-U.K. Political-Military Conversations, October 26, 1950, U.S. Department of State, *Foreign Relations of the United States* (hereafter *FRUS*), *1950* (Washington, DC: U.S. Government Printing Office [USGPO], 1977), 3:1696.

6. Substance of Discussion of State-JCS Meeting at the Pentagon Building, December 21, 1951, *FRUS, 1951* (Washington, DC: USGPO, 1978), 6:568–70; and JSPC Memorandum to JCS, "Conference with France and Britain on Southeast Asia," JSPC 958/58, December 22, 1951, RG 218, CCS 092 Asia (6-25-48), sec. 20.

7. Substance of Discussion of State-JCS Meeting at the Pentagon Building, July 10, 1953, *FRUS, 1952–1954* (Washington, DC: USGPO, 1982), 13:648ff.

8. JCS Paper, "The Situation in Indochina," February 7, 1954, RG 218, CCS 092 Asia (6-25-48), sec. 57.

9. Andrew J. Rotter, *The Path to Vietnam: Origins of the American Commitment to Southeast Asia* (Ithaca, NY: Cornell University Press, 1987); Lloyd C. Gardner, *Approaching Vietnam: From World War II to Dienbienphu, 1941–1954* (New York: Norton, 1988); William S. Borden, *The Pacific Alliance: United States Foreign Economic Policy and Japanese Trade Recovery, 1947–1954* (Madison: University of Wisconsin Press, 1984).

10. Army Position on NSC Action 1074-A, n.d., *USVN Relations*, bk. 1, II.B.1., p. B-10, and bk. 9, p. 333; Chief of Staff, USA, Memorandum to JCS, April 6, 1954, *FRUS, 1952–1954*, 13:1269–70; Ridgway quoted in Robert Asprey, *War in the Shadows: The Guerrilla in History* (Garden City, NY: Doubleday, 1975), 817–18; Ridgway Interview with Maurice Matloff, 2–6, Military History Institute (MHI), Carlisle, PA. See also JCS Memorandum for Secretary of Defense, "Indochina," April 8, 1954, RG 218, CCS 092 Asia (6-25-48), sec. 62; *The Pentagon Papers: The Defense Department History of United States Decisionmaking on Vietnam*, Senator Gravel Edition, 5 vols. (Boston: Beacon, 1971–72), 1:93; CSUSA Memorandum to JCS, "Reconnaissance of Indochina and Thailand," JCS 1992/359, July 14, 1954, July 15, 1954, RG 218, CCS 092 (6-25-48), sec. 75; and Matthew B. Ridgway, *Soldier: The Memoirs of Matthew B. Ridgway, as Told to Harold H. Martin* (New York: Harper, 1956), 276.

11. JCS Memorandum for Secretary of Defense, "French Request for Additional Aid," April 27, 1954, RG 330, Records of the Office of Assistant Secretary of Defense

for International Security Affairs (ASD/ISA), 091 Indochina, May–December 1954.

12. Gen. Thomas Trapnell, Comments at Debriefing, May 3, 1954, *USVN Relations,* bk. 9, pp. 406–20.

13. Supplement to Outline Plan for Conducting Military Operations in Indochina with United States and French Union Forces, Spring (April–May) 1954, RG 319, G-3 091 Indochina, TS (April 5, 1954), FW 23/5.

14. JCS 1992/334, "Military Situation in Tonkin Delta," June 7, 1954, RG 218, CCS 092 Asia (6-25-48), sec. 71; JCS 1992/348, "Rhee Offer of One Corps for Commitment in Indochina," June 29, 1954, RG 218, CCS 092 Asia (6-25-48), sec. 73; Wilson in 215th Meeting of National Security Council, September 24, 1954, Dwight D. Eisenhower Presidential Library (hereafter Eisenhower Library), Abilene, KS, Ann Whitman File—NSC Series, box 6; Gavin, G-3, Memorandum for Chief of Staff, USA, "Military Implications of Cease-Fire Agreements in Indochina," July 22, 1954, RG 319, G-3 091 Indochina. See also JCS memorandum for Secretary of Defense, Sub: Additional Aid for Indochina, June 24, 1954, RG 330, ASD/ISA, 091 Indochina, May–December 1954.

15. JCS 1992/287, "Preparations of Department of Defense Regarding Negotiations on Indochina for the Forthcoming Geneva Conference," March 11, 1954, RG 218, CCS 092 Asia (6-25-48), sec. 59. See also JCS Memorandum for Secretary of Defense, March 12, 1954, *USVN Relations,* bk. 9, pp. 266–70. On the inevitability of Communist victory in any elections in Vietnam, see George McT. Kahin, *Intervention: How America Became Involved in Vietnam* (Garden City, NY: Anchor/Doubleday, 1987), 53, 450; Adm. Edwin T. Layton, Deputy Director for Intelligence, Joint Staff, Memorandum for Director Joint Staff, December 22, 1955, "Emerging Pattern—South Vietnam," RG 218, CCS 092 Asia (6-25-48), sec. 17.

16. Collins to Dulles, January 20, 1955, *Declassified Documents Reference System* (*DDRS*), 78, 295A; Collins to Dulles, December 13, 1954, *USVN Relations,* bk. 1, IV.A.3., pp. 20–22. Many of Collins's reports from Vietnam can be found in *FRUS, 1955–1957* (Washington, DC: USGPO, 1985), 1:200–370. See also David Anderson, "J. Lawton Collins, John Foster Dulles, and the Eisenhower Administration's 'Point of No Return' in Vietnam," *Diplomatic History* 12 (Spring 1988): 127–47.

17. To Eisenhower and Dulles, it was Collins, not Diem, who might have to be replaced. Eisenhower told Dulles during an early March 1955 meeting to consider replacing Collins with Maxwell Taylor and suggested that a special law be developed to allow the general to serve as special ambassador without giving up his military rank. Taylor, however, became the army chief shortly thereafter, while Collins was replaced by Elbridge Durbrow, who became ambassador to the RVN. Dulles's Memorandum of Conversation with the President, March 7, 1955, White House Memorandum Series, John Foster Dulles File, folder: Meetings with the President (7), Eisenhower Library.

18. David L. Anderson, *Trapped by Success: The Eisenhower Administration and Vietnam, 1953–1961* (New York: Columbia University Press, 1991), chaps. 5–6.

19. F. W. Moorman, Memorandum to Gavin, "Indochina," May 11, 1954, RG 319, CS 091 Indochina; JCS 1992/367, "U.S. Assumption of Training Responsibility in Indochina," August 3, 1954, RG 218, CCS 092 Asia (6-25-48), sec. 77. See also *USVN Relations,* bk. 1, III.A.2., pp. A-19–A-20; Cable, CH MAAG to DEPT AR, June 20, 1954, NR: MG1750A, RG 218, CCS 092 Asia (6-25-48), sec. 72; *USVN Relations,* bk. 1, IV.A.3., pp. 7–9, and bk. 10, pp. 701–2; and Gavin and Adams to Ridgway, "U.S. Policy toward Indochina," August 10, 1954, RG 319, G-3 091 Indochina. For background on military criticism regarding training, see *USVN Relations,* bk. 2, IV.A.4., pp. 2–5; Brink to Gen. Reuben Jenkins, Office of Assistant Chief of Staff, G-3, Department of Army, April 16, 1952, 091 Indo-China 1952, RG 218, Chair's File, General Bradley; Memorandum of Conversation, Director PPS (Nitze), May 12, 1952, *FRUS, 1952–1954,* 13:141–44; JSPC memorandum to JCS, "Report of U.S. Joint Military Mission to Indochina," JCS 1992/246, November 3, 1953, RG 218, CCS 092 Asia (6-25-48), sec. 48; and Admiral Davis, Memorandum to Nash, "U.S. Military Advisors in Indochina," November 27, 1953, RG 330, 012.2-742 Indochina.

20. Gavin and Adams to Ridgway, "U.S. Policy toward Indochina" (n. 19 above).

21. CH MAAG, Vietnam, Telegram to CINCPAC, June 9, 1956, RG 218, CCS 092 Asia (6-25-48), sec. 23.

22. CS Bulletin, MAAG, n.d., Williams Papers, box 1, folder 138, MHI.

23. Arleigh Burke Oral History (Columbia Oral History Project), 165–72, Eisenhower Library.

24. Lyman Lemnitzer Oral History (Columbia Oral History Project), 46–48, Eisenhower Library.

25. Collins Interview at Combat Studies Institute, Army Command and General Staff College, 14, MHI.

26. Anderson, *Trapped by Success,* 133.

27. Hilsman Memorandum, May 9, 1962, Hilsman Papers, box 2, folder 6, John F. Kennedy Presidential Library, Boston. This document, a hectically written, somewhat stream-of-consciousness effort, was untitled, but a close reading indicates that Hilsman, who referred to himself in the third person singular throughout, was the author. Hilsman is also quoted in Stephen E. Pelz, "Documents: 'When Do I Have Time to Think?' John F. Kennedy, Roger Hilsman, and the Laotian Crisis of 1962," *Diplomatic History* 3 (Spring 1979): 22. It is, indeed, ironic that Hilsman would score the military's alleged softness in Indochina in May 1962, for the JCS—urging a military emphasis in Vietnam—had criticized his "Strategic Concept for South Vietnam," which had viewed the insurgency as primarily a political problem and urged a program of civic action. Hilsman Report, "A Strategic Concept for South Vietnam," February 2, 1962, *FRUS, 1961–1963* (Washington, DC: USGPO, 1990), 2:73–90; "Memorandum of a Discussion at Department of State–Joint Chiefs of Staff Meeting," February 9, 1962, ibid., 113–16.

28. McGeorge Bundy to Johnson, January 27, 1965, NSC History—Troop Deployment, Lyndon Baines Johnson Presidential Library (hereafter LBJ Library), Austin,

TX (available on microfilm through University Publications of America [UPA]). See also M. Bundy 1557 to Taylor, January 28, 1965, NSC History—Troop Deployment, LBJ Library; and Lyndon B. Johnson, *The Vantage Point: Perspectives of the Presidency, 1963–1969* (New York: Holt, Rinehart & Winston, 1971), 122–23.

29. Maxwell Taylor Oral History, interview by Ted Gittinger, September 14, 1981, interview 3, 2–5, LBJ Library.

30. McGeorge Bundy to Johnson, July 24, 1965, "The History of Recommendations for Increased US Forces in Vietnam," VN C.F., NSF, box 74–75, folder: 2 E, 5/65–7/65, 1965 Troop Decision, LBJ Library.

31. Maxwell D. Taylor, *Swords and Plowshares* (New York: Norton, 1972), 333–34.

32. Westmoreland analysis in Taylor 2058 to Johnson, January 5, 1965, *The War in Vietnam: Classified Histories by the National Security Council,* LBJ Library (available on microfilm through UPA); and "Deployment of Major U.S. Forces to Vietnam: July 1965," *DDRS,* 83, 2793.

33. Harold K. Johnson, MHI Oral History Program, 8, Center of Military History (CMH), Washington, DC.

34. Taylor to Johnson, January 6, 1965, NSC History—Troop Deployment, LBJ Library. See also Taylor to Johnson, January 27, 1965, ibid.; Taylor to Johnson, February 2, 1965, *DDRS,* 77, 34D.

35. Taylor to M. Bundy, February 1, 1965, NSC History—Troop Deployment, LBJ Library. Westmoreland also pointed out that, amid the political turmoil of late January, ARVN soldiers in Da Nang were participating in anti-U.S. demonstrations. Westmoreland Memorandum for the Record, January 28, 1965, "Discussion with General Khanh," Westmoreland Papers, box 5, folder: #13 History Backup (I), LBJ Library.

36. Taylor 2052 to Johnson, January 6, 1965, NSC History—Troop Deployment, LBJ Library; Taylor, *Swords and Plowshares,* 329–38.

37. Bundy quoted in David Halberstam, *The Best and the Brightest* (New York: Random House, 1972), 646.

38. McGeorge Bundy to Johnson, February 7, 1965, "The Situation in Vietnam," NSF, NSC Meetings File, box 1, folder: volume 3, tab 29, LBJ Library. See also Johnson, *Vantage Point,* 125–28.

39. Mark Clodfelter, *The Limits of Air Power: The American Bombing of North Vietnam* (New York: Free Press, 1989), 56–62.

40. Col. H. M. Darmstandler, December 15, 1967, "Chronology of Significant Requests and Decisions Affecting the Air War against North Vietnam," Warnke-McNaughton, box 7, folder: VNS 2 (Vietnam, 1966–1968) (1), LBJ Library; JCS to CINCPAC, February 12, 1965, "Courses of Action Southeast Asia—First 8 Weeks," NSC History—Troop Deployment, LBJ Library. For the JCS's air plans, see Annex to JCS to McNamara, March 7, 1965, "Air Strike Program against North Vietnam," VN C.F., NSF, box 193, folder: Vietnam, JCS Memos, volume 1 (2 of 2), LBJ Library.

41. Vincent Demma, "Suggestions for the Use of Ground Forces, June 1964–March 1965," CMH.

42. William C. Westmoreland, *A Soldier Reports* (Garden City, NY: Doubleday, 1976), 115.

43. Westmoreland to Sharp, February 27, 1965, "Use of U.S. Air Power," Westmoreland Papers, box 5, folder: #13 History Backup, LBJ Library. See also Westmoreland, *A Soldier Reports,* 123.

44. Demma, "Suggestions for Ground Forces"; DePuy quoted in William Gibbons, *The U.S. Government and the Vietnam War: Executive and Legislative Roles and Relationships, pt. 3, 1965–1966* (Princeton, NJ: Princeton University Press, 1989), 125.

45. Taylor 2699 to Rusk, February 22, 1965, NSC History—Troop Deployment, LBJ Library.

46. Taylor 3003 to Secretary of State, March 16, 1965, ibid.

47. Gen. Norman Anderson, Oral History, 170–72, Marine Corps Historical Center, Washington, DC.

48. Gibbons, *Government and Vietnam War,* 170.

49. Ironically, McGarr has been essentially ignored in all major works on Vietnam, but, with the publication of the *FRUS* volumes on Vietnam, the MAAG chief's insight and worries about the war are clear.

50. Valenti to Johnson, November 14, 1964, CF, CO 312, VN, box 12, folder: CO 312, Vietnam, 1964–65, LBJ Library. A handwritten note at the bottom of the document indicates that the president discussed this memorandum with Valenti.

51. McDonald quoted in Richard K. Betts, *Soldiers, Statesmen, and Cold War Crises* (Cambridge, MA: Harvard University Press, 1977), 11.

52. U. S. G. Sharp to Westmoreland, in NMCC to White House, June 13, 1965, NSC History—Troop Deployment, LBJ Library. For background, see Westmoreland to Taylor, June 3, 1965, "Authority for the Commitment of US Ground Combat Forces," Westmoreland Papers, folder 511: #16 History Backup, 10 May–30 June 1965, Washington National Records Center (WNRC), Suitland, MD; and Taylor 4036 to Secretary of State, June 3, 1965, NSC History—Troop Deployment, LBJ Library.

53. Bromley Smith, Summary Notes of 552d NSC Meeting, June 11, 1965, NSF, NSC Meetings File, box 1, folder: volume 3, tab 34, LBJ Library. See also Kahin, *Intervention,* 348–52.

54. Sharp to Westmoreland, June 13, 1967, Westmoreland v. CBS, LC, box 18, folder: MACV Backchannel Messages to Westmoreland, 1–30 June 1967, WNRC.

55. Westmoreland MAC 5601 to Sharp, June 13, 1967, ibid.; U. S. G. Sharp, *Strategy for Defeat: Vietnam in Retrospect* (San Rafael, CA: Presidio, 1978).

56. Johnson WDC 8419 to Westmoreland, June 27, 1967, Westmoreland v. CBS, LC, box 18, MACV Backchannel Messages to Westmoreland, 1–30 June 1967, WNRC.

57. Wheeler quoted in Merle Miller, *Lyndon: An Oral Biography* (New York: Putnam, 1980), 611; Dave Richard Palmer, *Summons of the Trumpet: U.S.-Vietnam in Perspective* (San Rafael, CA: Presidio, 1978), 261; Record of COMUSMACV Fone-

con with General Palmer, 0850, February 25, 1968, Westmoreland Papers, folder 450: Fonecons, February 1968, WNRC.

58. Westmoreland added, disingenuously it would seem, that he and Wheeler "had developed our plans primarily from the military viewpoints, and we anticipated that other, nonmilitary considerations would be brought to bear on our proposals during an intensive period of calm and rational deliberation." Westmoreland Paper, "The Origins of the Post-Tet 1968 Plans for Additional Forces in the Republic of Vietnam," April 1970, Westmoreland Papers, folder 493 (1 of 2): #37 History Files, 1 January–31 June 1970, WNRC; Westmoreland, *A Soldier Reports,* 469. Ironically, both Westmoreland and Gabriel Kolko believe that Wheeler was trying to exploit the circumstances of Tet with his alarmist reports in order to get reinforcements and a reserve call-up. Kolko, however, argues that Wheeler was "conniving" for more troops principally to meet U.S. needs elsewhere. See Gabriel Kolko, *Anatomy of a War: Vietnam, the United States, and the Modern Historical Experience* (New York: Pantheon, 1985), 315.

59. Harold K. Johnson Interview, MHI Senior Officer Debriefing Project, sec. 11, pp. 14–15, CMH.

60. Notes of the President's Meeting with Senior Foreign Policy Advisors, February 9, 1968, Tom Johnson's Meeting Notes, box 2, folder: February 9, 1968—10:15 P.M., LBJ Library.

61. Johnson quoted in *New York Times,* February 2, 1968; Notes of the President's Meeting with Senior Foreign Affairs Advisory Council, February 10, 1968, Tom Johnson's Meeting Notes, box 2, folder: February 10, 1968—3:17 P.M., LBJ Library.

10

Unpopular Messengers

Student Opposition to the Vietnam War

Joseph A. Fry

President Lyndon B. Johnson assured Undersecretary of State George Ball, "I don't give a damn about those little pinkos on the campuses; they're just waving their diapers and bellyaching because they don't want to fight." Johnson's successor, Richard M. Nixon, agreed that student protesters opposed the Vietnam War not out of "moral conviction" but, rather, "to keep from getting their asses shot off." Nixon further vowed that "under no circumstances will I be affected whatever" by campus dissent. Despite their contentions to the contrary, the two American presidents who presided over America's longest and most unpopular war monitored student protests carefully. What they observed and struggled to counter was easily the most widespread student activism and protest in American history—an activism that was motivated by far more than immediate self-interest and that helped keep the agony of the war before the public, challenge the morality of U.S. actions, constrain executive policy options, and erode national support for the conflict. This final influence resulted not from general public support for the young dissenters, who actually elicited a distinctly negative response from the broader American public, but, rather, from the student contribution to a general national distress and anxiety. This national mood helped convince many Americans of the validity of the basic antiwar message that U.S. intervention was not in the national interest and that losing did not entail irreparable harm to the nation or its security.[1]

Students at the University of Nevada, Las Vegas, express a common antiwar message. Courtesy of Special Collections, Lied Library, University of Nevada, Las Vegas.

Ironically, few educators or public officials foresaw this often-explosive activism from 1960s and early 1970s students. As the decade began, Clark Kerr, the president of the University of California, predicted: "Employers will love this generation [of students]. . . . They aren't going to press many grievances. They are going to be easy to handle. There aren't going to be any riots." While running for president in 1964, Johnson prodded college-age Americans to become more involved. LBJ rejected the "tags often applied to your age group, the 'quiet generation,' the 'apathetic generation,' the 'cool cookies'" or the perception that these young people were "interested only in sports cars, a split-level [house], and an annuity." Instead, he thought that college students seemed "ready and eager to take on the tasks which call for a real personal sacrifice. This country needs those virtues. We need your boundless energy." Kerr was simply wrong. Johnson was right about the students' boundless energy and willingness to make personal sacrifices; to his chagrin, they expended much of that energy lambasting his Vietnam policies.[2]

Student opposition to the war arose against the backdrop of dramatic changes in American higher education and a more general inclination of young people to question authority. As the "baby boomers," or the generation born near the end of World War II, came of age, the number of college-age students literally exploded. Between 1960 and 1972, 45 million Americans turned eighteen; and, during the 1960s, the number of college students ballooned from 16 to 25 million. In response to this influx of students, the number and size of colleges and universities grew accordingly. Prior to World War II, no American university exceeded fifteen thousand students; by the 1960s, at least fifty universities had grown beyond that figure. Eight exceeded thirty thousand, and the University of Minnesota topped forty thousand. Both the vast increase in the number of students and their greater concentration at the "megaversities" created the environment for a youth culture distinguished by its music, dress, and attitudes toward drug use and sexual relations. The boomers came to question their elders on a broad array of issues ranging from the length of one's hair to economic injustice, civil rights, and U.S. foreign policy. In addition to fostering a youth culture, larger universities often spawned a stultifying bureaucracy and far too many large, boring classes (one at the University of Minnesota incarcerated two thousand students) that left students alienated and restless.

Having gone to college at least in part to escape their parents' control, the boomers also resented university-imposed restrictions on their personal behavior. Acting in loco parentis, various universities imposed curfews on men and especially on women, dictated that a man and a woman together in a dormitory lounge keep three of their four feet on the floor at all times, and prohibited kissing good night while leaning against a building (to prevent potential "bumping and grinding"). At church-affiliated schools, small colleges, and many Southern universities, rules were even more restrictive, calling for obligatory chapel attendance and, in extreme cases, regulating the length of men's sideburns, requiring that women wear bras, and outlawing jeans, shorts, and T-shirts—even for men. Sex, dress, and church attendance were not the only areas of concern. In Tallahassee in the early 1960s, white students at Florida State University and black students at Florida A&M University could not visit one another without written permission. Students grew more frustrated when their challenges to bureaucratic anonymity; a stultifying, seemingly irrelevant curriculum; or juvenile, personal restrictions elicited the response that they had no valid role in establishing university policies or governance.

These grievances, when combined with issues of race and the civil rights movement and especially the war, produced unprecedented student activism. Despite this fundamental change in the level of student involvement, protesters were always a minority on every issue and on every campus, even at the most boisterous and elite private universities in the Northeast or large public schools in the Midwest and West. By the end of the 1960s, only 20 percent of students polled professed to have taken part in even one antiwar demonstration. The majority of students were apathetic, supportive of the war, or simply too busy working and balancing their family obligations while attending urban, commuter schools or community colleges to have time for antiwar protests.

Antiwar students were more likely to have been from middle- or upper-middle-class than from working- or lower-middle-class households; to have been majoring in the humanities or social sciences than in business, engineering, or the sciences; and to have been political independents or Democrats than Republicans. Most antiwar students were liberal or moderate politically rather than conservative or radical, and they viewed U.S. intervention in Vietnam as a correctable foreign policy

University of Nevada, Las Vegas, students protest U.S. involvement in Vietnam in 1970. Courtesy of Special Collections, Lied Library, University of Nevada, Las Vegas.

mistake rather than the result of a irreparably flawed capitalistic system that should be overthrown. Few protesters belonged to an official or national antiwar organization since most dissident activity was essentially local in its origins and organization.[3]

Students for a Democratic Society (SDS), which was founded in 1960 and constituted the most active and visible national "New Left" group, claimed a membership of only 100,000 by the end of the 1960s, when it broke apart over internal squabbles. To be sure, SDS members played prominent roles in numerous important protests during the decade, but few of these events resulted from any true central strategy or direction. Moreover, Young Americans for Freedom, the principal, national conservative group, also founded in 1960, enrolled at least fifty thousand students by 1970, and some historians assert that its membership surpassed that of SDS. Even if that were true, the membership of neither group represented a significant percentage of 1960s students.

Diverse motives prompted the activist minority to oppose the war. Presidents Johnson and Nixon were correct in asserting that antiwar sentiment derived in part from the male students' desire to avoid combat. Beginning in 1966 the Johnson administration opted to draft undergraduate men whose grade point average fell below a C and the next year ended deferments for graduate students. These changes made the prospect of serving in Vietnam all too real for these students and their families. More ephemeral, social attractions brought other students to antiwar rallies. An often-repeated boomer recollection held, "Protesting was a great place to get laid, get high, and listen to some great rock."[4]

Self-preservation and more trivial social concerns hardly exhausted the bases for student opposition to the war. As one University of South Florida activist declared, "Some people were there just for the drugs and good times, but the people I knew were really not. We were committed to higher ideals." In the most general sense, antiwar students challenged the nation to live up to its professed and highest ideals, and these young people believed optimistically in the possibility of positive changes, whether in the realm of foreign policy, race relations, or women's rights. Students were more inclined than the general population to object to the war on moral grounds, to express concern over the loss of both Vietnamese and American lives, and to decry the destructive impact of the U.S. military presence in Southeast Asia. For these young people, the path to activism had involved both an emotional and an intellectual transformation, and the latter had often come after reading and attending lectures, discussions, and teach-ins. Many acted, according to one Iowa student who protested and risked arrest, to demonstrate "personal commitment to the cause." One Iowa coed recalled her participation in a campus sit-in as a "small thing, nearly insignificant, but symbolic." Later, she picketed the local draft board to express that she was "not going to support a government that goes around killing its students. . . . Being at the draft board was a time for me to say, 'No. This has to stop.'" Other students believed that the war diverted attention and resources from pressing domestic needs. A Tennessee man observed, "You couldn't fight poverty, you couldn't fight racism . . . 'cause everything was being poured into—emotionally, fiscally—everything was being poured into this damn war over in Vietnam." Others were convinced that U.S. involvement in Vietnam was simply bad policy. A North Carolina student declared, "We had no business in Vietnam. We had no national interest, we had no interest as working people. It was an unconstitutional war, it was an undeclared war, it was undemocratically decided, and it only benefited the rich folks—the war machine, the military-industrial complex."[5]

While subscribing to most of these same sentiments, Vietnam veterans added an especially powerful voice to the antiwar chorus. The leaders of the University of Georgia's Vietnam Veterans against the War chapter declared, "Although we have been honorably discharged from active duty in Southeast Asia, we have voluntarily enlisted ourselves in the United States to end the war and to see that all Americans are brought home where they may join us in working for a just and peaceful world." Later, they urged fellow students to attend a rally in Atlanta to highlight the "suffering of the Indochinese people," the "plight of our brothers in uniform," and the misery of "American POWs."[6]

The police and FBI surveillance of protesters and the abuse those protesters often endured further revealed both the reality of their minority status and the seriousness of their commitment. Covert police and FBI agents frequently monitored and infiltrated antiwar groups. Undercover cops were present on at least sixteen of the campuses with the most significant unrest in 1969—ranging from the University of California, Berkeley, and Harvard University to the University of Minnesota and Kent State University. The administration at Pennsylvania State University cooperated actively with the fourteen FBI agents assigned to the campus and organized its own surveillance squad of two hundred conservative students. When Kent State SDS members ran out of money and canceled their phone service in 1969, the FBI quickly paid the bill since it had tapped the students' phone. Not even the completely nonviolent and calm commuter campus of nine thousand at Louisiana State University in New Orleans (now the University of New Orleans) escaped the FBI's attention. In 1970, the agency recruited a student informant and provocateur who attempted unsuccessfully to incite a violent demonstration.

Nor were student protesters necessarily well received by their families or fellow students. To join the Southern Student Organizing Committee (SSOC), the principal antiwar and civil rights organization for white students in the South, "required great courage," according to the historian Gregg L. Michel. "SSOC students faced the sobering reality that their actions could lead to loss of friends, condemnation and rejection by one's family, and expulsion from school." Jeff Shero, an SDS organizer at the University of Texas, explained that joining SDS in Texas meant "breaking

with your family, it meant being cut off—it was like in early Rome joining a Christian sect. . . . If you were from Texas, in SDS, you were a bad
motherfucker, you couldn't go home for Christmas. . . . In most of those
places it meant, '*You Goddamn Communist*.'"[7]

Conflict was not confined to clashes with parents. The twenty-three
University of Virginia students who conducted the school's first antiwar
demonstration in February 1966 braved both the expletives of and a volley
of snowballs from a three-hundred-strong contingent of war supporters.
Three years later, SSOC students on a "peace tour" to southern campuses
encountered a pistol-wielding opponent at Erskine College in South Carolina. Such experiences extended beyond the comparatively conservative
South. A Penn State coed regularly received signed death threats. In 1967,
pro-ROTC students at Kansas State University bombarded protesters with
eggs and manure from nearby campus barns. In response to Kent State's
first antiwar protest in February 1965, more than one hundred hawkish
students hurled apples and oranges at embattled opponents, seized their
placards, and kicked one young woman in the face. Three years later,
little had changed. In April 1968, seven hundred conservative students,
some armed with chains and baseball bats, assaulted approximately two
hundred Kent State antiwar demonstrators. Incidents such as these and
subsequent clashes with police and national guard units that infringed
on protesters' freedom of speech and assembly helped enlist additional
dissidents and incited others to become more radical and violent. These
episodes also demonstrated graphically that opposing the war on college
campuses frequently fell far short of being a uniformly popular or glam-
orous experience.

Prompted by these diverse motives, students initiated sustained opposition to the war in 1965. Although students at the University of California,
Berkeley, had organized rallies denouncing the war early in the new year,
national protests arose in response to the Johnson administration's initia-
tion of continuous bombing of North Vietnam in February and March.
These protests took the form of university teach-ins devoted to discussing
and understanding the war and seeking ways to end U.S. involvement.
Organized by antiwar faculty, the first of these sessions at the University
of Michigan attracted an audience of nearly three thousand over the night
of March 24–25. This strategy quickly spread to more than one hundred
campuses, and the sessions stretched into the fall. Three thousand gath-

ered at the University of Oregon, fifteen hundred at the State University of New York at Buffalo, one thousand at Emory University (in one of the South's first protests), and twenty thousand at Berkeley in the largest and longest of the teach-ins. Although the teach-ins signaled the start of student dissent directed at the war, protesters were greatly outnumbered by supporters of U.S. involvement. In response to the teach-in at the University of Wisconsin at Madison, more than six thousand students signed a petition backing LBJ's policies. Prowar students decisively held sway with a similar petition at Yale University, and a subsequent poll revealed that 75 percent of the students at the University of Wisconsin at Madison backed President Johnson. Indeed, as late as 1967, only 35 percent of students nationally declared themselves doves opposed to the war.

Over the next two years, antiwar students adopted far more aggressive tactics. Indeed, their hostility toward the top Johnson and, eventually, Nixon administration leaders prevented key U.S. officials from visiting college campuses. Secretary of Defense Robert S. McNamara's trip to Harvard in November 1966 provided a telling example. Having taught at Harvard Business School in the 1940s, McNamara agreed to meet privately with a small group of the elite university's students; but, as he left the meeting, a much less friendly crowd surrounded and began rocking his car and demanded that he answer questions about the war. Fearing physical attack, the secretary agreed and braved what he considered a most disrespectful mob, many of whom screamed "bullshit" in response to his every assertion. The following year, Vice President Hubert H. Humphrey endured a similar reception at Stanford University, and Secretary of State Dean Rusk was booed off the stage at Indiana University. President Johnson ruefully discovered that virtually any appearance before a crowd from which students had not been excluded brought taunts and placards asking, "HEY, HEY, LBJ, HOW MANY KIDS DID YOU KILL TODAY"? While still a presidential candidate in October 1968, Nixon was dogged by equally belligerent protesters chanting, "Ho, Ho, Ho Chi Minh, Ho Chi Minh is gonna win." On becoming president, Nixon declared that he was "not going to end up like LBJ, holed up in the White House afraid to show my face on the street." But that was exactly what happened. As students declared "DICK . . . a four-letter word," the president canceled a scheduled speech at Ohio State University in 1969 and chose not to attend his daughter's graduation from Smith College the following year.[8]

In addition to besieging national leaders, antiwar students sought to sever what they considered university connections to the war machine. They objected to university cooperation with the draft system, to the ROTC presence on campuses, to Dow Chemical Company (the manufacturer of napalm) recruiting new employees at universities, and to defense-related research at their institutions. Dissidents at the University of Chicago in May 1966 conducted a futile two-day sit-in denouncing the school's practice of providing the Selective Service System with student grades and class standing, and widespread demonstrations continued against the draft until its conversion to a lottery system in the fall of 1969. Other students chose the more extreme route of publicly burning their draft cards or simply refusing induction, both of which aroused the indignation of conservative politicians and large segments of the general public. Nearly 210,000 men were accused of draft-related offenses, and over 25,000 were indicted. At least 30,000 young people left the country and went into exile, primarily in Canada, Sweden, and Mexico. Far greater numbers "avoided" the draft by staying in school, by joining the national guard or the reserves, or by exploiting ambiguities or loopholes in the draft law. Draft counseling centers were established in virtually every university town and major city, and most counselors maintained a success rate of 90 percent in steering their clients safely through the Selective Service System maze.

Antiwar students also objected to the ROTC, and attempts to rid campuses of military training ranged from boycotting mandatory ROTC classes at the University of Mississippi to firebombing buildings across the country. Beginning in 1966, protesters ditched classes in Oxford, Mississippi, picketed ROTC functions such as a final review ceremony at Columbia University, and ran through the ranks and heckled the cadets as they conducted drills at the University of Virginia. Antiwar students at Furman University, a small Baptist school in South Carolina, organized the Furman University Corps of Kazoos, or "F.U.C.K.," to lampoon an ROTC parade and visiting military officials. Antiwar students at Florida State University held "antimilitary balls" to mock the ROTC's traditional military dances. After women checked their bras at the door for the 1971 event, they and their escorts elected a king and queen of the ball and were treated to antiwar films and Tweety Bird cartoons. As the war ground on and student frustrations mounted, a more violent minority of protesters sought to destroy ROTC buildings. During 1969–70, at the height of student protests, 197 ROTC buildings were attacked. In October 1969, protesters at SUNY-Buffalo invaded the air force ROTC offices, broke the windows, destroyed office equipment, and burned files. ROTC quarters were firebombed at Berkeley, the University of Washington, and the University of Delaware, the air force ROTC building at the University of Kentucky was burned to the ground, and attempts to burn ROTC buildings at the University of Virginia and the University of Georgia (twice) failed.[9]

Student opposition to defense-related activities extended to efforts of the CIA and Dow to recruit new employees from university student bodies. Dow elicited the intense ire of antiwar students by producing and selling napalm, the jellied gasoline that the United States dropped from planes on its enemies (and nearby civilians) in Vietnam. Here again, picketing and efforts to disrupt recruiting occurred nationwide. By the end of 1967, Dow recruiters had faced nearly five hundred hostile receptions, often at otherwise quiet campuses. For example, at conservative Iowa State University, frequently dubbed "Moo U" because of its founding as the Iowa Agricultural College, a Dow action was one of three small demonstrations before 1970. UCLA students carried signs that decried "MAKING MONEY BURNING BABIES," and protesters at numerous schools distributed flyers urging "DOW SHALL NOT KILL." The most dramatic of the anti-Dow actions took place at the University of Wisconsin in October 1967, when three hundred students barricaded the doors to the job-recruiting area. Madison city police dressed in riot gear battered the students and dragged them out of the building, where an angry crowd of several thousand had gathered. Reinforced by additional police and dogs and using tear gas and mace, the police dispersed the students, some of whom responded by throwing rocks and bottles. Three police and sixty-five students were injured, and, after a two-day student strike, Dow was temporarily banned from the campus. Although these nonuniversity police had overreacted and tear gas had been used for the first time on a college campus, a Wisconsin state assemblyman voiced the growing sentiment of many Americans toward student protesters: "Shoot them if necessary. I would. . . . It's insurrection."[10]

Student efforts to separate their universities from the war effort also encompassed campaigns to curb defense-related research sponsored by the federal government. This government-university relationship involved huge sums of money and was integral to the expansion of American higher education during the Cold War. At the height of the Vietnam conflict in 1968, universities devoted $3 billion to research and development. Washington-sponsored projects accounted for 70 percent of this figure, and 50 percent of the federal dollars were defense related. This translated into one-third of overall university research spending and amounted to 80 percent of the Massachusetts Institute of Technology's budget in 1969 and 43 percent of the budget at the University of Michigan. Most of this federal spending fell under the program designated Project Themis.

Campus dissidents regularly demanded that this highly profitable relationship be ended, and on occasion they resorted to violence to make their point. In March 1969, several hundred students destroyed building materials at a Themis construction site on the SUNY-Buffalo campus. The bombing of the University of Wisconsin's Army Mathematics Research Center in August 1971 proved far more tragic. Led by Karlton Armstrong, a former student, and his brother, Dwight, militants exploded a van loaded with a ton of explosives next to the six-story building. The explosion gutted the structure and killed a postdoctoral student doing research.

Armstrong's effort to "bring the war home" by making a "dent in the war machine," less tragic attacks on Themis facilities or ROTC buildings, and numerous more peaceful demonstrations failed to force university administrators to stop funneling grades to draft boards, banish the ROTC from campuses, or end the lucrative research projects. But the violence had a profound impact on national public opinion. Actual bombings on college campuses were the clear exception. During the war, only 10 percent of the nation's twenty-five hundred colleges and universities experienced violent protests. Still, when combined with mysterious events such as the burning of the Nichols Gymnasium at Kansas State University in December 1968 or the highly visible and violent clashes of students with police at Columbia University in April 1968, in the streets of Chicago in August 1968 during the Democratic National Convention, and at San Francisco State University in 1968–69, such incidents left older Americans shocked and fearful that the nation's political and social fabric was being ripped apart.[11]

Much of this public distress resulted from the media's portrayal of antiwar students and their actions. Although media attention to the antiwar movement was crucial to the protesters' impact on the thinking of presidents Johnson and Nixon and, thereby, on American policy, the reporters devoted far more scrutiny to the exceptional incidents of violence than to the other 90 percent of the peaceful, more sedate demonstrations. Adult America's discomfort with antiwar students intensified in 1967 and after when the media and public tended to associate these dissidents with "hippies" or those, young and sometimes not so young, who rejected mainstream, suburban values and opted instead for a counterculture. Although quite diverse in outlook, the hippies were most often identified with sex, drugs, and rock and roll. The "summer of love" in San Francisco's Haight-Ashbury district brought hippies and their long hair, sandals, jeans, and proclivity for pot and free love to national attention. When many college students and protesters adopted the hair style and clothes, if not always the drugs and sexual promiscuity, middle America was horrified. College students seemed to have lost respect for proper politics, morality, society, and decorum. All such affronts to consensus culture and the nation's Cold War foreign policy and defense establishment were seemingly put on display by the shaggy student contingent that participated in the march on the Pentagon on October 21–22, 1967. Some carried signs proclaiming "LBJ SUCKS," others demanded that "LBJ PULL OUT LIKE YOUR FATHER SHOULD HAVE DONE," and a few thousand participated in the sit-in at the Pentagon, only to be brutally removed by troops from the Eighty-Second Airborne Division. Long hair, profanity, violence, and opposition to the war effort all received particular emphasis in the media and incited disgust and fear among older and more conservative Americans.[12]

Student activism continued during 1968, termed appropriately by one historian as "a very bad year." On many levels, it certainly was—the Rev. Martin Luther King Jr. and Robert F. Kennedy were assassinated; Washington, DC, experienced a major race riot; student dissidents occupied five buildings for seven days at Columbia University, primarily protesting issues other than the war, and were violently expelled by the New York City police; and protesters, including five thousand young people, battled police and national guard troops in the streets of Chicago in late August during the Democratic National Convention. As these events reinforced the sense of national crisis, students sustained a variety of protests. Thousands trooped to New Hampshire, where they shaved their beards and changed out of miniskirts to campaign for Senator Eugene McCarthy in the Democratic presidential primary. The "clean for Gene" brigade helped

Police club a student protestor in Austin, Texas. Courtesy of the Vietnam Archive, Texas Tech University, Terry J. Dubose Collection.

the colorless candidate and his one-issue campaign in opposition to the war to a near victory over President Johnson. Later, on April 26, a million college and high school students and faculty boycotted classes to demonstrate their opposition to the U.S. role in Southeast Asia. In total, over the spring semester, some forty thousand students participated in more than two hundred other demonstrations on one hundred campuses. Still, opponents of the war remained a distinct minority. A survey of 859 colleges at year's end found that almost two-thirds reported no antiwar demonstrations and that only 2 percent had experienced protests involving more than 10 percent of their students.[13]

Over the next year, majority student opinion changed, and many more undergraduates protested against the war. By the end of 1969, 69 percent of students declared themselves doves, and students nationally were active participants in the October and November moratoriums denouncing the war. This overall trend occurred as student activism and violence increased markedly. During spring 1969, nearly four hundred protests disrupted college campuses. Vietnam continued to stimulate student unrest, but objections to the lack of student rights and independence and racial tensions prompted the clear majority of these incidents. Student arrests, which totaled four thousand for the 1968–69 school year and nearly eight thousand for 1969–70, reflected this heightened campus unrest. As had been the case the previous spring at Columbia, three high-profile clashes that had little relation to the war intensified public hostility toward student protesters irrespective of the issue in question. At San Francisco State, a strike begun in December by black students demanding a black studies department continued for 134 school days and resulted in the arrest of seven hundred students, supportive faculty, and community activists. In April, one hundred black students seized the student union at Cornell University. Thirty-six hours later, after gaining assurances regarding the continuation of an African American center and curriculum, they marched from the building brandishing shotguns and rifles. The next month, several thousand students, community activists, and hippies clashed with the Berkeley police over access to a "people's park" on the edge of campus. The crowd threw rocks and bottles; the police fired their shotguns. Twenty police officers were injured, thirty protesters were shot, and one student died. The next day, the national guard, acting on Governor Ronald Reagan's orders, cleared all remaining protesters from the park by spraying them with tear gas from helicopters. Incidents such as these caused many Americans to fear a possible war at home as well as in Vietnam. Eighty percent of respondents to a Gallup poll favored expelling student protesters, and more than 50 percent opposed even peaceful campus demonstrations.

Ironically, even as public hostility toward student protesters mounted, the students' most significant opposition to the war in 1969 took far more conventional forms. In April, 253 student body presidents and student newspaper editors signed and sent a "Declaration of Conscience" to President Nixon. Representing colleges and universities from thirty-eight states, Puerto Rico, and the District of Columbia, these "campus leaders" characterized the war as "immoral and unjust" and expressed their "intention to refuse induction and to aid" others with similar intentions. Students also participated actively in what had become the annual Easter Sunday demonstrations against the war, which attracted more than 150,000 participants in cities across the country.[14]

These peaceful actions were merely a prelude to the Vietnam Moratorium Day on October 15, 1969. Even as the "Declaration of Conscience" was being presented to the Nixon administration, Sam Brown and David Hawk, who had worked on the McCarthy campaign and conceived of the declaration, were devising a far more significant antiwar protest. In decided contrast to the attacks on ROTC buildings or clashes with university administrators and police, they envisioned a day during which people stopped their regular activities—declared a moratorium—to express opposition to the war. By early fall, Brown, Hawk, and other veterans of the McCarthy campaign had established organizations on at least three hundred campuses when the idea "caught on like wildfire" and spread to schools across the nation. Even more important, what "began as a day of student protest spilled out into the adult community." Described as the "largest public protest" in the nation's history and the "single most important one day demonstration of the entire war," the moratorium included at least 2 million participants. Moratorium activities, marked primarily by a "spirit of sadness and loss," included silent vigils, the planting of memorial flowers and trees, quiet prayers, speakers and discussions, and disciplined marches and demonstrations. The tone harkened back to the teach-ins of 1965.[15]

Referring to the rock music festival in upstate New York earlier that summer, *Time* characterized this unprecedented national event as a "sedate Woodstock Festival of Peace," and college students participated in ways much like the rest of the nation. Now eighty-nine years old, Jeanette Rankin, who was the first woman elected to the U.S. House of Representative and who had voted against U.S. entry into both World War I and World War II, spoke to a massive audience at the University of Georgia. Eight thousand Cornell students listened to a speech by Senator Charles Goodell; five thousand University of Minnesota students marched with five thousand community members to protest at the federal building; seventy-five hundred marched from the campus to the state capitol in Austin, Texas; twenty-five hundred attended a solemn convocation at Iowa State University; following an all-night prayer vigil, forty-four Louisiana State University undergraduates implanted white crosses on the campus "drill field" symbolizing the forty-four thousand U.S. war deaths; twelve hundred University of Louisville students joined with the university president in planning a "peace tree"; undergraduates at Bethel College in Kansas rang the campus bell every four seconds for six days to honor each American soldier killed in Vietnam; and students from all over the country signed antiwar petitions and wrote letters to their senators and congressmen.[16]

Much to the consternation of antiwar activists on and off college campuses, President Nixon effectively countered the moratorium and the subsequent 500,000-person demonstration in Washington in mid-November. On November 3, he deftly appealed to the "great silent majority" of Americans to stand with him against the minority of protesters and troublemakers who endangered the nation's "future as a free society." Playing on and reinforcing the general public's hostility toward the protesters, Nixon declared, "North Vietnam cannot defeat or humiliate the United States." Only unpatriotic, disloyal "Americans" who opposed his war policies could "do that." When the president's efforts were combined with the vitriolic attacks on students and other dissenters by Vice President Spiro Agnew and other defenders of the war, the administration's intimidation of the press, and declining numbers of Americans serving and dying in Vietnam, Nixon had seemingly won the battle for public opinion by early 1970. Many protesters were exhausted and frustrated after years of dissent. Vietnamization, or the turning of the ground war over to the South Vietnamese, had reduced the number of Americans serving and dying; and the draft lottery, which was initiated in December 1969, made men subject to the draft for only one year and ostensibly ended favoritism based on income, education, or race. All these developments had defused student opposition to the war.[17]

Nixon then squandered his seeming public relations coup by dispatching U.S. troops into Cambodia and provoking "easily the most massive and shattering protest in the history of American higher education." Outraged that the president appeared to be expanding rather than contracting the war, as he had promised, students lashed out following his nationally televised announcement of his decision on April 30 and his disparaging reference the next morning to "bums" who were "blowing up the campuses." As eleven Northeastern student editors called for a national student strike, walkouts spontaneously erupted at numerous campuses, including Columbia, Princeton, the University of Virginia, and Brandeis. Violence flared at Stanford, the University of Maryland, Michigan State, and Wisconsin. At Ohio State, a national guard trooper shot a student, and at Kent State, the ROTC building was burned and sixty-nine students arrested. The following day, May 4, nervous and exhausted Ohio national guardsmen fired on Kent State students (some demonstrators who had hurled bricks and insults and others who were just on their way to class). Nine were wounded and four killed. Once again, Nixon intensified student indignation by declaring that the events at Kent State "should remind us all . . . that when dissent turns to violence, it invites tragedy."[18]

Nine days later, partly in response to the invasion of Cambodia and the shootings at Kent State, a group of about three hundred students at Jackson State College, an all-black school in Mississippi, threw rocks at passing cars and attempted to burn the ROTC quarters. When unrest resumed the next night, May 14, state police fired on the students. Three hundred rounds hit a dormitory, twelve students were wounded, and two young women inside the dorm were killed. The deaths at Jackson State received far less attention than those at Kent State, but the young women's fate said much about the temper of the times and further stimulated national protests.

Following the deaths at Kent State, student opposition to the war rose to its crescendo. More than 2 million students demonstrated, and approximately 450 colleges and universities experienced strikes or closures. Governor Ronald Reagan closed the University of California campuses for five days, and the University of Pennsylvania system shut down for the remainder of the school year. Student "frustration" and the "volatile, angry crowd" stunned a Florida State University protester, and the FSU chancellor voiced a national perception that university presidents had "never seen students so angry." Students damaged ROTC buildings at more than thirty schools, and governors in sixteen states called out the national guard to protect campuses. Violent outbursts at Berkeley or the University of Wisconsin were perhaps predictable, but attacks on ROTC buildings at the University of Virginia or Central Michigan were more surprising. Students at the University of South Carolina occupied two buildings, destroyed files, and battled with the national guard and state police. Two thousand SUNY-Buffalo students blocked traffic and broke local bank windows. In far less contentious demonstrations, three to four thousand University of Georgia students rallied in protest; students joined townspeople in a crowd estimated at between three and seven thousand to march to the state house in Iowa City to listen to an address by the U.S. senator Harold E. Hughes; nearly twenty thousand University of Texas

HAWKS COME AND THEY GO
BUT DOVES
STAY ON YOU KNOW

THANKS SHOULD BE EXTENDED TO
SPIRO T. AGNEW
——THE END——

The students' final word in their 1970 yearbook, *The Epilogue,* at the University of Nevada, Las Vegas. Courtesy of Special Collections, Lied Library, University of Nevada, Las Vegas.

students again trooped from the campus through downtown Austin; and students made up the bulk of a 130,000-strong march in Washington on May 9.[19]

As had been the case since the first student protests in 1965, general public response to the anti-Cambodia and –Kent State protests was decidedly negative. In a June 1970 Gallup poll, 82 percent of Americans consulted disapproved of "college students going on strike as a way to protest the way things are run in this country." Construction workers in New York City expressed this disapproval more directly on May 8 by attacking several hundred student demonstrators on Wall Street. Shouting, "Kill the Commie bastards," the blue-collar workers injured seventy of the marchers. Ironically, the workers, like much of the nation, were coming to agree with much of the antiwar message despite their contempt for the young protesters, whom they considered arrogant and disrespectful. One worker expressed this simultaneous frustration with the war and dislike for the financially better-off students and their criticisms of the nation and its foreign policy: "I think we ought to win that war or pull out. What the hell else should we do—sit and bleed ourselves to death, year after year?" But he continued: "I hate those peace demonstrators. Why don't they go to Vietnam and demonstrate in front of the North Vietnamese? . . . The whole thing is a mess. The sooner we get the hell out of there the better."[20]

The unprecedented demonstrations in response to the invasion of Cambodia and the deaths at Kent State and Jackson State marked the apogee of student opposition to the war. Two years later, in the spring of 1972, student protesters opposing Nixon's decision to mine Haiphong Harbor prompted governors to declare a state of emergency at the University of New Mexico and to activate the national guard at the University of Minnesota. But these incidents had become the exception rather than the rule. Exhausted and disillusioned, many student activists concluded by the early 1970s that they could not influence President Nixon. Others deemed the lottery more equitable than the previous draft and, therefore, less objectionable. Nixon's Vietnamization program, which steadily reduced the number of Americans serving and dying in Southeast Asia, also eased student dissatisfaction. The downturn in the economy in the early 1970s reinforced these war-related influences by focusing students' attention on finding jobs and starting careers. But, perhaps most important, as the historian Terry Anderson has aptly observed, "such activism was no longer necessary [by 1971]. The call for peace, which a majority considered unpatriotic as late as 1968, now was patriotic." President Nixon repeatedly proclaimed his desire for peace as he implemented Vietnamization, and national majorities had come to consider U.S. intervention in Vietnam a mistake and to favor withdrawal.[21]

The nation's ultimate adoption of the antiwar students' message to leave the war while loathing the messengers embodies the difficulty of assessing the young protesters' influence. They were termed correctly the "footsoldiers" of the antiwar movement: "far more college students actively protested the war than any other single group." Their sheer numbers and presence were critical to demonstrations on and off campuses. Neither this presence nor their actions and arguments immediately convinced the majority of their fellow students or nonstudent America to oppose the war. But student protesters did help keep this tragic war in the public eye, challenge the morality of U.S. intervention and actions, and heighten "a general perception of national malaise and crisis that made ending the war even more urgent."[22]

Although these facets of student influence were at best indirect, the young activists had a more discernible impact on presidents Johnson and Nixon and other elite policymakers. Despite their denials, both presidents were deeply troubled by the student opposition, which, together with the larger antiwar movement, constituted an ongoing restraint on executive freedom of action. Both presidents ruefully discovered that major escalations, such as the beginning of sustained bombing in 1965 or the invasion of Cambodia in 1970, were met with massive student opposition. Moreover, the children of policymakers within both administrations and other influential members of the "establishment" often attended the elite private schools or major state universities where student opposition to the war was most intense. These students frequently adopted antiwar positions. For example, the sons of both Secretary of Defense McNamara and Secretary of State Rusk and the children of several Nixon White House staffers demonstrated against the war. According to one member of the State Department, "*All* of us . . . had sons or daughters who were involved in this. . . . All of us were torn in our own family lives." If these officials and other important people in business, the media, and education were not converted to an antiwar stance, they certainly were exposed to passionate antiwar arguments and were very worried that many of their children had become so alienated from the government during wartime. This in turn reinforced the sense that the need to alleviate the war's domestic ramifications outweighed the foreign policy arguments for involvement.[23]

Ironically, even as student protests helped extricate the United States from the Vietnam War, they also helped spawn the "backlash politics" that aided the Republican Party and contributed to the election of Richard Nixon as president in 1968. In the wake of three years of student demonstrations and urban rioting, respondents to a Gallup poll in early 1968 cited "crime and lawlessness" as the principal domestic problem and just behind Vietnam as the nation's most troubling issue. After appealing successfully to the public desire for "law and order" in the presidential election, Nixon subsequently sought, with some success, to divert attention from the war itself by focusing on domestic dissent. Although the contention that this ploy enabled him to prolong the war is problematic, his campaign tactics and domestic political strategy, his election in 1968, and his reelection in 1972 do illustrate the complexity of the antiwar students' impact.[24]

While this complexity should be recognized, it should also be remembered that the Vietnam War had provoked the most massive protests in American history. Although always a minority on college and university campuses and the proponents of an unpopular message that often elicited ridicule or outright physical attacks by prowar peers and conservative political figures, these young people summoned the courage to challenge their elders and to question America's most tragic Cold War military intervention abroad. Most important, they were correct in proclaiming that the nation would be best served by ending its misguided involvement in Vietnam, a conclusion that national leaders, ostensible foreign policy experts, and the general public only belatedly accepted.

Notes

1. Walter LaFeber, "Johnson, Vietnam, and Toqueville," in *Lyndon Johnson Confronts the World: American Foreign Policy, 1963–1968,* ed. Warren I. Cohen and Nancy Bernkopf Tucker (New York: Cambridge University Press, 1994), 50; Melvin Small, *Antiwarriors: The Vietnam War and the Battle for America's Hearts and Minds* (Wilmington, DE: Scholarly Resources, 2002), 102; Nancy Zaroulis and Gerald Sullivan, *Who Spoke Up? American Protest against the War in Vietnam* (Garden City, NY: Doubleday, 1984), 33–34.

2. Terry H. Anderson, *The Movement and the Sixties: Protest in America from Greensboro to Wounded Knee* (New York: Oxford University Press, 1995), 39; Walter LaFeber, *The Deadly Bet: LBJ, Vietnam, and the 1968 Election* (Lanham, MD: Rowman & Littlefield, 2005), 33–34.

3. This family background for protesters was consistent with the composition of university and college student bodies, since only 17 percent of students were from working- or lower-middle-class homes. For these materials on student numbers and characteristics and subsequent information on the university–Department of Defense relations, see esp. Kenneth J. Heineman, *Campus Wars: The Peace Movement at American State Universities in the Vietnam Era* (New York: New York University Press, 1993), and *Put Your Bodies upon the Wheels: Student Revolt in the 1960s* (Chicago: Dee, 2001).

4. Myra MacPherson, *Long Time Passing: Vietnam and the Haunted Generation* (Garden City, NY: Doubleday, 1984), 39.

5. Todd V. Scofield, "History and a Slice of Social Justice: The Anti–Vietnam War Movement in Tampa and USF: 1965–1970" (M.A. thesis, University of South Florida, 1988), 18; Clyde Brown and Gayle K. Pluta Brown, "Moo U and the Cambodian Invasion: Nonviolent Anti-War Protest at Iowa State University," in *The Vietnam War on Campus: Other Voices, More Distant Drums,* ed. Marc Jason Gilbert (Westport,

CT: Praeger, 2001), 134; Gregg L. Michel, *Struggle for a Better South: The Southern Student Organizing Committee, 1964–1969* (New York: Palgrave Macmillan, 2004), 110, and "'We'll Take Our Stand': The Southern Student Organizing Committee and the Radicalization of White Southern Students, 1964–1969" (Ph.D. diss., University of Virginia, 1999), 415.

6. *Red and Black* (University of Georgia student newspaper), November 2, 19, 1971.

7. Michel, *Struggle for a Better South*, 3; Heineman, *Campus Wars*, 82.

8. Melvin Small, *The Presidency of Richard Nixon* (Lawrence: University Press of Kansas, 1999), 67; Stephen Eugene Parr, "The Forgotten Radicals: The New Left in the Deep South, Florida State University, 1960–1972" (Ph.D. diss., Florida State University, 2000), 306.

9. Michel, "'We'll Take Our Stand,'" 480.

10. Anderson, *The Movement and the Sixties*, 177–78.

11. Ibid., 367.

12. Melvin Small, *Covering Dissent: The Media and the Anti-Vietnam War Movement* (New Brunswick, NJ: Rutgers University Press, 1994), 82.

13. Mark Hamilton Lytle, *America's Uncivil Wars: The Sixties Era from Elvis to the Fall of Richard Nixon* (New York: Oxford University Press, 2006), 217.

14. Zaroulis and Sullivan, *Who Spoke Up?* 243–44.

15. Ibid., 265, 269; Melvin Small, *Johnson, Nixon, and the Doves* (New Brunswick, NJ: Rutgers University Press, 1988), 183; Charles DeBenedetti and Charles Chatfield, *An American Ordeal: The Antiwar Movement of the Vietnam Era* (Syracuse, NY: Syracuse University Press, 1990), 255.

16. Small, *Antiwarriors*, 111; *Red and Black*, October 16, 1969; *Daily Texan* (University of Texas student newspaper), October 16, 1969; *Daily Reveille* (Louisiana State University student newspaper), October 16, 1969; *Louisville Courier-Journal*, October 16, 1969.

17. Anderson, *The Movement and the Sixties*, 331; Jeffrey Kimball, *Nixon's Vietnam War* (Lawrence: University Press of Kansas, 1996), 174.

18. DeBenedetti and Chatfield, *An American Ordeal*, 280; Zaroulis and Sullivan, *Who Spoke Up?* 319; Kimball, *Nixon's Vietnam War*, 216.

19. Parr, "The Forgotten Radicals," 270; *Cavalier Daily* (University of Virginia student newspaper), May 5, 1970; *Red and Black*, May 5, 1970; *Daily Texan*, May 9, 10, 1970.

20. Rhodri Jeffreys-Jones, *Peace Now! American Society and the Ending of the Vietnam War* (New Haven, CT: Yale University Press, 1999), 88; Zaroulis and Sullivan, *Who Spoke Up?* 334; Lytle, *America's Uncivil Wars*, 356.

21. Anderson, *The Movement and the Sixties*, 380.

22. Small, *Antiwarriors*, 85; David Farber, *The Age of Great Dreams: America in the 1960s* (New York: Hill & Wang, 1994), 160; Kimball, *Nixon's Vietnam War*, 220.

23. Tom Wells, *The War Within: America's Battle over Vietnam* (Berkeley and Los Angeles: University of California Press, 1994), 373–74.

24. Jeffreys-Jones, *Peace Now!* 80–81; LaFeber, *Deadly Bet,* 29; Kenneth Heineman, "The Silent Majority Speaks: Antiwar Protest and Backlash, 1965–1972," *Peace and Change* 17 (October 1992): 402–33.

Suggestions for Further Reading

For excellent treatments of the 1960s, including student opposition to the war, see Terry H. Anderson, *The Movement and the Sixties: Protest in America from Greensboro to Wounded Knee* (New York: Oxford University Press, 1995); David Farber, *The Age of Great Dreams: America in the 1960s* (New York: Hill & Wang, 1994); and Mark Hamilton Lytle, *America's Uncivil Wars: The Sixties Era from Elvis to the Fall of Richard Nixon* (New York: Oxford University Press, 2006). Student culture and campus life are examined in Helen Lefkowitz Horowitz, *Campus Life: Undergraduate Cultures from the End of the Eighteenth Century to the Present* (New York: Knopf, 1987), chap. 10; and Edward K. Spann, *Democracy's Children: The Young Rebels of the 1960s and the Power of Ideals* (Wilmington, DE: Scholarly Resources, 2003). For the draft and its impact, consult Lawrence M. Baskir and William A. Strauss, *Chance and Circumstance: The Draft, the War, and the Vietnam Generation* (New York: Vintage, 1978). The most important analyses of the antiwar movement and the student role include Charles DeBenedetti and Charles Chatfield, *An American Ordeal: The Antiwar Movement of the Vietnam Era* (Syracuse, NY: Syracuse University Press, 1990); Tom Wells, *The War Within: America's Battle over Vietnam* (Berkeley and Los Angeles: University of California Press, 1994); Rhodri Jeffreys-Jones, *Peace Now! American Society and the Ending of the Vietnam War* (New Haven, CT: Yale University Press, 1999); and Melvin Small, *Antiwarriors: The Vietnam War and the Battle for America's Hearts and Minds* (Wilmington, DE: Scholarly Resources, 2002). Small's excellent overview draws on his extensive work on the peace movement, including *Johnson, Nixon, and the Doves* (New Brunswick, NJ: Rutgers University Press, 1988) and *Covering Dissent: The Media and the Anti-Vietnam War Movement* (New Brunswick, NJ: Rutgers University Press, 1994). Kenneth J. Heineman's *Campus Wars: The Peace Movement at American State Universities in the Vietnam Era* (New York: New York University Press, 1993) provides extensive information on and acute analysis of developments at Kent State, Penn State, and SUNY-Buffalo. His *Put Your Bodies upon the Wheels: Student Revolt in the 1960s* (Chicago: Dee, 2001) is more critical of the students than my analysis or most of the other volumes cited here. William J. McGill's *The Year of the Monkey: Revolt on Campus, 1968–1969* (New York: McGraw-Hill, 1982) provides another sometimes biting account from the perspective of a university president. Joel P. Rhodes's *The Voice of Violence: Performance Violence as Protest in the Vietnam Era* (Westport, CT: Praeger, 2001) examines the origins and implications of the violent aspects of student dissent. W. J. Rorabaugh's *Berkeley at War: The 1960s* (New York: Oxford University Press, 1989) and Mary Ann Wynkoop's *Dissent in the Heartland: The Sixties at Indiana University* (Bloomington: Indiana University Press, 2002) are perceptive case studies. Student activism in the South has received far less scholarly attention than that in the remainder of the country. Gregg L. Michel's excellent study *Struggle for a Better South: The Southern Student Organizing Committee, 1964–1969* (New York: Palgrave Macmillan, 2004) and his "'We'll Take Our Stand': The Southern Student Organizing Committee and the Radicalization of White Southern Students, 1964–1969" (Ph.D. diss., University of Virginia, 1999), on which *Struggle for a Better South* is based, help remedy this problem. Other dissertations, such as Stephen Eugene Parr's "The Forgotten Radicals: The New Left in the Deep South, Florida State University, 1960–1972" (Ph.D. diss., Florida State University, 2000), and articles, such as Mitchell K. Hall's "'A Crack in Time': The Response of Students at the University of Kentucky to the Tragedy at Kent State, May 1970" (*Register of the Kentucky Historical Society* 83 [Winter 1985]: 36–63), Gregory Kuhe's "The FBI and Students for a Democratic Society at the University of New Orleans, 1968–1971" (*Louisiana History* 43 [Winter 2002]: 53–74), and John Ernst and Yvonne Baldwin's "The Not So Silent Minority: Louisville's Antiwar Movement, 1966–1975" (*Journal of Southern History* 73 [February 2007]: 105–42), also broaden our understanding of student dissent in the South. For the deaths at Jackson State College (now University), see Tim Spofford, *Lynch Street: The May 1970 Slayings at Jackson State College* (Kent, OH: Kent State University Press, 1988). Finally, *The Vietnam War on Campus: Other Voices, More Distant Drums* (Westport, CT: Praeger, 2001), a collection edited by Marc Jason Gilbert, includes useful essays on the South and other less-well-studied universities, such as Ball State and Iowa State.

11

Vietnam Is Here

The Antiwar Movement

Terry H. Anderson

In October 1967, during the events of Stop the Draft Week in Washington, DC, the activist Dave McReynolds declared, "Vietnam is here." He was right; opinion polls at that time demonstrated that Vietnam had eclipsed civil rights as the nation's top problem. The war in Southeast Asia was overwhelming America.

The antiwar movement, however, had developed slowly during the first part of the 1960s. That was because the United States was involved in a cold war with the forces of communism—the Soviet Union and its Eastern European allies, and China and its Asian neighbors North Korea and North Vietnam. Since the late 1940s, and especially since President Harry Truman sent troops to defend South Korea in 1950, the United States had practiced a policy of containing Communist expansion. Most citizens throughout the 1950s and until the late 1960s agreed with Truman when he told the nation, "We are fighting in Korea so we won't have to fight in Wichita, or in Chicago, or in New Orleans, or on San Francisco Bay." Thus, during the first part of the 1960s, most Americans saw the war in South Vietnam as stopping the flow of communism from North Vietnam; taking a different stance from the government's position resulted in scorn or charges of disloyalty.

Initially, events in South Vietnam bolstered support for the war. In August 1964, North Vietnamese patrol boats attacked an American destroyer, the USS *Maddox,* in the Tonkin Gulf. The president declared that our ship had been assaulted in international waters and that he was retaliating by ordering air strikes on naval installations in North Vietnam. The nation rallied around the flag. The *New York Times* declared that the attack on the warship was the "beginning of a mad adventure by the North Vietnamese Communists" and that the United States must "assure the independence of South Vietnam." The president's approval rating soared to over 70 percent, and Congress overwhelmingly passed the Tonkin Gulf Resolution, which supposedly gave Johnson authority to use U.S. armed forces in South Vietnam. Two-thirds of the public supported the resolution, including at least that percentage of college students. The editors of the *Michigan State News* were happy that LBJ had not "patted North Vietnam's leaders on the head for launching an unprovoked attack on our ships."

Next spring, the Viet Cong intensified their attacks on American forces, this time a U.S. base at Pleiku, and that angered Johnson. "I'm not going to be the first president to lose a war," he declared, and he changed U.S. policy by ordering Operation Rolling Thunder—air strikes against North Vietnam—which also was popular in the United States.

Yet the bombing provoked some citizens. Throughout the first half of the decade, a few peaceniks had spoken out against military action in Southeast Asia. Dr. Benjamin Spock, a founder of the Committee for a Sane Nuclear Policy, and A. J. Muste, who often volunteered with the Committee for Non-Violent Action, held rallies that attracted small crowds. In those gatherings were members of older peace groups, such as the American Friends Service Committee, Clergy and Laity Concerned, and the War Resisters League, or newer organizations, like Women Strike for Peace and Students for a Democratic Society. LBJ's bombing during spring 1965 also aroused some other Americans, especially on university campuses. At the University of Michigan, professors decided to hold a "teach-in." Inspired by civil rights sit-ins, two hundred professors took out an ad in the *Michigan Daily* appealing to students to join them in an attempt to "search for a better policy." Throughout the night of March 24–25, more than three thousand students and faculty participated in lectures, debates, and discussions, an idea that spread to other campuses. Some thirty-five universities, from Columbia to Oregon, from Rutgers to Berkeley, held teach-ins that semester. In April, the budding peace movement arrived in the nation's capital. Bused in from campuses all over the country, twenty thousand protesters appeared on a warm, beautiful Sunday. They picketed the White House, marched to the Washington Monument, sang with folksingers Judy Collins and Joan Baez, and eventually walked to the Capitol, where they presented Congress with a petition: "The problems of America cry out for attention, and our entanglement in South Vietnam postpones the confrontation of these issues. . . . We call on you to end, not extend, the war in Vietnam."[1]

The small but emerging antiwar movement had no impact on the Johnson administration; the president had popular support. Opinion polls demonstrated that 80 percent supported bombing North Vietnam, and the same percentage thought that it was "very important" to prevent a Communist South Vietnam. That being the case, most citizens, including most students, considered peace marchers as beatniks, kooks, or Communists. When thirty activists at Kent State protested the war, an angry crowd five times larger pelted them with rocks. A teach-in at Wisconsin resulted in six thousand students signing a letter supporting the president, and a fourth of the student body did the same thing at Yale. A survey of student opinion demonstrated that only a quarter supported negotiations or withdrawal from Vietnam.

With public support, LBJ enlarged America's role in South Vietnam. In July, he announced that he was increasing the number of U.S. troops from about 25,000 to 125,000. Significantly, he did not admit that he had already authorized an escalation to 200,000. Previously, the American soldiers were there to advise the South Vietnamese army (the Army of the Republic of Vietnam, or ARVN), but LBJ gave the field commander, Gen. William Westmoreland, permission to conduct independent combat missions against the enemy—clearing the way for the U.S. Army to replace the ARVN as the primary combat organization and, thus, Americanize the war. Citizens and the press cheered. *Life* proclaimed that it was wise and moral to "fulfill a promise to defend a victim of attack," South Vietnam, and *Time* editorialized that the conflict was the "crucial test of American policy and will. . . . The Right War at the Right Time."

Most Americans agreed, especially that autumn when U.S. troops engaged the enemy in the first major battle of the war—the Ia Drang Valley. The Viet Cong and the North Vietnamese army (NVA) launched an offensive in what appeared to be a plan to cut South Vietnam in half, and General Westmoreland met the challenge by sending his soldiers to stop the advance in the valley. Americans, sometimes outnumbered seven to one, withstood attacks for five weeks, in an area one survivor called the "devil's butcher shop." The battle convinced the enemy to avoid conventional attacks on well-armed U.S. forces; they shifted back to guerrilla warfare and employed tactics of ambush, hit-and-run, before vanishing into the jungle. To Westmoreland, Ia Drang confirmed his strategy; he would search for and destroy the enemy, "bleeding them until Hanoi wakes up to the fact that they have bled their country to the point of national disaster." Then, supposedly, they would give up. The president quietly raised the ceiling of U.S. troops in Vietnam to 375,000, as Pentagon officials proclaimed Ia Drang a "resounding military success."

Ia Drang rallied the American people. "Fury at Ia Drang," *Newsweek* declared, and the magazine pictured two soldiers helping a wounded man with the caption "Red Badge of Courage." The journalist Joseph Alsop called Ia Drang a series of "remarkable victories," and *U.S. News* boasted about America's tenacious fighters who beat the "best the Communists could throw at them." The pollster Louis Harris reported that about 65 percent approved of LBJ's handling of the war; only 11 percent favored negotiations or withdrawal. According to Harris, the "most hotly debated issue among Americans was whether they should first carry the ground war North or destroy the Vietcong in the South."[2]

"We'll lick them," declared Secretary of State Dean Rusk, and, given the popular mood, antiwar demonstrators provoked resentment. War supporters in Washington, DC, held "BURN THE TEACH-IN PROFESSORS" signs, and over twenty-five thousand prowar New Yorkers marched behind five winners of the Medal of Honor while a World War II veteran carried a sign reading, "SUPPORT OUR MEN IN VIETNAM—DON'T STAB THEM IN THE BACK." During that autumn, less than one-tenth of 1 percent of the population participated in an antiwar demonstration, and, on campus, students favored the war at higher rates than did their parents; a remarkable 75 percent of twenty-somethings favored sending troops to Southeast Asia.

Yet even the small number of protesters concerned the government. In the mid-1960s, it was one thing to demonstrate for civil rights or student issues, causes that moderates and liberals could support, but it was another thing to question American foreign policy during the Cold War. Who were these dissidents? Attorney General Nicholas Katzenbach stated that there were "some Communists involved," and FBI director J. Edgar Hoover declared that subversives participated in the demonstrations. The Senate Internal Security Subcommittee held hearings and then proclaimed that the control of the antiwar movement had passed from the liberals to the "Communists and extremists who favor the victory of the Vietcong and are openly hostile to the United States."

That was not true. Actually, antiwar activists at that time were not organized into any group, certainly not by the Communists. There were numerous local and national organizations that got out the word about a demonstration, printed up leaflets, sent letters to newspaper editors, or invited antiwar speakers to cities or campuses. In the mid-1960s, those people usually were liberals and students who were concerned about a conflict on the other side of the world against people of a different culture, and they raised important questions: Was a war in Vietnam in the national interest, and did fighting there have anything to do with American security? Was this undeclared war legal, and was the way the nation raised an army—the draft—fair? The United States had not been attacked, so pacifists wondered whether young people should put their lives in harm's way for what they considered a dubious cause, a military government in Saigon led by Gen Nguyen Van Thieu and Gen. Nguyen Cao Ky. Was the Thieu-Ky regime any better or worse than North Vietnam's Communist government led by Ho Chi Minh? Many demonstrators were angry that in the last election they had voted for Johnson—who assured the public that he had no intention of expanding the U.S. role in the war (it "ought to be fought by the boys of Asia to help protect their own land")—only to have him Americanize the war in Vietnam.

Questions raised by antiwar activists would be debated for the next eight years, but in 1965, most Americans understood little about the war and had no idea how to win it. Few felt that Viet Cong peasants or the NVA would be a match for the "greatest nation on earth." Faced with an army of John Waynes, the enemy would give up quickly, many thought in a year. How could America lose? Furthermore, Americans trusted the president and his advisers, and LBJ had assured the nation that he was prepared to "go anywhere at any time" to talk peace, that he supported "unconditional negotiations" with Hanoi. His subordinates added that, although the administration shared the same goals as the dissidents, they had "secret information" that justified their policy.

Thus, Johnson continued what citizens learned in 1971 with the publication of the Pentagon Papers were a long string of lies concerning Vietnam. The president had no secret information or any knowledge about
the Vietnamese people. The Texan once said that Vietnam was "just like
the Alamo," and at another time he tried to cut a deal with Ho Chi Minh,
proposing massive public works for North Vietnam if Ho would withdraw his troops and stop fighting in the South. Ho and his followers had
been fighting the Japanese, the French, and now the Americans for thirty
years, not for public works, but for independence—for a unified nation.
As far as war was concerned, Ho told a Western reporter, "The Americans
greatly underestimate the determination of the Vietnamese people."[3]

Throughout 1966, the United States sank deeper into the Vietnam
quagmire. Satisfied that this increasing involvement was justified by the
vague aim of stopping communism, citizens watched and waited, hoping for some sign of victory. In September, three-fourths supported and
only a quarter opposed the war; about the same percentage wanted to
expand the war and attack North Vietnam as wanted to withdraw the
troops. That same month, *Time* summarized the national mood: "Along
with most other people, the politicians are letting Lyndon Johnson take
the responsibility, and waiting for something to happen."

By early 1967, however, antiwar activism was getting more attention
and volunteers, especially from the civil rights movement. Vietnam was
expensive, and the conflict was draining appropriations from Johnson's
Great Society and War on Poverty, social programs that often helped
minorities. In February, Martin Luther King Jr. spoke out, calling on all
"creative dissenters to combine the *fervor* of the civil rights movement
with the peace movement . . . until the very foundations of our nation
are shaken." A month later, he led a procession of over eight thousand in
Chicago, and in April he gave a memorable address, proclaiming that the
"Great Society has been shot down on the battlefields of Vietnam."[4]

The antiwar movement was also expanding because of the way the
nation raised an army—selective service, or the draft. By that time, it was
becoming obvious that the draft was unfair. Supposedly, all men from
their eighteenth birthday until they turned twenty-six could be drafted,
but there were numerous deferments available (college, medical, hard-
ship, occupational), and only individuals who lived in the United States
could be drafted, so numerous men went off to Canada or Europe. More-

over, local draft boards were composed of upstanding citizens, meaning that they were 99 percent white. In several Rio Grande Valley counties in Texas, with populations that were over 50 percent Mexican American, not one Mexican American sat on the draft board, and the same was true for southern boards and African Americans. Selective Service System officials, naturally, did not want to draft their own sons or their friends' sons, and, since minorities were usually the least educated and skilled and were usually not attending college (and, thus, were ineligible for student deferments), they were the first to receive their induction notices. Once in the army, they were perfect candidates, first for infantry training and then for Vietnam. In Vietnam, there was additional discrimination. A much higher proportion of whites than blacks held rear support positions, most blacks being stationed on the front lines. While blacks constituted only 12 percent of U.S. citizens, the army in Vietnam was a quarter black, and many frontline units were 50 percent black; at times, forward bases were called *soulvilles*. Naturally, minority troops took a disproportionate percentage of casualties. In 1966, Hispanic servicemen from San Antonio (40 percent Latino then) took over 60 percent of that city's casualties, and, that same year, the government reported that black soldiers suffered a quarter of the casualties incurred while fighting the Viet Cong.

"I got no quarrel with them Vietcong," declared the boxing champ Muhammad Ali, who refused to register for the draft and was stripped of his heavyweight crown. By spring 1967, Martin Luther King called out to citizens, "We are at a moment when our lives must be placed on the line if our nation is to survive. Every man of humane convictions must decide on the protest that best suits his convictions—but we must all protest."[5]

Many more citizens were protesting in 1967, especially as the nation watched the war taking its deadly toll. Fewer than fourteen hundred Americans had died in Vietnam in 1965, but that number soared to over five thousand in 1966 and to over nine thousand in 1967, for a total of about sixteen thousand. And, unlike previous wars, Vietnam was televised. The three networks showed the carnage on the evening news. Exploding napalm, firefights, body bags, coffins—frightening scenes streamed into American living rooms, which naturally provoked more citizens to question the war.

The antiwar movement blossomed in spring 1967. In April, the nation witnessed the largest demonstration until that time. Coretta Scott

The March on the Pentagon, October 1967, which was the largest protest in decades. LBJ responded by trying to sell the war and predict victory in Vietnam, but his efforts to portray success ended at Tet, January 1968. Courtesy of Corbis.

King addressed 50,000 in San Francisco, and her husband marched with 200,000 in New York City. The movement was expanding beyond peaceniks, liberals, and students to civil rights activists, religious leaders, politicians, and even some from a new group—Vietnam Veterans against the War (VVAW). A few former career officers began dissenting against the war. These included the retired Marine Corps general David M. Shoup, who declared that all Southeast Asia was not "worth the life or limb of a single American." Women Strike for Peace marched on the Pentagon demanding to see "the generals who send our sons to Vietnam," and Another Mother for Peace began printing up posters, buttons, and T-shirts with what became one of the most popular slogans of the era: "WAR IS NOT HEALTHY FOR CHILDREN AND OTHER LIVING THINGS."

A few young protesters were becoming more frustrated with the war, and that usually resulted in more radical behavior, especially after the regimented and polite 1950s. Some Harvard activists confronted Secretary of Defense Robert McNamara, surrounding his car, and chanting

"Bullshit." At Howard University, students jeered the director of the Selective Service System, Gen. Lewis Hershey, and burned his effigy. At Indiana University, some students booed for so long when Secretary of State Dean Rusk appeared at the podium that he left without making his speech. In New York's Central Park, about 175 young men burned their draft cards while protesters chanted "We won't go!" A couple of demonstrators carried Viet Cong flags—and one burned the Stars and Stripes.

"The American people are not going to let this go on," declared Congressman L. Mendel Rivers. "They want this treason stopped." Was it treason? Many who doubted the wisdom of the war asked, What is patriotism? General Westmoreland returned to Washington in April and announced his dismay over "recent unpatriotic acts here at home," and the president stated later that the nation must unite behind his policy as a "family of patriots." Dissidents disagreed. The Arkansas Democratic senator J. William Fulbright, who was publicly questioning the war, stated that dissent "is more than a right; it is an act of patriotism, a higher form of patriotism." The clergyman Robert McAfee Brown agreed: "The question is not what right have we to be speaking, but what right have we to be silent."

Patriotism would be debated for the remainder of the era, but, in 1967, most politicians still desired Cold War obedience. A hint of disloyalty was outrageous, and Congress overwhelmingly passed a bill making desecrating the flag a federal crime (the law was later found unconstitutional by the Supreme Court). Millions of Americans bought a record number of flags, many putting flag decals on their car bumpers. Prowar posters appeared: "MY COUNTRY, RIGHT OR WRONG"; "LOVE IT OR LEAVE IT."

Flags and bumper stickers had no impact on the antiwar movement, and, in 1967, it reached its peak on Saturday, October 21, when Stop the Draft Week climaxed with the March on the Pentagon. This event stunned the public. While some radicals proclaimed that they were now going to attack the military headquarters, hippies of the emerging counterculture joked that they planned to exorcize demons from the building by chanting *om* and levitating the Pentagon. About fifty thousand assembled on that sunny Saturday in front of the Lincoln Memorial. The activist David Dellinger announced that the march was the end of peaceful protest: "This is the beginning of a new stage in the American peace movement in which the cutting edge becomes active resistance."

The crowd began walking across the Arlington Bridge and toward the Pentagon. The federal government was prepared; for the first time since the Bonus March of 1932, it ordered its armed forces to protect the nation's capital against Americans. On arriving at the Pentagon, a few dozen radicals attacked; the military easily repulsed them and won the first battle. At the same time, a few hundred others began a sit-down in the Pentagon parking lot. "Soon diggers started bringing in food and joints," wrote a participant. "A real festival atmosphere was in the air. People laughed and hugged." Many talked to other troops, chanting "join us," singing "we'd love to turn you on." A few put flowers in the troop's rifle barrels—flower power. Some smoked dope into the evening; others sipped wine and built campfires. A few sang "Silent Night." Others sat in the lotus position and hummed *om*. By most reports, the Pentagon did not levitate. Instead, it ordered an attack. "The brutality was horrible," reported an activist. "Nonresisting girls were kicked and clubbed by U.S. marshals old enough to be their fathers . . . cracking heads, bashing skulls."

Stop the Draft Week had an impact on the administration. Johnson believed that the peace movement was turning citizens against the war, and he responded by announcing to his cabinet, "It is time that the administration stopped sitting back and taking it from the Vietnam critics." LBJ took the offensive, privately instructing the FBI to watch antiwar leaders and conduct investigations. The CIA began Operation Chaos, which violated federal law excluding that agency from domestic investigations. Agents infiltrated civil rights and antiwar groups in an attempt to find proof that they were controlled by foreign governments or Communists. They found no such evidence, so the president ordered more studies while he and his aides leaked fabrications to hawkish politicians. The House Democratic leader, Carl Albert, declared that the March on the Pentagon was "basically organized by International Communism," and the House Republican leader, Gerald Ford, added that it was "cranked up" in Hanoi.

Johnson, therefore, attempted to change opinion in America instead of changing policy in Vietnam. It was time to rally the nation. The president had not wanted the war, but, once committed, he could not back away. He would shoulder the burden: Stay the course! He continued the same policy in 1967, the historian George Herring has written, "for the same reasons he had gone to war in the first place—because he saw no alternative that did not require him to admit failure or defeat." For the Texan, the war had become a matter of pride.

The president flew to South Vietnam, shook hands with the troops, and declared, "We are not going to yield. We are not going to shimmy." Back home, he privately told his advisers, "Sell our product to the American people." Officials became salesmen. "We're winning the war," declared the army chief of staff, and the U.S. ambassador to Vietnam proclaimed, "We are making steady progress." General Westmoreland added, "It is significant that the enemy has not won a major battle in more than a year." The administration could see "the light at the end of the tunnel."

Two months later, on January 31, 1968, Tet, the Buddhist lunar new year, the enemy troops launched their most massive offensive of the war. The Viet Cong and the NVA attacked most towns, villages, and bases controlled by the South Vietnamese government and U.S. armed forces. Significantly, the attack was televised, and so was General Westmoreland, who assured American viewers that the enemy suffered heavy casualties and had been defeated. That might have been true, but it was meaningless, for Tet really demonstrated that Westmoreland's search-and-destroy strategy had failed. U.S. forces were no closer to victory in 1968 than they were in 1965, before a half million American forces entered Vietnam. Tet was a shocking psychological defeat. It shattered the illusion of progress in Vietnam, and it forced the public to consider the agonizing possibility that the war might go on for many more years.

"What's going on here?" CBS anchorman Walter Cronkite asked millions of viewers during Tet. "I thought we were winning the war." Had the government been telling the truth? "The American people have been pushed beyond the limits of gullibility," declared the *New York Times.* The press—which, like most citizens, had been supporting the administration's policy—now began questioning the war. The "U.S. must accept the fact that it will never be able to achieve decisive military superiority in Vietnam," declared *Newsweek,* and even conservative editors at the *Wall Street Journal* warned that "everyone had better be prepared for the bitter taste of a defeat." Late in February, Cronkite summarized the gloomy mood: "To say that we are mired in stalemate seems the only reasonable, yet unsatisfactory conclusion."

"If I've lost Cronkite," LBJ said to an aide, "I've lost the country." Indeed, disillusionment soared in the weeks after Tet. Polls from January to March recorded one of the most profound opinion shifts in history. Earlier, hawks had outnumbered doves 60 percent to 24 percent; a month later, doves led hawks 42 percent to 41 percent. Furthermore, those approving LBJ's handling of the war plummeted to a record low, only 26 percent. Before Tet, a majority of citizens supported the administration's policy; after, a majority opposed it.

The swing in opinion was also apparent in Congress. "Can we afford the horrors which are being inflicted on the people of a poor and backward land to say nothing of our own people?" asked Senator Fulbright. "Can we afford the alienation of our allies, the neglect of our own deep domestic problems and the disillusionment of our youth?" And the senator asked the most important question: "Can we afford the sacrifice of American lives in so dubious a cause?"

Eugene McCarthy didn't think so. The obscure senator from Minnesota was in New Hampshire challenging the president in the state's Democratic primary. He had inspired hundreds of college students to take off a semester and campaign for him, go door-to-door talking about the war, and the results startled the nation—the sitting president beat the senator by only a few percentage points, which political pundits considered a major upset and a defeat for LBJ. Thus, on March 31, President Johnson addressed the nation on television. He discussed the "divisiveness among all of us tonight" and the Vietnam War and then shocked the audience by declaring, "I shall not seek, and I will not accept, the nomination of my party for another term as your president."[6]

LBJ became the most notable casualty of his own policy in Vietnam, and eventually that resulted in a three-way race for president in 1968 between the sitting Democratic vice president, Hubert Humphrey, the Republican challenger, Richard Nixon, and the third-party candidate, the former Democratic Alabama governor George Wallace. The most important issue was Vietnam, and, before the election, Humphrey talked about deescalation; Nixon had a "secret plan" to achieve "peace with honor," the best slogan of the campaign; and only Wallace wanted to escalate. "I think we've got to pour it on," he proclaimed, and then for his running mate he picked the tough-talking retired air force general Curtis LeMay, who advocated that it would be "most efficient" to use nuclear weapons against the enemy and "bomb 'em back to the stone age."

In a very close election, Nixon barely won. "If the United States gives up on Vietnam," Nixon once said, "Asia will give up on the United States and the Pacific will become the Red Sea." Like Johnson, the new president had no knowledge of the Vietnamese and felt that victory depended on "the will to win—the courage to use our power." Apparently, victory had nothing to do with the will of the enemy or the South Vietnamese. In 1969, Nixon said the same thing as LBJ in 1965: "I will not be the first President of the United States to lose a war."

Nixon announced his plan—Vietnamization. U.S. forces would train the ARVN to fight and win the war against the Viet Cong and the NVA, a policy that the Americans had been following for years. Supposedly, that would allow the president to bring home U.S. troops and, thus, claim that he was "winding down the war." Yet it would be difficult to win while de-escalating, so he quietly escalated the bombing campaign. In Nixon's first two years, the United States dropped more bombs on Southeast Asia than the entire tonnage used on all its enemies in World War II.

The public did not know about the massive bombing, and most agreed that the president deserved some time to wind down the war. Activists attempted to convince the administration to end the conflict as soon as possible, and, on Easter Sunday 1969, hundreds of thousands marched in the first major antiwar demonstration during the new administration. Enormous crowds appeared in New York, Philadelphia, and San Francisco; the largest parades to date were held in Chicago, Atlanta, and Austin.

The administration at first tried to placate critics. "Give us six months," the presidential adviser Henry Kissinger told peace activists, "and if we haven't ended the war by then, you can come back and tear down the White House fence." Nixon, who told an aide that he could end the war by the 1970 elections, publicly pledged to cut draft calls and announced the first withdrawal—25,000 troops of about 540,000 in Vietnam.

Yet placating critics ran counter to Nixon's usual modus operandi. The president told subordinates that he was "appalled" by protesters, "mindless rioters and professional malcontents." Supposedly to maintain law and order, he began a domestic policy aimed at silencing his critics. "Those who are against us," the presidential aide Egil Krogh said, "we will destroy." The administration enlarged investigations aimed at proving that the movement had links with Hanoi or Moscow. The CIA could not find any foreign ties, but, as we have seen, the White House ordered the agency to break its charter and conduct domestic infiltration of anti-

Kent State, May 1970. National guardsman, many the same age as the students, fired tear gas and, later, over sixty bullets at protestors, killing four and wounding America. Courtesy of Kent State University.

war organizations, code name Operation Chaos. Nixon also formed the Committee of Six. Composed of young conservatives such as Pat Buchanan, the committee encouraged the IRS to harass movement organizations. Moreover, the administration boosted the counterintelligence, or COINTELPRO, program, eventually employing two thousand agents who infiltrated, provoked disturbances, and began a massive program of "disinformation," a euphemism for spreading lies. After someone in the administration leaked the secret U.S. bombing of Cambodia to the press, the White House instructed the FBI to conduct illegal wiretaps of several government officials, journalists, and activists—even the musician John Lennon.

Just months after his inauguration, then, the new president was breaking the law, yet to no avail, for his actions did not stifle the movement. In fact, the number of protesters soared because there were more baby boomers and because the reasons for activism had not disappeared: the war dragged on; there was no end in sight. To prompt Nixon to bring the boys home, activists declared a one-day pause in their usual business, a peaceful moratorium on October 15, 1969, for the purpose of generating popular support for either immediate withdrawal or a fixed date to evacuate all U.S. troops. The moratorium was the largest one-day protest of the era. Millions participated, some attending church services or joining processions through their cities, others simply wearing black armbands or peace symbols. Thousands conducted quiet candlelight processions, one of the largest being from the Washington Monument to the White House. A "political Woodstock," declared the *Boston Globe,* for, more than ever before, the massive, peaceful moratorium revealed a yearning in America, as many marched and sang, "All we are saying, is give peace a chance."

Nixon was upset. He told colleagues that he was "not going to be pushed around by the demonstrators and the rabble in the streets," and he unleashed his vice president, Spiro Agnew, who attacked the "mob," the "strident minority" who did not support the president. Agnew also assailed the press, charging that "a small and unelected elite" distorted the news and raised doubts about the president's policies; these "nattering nabobs of negativism" promoted dissent. Agnew's attack had an impact on the media. On November 15, when 250,000 demonstrated against the war in Washington, DC, there was no live coverage on television.

Yet, no matter what Nixon did or said, most people were losing confidence in victory and remained bewildered about Vietnam. By the end of 1969, half those asked felt that the war was "morally indefensible," 60 percent said that it was a "mistake," and 80 percent were "fed up and tired" of the conflict. Other polls showed contradictions. Eighty percent felt antiwar activists raised important issues that should be discussed, but over 60 percent agreed with Nixon that demonstrations harmed the prospects for peace.

The peace movement smoldered during spring 1970. Many activists had become more interested in other movements of the era—black and Chicano power, women's liberation, environmentalism, or the flourishing counterculture. Moreover, the president had defused antiwar critics by continuing negotiations with the North Vietnamese, cutting draft calls, announcing the withdrawal of another 150,000 troops, and promising that he was "winding down" the war. Many activists were getting tired of demonstrations; others realized that they would not have much impact on the Nixon administration.

Then, on April 30, Nixon went on television and told the public that he had ordered the invasion of South Vietnam's neighbor, Cambodia. His "incursion," supposedly, was aimed at destroying enemy bases and cutting supply lines. That sparked protests across the nation.

Most rallies were peaceful—until Kent State. On May 4, nervous Ohio national guardsmen fired over sixty times into a crowd of about two hundred students, wounding nine and killing four. In ten terrifying seconds, *Time* reported, the usually placid campus was converted "into a blood-stained symbol of the rising student rebellion against the Nixon Administration and the war in Southeast Asia."

In the week after the Kent State incident, students at 350 universities went on strike, and protesting resulted in the closing of about five hundred campuses, fifty of them for the remainder of the semester. The governors of Ohio, Michigan, Kentucky, and South Carolina declared their universities in a state of emergency, and governors of sixteen states activated the national guard to curb rioting at twenty universities. In other words, the government was forced to employ its military to occupy the nation's campuses in order to quell the insurrection of its own youth.

That summer, the Campus Commission on Student Unrest surveyed universities and reported the main reason for campus demonstrations: Nixon's policies in Vietnam. The president immediately rejected such views and blamed the riots on "the rock throwers and the obscenity shouters" who wanted to "tear America down."[7]

Nixon's statements had no impact, for the beginning of the end of the war was during the first half of 1971, and it was broadcast live on television. In January, the nation watched the trial of Lt. William Calley Jr., charged for murder in the Vietnam village of My Lai, where his soldiers went berserk and shot over three hundred unarmed civilians, mostly women and children. Next month, more than 130 vets, many VVAW members, testified before Congress. Their war tales were horrifying—beating enemy prisoners, rape, even murder. "When you shot someone you didn't think you were shooting at a human," one vet testified, while another told of tossing enemy prisoners out of helicopters: "Don't count prisoners when loading, only upon landing."[8]

The statements repulsed the American public, and so did other revelations coming from the war zone that spring. The ARVN invaded Laos to cut off supply lines from the North and to demonstrate that Vietnamization was working, and the NVA counterattacked, smashing the ARVN, demonstrating that, after years of training, the ARVN was no match for the NVA. As for the U.S. Army in-country, the Pentagon admitted that morale was in sharp decline, that drug usage was up, and that there was fragging. The term *fragging* was taken from the fragmentation grenade, meaning assassination attempts against superiors, eventually resulting in at least six hundred and perhaps as many as one thousand murders of career enlisted men and officers in Vietnam. The army was at war with itself over the war in Vietnam.

Antiwar feelings had invaded the U.S. Army. Soldiers signed petitions, joined the VVAW, and even marched against the war in 1971. On July 4, over one thousand GIs at Chu Lai held a peace rally, which they reported as the "largest pot party in the history of the army." The troops hated the war, one veteran predicting, "If Nixon doesn't hurry up and bring the GIs home, they are going to come home by themselves."

To most Americans, the Vietnam War ended during the first half of 1971. The revelations about the U.S. military, the failure of Vietnamization, and the publication of the Pentagon Papers, revealing that the Kennedy and Johnson administrations had lied about how we got involved in South Vietnam—all ended lingering doubts. The effort was no longer worth the price. Over fifty thousand U.S. troops had made the ultimate sacrifice. Opinion polls between March and June revealed that only 15 percent wanted to continue the war, almost 60 percent thought that U.S. involvement was "immoral," and over 70 percent thought that the war was a "mistake" and favored withdrawal. Over 60 percent favored withdrawal, even if that meant the collapse of South Vietnam. "Everybody's just sick and tired of the war," said a conservative. Business complained that the war was hurting profits and creating labor unrest. Unions said that it was fueling inflation and hurting workers. The foreign policy establishment preached that it was no longer strengthening but weakening U.S. credibility and alliances.

Nixon had no recourse; he had to get out of Vietnam. He sent his negotiator, Henry Kissinger, to hold talks with enemy representatives in Paris, and, after the president was safely reelected, the administration signed a treaty with the enemy in January 1973.

As the administration scrambled for a way out of an unpopular war, the antiwar movement naturally faded. The administration's attacks on the "liberal media" had taken a toll; news executives told their journalists to cut reporting antiwar activities, and televised coverage of demonstrations significantly decreased. Antiwar protests were no longer "news." Moreover, fewer college students participated. A journalist surveyed forty universities and found that, "while student opposition to the war and the Nixon Administration is as monolithic as it ever was," activists were no longer enthusiastic about mass demonstrations, especially at colleges that had witnessed years of upheaval. Many students realized that troops were coming home, casualties were declining, and Nixon had ended the draft and established voluntary armed forces; they would not have to serve.

The remaining troops came home in 1973, and ever since the question has lingered: How much impact did the antiwar movement have on ending the war?

Did the antiwar movement end the war? Some who had spent years marching and speaking out, activists like Dave McReynolds, thought that it did, while others, such as Nixon's adviser Bob Haldeman, argued that the movement encouraged the enemy and "prolonged the war three-and-one-half years."

The answer is more complicated. The antiwar movement alone did not end U.S. participation in Vietnam, nor did it lead to victory for the enemy; they would have fought forever to unify their nation. Most likely, the frustrating conflict that George Herring labeled *America's longest war* eventually generated the question, Why aren't we winning? And that increased public opposition. After Tet, most Americans eventually agreed with the movement—the war was not necessary for U.S. security, and the carnage was not worth saving South Vietnam from being united under the North. The movement also influenced presidents Johnson and Nixon, men of enormous egos. LBJ would not have quit the presidency, and Nixon would not have withdrawn from Vietnam, if there was no antiwar movement massing enormous demonstrations throughout America. "The reaction of the noisy radical groups was considered all the time," said Adm. Thomas Moorer, chairman of the Joint Chiefs of Staff during the Nixon years. "And it served to inhibit and restrain the decision makers." More specifically, the historian Mel Small concluded, after numerous interviews with administration officials, that there were at least two times when the antiwar movement directly influenced presidents. The first was after the March on the Pentagon in 1967. Johnson then decided to sell the war to the public, a move that backfired since the premature victory speeches resulted in a massive loss of support for the conflict two months later, after Tet. The second time was the October 1969 moratorium. The size of that event and the number of middle-class marchers (whom Nixon needed in his political base) involved convinced the president not to attack North Vietnam in November with a "savage blow," which he was planning. The movement restrained Nixon, and it also demonstrated the inequities in selective service, which Nixon ended. That resulted in voluntary armed forces, which, unfortunately, also meant much less popular—and student—interest in and concern about U.S. intervention in foreign countries.

In the long run, then, the antiwar movement provoked citizens out of Cold War allegiance and stimulated thoughtful people to question military action and to ask significant questions: Is our involvement necessary? Is it in the national interest? Will it enhance our security? Is it worth American lives?

Notes

1. Among the best overviews of the antiwar movement are Charles DeBenedetti and Charles Chatfield, *An American Ordeal: The Antiwar Movement of the Vietnam Era* (Syracuse, NY: Syracuse University Press, 1990); and Melvin Small, *Antiwarriors: The Vietnam War and the Battle for America's Hearts and Minds* (Wilmington, DE: Scholarly Resources, 2002).

2. A good military examination of the Ia Drang battle is Harold G. Moore and Joseph L. Galloway, *We Were Soldiers Once and Young: Ia Drang, the Battle That Changed the War in Vietnam* (New York: Random House, 1992).

3. For an inside perspective on the Pentagon Papers, see Daniel Ellsberg, *Secrets: A Memoir of Vietnam and the Pentagon Papers* (New York: Viking, 2002).

4. To understand the antiwar movement in the framework of the protest era, see Terry H. Anderson, *The Movement and the Sixties* (New York: Oxford University Press, 1995).

5. For discussions of the profound effect the draft had on the working class and minorities, see Lawrence A. Baskir and William A. Strauss, *Chance and Circumstance: The Draft, the War, and the Vietnam Generation* (New York: Vintage, 1978); Myra MacPherson, *Long Time Passing: Vietnam and the Haunted Generation* (Bloomington: Indiana University Press, 2001); and James E. Westheider, *Fighting on Two*

Fronts: African Americans and the Vietnam War (New York: New York University Press, 1997).

6. Lyndon Johnson's handling of the Vietnam conflict is thoughtfully examined in George C. Herring, *LBJ and Vietnam: A Different Kind of War* (Austin: University of Texas Press, 1994).

7. Jeffrey Kimball's *Nixon's Vietnam War* (Lawrence: University Press of Kansas, 1998) is an in-depth study of Richard Nixon's management of the conflict. Melvin Small's *Johnson, Nixon, and the Doves* (New Brunswick, NJ: Rutgers University Press, 1988) focuses on both presidents and the antiwar movement.

8. For a fascinating study of My Lai from varied perspectives, see David L. Anderson, ed., *Facing My Lai: Moving beyond the Massacre* (Lawrence: University Press of Kansas, 1998).

12

The Media and the Vietnam War

Clarence R. Wyatt

The role of the news media remains one of the most controversial aspects of American involvement in Vietnam. Understanding what the press did (and did not do) and why is, of course, important to achieving a clearer sense of how and why American society approached the conflict in Vietnam, and the parallel conflict at home, as it did.

This issue of the press and the Vietnam War also has implications for today. First, the issue of government information policy, especially regarding national security information, is still very much with us. From the Grenada operation in 1983 through the Gulf War to the current conflict in Iraq and the global war on terror, information policy and press access have been a major part of government and military planning. The degree to which the public has confidence in the information that it receives, whether from the government, the military, and news organizations, greatly affects the degree to which it will support any military conflict.

In addition, ideas about the role of the press are an important part of the mythology that has developed around the Vietnam War. As it has for all previous major U.S. military engagements, American society has developed a kind of public "consensus of memory" that designates certain topics and conclusions as safe while dismissing, or ignoring altogether, others. That consensus has evolved over time, but, at each step, it has limited the questions that we can ask of that experience and the answers that might help us view current and future conflicts more clearly.

Background

Since the end of the Vietnam War, two images of the press have presented themselves in this public memory. The first appeared only briefly, toward the end of the war and immediately afterward. In that conception, the press was something of a deliverer, dispelling government lies and enabling the American people to bring an ill-advised, unjust war to an end.

But that image was soon replaced by that of betrayer. In this latter manifestation, individual journalists and entire news organizations deliberately distorted news of the war to suit their own political biases. In this view, the press downplayed or ignored progress in the conflict and emphasized (or outright invented) negative reports. Over time, this barrage of bad news eventually sapped the public's will to bring the "noble cause," as President Ronald Reagan called it, to a successful end. Thus, the news industry became a villain that misled the American public, dishonored the sacrifice of American soldiers, and abandoned the people of South Vietnam to Communist oppression.[1]

Neither image, however, is based on a real understanding of two larger issues. First, they are not based on a thorough sense of the institution of U.S. journalism. Over the course of the twentieth century, the news media in America underwent some significant changes. The institutional characteristics that developed derived from economic and cultural issues rather than the supposed political motivations on which the two images of the press are based. Second, during the Cold War a "national security mentality" developed. The potential Armageddon represented by a Soviet Union in possession of nuclear weapons encouraged and justified a culture of official secrecy. The ability and willingness of the federal government, especially the executive branch, to control and manipulate information—often for legitimate security reasons, but frequently for more self-interested political reasons—grew dramatically. An exploration of the relationship between the press and government and the role that that relationship played in American involvement in Vietnam should include these two elements.

American Journalism

Journalism in the United States possessed several key characteristics during the period of the Cold War and the war in Vietnam. The first is *ethnocentrism,* what Herbert Gans described as the tendency of news organizations to focus on stories featuring the members of their "home" societies as one of the "enduring values of the news."[2] For American editors and news directors, this meant that a story was really news only if Americans were somehow involved. Other stories that did not directly affect or involve Americans were shunted to the background, if they were covered at all. American news organizations were not alone in exercising such judgments. A British editor once declared that it would take the deaths of a thousand Africans or fifty Frenchmen to equal the newsworthiness of the death of one Englishman: "1,000 wogs equals 50 frogs equals one Englishman," in his more colorful phrasing.

This ethnocentrism played into how news organizations allocated resources. Believing that coverage of domestic issues and domestic stories was what readers, listeners, and viewers wanted and that this was where the profits would be made, editors and news directors kept the bulk of their resources at home. This meant that relatively little attention was devoted to foreign coverage, especially of Asia, in the late 1950s as the United States was becoming involved in Vietnam. Most of the meager foreign assets were devoted to Europe. For example, *Time* had fourteen overseas bureaus, but only two (Hong Kong and Tokyo, with a total of three reporters between the two) were in Asia. In the same year, *Newsweek* had two reporters in Tokyo, and *U.S. News* covered all East Asia with one regional editor. The *New York Times* had twenty-eight foreign offices, only three of which were in Asia.

The danger of this practice was not lost on news and media professionals, even at the time. A 1960 study of public relations work in the United States on behalf of foreign governments concluded that "the economics of U.S. news coverage" resulted in "hordes of reporters" following the American president's every move while "the ranks of American journalists covering the rest of the world are remarkably thin. . . . The facts we need to know are often concealed from us or get to us too late. All of a sudden there may be a blow-up in a country with which we have been deeply involved." Otto Friedrich, working for United Press during the French war in Vietnam, said, "The basic fact is that it would have cost a lot of money to support one of those red-blooded American reporters in Vietnam. Figure at least $100 a week in salary and at least $50 a week in expenses, and is it worth it? It might be, if an American newspaper really wanted to know what was going on in Indo-China. . . . But that is not what American editors wanted. They wanted stories of good guys fighting Reds, and that is what they got."[3]

During this post–World War II period, growing national literacy, mobility, and prosperity led to two other important changes in the economics of American journalism. First, news became a big and profitable business. Newspapers evolved from being the creature of one owner/publisher to being publicly owned, corporate entities. This phenomenon was particularly true in television. Also, journalism changed from being a barely respectable craft to being a profession. It developed a canon of standards and a system of professional education. Reporters were increasingly college and graduate school trained, the professional and social peers of the political leaders whom they covered.

The Rise of the National Security Mentality

American officials had from the beginning of the Republic attempted to conduct certain business in private. But, because the federal government was so limited for most of our history, there was little concern over the maintenance of government secrets. However, this began to change in the 1930s and 1940s as the power of the federal government increased, especially with the advent of the atomic age and the Cold War. With the fear of subversion from within and the profound threat from without, with massive death and destruction just hours or minutes away, presidents felt the need to control information, lest any slip signal weakness or overaggressiveness. This led to a deference on the part of the press and public to the presidency, especially on matters of national security. Presidents Harry Truman and Dwight Eisenhower greatly expanded the ability to classify information and hold it from public, even congressional, view. In late 1945, the McMahon Act put severe restrictions on access to information about nuclear technology. In September 1951, President Truman issued Executive Order 10-290, giving hundreds of executive branch employees authority to classify information. Executive Order 10-501, issued in November 1953 by President Eisenhower, created thirty new levels of classification and formed the basis of federal information policy for the next fifteen years.

These developments raised concerns among congressional leaders, the press, and public figures. The *U.S. News* editor David Lawrence called Truman's order "our own iron curtain" and predicted that "the only information the public may get officially will be that which the President and his political advisers deem good for the Administration's political fortunes." Responding to Eisenhower's order, Sigma Delta Chi, the press fraternity, declared, "The imposition of secrecy on the broad and undefined ground of 'Executive Privilege' has reached a new peak . . . posing the most serious threat to the theory of open government so far in U.S. history."[4]

While this increased control did serve legitimate security concerns, it also served to provide political cover for administrations. A prominent example is the May 1960 U-2 incident, in which the American pilot Francis Gary Powers was shot down and captured while flying photo reconnaissance missions over the Soviet Union. Such flights had gone on for years; the Soviets knew about them, as did key journalists and congressional leaders. Still, Eisenhower hoped to avoid embarrassment. Assuming that the pilot was dead and the plane destroyed, the White House issued a cover story that described the mission as NASA weather research. However, when Khrushchev produced pictures from the plane's cameras and a live pilot before the Supreme Soviet, it became clear that only the American public had been deceived.

Eisenhower's successor, John F. Kennedy, raised information management to a high art. He understood how journalism had changed and how journalists worked much better than did his immediate predecessors. After all, he had worked as a reporter himself; he listed his occupation on his National Press Club bio as "a former newspaperman now in politics." Kennedy understood reporters' need for access, for a steady supply of information (or at least the appearance of it).

Kennedy cultivated relationships with key news organizations and journalists. During the 1960 presidential campaign, he met several times with Henry Luce, hoping to at least neutralize the staunchly Republican publisher of *Life* and *Time*. His attentions had at least some effect—Luce told an aide that Kennedy "seduces me": "When I'm with him I feel like

a whore." Ben Bradlee, of *Newsweek* and the *Washington Post*, was JFK's
neighbor and drinking buddy. Charles Bartlett, the Washington correspondent for the *Chattanooga Times*, was a longtime Kennedy intimate,
having introduced him to Jacqueline Bouvier. One White House reporter,
in describing Bartlett's close relationship to Kennedy, said that Bartlett
was "a tomb of secrets."[5]

Kennedy also understood the rising influence of television and the
ability it gave him to go over the heads of the press. On January 25, 1961,
he held the first presidential press conference to be broadcast live on television, and the event represented a major change. Kennedy moved the
event from the Indian Treaty Room, where reporters could see every gri-
mace and twitch in the presidential face, to the State Department audi-
torium, which created a physical distance between the president and the
press, and which was also much more suited to the needs of television.
Also, reporters were told not to identify themselves or their employers
when asking questions, supposedly to save time and allow more journalists to pose inquiries. Of course, the practice also kept the focus on the
star of the show, Kennedy himself. Many journalists hailed the live press
conference as a move to greater openness, but it actually gave a president,
especially a natural performer like JFK, even greater ability to shape the
news and public perception.

If this program of control through the appearance of spontaneity
and candor did not work, however, Kennedy also showed a willingness
to clamp down. He once denied Hugh Sidey, *Time's* White House correspondent and Washington's most influential reporter, access to the White
House for weeks in retaliation for an irksome story. He also used federal
investigators to find sources of unauthorized leaks.

Despite Kennedy's personal relationships with key journalists and his
understanding of the journalistic process, his information practices eventually created resentment. His attempts to suppress the *New York Times*
story on the Bay of Pigs invasion and the Cuban missile crisis brought
critical responses. New policies regulating contacts between executive
branch officials and reporters also drew fire, even from Kennedy's friends.
In a private letter to the president, the columnist Joe Alsop, whose home
had been the Kennedys' last stop on inauguration night, decried the regu-
lations, saying that openness was "the chief safeguard of the public interest." Less friendly critics also weighed in. A Republican Party publication

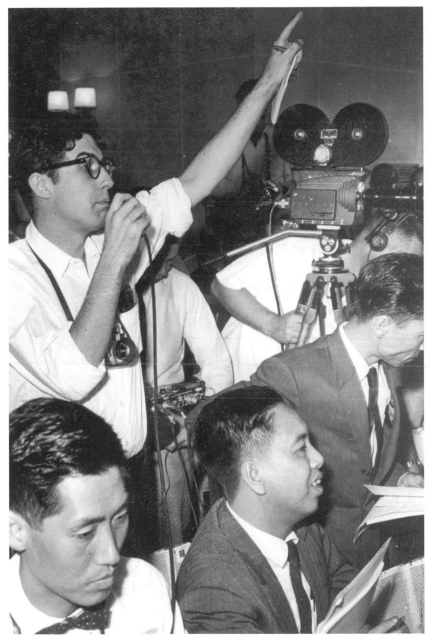

Neil Sheehan of United Press International during a press conference, ca. 1966. Courtesy of the Vietnam Archive, Texas Tech University, Douglas Pike Photograph Collection.

quoted a joke involving the Defense Department spokesman, Arthur Sylvester, and the presidential press secretary, Pierre Salinger, that was making its way around Washington: "When Sylvester says the government is lying, he's telling the truth. When Salinger says the government is telling the truth, he's lying."[6]

The American Press Comes to Vietnam

President Kennedy brought these approaches to information management to his handling of the situation in Vietnam. The Viet Cong had become much more aggressive in 1959 and 1960, putting greater pressure on the increasingly fragile regime of South Vietnamese president Ngo Dinh Diem. Kennedy's policies toward Vietnam were shaped by two major priorities: don't lose South Vietnam, but also don't appear to be taking over the effort. Following the October 1961 fact-finding mission by the military adviser Maxwell Taylor and the special assistant Walt Rostow, Kennedy responded to the higher level of insurgent activity by increasing military and financial aid to Diem as well as increasing the number of American advisers working directly with South Vietnamese combat units.

The increase in combat activity sparked greater interest among the American public. Combat reporting—simple, direct, and dramatic—had appeal to editors and readers. Vietnam also emerged as a more prominent part of the continuing Cold War drama between Kennedy and Khrushchev. This heightening U.S. involvement made Vietnam more of an "American" story, and the press increased its commitment in South Vietnam parallel with that of the Kennedy administration. In 1961 and early 1962, major news organizations began to establish full-time offices in the South Vietnamese capital of Saigon. Among some of the early group were Homer Bigart for the *New York Times,* Peter Arnett and Malcolm Browne for the Associated Press, Neil Sheehan for United Press International, Nick Turner for Reuters, Francois Sully for *Newsweek,* and Charles Mohr and Mert Perry for *Time.*

However, Kennedy also did not want Vietnam to be seen as an American war. In an effort to create the appearance of distance, the Kennedy administration issued orders in November 1961 that U.S. officials were to provide the press with no information regarding military or political activity and were to refer all inquiries to South Vietnamese officials—who were usually reluctant to speak with reporters. Denial of access was tightened even more in early 1962, when Adm. Harry Felt, commander in chief of U.S. forces in the Pacific, banned reporters from helicopter combat missions piloted by Americans. This practice made it more difficult for reporters to assess the effectiveness of this new tool and of the South Vietnamese troops it took into battle.

Also in early 1962, the policy of stonewalling was codified. On February 20, the State Department issued Cable 1006, which set out for U.S. government and military personnel in South Vietnam the official information policy that they were to follow. The first two of the cable's seven points urged Americans not to "grant interviews or take other actions implying all-out U.S. involvement." The third declared that stories on civilian casualties "are clearly inimical to national interests." The fourth and fifth points emphasized the need to support Diem and said "that articles that tear down Diem only make our task more difficult."[7]

The sixth and seventh guidelines held the key to the whole memorandum and provided the muscle by which the U.S. government could withhold or manipulate information. The sixth said: "Operations may be referred to in general terms, but specific numbers—particularly numbers of Americans involved—and details of material introduced are not to be provided. On tactical security matters, analyses [of] strengths and weaknesses and other operational details which might aid the enemy should be avoided." The final guideline said: "Correspondents should not be taken on missions whose nature is such that undesirable dispatches would be highly probable."[8] These two statements essentially denied the American people information on the greater role that their fathers, sons, and brothers were playing in the conflict while also preventing them from hearing of any but the most favorably stage-managed operations.

In the meantime, the government of South Vietnamese president Ngo Dinh Diem also cracked down on reporters. Government officials refused to speak with them, military commanders denied them access to their areas of operations, and they were followed and harassed by Diem's secret police. The regime even expelled reporters like *Newsweek*'s Francois Sully on trumped-up charges of being a Viet Cong spy, an opium smuggler, and a patron of sex orgies.

It is at this point that most of the mythology surrounding the press's role in Vietnam began to take shape. Reporters like Bigart, Sheehan, and

Browne represented a significant commitment of human and financial resources by their employers, who expected steady coverage of the conflict in return. Needing to satisfy this demand, but being shut off from American and South Vietnamese official information, reporters turned to the only available sources—American advisers in the field.

It was not surprising that a partnership developed between the Saigon press corps and the young captains, majors, and lieutenant colonels who made up the advisory force. They were peers in age—mainly in their twenties and early thirties. The advisers and the reporters also shared a background of advanced professional training in their respective fields; they were all rising stars. Shaped by the legacy of World War II, they shared similar views regarding the need to oppose aggression early and firmly as well as the U.S. responsibility to lead the way. They also held similar ideas on American power and, by extension, their own capabilities, sharing a sense of "can-do-ism." The reporters and the advisers were committed to drawing the line against communism.

Each group also satisfied professional needs of the other. The advisers, frustrated with the ineffectiveness of U.S. policy, especially the commitment to the increasingly isolated Diem regime, needed an outlet by which to get their concerns aired in public. The reporters needed reliable sources to support the coverage that their employers demanded. The journalists did not wish for South Vietnam to fall to the Communists or have an innate desire to criticize U.S. policy. They were motivated, not by political or ideological bias, but, rather, by the need to satisfy the imperatives of the American news industry.

The best-known example of this relationship involved Lt. Col. John Paul Vann, Neil Sheehan, and David Halberstam. Vann, the chief adviser to the commander of the South Vietnamese army's Seventh Division, was a star among the American advisers, and the press gravitated toward him and the success that the Seventh Division was having against the Viet Cong. But that success quickly unraveled as Huynh Van Cao, the commanding general of the Seventh, grew cautious, fearing that aggressive action and the resulting casualties might jeopardize his political ambitions. Vann began to voice his frustrations, particularly to Sheehan of United Press International and Halberstam of the *New York Times*, who had won Vann's confidence by sharing the hardships of life in the field.

Peter Arnett, Associated Press, ca. 1960s. Courtesy of the Vietnam Archive, Texas Tech University, Douglas Pike Photograph Collection.

Reflecting the perspectives of these sources, coverage of the conflict became more and more critical of the Diem regime and the U.S. commitment to it. The U.S. and South Vietnamese governments responded by continuing to stonewall the Saigon press corps. Kennedy also sought to divide the press and discredit the reporters working in Vietnam. He cultivated editors and prominent columnists, encouraging them to reassign bothersome reporters or to dismiss them as inexperienced and their coverage as overly dramatic. For example, Joe Alsop was granted access to helicopter missions during a visit to Vietnam in the spring of 1962, an opportunity denied resident reporters. Marguerite Higgins, a columnist for the *New York Herald-Tribune,* went on a similar VIP tour in July 1963. She was given access to top American and South Vietnamese officials, including a rare interview with Diem himself. On the basis of these sources, Higgins concluded that the effort in South Vietnam was going quite well and that reporting to the contrary by the resident press corps was due to its collective inexperience and gullibility.

Otto Fuerbringer, the managing editor of *Time,* went so far as to disavow his reporters' coverage in the very pages of the magazine. Charles Mohr and Merton Perry had been working in Vietnam for months. Their reporting, which had grown increasingly critical, was repeatedly rewritten to take on a more positive tone. In the fall of 1963, Fuerbringer asked the two to file a status report on the conflict. Seizing the opportunity, Mohr and Perry filed a major assessment of the state of the South Vietnamese government and the effectiveness of the American effort. Holding no punches, the piece began: "The war in Vietnam is being lost." An enraged Fuerbringer rejected the dispatch and then dictated a story for *Time*'s "Press" section. "The newsmen themselves have become a part of South Vietnam's confusion," he wrote. "They have covered a complex situation from only one angle, as if their own conclusions offered all the necessary illumination." In the resident press's eyes, Fuerbringer said, Diem was automatically "stubborn and stupid," while his critics were treated with "sympathy." The reporters also downplayed South Vietnamese successes as contrary to "the argument that defeat is inevitable as long as Diem is in power."[9] Not surprisingly, Mohr and Perry resigned.

Diem took a more direct approach. His brother and chief adviser, Ngo Dinh Nhu, unleashed his secret police on reporters. Halberstam and Sheehan discovered that their names were on an assassination list kept by Nhu. On July 7, police attacked reporters, including Peter Arnett of the Associated Press, who were covering an anti-Diem demonstration. Four policemen knocked Arnett to the ground and kicked him viciously until Halberstam, yelling, "Get back, get back you sons of bitches, or I'll beat the shit out of you," rescued him.[10]

From January to September 1963, the conflict between American reporters and American officials in Vietnam became acute. At the beginning of the year, an operation near Ap Bac in the Mekong Delta had been designed as a showpiece of South Vietnamese prowess. When it failed owing to the incompetence of the South Vietnamese commander, American officials still tried to claim it as a success and dismiss the coverage of the battle. Admiral Felt, on a visit to Vietnam at the time of the operation, characterized Neil Sheehan's coverage as an example of "bad news . . . filed immediately by young reporters without checking the facts." On seeing Sheehan two days later, Felt snapped, "So you're Sheehan. You ought to talk to some of the people who've got the facts." "You're right," Sheehan shot back, "and that's why I went down there every day."[11]

Over the following weeks, tensions increased. On hearing that John Mecklin, the U.S. Information Agency chief in Saigon, had returned to the States for surgery, one reporter said, "I hope the son of a bitch dies." Reacting to the news that a reporter had narrowly avoided being shot, one embassy staffer snapped his fingers and said, "Darn." The press corps created a little jingle, sung to the tune of "Twinkle, Twinkle, Little Star": "We are winning / This I know / General Harkins told me so / If you doubt it / Who are you / McNamara says so, too."[12]

The crisis for the Diem regime and within the American community came to a head in the summer and fall of 1963. In May, a parade in Hue, the old capital city, celebrating the anniversary of Archbishop Ngo Dinh Thuc's appointment to the bishopric had included the display of Vatican flags. Thuc's brother, Ngo Dinh Diem, attended the parade and reminded his brother of the law against flying any flag but that of South Vietnam. Diem even issued a statement saying that the Vatican flags had flown in error. But a few days later, when they were denied the right to display their flags during the celebration of the Buddha's birthday, Buddhist priests launched nationwide protests. Within days, what would become known as the Buddhist Crisis would attract opponents of the Diem regime from across South Vietnamese society. The Kennedy administration was shaken by the depth of the anti-Diem actions, illustrated most vividly by photographs of a Buddhist monk burning himself to death at a Saigon intersection on June 11.

When Diem and his brother Nhu struck back by beating and arresting hundreds of Buddhist monks on August 21, Kennedy realized that the Diem regime was self-destructing. He replaced discredited Ambassador Frederick Nolting with Henry Cabot Lodge. Lodge privately signaled to a group of generals that the United States would recognize a new government that they might establish in South Vietnam, giving the green light to a coup. More publicly, Lodge signaled a new relationship with the Saigon press corps. Immediately on arriving in Saigon, he began to meet with reporters, with blunt questions and candid answers being exchanged. He agreed with the reporters' assessment of Diem and, as a savvy politician, knew the value of a sympathetic press. The embassy took a much tougher stand in response to attacks on reporters by the police, and Lodge even allowed reporters to use the embassy's communications equipment to file stories when Diem shut off the government facilities.

Various plans by groups of South Vietnamese officers finally came to fruition on November 1, when Diem's government was overthrown. Despite U.S. calls for safe passage for Diem and his family, Diem and Nhu were murdered. Exactly three weeks later, an assassin killed President Kennedy.

The Rise of Maximum Candor

In its last days, the Kennedy administration had realized that its policy of denying reporters access to official information only drove them to other, less controllable sources. The shift in approach was becoming evident by the time of President Kennedy's death. As the United States became more deeply and directly involved in the war in Vietnam under President Lyndon Johnson, that new policy, known as Operation Maximum Candor, would form the basis of information policy until U.S troops began their gradual withdrawal from Vietnam in 1969.

Although several officials in the government and military argued for a change in press policy, Assistant Secretary of State for Public Affairs James Greenfield was the most forceful and articulate advocate. He told his counterparts at the Defense Department and the White House, "The press will write whether we brief or not. You can't prevent stories by not providing information. . . . Whenever we have taken pains to keep the press abreast of what is happening it has worked to our advantage."[13]

Beginning in the summer of 1964, the new policy sought to remove the chief irritants between the resident press and American officials in Vietnam. Barry Zorthian, a senior U.S. Information Agency official, was named coordinator of information for the entire U.S. effort in Vietnam. The staffs of the civilian and military information operations were significantly increased. The Military Assistance Command, Vietnam (MACV), expanded its briefings and distributed a much greater volume of information, and access to top officials was made easier. Reporters received more help in getting out to the field, and facilities for the press, in Saigon and other locations, were improved.

Over the following months, a coordinated information effort, operating as the Joint U.S. Public Affairs Office (JUSPAO), evolved. Working under Zorthian was a small army of information officers, all the way down to provincial and battalion levels. This apparatus quickly became extremely effective at furnishing the American press what it needed most—the information and logistic support needed to report the hard news of American activity in Vietnam.

To work in Vietnam, a journalist had to receive accreditation from JUSPAO and the South Vietnamese government. This required only a valid passport and a visa, a letter of employment, and a current immunization card. Accreditation gave journalists access to the full range of facilities provided by the U.S. effort in South Vietnam—commissary and post exchange stores, officers clubs, military transportation, and press facilities. At the height of U.S. combat involvement, more than six hundred people held official press accreditation.

In addition to such assistance, the press in Vietnam worked under extremely light official restrictions. Formal military censorship was considered briefly in the spring of 1965 but rejected as legally unworkable and politically problematic. Instead, reporters in Vietnam agreed to abide by a set of ground rules detailing the types of information that could and could not be released. Although these ground rules changed slightly from time to time, restricted information generally fell into the following categories: (1) future plans, operations, or strikes; (2) rules of engagement; (3) amounts of ordnance and fuel on hand in combat units; (4) exact numbers and types or identification of casualties suffered by friendly units; (5) during an operation, unit designations and troop movements, tactical deployments, name of operation, and size of friendly force involved, until officially released by MACV; (6) intelligence unit activities; and (7) air operations against North Vietnam.

As the number of American troops and the level of combat action grew, the press corps faced an increasingly daunting task. The war spread all across the difficult terrain of South Vietnam and was made up mainly of small unit actions that lasted a few minutes or hours. Even with access to military transportation, it was hard for reporters to reach many of these engagements while they were in progress. Also, even though, as we have seen, the number of accredited news personnel eventually grew to over six hundred, that figure does not accurately reflect the press corps' news-gathering capability. Everyone who worked for a news agency, from the bureau chief to the driver, had to be accredited. Even at the height of the press presence in Vietnam, probably no more than thirty or forty people were actually involved in gathering and producing news for news organizations with national audiences. Finally, American editors and producers made covering the day-to-day action of Americans in combat their first priority. All these factors made it impossible for news organizations to gather and verify independently all information about combat action. As a result, they came to depend on the flood of information provided by the official U.S. information machine.

All this points to the central factor—and the central problem—of the relationship between the American press and the American government and military over information about the war in Vietnam. Taking advantage of the characteristics of the American news industry, the Maximum Candor approach largely achieved its goals. It made the press dependent on the government for information concerning the war and, consequently, allowed the government to shape the news. As one of James Greenfield's aides told him, "The preoccupation of the press with each day's story can be made to our advantage to minimize the impact and duration of unfavorable events, but only if we tell the story whole, all at once. It's never a good idea to conceal from reporters what they may find out for themselves—because in Viet-Nam they will. And when they do they'll write it *their* way, not in a context of our choosing."[14]

To be sure, some minor incidents occurred. In the summer of 1965, reporters were denied access to the air base at Da Nang, a chief staging point for the bombing campaign against North Vietnam. Later that year, military efforts to downplay growing American casualty rates and inflate those of the enemy, especially following the fierce fighting in the Ia Drang Valley, inspired anger and sarcasm from reporters. In June 1968, John Carroll of the *Baltimore Sun* had his accreditation suspended for six months for violating a news hold on Operation Pegasus along the demilitarized zone. One of the most famous incidents occurred in August 1965. Morley Safer of CBS filmed a group of marines setting fire to thatched huts. On the morning after the film had aired, CBS President Frank Stanton was awakened by a phone call. "Frank, are you trying to fuck me?" the voice bellowed. "Who is this?" asked the groggy Stanton. "Frank, this is your president and yesterday your boys shat on the American flag." Lyndon Johnson followed up his tirade with an investigation into Safer's background as well as pressuring Stanton to reassign Safer from Vietnam.[15]

Many journalists expressed growing concern and frustration over this dependence and its consequences. In a 1967 assessment of the press's performance, *Newsweek* lamented the fact that "coverage of Vietnam . . . suffers from undue reliance on centralized sources." *New York Times* Saigon bureau chiefs repeatedly asked their editors to allow them to stop writing a daily summary of combat action—"a tedious collection of largely meaningless scraps," as Charles Mohr called it. The emphasis on the "bang-bang," Mohr continued, "severely limits our ability to do the deep, thoughtful, interesting, funny, investigative, and analytical report- ing which will be our real record here." When he made a similar request, R. W. Apple was told, "We get an arbitrary space allotment and the spot news has to be covered."[16]

All this added up to a sense of near helplessness on the part of many journalists. "It's the only story I've been on in my life where I get a hope- less feeling when I try to get on top of things," said CBS's Dan Rather. Wil- liam Tuohy of the *Los Angeles Times* said, "We're drowning in facts here, but starved for information."[17]

Despite these frustrations, the journalistic/information system in Vietnam gave each participant what it needed in a largely complemen- tary relationship—not the adversarial one that has come down to us as conventional wisdom. For example, from 1965 through 1972, fewer than a dozen reporters had their accreditation suspended or revoked for violating the ground rules. Also, for several reasons, major news organizations had become, as institutions, more cautious and conserva- tive. Especially as regarded stories involving foreign policy and national security, the press was reluctant to appear disloyal in the face of the threat from the Soviet Union. The professionalization of journalism, with its quest for objectivity, was part of this trend, as was the need to maintain access to sources within the government. Also, major news organizations had become big, profitable businesses subject to all the pressures that stockholders and the marketplace brought to bear. This was particularly true for the television networks, subject to Federal Commu- nications Commission regulation and licensing.

A number of examples illustrate this caution. In late 1966 and early

1967, Harrison Salisbury, a veteran foreign correspondent for the *New York Times,* became the first reporter from a major American news organization to visit North Vietnam. In his dispatches, he acknowledged that he was being shown what his hosts wanted him to see. Still, his fellow *Times* correspondent Hanson Baldwin, concerned about "the effect that these stories will have upon the country and upon the *Times,*" wrote a refutation of Salisbury's reporting and pressured editors into publishing it on the front page of the paper. Among other attacks, he referred to Salisbury's reports as "grossly exaggerated." A few days later, a *Times* editorial further distanced the paper from Salisbury, and the editor Clifton Daniel instructed his staff to "do everything we can in the coming weeks to balance the Salisbury reports."[18]

Reluctant to jeopardize access or profits, major news organizations also approached the big stories that supposedly defined the adversarial relationship between the press and the government with similar caution.

My Lai

The My Lai massacre took place on March 16, 1968, in a small village on the northern coast of South Vietnam. According to charges later filed against Lt. William Calley, American troops murdered several hundred Vietnamese civilians. No reporters were present that day, only the army photographer Sgt. Ronald Haeberle. Following the incident, officers, running up to the division commanding general, invoked a "conspiracy of silence" that held for over a year. A soldier named Ron Ridenhour, who had not been present at My Lai, pieced together enough bits of stories from other troopers to conclude that something terrible had happened. He wrote President Nixon, the secretaries of state and defense, the chairman of the Joint Chiefs of Staff, and several members of Congress. His letters led to an army investigation and the filing of charges against several officers involved in the alleged incident, principally the platoon commander, Calley.

Even then, no major news organization picked up the story, leaving the field to the former Associated Press reporter Seymour Hersh. From interviews with Calley and other participants and witnesses, Hersh put together a detailed account of the day. However, no major news outlet would touch the story. Only after the tiny Dispatch News Service, an alternative media organization based in California, marketed the story did the big organizations, now able to blame any problems with the story on Dispatch, pick it up.

The Pentagon Papers

In 1967, Secretary of Defense Robert McNamara was growing more and more concerned about the direction and prospects of U.S. policy in Vietnam. In an effort to figure out how the situation had reached its current point, he authorized the compilation of a top secret documentary history of U.S. involvement that would come to be known as the Pentagon Papers.

One of the authors of the papers was the political scientist Daniel Ellsberg, who had worked in the Pentagon and in Vietnam as a pacification analyst. Before going to Vietnam, Ellsberg had been an ardent supporter of the war, but his exposure to the actual thing turned him into a similarly passionate opponent. By 1971, he was convinced that, if the Pentagon Papers were released to the public, a popular outcry would bring the war to a quick end. Still possessing his security clearance, Ellsberg copied significant portions of the papers and began to look for an outlet. He began with antiwar members of Congress, none of whom would touch the papers. He finally found a kindred soul in Neil Sheehan, who now worked for the *New York Times*. Sheehan convinced his editors and the *Times* publisher, Arthur Sulzberger, to authorize a series of articles based on the papers. Sulzberger devoted a team of reporters and over $100,000 to the series, which began on June 13, 1971. The *Times* would endure immense political and economic pressure, as well as a legal challenge by the Nixon administration, in order to continue publishing the series.

As dramatic as these stories were, and as courageous as were the journalists involved, they still point out the limits on reporting of the Vietnam story. First, neither of these stories broke in Vietnam. Reporters there, committed to covering the day-to-day action of the war, didn't have the time to take on long-term investigative projects. Second, insiders broke both stories. Sy Hersh and Neil Sheehan displayed significant courage and industry, but, without Ron Ridenhour, the massacre might yet be unknown to all but a few Americans, and, without Daniel Ellsberg, the Pentagon Papers could well be gathering dust in the bowels of the National Archives.

Even with these stories, the interest of the American public in Vietnam began to wane. Richard Nixon came into office determined to stabilize American power in the world by achieving some degree of rapprochement with the Soviet Union and the People's Republic of China. The war in Vietnam represented a major inconvenience standing in the way of achieving this goal. Nixon first attempted to bring the war to a quick end through increased bombing of North Vietnam. When that failed, he announced in November 1969 the beginning of a gradual withdrawal of U.S. troops and a buildup of the South Vietnamese military. As the process of Vietnamization continued, the number of American troops—and of American casualties—steadily declined. Declining with them was the interest of the American public and press in the conflict. The antiwar movement lost momentum and fractured. A survey of college freshmen in the fall of 1970 revealed that the environment, not the war, was their top public policy concern. News organizations began to reduce or eliminate altogether their presence in Vietnam. The elaborate information apparatus that had once issued reams of statistics and summaries each day had less and less American activity to report. On January 9, 1971, a MACV press officer took the podium at the daily briefing in Saigon. He said that there would be no morning release that day. "Normally we report B-52 strikes in Vietnam," he said. "There were no indirect fire attacks. Normally we report ground action involving U.S. troops. There were no ground actions. There just wasn't anything to report."[19]

The war would, of course, continue for another four years and, on occasion, still intrude itself into the headlines—later in January 1971 with the failed invasion of southern Laos by the South Vietnamese military; in spring 1972 with the Easter Offensive, in which the North Vietnamese seized control of the northern provinces of South Vietnam; and in March and April 1975 with the final, tragic collapse of South Vietnam. The press enjoyed a temporary glow of public acclaim during the Watergate period. However, news organizations proved not to be immune as the public lost confidence in the major institutions of American life—government, big business, education, and the press. With the end of the war, the process of assigning blame and drawing lessons began. With the conservative ascendancy of the 1980s, criticism of a supposedly liberal press became the conventional wisdom and came to shape assessment of the press's role in the failure of American will in Vietnam.

Basing their thinking about the press on this characterization, military and civilian leaders determined to keep the press on a tight leash in future conflicts. During the October 1983 invasion of Grenada, the press was banned entirely for the first two days; when some reporters tried to approach on their own in small boats, they were turned away at gunpoint. Under great pressure, the military allowed fifteen reporters, out of the seven hundred staging on Barbados, access to the island. Following Grenada, Chairman of the Joint Chiefs Gen. John Vessey appointed a commission headed by the former MACV chief information officer Winant Sidle to draft a press policy. The main result was the development of the National Media Pool, an "emergency response team" of press from major media organizations. Panama was the first test of this new policy, and it did not work well as the military deliberately did not mobilize the pool until after the initial invasion. The pool was mobilized at the beginning of Operation Desert Shield/Desert Storm in August 1990 and accompanied the first troops into Saudi Arabia. But, as U.S. troops poured into the region, so did journalists. The press corps soon exceeded sixteen hundred, and the pool arrangement crashed and burned. Reporters had very limited pool access to the battlefield—and then only under the most tightly controlled conditions. Most coverage came from reporters at the briefings by the commanding general, "Stormin'" Norman Schwarzkopf. This stonewall approach worked in Grenada, Panama, and Desert Storm only because the periods of intense combat were short, with journalistic and public attention shifting elsewhere before the controls began to crack. Even in Desert Storm, journalists began to strike out on their own in an effort to reach the battlefield. The most notable case was CBS's Bob Simon, who was captured and held for forty days by Iraqi troops.

Beginning in 2002, officials in the Defense Department came to the same realization that Assistant Secretary of State James Greenfield had back in late 1963 and early 1964. They understood that any war in Iraq aimed at removing Saddam and instituting new political and social structures would be longer than Desert Storm. They also understood that the characteristics of American journalism that had operated in Vietnam—the draw of covering American troops under fire, the "police beat" approach that the media would take, justifying the massive economic investment that would ensue, and the need to fill the even bigger newshole created by 24-7 news networks and the Internet—were still present and gave the government and military the same opportunity to shape the story. Assistant Secretary of Defense for Public Affairs Victoria Clarke and her deputy, Bryan Whitman, developed an approach that greatly resembled Operation Maximum Candor. The heart of this approach was the embedded media policy—assigning reporters to units for extended periods. Eventually, over six hundred reporters were placed with units, with ground rules calling for relatively few limits on what could be reported, similar to the ground rules used during the Vietnam War.

But, as was also the case in Vietnam, the American public's support for the war in Iraq rests ultimately on some hardheaded judgments. Is the goal achievable? And is it achievable at a price we are willing to pay? In Vietnam, the reality of a complex struggle with no simple solutions eventually led the majority of Americans to answer no. What judgment Americans will make regarding the war in Iraq remains to be seen.

For a brief period at the end of the Vietnam War, Americans engaged in a consideration of the appropriate uses, and the limits, of American power. But, in a few years, the desire for simple answers to complex questions won out, and Americans began to compartmentalize and sanitize their experience in Vietnam. They eventually made the veteran of that war the focal point of their shared memory of it. Of course, honoring the service and sacrifice of these men and women was more than appropriate. But it also allowed us to ignore the hard questions that confront us once again. The American people have a right to expect their government, their military, and, yes, their press to provide honest information. But the answers regarding right or wrong, the worthiness and the effectiveness of the sacrifice of blood and treasure, rests, ultimately, with a wary, skeptical citizenry.

Notes

1. William C. Westmoreland, *A Soldier Reports* (New York: Dell, 1980), 553–58; Robert S. Elegant, "How to Lose a War," *Encounter*, August 1981, 73–90.

2. Herbert J. Gans, *Deciding What's News: A Study of CBS Evening News, NBC Nightly News, Newsweek, and Time* (New York: Pantheon, 1979), 42–43.

3. Douglass Cater and Walter Pincus, "The Foreign Legion of U.S. Public Relations," *Reporter*, December 12, 1960, 20; Otto Friedrich, "How to Be a War Correspondent," *Yale Review* 48 (March 1959): 474–80.

4. David Lawrence, "Our Own 'Iron Curtain,'" *U.S. News and World Report*, October 5, 1951, 6; "Journalism Group Scores U.S. Secrecy," *New York Times*, November 12, 1959, 12.

5. David Halberstam, *The Powers That Be* (New York: Knopf, 1979), 352–55;

Herbert S. Parmet, *Jack: The Struggles of John F. Kennedy* (New York: Dial, 1980), 258.

6. Joseph Alsop to John F. Kennedy, November 24, 1962, Joseph Alsop Papers, folder 5, box 18, Library of Congress; Karl E. Meyer, "Kennedy and the Press," *New Statesman,* April 12, 1963, 513.

7. Rusk to Nolting, February 20, 1962, Kennedy Papers, National Security File, box 195, John F. Kennedy Presidential Library (hereafter JFK Library), Boston.

8. Ibid.

9. Marguerite Higgins, *Our Vietnam Nightmare* (New York: Harper & Row, 1965), 108; "The View from Saigon," *Time,* September 20, 1963, 62; David Halberstam, *The Making of a Quagmire* (New York: Harper & Row, 1965), 273–74.

10. Neil Sheehan, *A Bright, Shining Lie: John Paul Vann and America in Vietnam* (New York: Random House, 1988), 352–53, 356–57.

11. Ibid., 314.

12. John Mecklin, *Mission in Torment: An Intimate Account of the U.S. Role in Vietnam* (Garden City, NY: Doubleday, 1965), 126; Halberstam, *Making of a Quagmire,* 28–32.

13. James Greenfield, Memorandum for Discussion, December 8, 1964, Thomson Papers, box 24, JFK Library.

14. Sieverts to Greenfield, April 30, 1965, James Thomson Papers, box 25, JFK Library.

15. Halberstam, *The Powers That Be,* 490; Memorandum of Discussion on Meeting in Mr. Moyers' Office, August 10, 1965, Lyndon B. Johnson Papers, NSF, boxes 196–97, Lyndon Baines Johnson Presidential Library, Austin, TX.

16. "The Press: Room for Improvement," *Newsweek,* July 10, 1967, 76; Topping to Daniel, February 6, 1966, Apple to Topping, February 27, 1967, and Topping to Apple, February 27, 1967, September 23, 1967, Foreign Desk Papers, *New York Times* Archives, New York.

17. "Crud, Fret, and Jeers," *Time,* June 10, 1966, 53.

18. Baldwin to Daniel, December 27, 1966, Baldwin Papers, box 11, Yale University Library; Hanson W. Baldwin, "Bombing of the North," *New York Times,* December 30, 1966, 1; "The Tragedy of Vietnam," *New York Times,* January 2, 1967, 18; Daniel to Gerstenzang, January 16, 1967, Daniel Papers, *New York Times* Archives.

19. "U.S. Command Finds Nothing to Report," *New York Times,* January 10, 1971, 2.

13

Congress and the Vietnam War

Senate Doves and Their Impact on the War

Kyle Longley

"In our differences over Vietnam, we have let ourselves become hypno-tized into self delusion," Senator Albert A. Gore of Tennessee wrote in 1970. "We have gradually accepted the unholy, autistic reality that war creates. We have let Vietnam become a matter of partisan politics; and frequently we have devalued our moral currency to compound political nostrums and cater to prejudices, resorting to crude face-saving devices which counterfeit our highest traditional values and violate our pride in being the world's greatest democracy." "We must de-mesmerize our-selves," he concluded, "break through the shell of public relation formulae and jingoist slogans, and dispassionately analyze the kernel of our na-tional interest. What we must be really concerned about is saving the soul of our country and our individual honor and conscience."[1]

Since 1959, when he took a position on the Senate Foreign Relations Committee (SFRC), Gore had taken an often-contrary view to that of the various presidential administrations over South Vietnam. He worked with other senators, a group labeled *doves,* so named because they be-came leading advocates for a negotiated, peaceful solution to the conflict in Southeast Asia. Members included Wayne Morse (D-OR), Ernest Gru-ening (D-AK), George McGovern (D-SD), Frank Church (D-ID), Mike Mansfield (D-MT), and, ultimately, the powerful chair of the SFRC, J. William Fulbright (D-AR), who questioned the wisdom of escalation in

Senate Foreign Relations Committee, 94th Congress. Courtesy of the U.S. Senate Historical Office.

Vietnam. These senators, joined by others such as John Sherman Cooper (R-KY), Mark Hatfield (R-OR), Joseph Clark (D-PA), Stephen Young (D-OH), George Aiken (R-VT), Gaylord Nelson (D-WI), and Eugene McCarthy (D-MN), while remaining primarily in the minority throughout the conflict, became powerful opponents of the war. Using various forums, including the Senate floor, SFRC committee hearings, and the press, these doves consistently raised insightful critiques of the U.S. involvement in Vietnam. The result was that one of the most conservative institutions in the United States became a major source of dissent.

To better understand the evolution of the Senate doves, this essay looks at three major debates over Vietnam, beginning with the Tonkin Gulf Resolution, which the majority supported despite vocal opposition from Gruening and Morse. Then, it reviews the 1966 nationally televised SFRC hearings organized by Fulbright that shone the spotlight on the conflict for many Americans. Finally, it focuses on the congressional debates on the Cooper-Church and McGovern-Hatfield amendments following the U.S. invasion of Cambodia in April 1970. The essay demonstrates that the constant pressure exerted by the doves ultimately helped lead to a U.S. withdrawal in 1973.

The Evolution of the Doves

Throughout American history, many dissenting voices have been raised in Congress over foreign policy matters. Among them was that of a young Illinois congressman, Abraham Lincoln (Whig-IL), who demanded that President James K. Polk show the exact spot on the U.S.-Mexico border where blood had been spilled in 1846. Williams Jennings Bryan (D-NE) was a vocal critic of the U.S. involvement in the Philippines, and Jeannette Rankin (R-MT) voted against American entry into both World War I and World War II. However, during World War II and the early Cold War, criticisms had abated as most Americans remained true to a bipartisan foreign policy that took America out of its traditional political and diplomatic isolationism and thrust the country into world leadership against the Communist threat.

The group in the Senate that ultimately became the cornerstone of dissent relating to Vietnam was hardly homogeneous, but there were some important similarities among its members. For example, Mansfield, Gruening, Morse, McGovern, and Gore had strong roots in the populist/progressive traditions of the late nineteenth and early twentieth century. Morse's neighbor while growing up in Wisconsin was Robert LaFollette (R-WI), and McGovern had studied under Arthur Link, a prominent historian of the progressive era and Woodrow Wilson. Gruening had been the editor of *The Nation* and a prominent critic in the 1920s of American intervention in Latin America. Gore's heroes were Bryan and his political mentor, the Tennessean Cordell Hull, an ardent Wilsonian who served as secretary of state under Franklin Roosevelt.[2]

In addition, most were well educated, with Mansfield and McGovern having Ph.D.s in history, the former in East Asian history, the latter in modern American history. Fulbright was a Rhodes scholar and former president of the University of Arkansas. Morse was a distinguished lawyer, and Church had practiced law after graduating from Stanford Law School. Only Gore, who had a degree from Middle Tennessee State

Teacher's College and a law degree from the Nashville YMCA, lacked impressive educational credentials.

Finally, with the exception of the southerners Gore and Fulbright, the senators represented states with traditions of dissent. Church's home state was that of William Borah, and Jeannette Rankin hailed from Mansfield's Montana. Morse always remembered LaFollette's tradition of dissent. The setting was important as the state political cultures encouraged opposition in foreign affairs and especially in issues relating to war.

With backgrounds that encouraged questioning the majority opinion, the group developed foreign policy disagreements with the administrations of Dwight Eisenhower and John Kennedy. It began to break with the internationalist consensus in the late 1950s over issues such as nuclear testing, American support of dictators such as Nationalist China's Chiang Kai-shek and Iran's Reza Shah Pahlavi Mohammad, and the growing volatility in Vietnam.[3] Dissenters often expressed their concerns privately, especially during the Kennedy administration, when most of the group maintained cordial relations with the White House. Yet, as conditions deteriorated in Vietnam after 1963, the critiques became more public and pointed.

The process began early for Mike Mansfield, who became the Senate majority leader when Lyndon Johnson became vice president in 1961. Since the debacle of the French in 1954 at Dien Bien Phu, Mansfield had watched with growing trepidation the increased commitment of the United States in South Vietnam. While an early supporter of South Vietnamese president Ngo Dinh Diem, Mansfield became more concerned after a trip to Vietnam in November 1962. On his return, he wrote a pessimistic report to Kennedy, stressing that the current problems could be addressed only if the Vietnamese pursued various remedies with "great vigor and self-dedication." He warned that, if the efforts failed, "it is difficult to conceive of alternatives, with the possible exception of a truly massive commitment of American military personnel and other resources . . . and the establishment of some sort of neo-colonial rule in South Vietnam." He added, "That is an alternative which I most emphatically do not recommend." To him, the key was reform and making it clear that "it is their country, their future which is most at stake, not ours."[4]

Gore joined Mansfield in voicing his concerns, building on earlier critiques of U.S. policy in South Vietnam that dated back to 1954. In October 1963, he told Secretary of Defense Robert McNamara in a session of the SFRC that he questioned the "enormous importance" placed by the military on South Vietnam, observing, "I know of no strategic material that it has, I know of nothing in surplus supply there except poor people and rice. It seems to me we have no need for either." "Why must we suffer such great losses in money and lives for an area which seems to me unessential to our welfare," he queried, "and to freedom, there being none there?"[5]

Others shared Mansfield's and Gore's concerns about the Diem government and the potential for the enormous deployment of American troops. They feared drawing the United States into a conflict that would swallow massive economic and military resources, weakening its ability to focus on containing communism on a global scale. Many, including President Kennedy near the end of his life, worried that South Vietnam had become a potential quagmire. The assassinations of Diem and Kennedy in November 1963 changed the dynamics and created a new volatility and sense of urgency for the doves.

The Gulf of Tonkin Debates

Less than a year after Kennedy's death, the situation in South Vietnam had deteriorated as the Viet Cong, with increasing assistance from the North Vietnamese, gained more control in the countryside. Diem's successors proved ineffective in combating the insurgency. While President Johnson wanted to focus on domestic issues, including civil rights and his campaign for reelection in 1964, Vietnam increasingly troubled the president and his advisers, especially in the wake of criticisms from the hard-line anti-Communist Republican challenger from Arizona, Barry Goldwater.

Despite the flurry of campaigning in 1964, international events gripped the country. On August 2, while supporting covert actions against North Vietnamese targets by South Vietnamese commandos, the USS *Maddox* came under attack by North Vietnamese torpedo boats. In response, Johnson ordered the USS *Turner Joy* to the area and promised, "If they do it again, they'll get another sting."[6] Two days later, in stormy weather, the two ships reported radar contacts and believed that they were under attack. This time, the administration wanted to retaliate, but not before Johnson sought some political cover.[7]

Working with Fulbright, Richard Russell (D-GA), and Everett Dirksen (R-IL), Johnson and his advisers built on some existing measures dating back years and produced the Tonkin Gulf Resolution, which granted the president the right to take "all necessary measures to repel any armed attacks against the forces or the United States and to prevent further aggression."[8] The administration demanded and received a promise that Congress would vote on the resolution in an expedited manner and with limited amendments.[9]

The resolution immediately went to Congress, where the House approved it unanimously after only forty-five minutes of discussion. Most senators also responded by rallying round the flag, although several voiced concerns. Gruening was an outspoken critic, calling the action a "predated declaration of war." He argued that the United States was continuing a colonial war begun by the French and that the "allegation that we are supporting freedom in South Vietnam has a hollow sound." The resolution to him was "an inevitable development of the U.S. steady escalation of our own military activities" and that "all Vietnam is not worth the life of a single American boy."[10]

Morse joined Gruening as the most passionate dissenter. For several hours spread over two days, mainly in a nearly empty Senate chamber, he critiqued the resolution, arguing that the South Vietnamese had provoked the response with its commando operations against northern targets.[11] He characterized the United States as ignoring its responsibilities under the UN Charter to settle disputes peacefully and predicted that the Johnson administration would deploy hundreds of thousands of troops and sustain substantial casualties. "The administration responsible" for such a conflict "will be rejected and repudiated," he asserted.[12] "Future generations will look with dismay upon a Congress which is now about to make such a historic mistake," he lamented.[13]

Finally, even those who ultimately voted for the measure, including Church, warned that the United States had failed during the Korean War to break the spirit of the North Koreans despite bombing "every house, bridge, road until there was nothing left but rubble." Church argued, "Expanding the war is not getting out, Mr. President. It is getting further in."[14]

Despite significant misgivings, senators such as Gore found themselves in a quandary, especially with a hard-fought campaign on the horizon in November against a hawkish Republican. Gore praised Church for raising his "reservations and doubts," but, when the debates started, he argued that "when U.S. forces have been attacked repeatedly upon the high seas . . . whatever doubts one may have entertained are water over the dam. Freedom of the seas must be preserved. Aggression against our forces must be repulsed."[15] Others expressed similar doubts but justified their decision to vote for the measure. McGovern emphasized that there was a "feeling in the country that we had to close ranks," especially after Kennedy's death. He also thought that "Johnson was too shrewd to get involved."[16]

Perhaps the most important turning point of the debates was the argument made by Fulbright that the resolution was a continuation of existing policy only, related to the attacks in the Tonkin Gulf, not the start of a massive escalation of American military capabilities.[17] While Johnson disputed Fulbright's rendition, George Reedy, LBJ's press secretary, noted that Fulbright "had very definite assurances from Johnson that the Tonkin Gulf Resolution was not going to be used for anything other than the Tonkin Gulf incident."[18]

Despite lingering skepticism among some senators, the administration easily won passage 88–2, with only Gruening and Morse dissenting. Within a short time, the Johnson administration proved Fulbright wrong. It struck back hard in 1964 with massive air strikes against North Vietnamese targets, and, once the election ended, it dramatically escalated the bombings, leading to new requirements for troops to protect the air bases. Within a year and a half, the American commitment to Vietnam had grown to several hundred thousand troops and billions of dollars.

Furthermore, over time, it became apparent that the second attack had not occurred, a point reinforced by the recent release of American and North Vietnamese documents.[19] Johnson and his military advisers wanted an excuse to strike back, and, while in the original stages they may not have knowingly misled Congress, they never rectified the mistake. Furthermore, much to the consternation of many people, the war increasingly became a quagmire.

Some immediately began to question the decision to escalate the American military presence. Speaking in Miami in late December 1964,

Gore openly clashed with the president. He publicly called for a negotiated settlement, sparking a walkout by some of the audience.[20] Gore continued to regret his vote for many years. Regarding the resolution, he wrote several years afterward: "Here the whole Congress was grievously remiss. I erroneously voted for the Tonkin Gulf Resolution in 1964." He stressed that he voted for it on the premise that there had been an "unprovoked attack" on a U.S. warship in international waters. "Later, I discovered and took a leading role in revealing that the events on that dark, murky, and fateful night in Tonkin Gulf provided but fragile, if any justification, for our subsequent actions."[21]

The problem was that, once Johnson began committing large numbers of troops, it was nearly impossible for Congress not to back them in the field with military appropriations. Once Congress in essence surrendered its constitutional ability to declare war, it found itself handcuffed. Furthermore, strong divisions developed between those who wanted full-scale war, those who supported President Johnson's limited efforts, and those doves who feared that the war would incite a confrontation with China and the Soviet Union, thus sparking World War III. The latter remained in the minority and found themselves fighting an uphill battle to shape U.S. policy for several years following the Tonkin Gulf Resolution.

The 1966 SFRC Hearings on Vietnam

After August 1964, President Johnson significantly increased the U.S. role in South Vietnam with the number of American troops in Vietnam and the intense bombing of North Vietnamese targets. He did so with the blessing of many congressmen, such as Senator Richard Russell (D-GA), who wanted to let the North Vietnamese "know they are in a war."[22] Others, such as Senator John Stennis (D-MS), a high-ranking member of the Armed Services Committee, told the Mississippi legislature in early 1966 that, ultimately, the war would require stationing more than 680,000 troops in Vietnam and the possible use of nuclear weapons if China intervened.[23]

However, dissenting views existed. Mansfield, recently returned from a presidential fact-finding tour in Vietnam, told Johnson that the "best chance of getting to the peace table is to minimize our military action." Fulbright, who had moved from administration supporter to dissenter

Senate Foreign Relations Committee, ca. 1960s. Courtesy of the U.S. Senate Historical Office.

after a clash with Johnson over the U.S. intervention in the Dominican Republic in 1965, also began pushing negotiation, asking, "If we win what do we do? Do we stay there forever?"[24] Others watched the escalation apprehensively but felt that they had little ability to change the administration's direction because, at the time, most Americans supported the president's decision.[25]

By the end of January 1966, however, a major confrontation developed between the doves on the SFRC and the White House. In response to the military buildup and the intensified bombing campaign, Fulbright opened to the public meetings on a $415 million supplemental foreign aid bill and arranged for the major networks to televise them during the afternoon. The powerful chairman had set the stage for the first major public debate on the war, much to the consternation of the White House.

Fulbright and his staff called sympathetic witnesses, including the primary architect of the containment policy, George Kennan, who argued against escalation largely because of his Eurocentric belief that it was a costly and questionable commitment of valuable resources in a peripheral area of limited strategic value to the United States. The distinguished diplomat emphasized: "The first point I would like to make is that if we were not already involved as we are today in Vietnam, I would know of no reason why we should wish to become so involved, and I could think of several reasons why we should wish not to." He expressed his opinion that the war had already damaged American prestige internationally and that "our country should not be asked . . . to shoulder the main burden of determining the political realities in any other country, and particularly not in one remote from our shores, from our culture, and from the experience of our people." He also stressed: "There is more respect to be won in the opinion of this world by a resolute and courageous liquidation of unsound positions than by the most stubborn pursuit of extravagant or unpromising objectives."[26]

From the beginning, Gore and others made their position clear. Gore grilled Secretary of State Dean Rusk, emphasizing, "Many people do not believe, many members of Congress do not believe, that the costs, the risk of nuclear war, the dangers of war with China or perhaps both China and Russia, are worth the endeavor." Next, he went after Rusk over the administration's liberal interpretation of the Gulf of Tonkin Resolution: "I certainly want to disassociate myself [from] any interpretation that this was a declaration of war . . . or that it authorized the Administration to take any and all steps toward an all-out war."[27]

Fulbright also lashed out at General Maxwell Taylor, who worked with administration stalwarts on the committee, including Thomas Dodd (D-CT), Frank Lausche (D-OH), and Bourke Hickenlooper (R-IA), to defend the White House's policies. In exchanges with Taylor, Fulbright underscored significant problems with the escalation. "I would regret to see us continue this war to the point where we engaged in an all-out war with China," he emphasized. Fulbright also pressured Taylor to explain the administration's opposition to negotiations with the Viet Cong and the North Vietnamese, stressing, "I would think a limited war would be where our real efforts are to seek a conference and propose a compromise in which we don't necessarily get our way and they don't surrender." When Taylor lamented that that would be tantamount to surrendering the 15 million South Vietnamese, Fulbright responded by asking why not liberate the Russians, Yugoslavs, or others. A frustrated Taylor responded, "That is not the issue for the moment."[28]

The event was the most important public television spectacle in Congress since the McCarthy-army hearings of 1954. The White House consistently tried to upstage the hearings by pressuring the major networks not to carry them and even orchestrating an impromptu meeting in Honolulu between the South Vietnamese leader, General Nguyen Cao Ky, and Johnson to shift the focus off the SFRC hearings. A Johnson aide, Mike Manatos, accused the senators of providing aid and comfort to the Viet Cong.[29] By February 19, Johnson ordered the FBI to "cover Senate Foreign Relations Committee television presentation with a view toward determining whether Senator Fulbright and other Senators were receiving information from Communists."[30] Everywhere, hawks criticized Fulbright, Gore, Church, McGovern, and the doves for being Communist dupes.

An estimated 22 million Americans watched the hearings. At one point, Gore told a story about a journalist who went home and found his wife transfixed on the hearings. She met her husband at the door with the greeting: "You have an unclean house but a highly informed wife."[31] Pat Holt, one of the SFRC staff members, stressed that he thought that "those initial hearings in early 1966 were significant" because "they contributed to . . . the erosion of support for the Johnson policy in the Senate." He added, "They also made public dissent more acceptable because the dissenters were no longer a bunch of crazy college kids invading deans' offices . . . they were people of substance."[32]

In his own family, Gore won the admiration of his son, the future senator and vice president, who skipped classes at Harvard to watch his father. He wrote his girlfriend, Tipper, that he had talked with his father, who "was so pleased when I told him I missed two or three days of classes to watch him on television": "He tried not to show it and said I shouldn't have missed classes, but he was awfully pleased." In addition, he recalled that his father's "TV appearances as a member of the Senate Foreign Relations Committee, when he challenged LBJ, made me swell with pride."[33]

Although Fulbright was heartened by the public's attention, the hearing would have only a limited impact, as he wrote in March 1966: "The most favorable thing the hearings can possibly accomplish is to prevent the enormous escalation of the war."[34] The doves found themselves again frustrated as Gen. William Westmoreland continued requesting more troops and funds to broaden the war. While there was growing opposition in both the House and the Senate, the doves continued to find that withdrawing troops once they had been committed was extremely difficult. Even the Tet Offensive of early 1968, which shook the country and helped ensure that LBJ did not seek reelection, left the doves desperately trying to push for withdrawal while still supporting the troops. Newly elected Richard Nixon's promise of a secret plan for extricating the United States from the quagmire left many wondering how quickly the extrication would occur. While often disheartened, especially as they saw Gruening lose his seat, partly in response to his opposition to Vietnam, the doves continued to try to find ways to push their agenda of ending U.S. involvement in Vietnam.

The Cooper-Church and McGovern-Hatfield Amendments

As 1970 opened and many members of Congress prepared for reelection campaigns, there was significant concern that the Nixon administration would expand the war in Southeast Asia. An unusual alliance had developed between Church and Cooper as the Idaho Democrat teamed with the older Kentucky Republican to try to limit the expansion of the war into Thailand, Laos, and Cambodia. In late 1969, they had pushed forward the first of the Cooper-Church amendments that passed in secret session to limit the introduction of ground troops into Laos and Thailand.[35]

Events intervened to accelerate the efforts of Cooper and Church. The situation in Cambodia had become unstable after Gen. Lon Nol overthrew the neutralist Prince Norodom Sihanouk. Nol received immediate recognition and secret military aid from the White House in return for trying to disrupt operations on the Ho Chi Minh Trail. By April 30, Nixon decided to launch an offensive into Cambodia to destroy the Central Office for South Vietnam and limit the offensive capabilities of the North Vietnamese army (NVA). He worried that, "if when the chips are down, the world's most powerful nation acts like a pitiful helpless giant, the forces of totalitarianism and anarchy will threaten free nations and free institutions throughout the world."[36]

An immediate outcry arose across the country. Antiwar activists denounced the action, leading to marches and confrontations at many university campuses. Ultimately, national guardsmen in Ohio and state police in Mississippi killed students at Kent State and Jackson State. Soon after, 100,000 protestors gathered in Washington, DC, in the first week of May to publicly criticize the invasion and the president.[37]

Doves in Congress also joined the chorus. An infuriated Church went to the Senate floor and characterized the invasion as Nixon's refusal to "acknowledge the futility of our continued military intervention in Vietnam." Arguing that the nation had to recognize "the impossibility of sustaining at any acceptable cost an anticommunist regime in Saigon, allied with, dependent on, and supported by the United States," Church concluded that the "policy itself was deeply unsound, extraneous to American interests and offensive to American values."[38]

Working in conjunction with others, including Church and Fulbright, Gore addressed the Senate immediately and complained that the president had promised only eleven days earlier that peace was in sight. "Can it possibly be that this major military operation was not in preparation 10 days ago?" Gore asked. He continued: "If, by reason and logic, the security of the United States impels an invasion of another nation, why should we pick upon neutral, little Cambodia?"[39] He denounced the action for merely widening the war and criticized the administration for failing to realize that the enemy's sanctuaries would extend from the Cambodian border to "all of Asia behind it."[40] "Today is a sad and bloody day," he concluded.[41]

For several months, doves clashed with the White House over the Cambodian invasion. On May 11, Cooper and Church introduced an amendment to a military sales bill cutting the appropriations for troops in Cambodia on July 1. Critics chastised them for providing Nixon some room to maneuver to remove the troops by the deadline. On the other side, some detractors complained that the amendment undermined the president's abilities to wage war, but Church and others responded that this remained a congressional power, especially when expanding an intervention into another sovereign nation.[42]

While the Nixon administration maneuvered to delay the Cooper-Church Amendment, the Senate repealed the Tonkin Gulf Resolution by a vote of 81–10. Nixon also waged a public relations campaign, declaring that the invasion of Cambodia was "the most successful operation of this long and difficult war" and that the "major military objectives have been achieved."[43] At the same time, he began withdrawing American troops and promised that the remainder would be out by the end of June.

As the doves moved the Cooper-Church Amendment forward, Church declared that he believed that it was the first step in moving the United States out of Vietnam by "setting the outer limits . . . to American involvement in Cambodia." He added, "Its adoption would also signal that Congress recognizes and stands willing to reassert its share of the responsibility for bringing the war to a close." He chastised the opponents who "would concede all power to the Presidency": "They would reduce the Congress of the United States to impotence, while making the President an autocrat supreme."[44]

Ultimately, just a few days before the effective date of implementation, the Cooper-Church Amendment passed 58–37. The House, however, hesitated. It would not pass the amendment, and then only a modified version, for nearly six months.[45] Nevertheless, Cooper, Church, and their allies declared victory, and despite some public and private pronouncements to the contrary, Nixon acknowledged that it was the "first restrictive vote ever cast on a President in wartime."[46]

In response, Nixon and the White House sought to retaliate against the doves. The president told several congressional leaders that, if "Congress undertakes to restrict me, Congress will have to assume the consequences."[47] The White House proposed the Huston Plan in July 1970, which allowed intelligence groups to use wiretaps, search mail, and burglarize offices of opponents suspected of cooperating with foreign governments. The FBI director, J. Edgar Hoover, immediately rejected it, but the proposal highlighted Nixon's growing paranoia and desire for retribution.[48]

A far more serious challenge than the Church-Cooper Amendment came from another quarter centered in the president's own party. Almost simultaneously with the U.S. encroachment into Cambodia, Mark Hatfield, a relatively recent, 1966 addition to the Senate who became a leading Republican critic of the war, joined with McGovern and attached an amendment to a military procurement bill. The Hatfield-McGovern bill, submitted in late April 1970, the so-called amendment to end the war, called for withdrawal from Cambodia in thirty days, a termination of military operations in Laos by December 30, 1970, and the removal of U.S. troops from Vietnam by June 30, 1971, with any appropriations after December 30, 1970, devoted only to the safe extrication of U.S. troops from the region.[49]

During the debates in early September, McGovern gave an impassioned speech on the Senate floor in which he emphasized that Vietnam was "the cruelest, the most barbaric, and the most stupid war in our national history" and that the Congress had allowed its constitutional authority "to slip out of our hands until it now resides behind closed doors [in] . . . the basement of the White House." He went on to say, "And every senator in this chamber is partly responsible for sending 50,000 young Americans to an early grave. This chamber reeks of blood. Every Senator here is partly responsible for the human wreckage at Walter Reed and Bethesda Naval and all across our land—young boys without legs, or arms, or genitals, or faces, or hopes. . . . And if we don't end this foolish, damnable war, those young men will some day curse us for our pitiful willingness to let the Executive carry the burden that the Constitution places on us."[50]

In the final tally, the amendment failed 55–39. A majority of Senate Democrats (thirty-two) voted in favor, as did seven Republicans. However, thirty-four Republicans and twenty-one Democrats voted to kill the bill; Hatfield believed that they thought it too "radical" in terms of usurping the president's power to make foreign policy. Nevertheless, Stephen Young stressed: "Thirty-nine senators today have spoken out in clear and convincing terms that the United States must disengage and withdraw combat troops from Vietnam next year."[51]

Despite the setback, Hatfield and McGovern introduced a similar bill in January 1971 titled "Vietnam Disengagement Act of 1971." It called for cutting funds to any troop levels exceeding 284,000 soldiers in May 1971 and afterward, the use of funds only for the withdrawal of troops, negotiations for the release of prisoners of war, and resettlement of Vietnamese. Hatfield declared on the Senate floor, "A negotiated settlement is the means for ending the war. A timetable for withdrawal is the means to enable authentic negotiations. It is also the means for assuring the return of our prisoners of war."[52]

After running into roadblocks, Hatfield and McGovern changed tactics and attached a rider to a selective service bill that called for changes to the "Vietnam Disengagement Act." It moved beyond withdrawing troops only from Vietnam to withdrawing them from all Indochina. Trying to win more moderate support, the rider tied funding restrictions to North Vietnamese concessions on the prisoner-of-war issue. As the debates began in June, Hatfield emphasized that, since the last debates on

Senate Foreign Relations Committee, ca. 1960s. Courtesy of the U.S. Senate Histori-cal Office.

the stop-the-war amendment, more than "2,811 Americans have died in Indochina," that "11,250 Americans have been wounded," and that "we are no closer to peace."[53]

The opposition fought back. Senator Robert Dole (R-KS) complained that the amendment's supporters "read like a Who's Who of has-beens, would-bes, professional second-guessers, and apologists for the policies which led us into this tragic conflict in the first place." Stennis also la-mented that the amendment would "be tantamount to desertion of our American boys on the battlefield."[54]

Despite the eloquent pleas of Hatfield and many others, the measure failed 55–42, with the coalition gaining only three votes since the Sep-tember 1970 vote, a process made more difficult by the defeat in 1970 of several dovish senators and the approaching midterm elections, when some others faced major challenges. Still, the continued debate kept the pressure on the Nixon administration to prevent an escalation of the war and to find a way to extricate the United States from Vietnam.

The passage of the Cooper-Church Amendment, the repeal of the Tonkin Gulf Resolution, and the continued support among a large and prominent minority of senators of the Hatfield-McGovern Amendment were significant achievements, although not powerful enough to force the United States immediately out of South Vietnam. In the White House, National Security Adviser Henry Kissinger bitterly complained about the emerging pattern in which doves "would introduce one amendment after another, forcing the Administration into unending rearguard actions."[55] The pressure affected the White House and led to renewed efforts in Paris to negotiate with the North Vietnamese for the withdrawal of U.S. troops and the return of prisoners of war, although the process was slow and contentious.

Withdrawal: The Doves' Final Victory?

After 1971, the Senate doves and their House allies continued pressuring the Nixon administration to withdraw from Vietnam. There were casualties in the process. In 1970, Gore had been defeated by the hawkish Nixon supporter Bill Brock after the Republican's campaign made Vietnam a central issue, tying it to law-and-order issues on college campuses. Nixon, Vice President Spiro Agnew, and U.S. Army chief of staff William Westmoreland made several visits during the campaign and even funneled illegal monies into Brock's coffers.[56] Other critics of Nixon's policies fell too, such as Ralph Yarborough (D-TX), Joseph Tydings (D-MD), and Charles Goodell (D-NY), although other issues weighed in heavily.[57]

Despite these setbacks in 1970, the efforts of the doves continued to be a constant source of irritation for Nixon and the White House, who faced a reelection campaign in 1972 against McGovern. The pressure, along with the disclosures of the My Lai massacre and the release of the Pentagon Papers, pushed the administration to pursue negotiations with the North Vietnamese and troop withdrawals. The threat of the passage of an "end-the-war" resolution restrained the White House during the Easter Offensive of 1972 and pushed the negotiators in early 1973. "We took the threats from Congress seriously," one White House aide later recalled. They knew they were "racing the clock" and faced possibly "stern action."[58] The pressure worked and pushed Kissinger to work harder to promulgate the Paris Peace Accords in 1973.[59]

Afterward, Congress sought to rein in the powers of the president. Nixon, weakened by the Watergate scandal, could not prevent Congress from passing the War Powers Act of 1973. That legislation, a watered-down version of the original one proposed by Senator Jacob Javits (R-NY), required the president to report to Congress within forty-eight hours the deployment of U.S. troops and to withdraw troops within sixty days unless Congress explicitly supported the intervention. Nixon vetoed the measure, but Congress overrode him. While many debates have followed on the effectiveness of the War Powers Act, it clearly sent a message to the floundering Nixon administration on where Congress stood on the war.[60]

Though Nixon resigned in 1974, after a congressional committee recommended articles of impeachment for his part in Watergate, Congress continued asserting its power. As the North Vietnamese and their Viet Cong allies moved steadily toward defeating the Army of the Republic of Vietnam (ARVN), the newly installed president, Gerald Ford, and Secretary of State Kissinger requested $1.5 billion for the Saigon government. Congress, however, appropriated only $700 million. In March 1975, the enemy launched a major offensive. As the ARVN collapsed, President Ford requested an emergency $300 million loan, but Congress rejected it. As the NVA and Viet Cong moved closer to victory, Ford asked for $722 million, but Congress granted only $300 million for humanitarian assistance and evacuation efforts. In response, Kissinger noted, "The Vietnam debate has run its course." By early May, South Vietnam no longer existed as the NVA overran Saigon, and President Ford concluded that the Vietnam War was "finished as far as the United States is concerned."[61]

Conclusion

In the final analysis, the doves in the Senate, working in conjunction with others in Congress opposed to the war, helped extricate the United States from the quagmire in Vietnam. They also helped prevent the conflict from expanding into a global one involving Communist China and the Soviet Union. There were many other forces at work, including the larger antiwar movement, divisions in the military and other government agencies, and, of course, the resistance of the enemy, but the opposition of the Senate doves was essential. It was a slow, frustrating, and often painful process that cost the political careers of several dissenters. The methods that the doves employed often took significant time and effort, including the use of the Senate floor, committee meetings, and other outside efforts to educate the American public. They often encountered significant opposition from more hawkish members of Congress and the White House, who questioned their patriotism and fortitude. Yet, in the final analysis, events vindicated their positions, and their efforts helped push several administrations away from war and toward a path out of Vietnam.

Notes

1. Albert A. Gore, *The Eye of the Storm: A People's Politics for the Seventies* (New York: Herder & Herder, 1970), 10.

2. Kyle Longley, *Senator Albert Gore, Sr.: Tennessee Maverick* (Baton Rouge: Louisiana State University Press, 2004); Don Oberdorfer, *Senator Mansfield: The Extraordinary Life of a Great American Statesman and Diplomat* (Washington, DC: Smithsonian Books, 2003); Robert D. Johnson, *Ernest Gruening and the American Dissenting Tradition* (Cambridge, MA: Harvard University Press, 1998); Mason Drukman, *Wayne Morse: A Political Biography* (Portland: Oregon Historical Society Press, 1997); LeRoy Ashby and Rod Gramer, *Fighting the Odds: The Life of Senator Frank Church* (Pullman: Washington State University Press, 1994); Randall Woods, *Fulbright: A Biography* (New York: Cambridge University Press, 1995).

3. Robert D. Johnson, "The Origins of Dissent: Senate Liberals and Vietnam, 1959–1964," *Pacific Historical Review* 65 (1996): 249–75.

4. Gore quoted in Oberdorfer, *Senator Mansfield,* 192–93.

5. Gore, *The Eye of the Storm,* 7.

6. Johnson quoted in George Herring, *America's Longest War: The United States and Vietnam, 1950–1975,* 4th ed. (Boston: McGraw-Hill, 2002), 134.

7. Edwin E. Moise, *Tonkin Gulf and the Escalation of the Vietnam War* (Chapel Hill: University of North Carolina Press, 1996), 73–142.

8. Resolution quoted in George Donelson Moss, *Vietnam: An American Ordeal* (Upper Saddle River, NJ: Prentice-Hall, 1998), 173.

9. Oberdorfer, *Senator Mansfield,* 246.

10. Gruening quoted in Johnson, *The American Dissenting Tradition,* 253–54. Gruening later complained, "In sum, while the Johnson administration was charging that its action was to repel and prevent aggression, it was itself the aggressor, a paradox applicable not only to the Tonkin Gulf incident but to the whole war in Southeast Asia." Ernest Gruening, *Many Battles: The Autobiography of Ernest Gruening* (New York: Liveright, 1973), 472. See also Ernest Gruening and Herbert Wilton Beaser, *Vietnam Folly* (Washington, DC: National Press, 1968).

11. H. R. McMaster, *Dereliction of Duty: Lyndon Johnson, Robert McNamara, the Joint Chiefs of Staff, and the Lies That Led to Vietnam* (New York: HarperCollins, 1997), 134.

12. Morse quoted in Robert D. Schulzinger, *A Time for War: The United States and Vietnam, 1941–1975* (New York: Oxford University Press, 1997), 152.

13. Morse quoted in Drukman, *Wayne Morse,* 413.

14. Church quoted in Ezra Y. Siff, *Why the Senate Slept: The Gulf of Tonkin Resolution and the Beginning of America's Vietnam War* (Westport, CT: Praeger, 1999), 61–62.

15. *Congressional Record* 110, pt. 19 (August 6, 1964): 18075.

16. George McGovern, telephone interview with the author, August 25, 2001.

17. Woods, *Fulbright,* 355. Partisanship also played a role for some Democrats, fearful of how Goldwater would exploit the attacks for political advantage.

18. Reedy quoted in Oberdorfer, *Senator Mansfield,* 247.

19. Robert S. McNamara, James G. Blight, and Robert K. Brigham, *Argument without End: In Search of Answers to the Vietnam Tragedy* (New York: Public Affairs, 1999), 202–4.

20. *Nashville Tennessean,* January 1, 1965.

21. Gore, *The Eye of the Storm,* 8–9.

22. Russell quoted in William C. Berman, *William Fulbright and the Vietnam War: The Dissent of a Political Realist* (Kent, OH: Kent State University Press, 1988), 53. Privately, Russell harbored reservations about the escalation and chances for a military victory, but, publicly, he supported Johnson.

23. Stennis quoted in ibid., 52–53.

24. Mansfield and Fulbright quoted in ibid. Mansfield's report indicated that the military escalation had accomplished little, other than further involving the United States, and that further escalation appeared unlikely to change the situation dramatically. Francis R. Valeo, *Mike Mansfield, Majority Leader* (Armonk, NY: Sharpe, 1999), 203–6.

25. Robert David Johnson, *Congress and the Cold War* (New York: Cambridge University Press, 2006), 120.

26. *The Vietnam Hearings* (New York: Vintage, 1966), 108–14.

27. Ibid., 15, 43–46.

28. Ibid., 206, 223.

29. Johnson, *The American Dissenting Tradition,* 274.

30. Athan G. Theoharis, ed., *From the Secret Files of J. Edgar Hoover* (Chicago: Dee, 1991), 237.

31. Melvin Small, *Johnson, Nixon, and the Doves* (New Brunswick, NJ: Rutgers University Press, 1988), 79.

32. "Pat M. Holt, Chief of Staff, Foreign Relations Committee," 203, Oral History Interviews, Senate Historical Office, Washington, DC.

33. Douglas Brinkley, interview with Al Gore, September 4, 1999, New Orleans,

Louisiana. (I thank Professor Brinkley for loaning me a copy of this unpublished interview.)

34. Fulbright quoted in Woods, *Fulbright,* 403.

35. Ashby and Gramer, *Fighting the Odds,* 300–302.

36. Nixon quoted in Herring, *America's Longest War,* 261.

37. Kenneth J. Heineman, *Put Your Bodies upon the Wheels: Student Revolt in the 1960s* (Chicago: Dee, 2001), 175–76.

38. Church quoted in David F. Schmitz, "Congress Must Draw the Line: Senator Frank Church and Opposition to the Vietnam War and the Imperial Presidency," in *Vietnam and the American Political Tradition: The Politics of Dissent,* ed. Randall B. Woods (New York: Cambridge University Press, 2003), 138.

39. *Congressional Record* 116, pt. 34 (May 1, 1970): 13835.

40. Gore quoted in Ashby and Gramer, *Fighting the Odds,* 309.

41. Gore quoted in Robert Mann, *A Grand Delusion: America's Descent into Vietnam* (New York: Basic, 2001), 659.

42. Schmitz, "Congress Must Draw the Line," 139.

43. Nixon quoted in Ashby and Gramer, *Fighting the Odds,* 315.

44. Church quoted in Schmitz, "Congress Must Draw the Line," 141.

45. Woods, *Fulbright,* 568–75.

46. Nixon quoted in Ashby and Gramer, *Fighting the Odds,* 330.

47. Nixon quoted in Henry Brandon, *The Retreat of American Power* (New York: Doubleday, 1974), 146–47.

48. Athan Theoharis, *Spying on Americans: Political Surveillance from Hoover to the Huston Plan* (Philadelphia: Temple University Press, 1978), 13–39.

49. Robert Eells and Bartell Nyberg, *Lonely Walk: The Life of Senator Mark Hatfield* (Chappaqua, NY: Christian Herald, 1979), 66.

50. *Congressional Record* 116, pt. 34 (September 1, 1970): 30567.

51. Young quoted in Thomas Knock, "'Come Home, America': The Story of George McGovern," in *Vietnam and the American Political Tradition,* ed. Woods, 116–17.

52. Hatfield quoted in Eells and Nyberg, *Lonely Walk,* 67–68.

53. Hatfield quoted in ibid., 68.

54. Dole and Stennis quoted in Johnson, *Congress and the Cold War,* 181.

55. Henry Kissinger, *White House Years* (Boston: Little, Brown, 1979), 513.

56. Longley, *Senator Albert Gore, Sr.,* 217–40.

57. Johnson, *Congress and the Cold War,* 172.

58. Charles Colson, *Born Again* (Old Tappan, NJ: Chosen, 1976), 77–79.

59. George C. Herring, "The Executive, Congress, and the Vietnam War, 1965–1975," in *Congress and United States Foreign Policy: Controlling the Use of Force in a Nuclear Age,* ed. Michael Barnhart (New York: State University of New York Press, 1987), 182; P. Edward Haley, *Congress and the Fall of South Vietnam and Cambodia* (Rutherford, NJ: Fairleigh Dickinson University Press, 1982).

60. Schulzinger, *A Time for War,* 314.

61. Ford quoted in Herring, *America's Longest War*, 336. Some analysts continue to critique Congress's role (as well as that of the press and the antiwar movement) and argue that it sold out the Vietnamese when it reduced assistance. For examples, see Melvin R. Laird, "Iraq: Learning the Lessons of Vietnam," *Foreign Affairs*, November/December 2005, 22–43, available online at http://www.foreignaffairs.org/20051101faessay84604-p10/melvin-r-laird/iraq-learning-the-lessons-of-vietnam.html; and Lewis Sorley, *A Better War: The Unexamined Victories and Final Tragedy of America's Last Years in Vietnam* (New York: Harvest, 2000).

14

In the Valley

The Combat Infantryman and the Vietnam War

Yvonne Honeycutt Baldwin and John Ernst

> The myth of a war tells what is imaginable and manageable; the soldiers' tale,
> in its infinite variety, tells the whole story.
> —Samuel Hynes, *The Soldiers' Tale: Bearing Witness to Modern War*

The American combat soldier's experience in the Vietnam War was, according to some, different from that in any other war in the nation's history.[1] Chosen by a draft that selected the nation's poor and working-class youths, shaped by a troop-rotation system that focused on individuals rather than units or regiments, confronted by an enemy who was at once everywhere and nowhere, disillusioned and frustrated by divisions on the home front, and ultimately blamed by an angry public for failing to win an unwinnable war, Vietnam veterans share a long list of stereotypes. Myths abound. Only those who experienced combat know the truth, and, even among that group, no consensus exists. As a number of soldiers and historians correctly concluded, Vietnam was a "time- and space-sensitive" conflict that affected individuals differently depending on when, where, and in what capacity they served.[2] In fact, one of the few historical truths concerning the war is that there was nothing monolithic about the soldiers' experience or, for that matter, about the Vietnam generation as a whole.[3]

That generation's war was different in its execution. Although large engagements took place in the Ia Drang Valley, at Khe Sanh, An Loc, and Hue, and later, around Saigon and elsewhere, the war was more often characterized by quick and grim one-on-one confrontations, ambushes, long-range patrols that stretched from days into weeks, blind searches in dark tunnels, and endless humping the boonies to draw enemy fire. It was deadly work, and, unlike the set-piece battles and large-scale strategic operations carried out at the division and battalion level in previous American wars, most Vietnam combat took place at the company, platoon, and squad level. The casualty rate for maneuver battalions, units that actually engaged the enemy, equaled or exceeded that of World War II and Korea, but the quick response and skill of aeromedical evacuation procedures meant fewer fatalities. The familiar "dust-off" helicopters carried an estimated 400,000 American wounded and a much larger number of Vietnamese to field hospitals and other medical facilities between 1963 and 1973, and over 81 percent of men wounded in battle in Vietnam survived, a full 10 percent higher than during World War II.[4]

In previous wars, people died taking and holding territory or liberating cities from the enemy. In Vietnam, soldiers took and retook the same territory time after time. The objectives were nebulous and became even more so as the war dragged on. The words *search and secure* conveyed no permanence as situations changed radically from morning to night. American soldiers served as bait to draw fire and expose enemy positions to the highly destructive U.S. air strikes that cratered the landscape but frequently missed human targets, who simply faded into the cover of villages and triple-canopy jungles to regroup and fight another day.

Frontline combat troops, aptly known as *grunts,* slogged through exhausting climate and terrain and faced a formidable opponent, the North Vietnamese army (NVA) and the Viet Cong (VC), the southern guerrillas who often selected the terms and time of battle. The experience took an immense physical and emotional toll. Americans suffered searing heat, monsoon rains, swamps, and rice paddies. Leeches, lice, mosquitoes, malaria, dysentery, fungus-like foot rot, and ringworm plagued grunts. Effectively using the jungle, the insurgents relied primarily "on the formless yet lethal nature of guerrilla warfare," including sniper fire, mines, and booby traps.[5] These deadly devices resulted in high rates of death and dismemberment and accounted for roughly one-fourth of all U.S. casual-

"Brother Howell," who served with the South Vietnamese regional forces, developed a close friendship with Tom Mullins. Mullins's unit housed troops with families in the nearby village of Ca Lu, and Tom often stayed with Brother Howell's family. Mullins recalls how hard the war was on villagers. "They had a baby we nicknamed 'Humphrey' because he looked like the vice president. Humphrey was killed when North Vietnamese sappers attacked the village." Courtesy of Tom Mullins.

ties in Vietnam. Apprehensive Americans could not always decide who was friendly and who was a guerrilla among the South Vietnamese. Most grunts spoke little Vietnamese, broadening the already painfully obvious cultural gap. The long, frustrating struggle between the powerful Western giant and what Lyndon Johnson termed the "raggedy-ass fourth-rate country" proved the wisdom of Aesop's fable of the bull and the mouse.[6]

The 365-day rotations for army personnel and thirteen-month tours for marines were considerably shorter than the time served by draftees in World War I, World War II, and, in most cases, Korea. Unlike their forebears at Ypres and the Battle of the Bulge, who knew they were in the war until it ended or they were carried from the field, those who served in Vietnam memorized their DEROS (date eligible for return from overseas), and simply living to see that day constituted the object of their war. Their departure from "the World" was not marked by cheering crowds assembled to celebrate their valor and wish them well, and their arrival "in-country" was more like a wake than a reception. No local or national officials stood ready to welcome them as liberators when their planes landed at Cam Rahn Bay, Bien Hoa, or Ton Son Nhut. And, for those who returned wounded or whole, quite often the only crowds greeting them at the airports had come to protest the war or conduct ritual spittings like those at Oakland, California. In general, the veterans came home to a quiet and indifferent nation that preferred to forget about the war and the unrest it had caused.

Spirited away on chartered airlines, most of America's warriors in Vietnam left their youth in the cabins of DC-10s marked World Airways, TIA, and Flying Tigers as they bade farewell to sad-eyed but smiling flight attendants and took in the fetid air of the place they called *the Nam*. As they left the plane and made their way to the processing area, most "FNGs" (fucking new guys) exchanged glances with at least one "salt," a homeward-bound veteran whose "old eyes" wore the "thousand-yard stare," an expression that said nothing but spoke volumes about what awaited replacement troops in the ground war in Vietnam. Most of the departees did not speak, but some heckled the new arrivals or wished them luck. The Kentuckian Barry Campbell recalled the day he arrived in Vietnam, although he has little memory of what he experienced there. It was "really really gloomy—just gray," he noted. It was July—monsoon season. Assigned to the Second Battalion, First Marine Division (2/1), Campbell flew from DaNang to Phu Bai, but this time he was not aboard a civilian charter. No smiling flight attendants served drinks on the C-130, and the webbed seats facing backward made him dizzy and disoriented. The airstrip "was terrible"—"about like a dirt road"—so the landing was rough. When he got to his unit, he stopped a young marine, trying to find out where to report. "Who's in charge?" he queried. "In charge of what?" came the reply. Some units established rituals to greet and initiate FNGs and integrate them into the unit, "married" to more experienced comrades. Others isolated them until they had learned the ropes on their own. Campbell's unit "never really greeted a new incoming," he asserted. "It was one man work."[7]

They called their location "The Hill," but it was "more like a pile of cinders." Each man had a rubber mattress for a bed and one blanket. The blanket went under the rubber mattress, to keep the cinders from poking holes in it. "Helicopters coming in would blow the tents away because tent pegs wouldn't go into the cinders," Campbell remembered, and several times a night they had to locate and reposition both tents and bedding. Campbell did not sleep at all the first night. However, like the seasoned men of 2/1, it soon dawned on him that "it was survive— kill or get killed. After that point you just go numb. You survive this hour. You were numb to everything—the weather included. The coldest

I ever remember being it was 76 degrees. Just standing there soaking wet, freezing."[8]

The journalist and author Charles Bracelyn Flood, who spent several months observing a rifle battalion near Tuy Hoa in the II Corps region of the central highlands, argued that soldiers quickly adjusted to the possibility that they might be killed. "I don't believe this stuff that every eighteen-year-old thinks he's immortal. It only takes seeing a very little bit to rid you of that notion." Campbell harbored no illusions about his own mortality. He knew he could die. He just hoped and prayed he would not. And, like many who saw combat in Vietnam, he, at some point, also took on a deeply felt sense of responsibility not just for his own survival but for that of his closest comrades. Like many others who survived the ground war in Vietnam, he wondered why he lived when others did not. "Probably my worst day was the day I left. Knowing I was leaving those guys behind. Knowing that they might not make it."[9]

Most soldiers recall with startling clarity their first engagement, the first time they came face-to-face with the enemy, or the first time their unit endured mortar rounds or incoming fire. "It had started raining at around nine or so, and I was laying there. . . . It was cold and I was soaking wet and it was dark. . . . My pillow was a rock. I said the most heartfelt prayer I've ever said in my life," recalled Grant Furnas as he described his first encounter with the enemy in Vietnam. "It was a real eye-opener." At twenty-two, and with three years of college behind him, Furnas was not a typical draftee. He was better educated than most and exceeded the average age of most draftees by three years. He also believed that those three years provided him an edge in both experience and insight. They caused him "to step back and look at things and think about it a little bit more."[10]

After eight weeks of infantry basic training, Furnas was selected for six months of officer candidate school (OCS) at Ft. Benning, Georgia. As the war intensified, the army dealt with the need for officers by promoting, offering more ROTC scholarships, raising the size of classes at West Point by 25 percent, and stepping up efforts to recruit enlisted men with some college into OCS. It also established training programs that produced thirteen thousand noncommissioned officers (NCOs) by 1968.[11] Many of the "ninety-day-wonder" lieutenants and "Shake 'n Bake" NCOs appeared less than competent to the men they led, and complaints against them weakened morale and eroded public confidence in the U.S. military. Nevertheless, Furnas thought that his own training was "excellent": "It covered a little bit of everything. I think I was well prepared . . . for what I encountered over there." Commissioned a second lieutenant with an infantry military occupational specialty, he underwent three additional months of jungle training in Panama before going to Vietnam. The training cycle was not easy. Not everyone could handle the intensity, and the attrition rate was high. Furnas's OCS platoon began with thirty-three candidates but ended with only eleven. "People can say what they want, but the [lieutenants] at the platoon level generally were very, very good and got the job done and were well trained for it," he recalled.[12]

Unlike those soldiers who considered the preparation for leadership or combat inadequate, Furnas believed that his training prepared him for his job as an infantry lieutenant. Moreover, he developed a great deal of respect for the officers with whom he served, particularly a second lieutenant named Joe Hooper, who commanded the reinforcements that freed Furnas's platoon when it stumbled onto a way station on the Ho Chi Minh Trail. Equipped as a field hospital with Russian and Polish surgical equipment and instruments, the station included a mess hall and even a burial ground. Furnas's platoon of seventeen men was pinned down by enemy fire. Twelve of them were wounded and three killed. Later, as they walked through the hospital compound, Hooper saved a number of additional lives when he stepped over a booby trap wired to a sixty-millimeter mortar round. He instructed Furnas and an NCO to disarm the mechanism, but they wanted to "blow it in place." Hooper disarmed the device, and, although they wanted to run away, Furnas and the NCO simply "had to stand there within three feet while this idiot disarmed this booby trap."[13] Hooper proved to be one of the tragic stories of the war. Awarded the Congressional Medal of Honor in 1969, and often called the Audie Murphy of Vietnam, he battled alcoholism and died in his early forties.[14]

Although many combat veterans recall positive experiences within their platoons, others criticize the command structure at the battalion and division levels. Many reserve the harshest criticism for civilian war planners, military strategists, and politicians in Washington who applied the concept of limited war, employing conventional tactics in a war of attrition. The best they could achieve was stalemate in the face of the unconventional revolutionary warfare waged by the NVA and the VC, but it was the army in the field that appeared at fault. A general but pervasive lack of confidence in combat leadership extended all the way to the top. Although "Westy," Gen. William Westmoreland, initially was highly regarded in the ranks, by the time he was replaced as MACV (Military Assistance Command, Vietnam) commander by his former deputy, Gen. Creighton Abrams, his image, like that of many officers at both the field and the company grade, had been tarnished. Especially late in the war, rumors of fragging (the killing of superiors, often with fragmentation grenades), accounts of troops disobeying direct orders, and stories of glory seekers, headline grabbers, and outright incompetents exposed a demoralized military establishment suffering from significant and, perhaps, irreversible breakdowns in discipline and traditional codes of military behavior. Barry Campbell recalls that many of his unit's replacement officers were green lieutenants, "ROTC grads—they knew the answer, but they didn't know what the question was." "There was a lot of internal killing," he said.[15] Certainly, no reliable statistics exist on the number of commanders who were murdered, but evidence suggests that such incidents occurred with greater frequency in Vietnam than in other American wars and happened not only in combat zones but in rear areas as well.[16]

Problems grew in frequency and severity as the United States staged its withdrawal from Vietnam. As troops sought to avoid becoming the last casualty in a collapsing war effort, their reluctance manifested itself in several ways. Individuals simply refused to do what they were told. Platoons refused to conduct search-and-destroy missions. Patrols refused to hump the boonies as sitting ducks for snipers or NVA rifle companies, and occasionally entire units appeared on the verge of mutiny. Particularly at the end of the war, discipline had so deteriorated that even good field commanders had difficulty carrying out their mission in units disrupted by drug and alcohol use, racial tensions, and questions regarding the legality and conduct of the war itself. Most analysts agree that Abrams faced a very different army than Westmoreland had commanded.

Discipline and leadership problems plagued the military in the late 1960s, particularly after the 1968 Tet Offensive. But, in the early years of the war, there was better morale and a degree of continuity between training and placement in Vietnam. Gen. Tom Lynch, an infantry officer, who as a lieutenant colonel commanded the Third Battalion, Eighth Infantry, for seven months at "the Hub" near Tuy Hoa, recalled, "People trained in the Third Battalion, Eighth Infantry, and then they all went to Vietnam in the Third Battalion, Eighth Infantry, so there was a camaraderie in there, and they knew the officers. Because they were targeted by snipers, officers generally wore no identifying insignia, and troops were instructed not to salute or identify them in the field." Lynch carried an M-16 just like his troops. A good commander "knew the faces and you knew the people," he said, so the insignia was not necessary.[17]

Despite the gradual deterioration of the U.S. military effort in Vietnam, the growing stalemate, and eventual U.S. withdrawal, Grant Furnas, like thousands of others, took pride in his own military service and believed that most who served did so honorably. He rejected the print and film media's depiction of American soldiers in Vietnam as trigger-happy, Zippo lighter–carrying bands of wanton killers who failed to distinguish between civilians and combatants and the stereotyping that has contributed to the creation of some of the war's most destructive myths. Making incompetence, insubordination, drug use, and the commission of atrocities and murder appear routine perpetrated a "terrible injustice" on those who served and obscured actual responsibility for the loss of life and property, misplacing it on GIs when, in fact, it belonged on military tactics and technology, the firepower that has been characterized as "unparalleled in military history."[18]

Atrocities occurred in Vietnam, almost from the war's beginning, because the nature of guerrilla warfare lent itself to such severe behavior. In some isolated cases, such as the infamous Tiger Force unit, soldiers adopted brutal tactics to combat the insurgency. Occasionally, grunts snapped. America's darkest moment, the March 1968 My Lai massacre, resulted in the deaths of "504 unresisting Vietnamese civilians" in South Vietnam's Quang Ngai Province.[19] Atrocities, however, were not standard operating procedure, and most units frowned on the practice. For example, when nine soldiers from the First Marine Division raped a South Vietnamese woman and murdered several villagers, including two babies and some adults, during a September 1966 night patrol, U.S. officials investigated. Moreover, other marines in the First Division condemned their comrades' behavior and referred to them as the "Nasty Nine."[20]

Accounts of atrocities, combined with growing disillusionment with the U.S. war effort, created a widespread tendency to blame the warrior for the war and caused some combat veterans to deliberately conceal their Vietnam service for many years, packing it away and waiting for the memories to die. As the war receded in time and distance, veterans often found that the combat experience had become a highly charged part of their personal and political identity, and its intensity still sparked heated controversy, debate, division, and personal pain. "Was the war justified?" asked one combat veteran. "No. Should we have been there? No. Was it worthwhile? No. Was I proud to be there? Yes." Speaking for many frustrated veterans, he concluded: "All any of us wanted was recognition for being there." But the political climate gradually changed in the 1980s. "Now," he remarked, "it's all right to have been a soldier [in the Vietnam War]."[21]

Although the figures are imprecise, those who actually engaged the enemy in Vietnam are part of a distinct minority, constituting less than 40 percent of all combat and combat support troops at any given time. General Lynch, like most fighting men, acknowledged the critical role of support troops but stressed the important difference between support and combat in a war zone. At any given time, 80–85 percent of the men in Vietnam were engaged in troop support, not combat. Frontline soldiers derogatorily referred to such personnel as *rear echelon motherfuckers* (REMFs).[22] "The most dangerous thing they've got is getting killed in a traffic accident or VD," remarked Lynch. "I never saw Saigon. There are different wars. There was a war in the delta and a war in the metro areas [like] Saigon, and then there is a war in the central highlands. So when we tell our experience, we are talking for the most part in the central highlands. We had no rest. We had no showers. I commanded [my unit] for seven and a half months, and it stayed in the field."[23]

Even in combat units, large numbers of soldiers performed administrative and service duties rather than engaging in actual combat. Johnson's failure to mobilize the reserves and the national guard meant that the services had to rely on the draft to meet engineering, logistics, and supply needs, a process that created critical delays during the rapid escalation of the war in 1965. Nevertheless, a "logistics miracle" soon took place, making the American forces in Vietnam the "best fed, best clothed, best equipped army the nation had ever sent to war."[24]

It is also important to note that those who served in Vietnam in any capacity are vastly outnumbered by the nearly 16 million draft-age men who did not serve. The bulk of this number were exempted or disqualified, although 570,000 evaded the draft illegally and an estimated 30,000 fled the country. Two-thirds of draft-eligible men attributed their lack of service to some deliberate dodge.[25] Of the nearly 27 million men who reached draft age between 1964 and 1973, approximately 40 percent saw military service. Selective Service System rules required registration of all males on their eighteenth birthday, but the impact of the baby boom on demographics meant that only 10 percent of the eligible male population actually served in Vietnam. Only 2 percent of that number actually served in combat, a group primarily composed of draftees or "reluctant volunteers," men who volunteered for military service hoping to exercise some control over their service assignment.

Lawrence Baskir and William Strauss's 1978 analysis of draft statistics shows that nonwhite, less well-educated men were more likely to be inducted and far more likely to serve in Vietnam than white, well-educated men. Baskir and Strauss concluded that minorities did more than their share of service and suffered casualties out of proportion to their share of the total military manpower and U.S. forces in Vietnam. The most serious inequities were social and economic, they argued.[26] The historian Christian Appy's 1993 book labeled Vietnam a *working-class war* and claimed that in it, more than in any other American war in the twentieth century, young men from prosperous families were able to avoid the draft. Class, not geography, Appy asserted, was the crucial factor in determining which Americans fought in Vietnam.[27] Troop strength in Vietnam went from 23,000 in 1964 to 543,000 in 1968, then declined again during President Richard Nixon's Vietnamization initiative. Draft calls rose from an annual 100,000 to approximately 300,000 per year, peaking at 340,000 in 1966. The U.S. Selective Service System drafted more than that each month during World War II and twice that during the Korean conflict.[28]

Men who were drafted between 1965 and 1967 more accurately represented a cross section of the country than did those drafted later in the war. The draft has been widely examined and generally criticized for its lack of fairness and overall failure to conscript a representative cross section of the U.S. population, but General Lynch recalled that he "had people in that rifle company carrying a rifle with a college degree because the draft . . . in '65/'66 was as fair as it ever was." At that time, he says, "We didn't have people figuring out ways to get out of it." By the late 1960s, however, youths in large urban areas often sidestepped the draft by failing to register, unknown thousands of dropouts and recent high school graduates rushed into marriage and early fatherhood to avoid conscription, and those who could afford it received deferments by enrolling in the nation's colleges and universities in record numbers. Although in the early 1960s intellectuals criticized draft deferments as an unfair advantage for those who could go to college, by 1967, when the ax fell on graduate school deferments, much of that altruism evaporated. Society did not value returning veterans, and the national interest did not appear to be at stake. "Many students defended their deferments—and their draft avoidance—with a measure of class arrogance," asserted Baskir and Strauss. At the time, Kingman Brewster, the president of Yale University, noted a "cynical avoidance of service, a corruption of the aims of education, a tarnishing of the national spirit, . . . and a cops and robbers view of national obligation."[29]

As draft calls tripled in response to U.S. escalation of the war effort, the nation's army grew in size between 1964 and 1968 from 2.7 million to 3.5 million.[30] Like most young men of his generation, Ralph Hale considered himself at the mercy of Uncle Sam, but he hoped to at least choose when and how he fulfilled his military obligation. The quality of marine basic training attracted him, and he enlisted after dropping out of college in Baltimore, Maryland. "If I had to go, I preferred to go into the branch of service that I wanted," he recalled. Like Grant Furnas, he acknowledged that many men simply did not make it through the rigorous training. At Parris Island, South Carolina, eighty men began training in his platoon, but, after eight weeks, only sixty-two graduated. At age twenty-one, Hale also opted for a second six-month tour of duty, which meant that he served nineteen months in-country. In his first assignment, he served in a line company, but, after special training in Okinawa, he came back to his original unit as part of an intelligence and reconnaissance team. He preferred the latter because it actually meant less time walking the front line.[31]

Although Furnas's and Hale's experiences illustrate important elements of the soldier's experience, both are somewhat atypical. Not only were they older and better educated, but both are also white. Black Americans bore a 30 percent higher proportion of the casualties than their statistical position suggested, accounting for 15.1 percent of total army casualties and 13.7 percent of total U.S. casualties. Moreover, especially early in the war, not only were black Americans more likely to sustain combat injuries; they were also more likely to die.[32]

Arthur E. (Gene) Woodley Jr. enlisted in 1968, leaving his poverty-stricken, primarily black Baltimore neighborhood to become an infantryman—a grunt in soldier parlance. He described himself as a "patriot," a passionate, healthy young American ready to do his duty. "Being from a hard-core neighborhood, I decided I was gonna volunteer for the toughest combat training they had. I went to jump school, Ranger school, and Special Forces training. I figured I was just what my country needed." Trained to lead long-range patrols (LURPs), Specialist Fourth Class Woodley was assigned to the First Field Force near An Khe. Haunted by the grim recollection of an American soldier his patrol found staked to the ground, stripped of portions of his skin, and left to die, Woodley says he became "a animal" in the bush. Because LURPs could not compromise their identity or location by calling in air support or evacuating wounded, he was instructed to take responsibility for handling the gravely wounded man. He agonized over what to do and finally decided that granting the man's request to die was the only feasible solution. The victim was too fragile to survive a medevac, and the team had to complete its mission. "I had to be as strong as he was, because he was askin' me to kill him, to wipe out his life. . . . We buried him. We buried him. Very deep," Woodley recalls. "Then I cried."[33]

Woodley related stories of enemy combat and told of gang rapes and murders of civilian women and children. He told of a game called *Vietnamese Roulette* in which captured VC were dangled and dropped from helicopters to encourage their counterparts to reveal information. He also described other actions that he and his team knew were atrocities. Moreover, he explored the changes wrought by the war on his psyche and his future and said that he had come to terms with his behavior, although he still struggled with nightmares and flashbacks. He believed the government lied to its young soldiers by telling them that Vietnam was a war for "democracy and independence," and he felt that black veterans "have been overlooked more than everybody": "We can't find jobs, because nobody trust us. Because we killers. We crazy. We went away intelligent young men to do the job of American citizens. And once we did, we came back victims."[34]

So who was the typical combat soldier? Did the war make him a victim, a villain, a hero, or a little of each?

In the thirty-plus years since the conflict ended, an elaborate and virtually irrefutable portrait of the Vietnam combat veteran has emerged. Only nineteen when he was drafted, the stereotypical serviceman saw action in the most emotionally and psychologically damaging type of warfare, and, because of widespread conscription of the very young, the relatively uneducated, and the highly inexperienced, he was the least emotionally and psychologically prepared soldier to serve in any American war. The insertion of individual replacement troops instead of unit rotations exacerbated the problem and isolated rookies in the critical first month in-country when they most needed effective leadership and camaraderie. The policy limiting the tour of duty in the war zone to twelve to thirteen months militated against unit cohesiveness, fostered a survival mentality, and assured that reentry into the World would be fraught with difficulty. With no time to decompress, no time to contextualize or rationalize the combat experience, returning veterans found themselves in the jungles of Vietnam one day and on their hometown streets the next.[35]

Serving under inept combat leaders whose primary concern was the body count, the vulnerable young soldier confronted a ubiquitous enemy who was both everywhere and nowhere. At home, he encountered a public that literally or figuratively spit on him and blamed him for losing the war. No parades and victory marches welcomed him home, and no programs aided his reintegration into society. Consequently, he degenerated into drug or alcohol addiction and unemployment, his wife divorced him, his children feared him, and even his parents held him in contempt for his inability to cope. Lingering psychological problems, including flashbacks, depression, horrible nightmares, and guilt over atrocities or his own survival, caused psychic numbing and occasionally even suicide. Ongoing health problems brought on by exposure to chemicals such as Agent Orange often combined with physical injuries to impair or limit adjustment to civilian life and a normal work routine. Delayed stress reactions sometimes surfaced, wrecking families and isolating veterans. This highly negative depiction of the Vietnam veteran as deeply disturbed, often homeless, and always alone and misunderstood shook the very foundations of patriotism and shared memory and threatened to destroy the nation's concept of military service and citizenship, to say nothing of its impact on those who served.

Many of the negative perceptions persist despite evidence to the contrary. For example, one of the broadest statistical studies of the war, Josefina Card's 1981 survey, found that, aside from a two-year delay in beginning their families, Vietnam veterans did not vary significantly from nonveterans in the rate of divorce, separation, or family dissolution. In fact, the nonveteran group was more likely to experience marital breakup in all but the vulnerable first year in which the veteran returned from Vietnam to a marriage begun prior to military service. Only in the category of job satisfaction did Vietnam service appear to significantly alter group responses, with respondents noting lower levels of satisfaction in terms of salary and overall success.[36]

The negative stereotyping of Vietnam combat veterans continued for many years and still continues in some respects, although a form of redemption came in the 1980s when the 1960s and the Vietnam War underwent a reinvention in U.S. popular culture. As the nation's veterans took responsibility for their place in history through the establishment of a memorial in Washington, DC, their apotheosis began. Steeped in the language of nostalgia, healing, and forgiveness, the mythic hero-survivor emerged fully drawn. In this interpretation, clearly illustrated by Gene Woodley's stories, not only had he lost everything in a crazy and impossible war, but the combat veteran had also done it all for a cynical and ungrateful nation headed by even more cynical and ungrateful politicians. Stabbed in the back by the media, his peace of mind destroyed by posttraumatic stress disorder, he nevertheless triumphed in his personal struggle and, in the process, reclaimed his identity as a man and as a citizen. Initially emblematic of the divisions among veterans' groups and veterans themselves, the Vietnam Veterans Memorial has, since its construction in 1982, focused attention on "precisely how wars should be remembered, and precisely who should be remembered in a war—those who died, those who participated, those who engineered it, or those who opposed it."[37]

Like most myths, the hero-survivor archetype represents some truthful elements. Military manpower policies during the war resulted in conscription of very young, relatively uneducated, and highly inexperienced fighting men whose extreme youth rendered them particularly susceptible to psychological trauma and almost guaranteed adjustment problems when they rejoined the World after their 365-day tour of duty, yet most veterans returned to productive lives. And, while the policy of individual replacement troops often isolated soldiers during their first month in-country, most survived and became seasoned members of the unit. Many young men also formed intense friendships that transcended military service. Certainly, the failure of the Johnson and Nixon administrations to clearly articulate a credible rationale for the conflict and escalating public opposition to it left many returning veterans wondering just what they were fighting and dying for in the jungles of Southeast Asia; nevertheless, many veterans report that they were proud to serve their country and would do so again if needed. The guerrilla-style war and the reliance on the number of kills as the only substantive measure of U.S. success definitely led to inflated body counts and produced the "mere gook rule," the assumption that, if it was dead and Vietnamese, it was enemy dead. But most veterans report by-the-book treatment of enemy soldiers and noncombatants alike. Most recall sharing their rations with Vietnamese children and having civil interactions with local populations. Most also report the expected encounters with bar girls and prostitutes, black marketers and mama-sans who did their laundry and worked in base camps. Card's study found that 89 percent of Vietnam veterans, roughly the same percentage as veterans who did not serve in Vietnam, attached a positive (56 percent) or equally positive and negative (33 percent) value to their military service. Nevertheless, those who categorized their experiences as negative were very vocal. "Perhaps," Card concluded, "the vocal minority speak in addition for the silent minority who cannot speak: the men who gave up their lives on the battlefields of this war and who could not be represented in this study."[38]

Although many Vietnam veterans look back on their service as a civic duty that they would repeat if called on to do so, others consider *reconciliation* a dirty word, a sham, or a tactic for silencing them. The poet W. D. Ehrhart questioned the entire process: "By reconciliation, do they mean I should embrace Henry Kissinger and Robert McNamara? I don't want to reconcile with people like that. . . . I'm going to keep talking about this till I think we learned something from it—and that means I'm going to keep talking until they're shoveling dirt in my mouth! Go on to what? Go on to Mogadishu? Go on to Baghdad? Not me!"[39]

An inescapable reality is that, if the combat experience did not take a soldier's life, it took part of it, significantly more than just the 365 days of a year in-country. It took his youth, perhaps his innocence, and, more than likely, his optimism; therefore, the combat experience must mean something. It took the lives of over fifty-eight thousand Americans, a figure made real by the names etched in the black granite of the memorial and seared in the memories of those left behind. One who gave his life was Paul Aton, who arrived in Vietnam on April 13, 1968. Reporting his first engagement with the enemy to his friend Lonnie on May 17, he said he was "so scared" all he did was shake. "But when I stopped shaking I guess I went crazy for a minute because I crawled all over the place and finally found a machine gun." He reported firing six or seven hundred rounds and taking out the sniper who had attacked from the base perimeter.[40] By July, Aton had been transferred to an infantry unit in the field. A radiotelephone operator, he was assigned to a "1st lutenant and about 6'6" know's his stuf [*sic*]." Aton's letters to his father report combat assaults in which he struggled through waist-deep mud and chest-deep water, holding his equipment overhead all the while. He told of seeing Fourth of July "fire works that nobody State side saw." "Combat isn't like it is in the movies or TV," he said, although he acknowledged some similarities. "We get dirtier because we aren't putting on a show. . . . When you get hit there is a lot of blood and the men fight Hard on both sides, harder in real life though. . . . When you hump you sweat . . . in the movie you don't see any sweat. Or here people don't just die like flies. They have to fight to fall and they don't give up." "War is Hell," he concluded.[41]

It was also physically and mentally exhausting: "I was so tired when the fighting and walking was over that I had to be dragged in to the chopper because it had started to lift off before I was in and the draft was pushing me away from the door." Although he jokingly signed his letters "the Jungle Fighter," "the Cong Killer," or "the rat patrol," Aton assured his father that he was with "good people": "I am a combat trouper. I am proud of that." He also believed that his combat experience had made him stronger: "I am tired but I at least have guts and I can hump as hard and as long as the grunts. I am at long last a man who can walk tall when I come home."[42] But Paul never again walked tall in his hometown of Franklin, Kentucky. Ten days after he wrote those words, his father, Loyd S. Aton,

Draped in ammunition, and holding a grenade, a young and apparently invincible Tom Mullins leans with a friend against a gun emplacement. The elegant relief work on the wall indicates that it had been built for a more pleasant purpose. Courtesy of Tom Mullins.

received a telegram notifying him that his son, Private First Class Paul D. Aton, had been last seen during a "combat operation when he slipped and fell into [a] river while crossing." A second telegram, confirming the "personal notification made by a representative of the secretary of the Army," informed Mr. Aton that his son's remains had been recovered and positively identified.[43] In his letters home, Aton shared some of his combat experiences with his father, inadvertently providing a legacy that may have helped his family deal with his death.

Others wrote home to help them deal with the realities of surviving in a war zone. Killing another human being is a life-altering experience even when legitimized by combat and sanctioned by society. It wreaks havoc with individual conscience. Needing to unburden himself, David Disney wrote to his father following his first kill. Because his father was also a combat veteran, he expected that he would understand. He told his father that the information was meant for his eyes only and asked that he keep it from his mother and his wife. A "lone VC" had crawled under the wire and tossed a hand grenade that exploded in front of their bunker, Disney wrote. The young American saw the enemy "on his knees coming at me": "God Dad I didn't want to kill him, I shot the M-60 with a long burst and he fell. Dad I cried like a baby after it was all over. . . . The captain shook my hand and said I did a great job. Is killing great?" he asked.[44]

Although David Disney tried to shield his mother and wife from the worst of his combat experience, in an ironic twist of fate he apparently mailed the letter intended for his father in an envelope addressed to his wife, Dot. She forwarded the letter to her father-in-law, asking that he not let David know what had happened. "Since you have been through a war, I know you will think of the right words to say to him. He loves and respects you very much. This will be our secret that I know about what happened."[45]

Killing did not come easily to David Disney, and it was even harder when he became certain that he had killed some Americans. In January 1970, he wrote to tell his father that he "killed or at least I feel as though I killed 5 GI's [sic]." During a continuous fire operation, he "was the one who yelled fire and sent the data to the guns. Dad, do you think I was at fault? I checked the data and it was right so the FO [forward observer] is as much to blame as I am." He reported a similar occurrence from Cambodia in May 1970. "The real reason for writing is to tell you that yesterday I killed four GI's [sic] when a guy misdirected our rounds and we shot on top of him. You'll probably see it in the papers. Well I was the one who computed the data, sent it to the guns and gave the command to fire. Dad, I'm going to go nuts. I've killed my own people, friendly villagers and God knows who else."[46]

The war didn't make a lot of sense to David Disney, and he began to fear that he wouldn't make it home. "I'm scared Dad, I've got 65 days of this hell left and I don't know if I'll make it or not. I've never been so scared of dying before. I just had to write this to you. I know you'll understand."[47] Following a fairly large operation in which three infantry companies swept a mountain and located an underground hospital and storage area, he wrote to his father of the heavy casualties. The unit claimed "a body count of 24 so they considered the operation a success." But the infantry companies sustained heavy casualties, with eighteen dead and many more wounded. "Dad, they had the dead in our mess hall. I went down there and it was awful. The guys were shot up awful. I got sick. . . . Their damn chicken fight makes my stomach turn. . . . It is all a bunch of bull."[48]

The typical private in Vietnam was nineteen, seven years younger than the average GI in World War II. Their youth and inexperience made some men reckless. It made others tough. Some young men could separate what mattered to them back in the World from what didn't matter in the bush, and the whole experience could be packed away in the phrase, *It don't mean nothin'!* Although early in the war there was the usual tendency to gloss over the details and make the war appear noble and heroic, the actual stories of some of America's young warriors were told for the first time in *Newsweek*'s searing oral history, *Charlie Company: What Vietnam Did to Us,* by Peter Goldman and Tony Fuller. The book broke new ground in 1983 when it was released. Goldman and Fuller pieced together the narratives of sixty-five members of Charlie Company, First Infantry Division, Second Battalion, Twenty-Eighth Infantry Regiment. "It is the most real book written about Vietnam," claimed Thomas Mullins, a fifty-something veteran who took college history classes to help him better understand the war he had fought as a young man. "It captures what it was really like better than anything else I've read."[49] Mullins brought along his copy of the book when he was interviewed. His name is printed in block letters inside the front cover, and the well-worn volume falls open to this passage: "They were boys at play in those interludes when the war did not require them to be men; their sport and their memory of it were all beer, smoke and braggadocio. But there was a strain of desperation in their comedy as well, a primal scream of laughter in the valley of the shadow of death."[50]

The time spent in that valley acquainted young men with war and mortality, and many carried the memories like deadweight into midlife and beyond. "I knew I would someday write about Khe Sanh," says Michael Archer, although he did not begin until nearly thirty years after the siege of the marine base camp. Like many who experienced combat, he recalls praying—bargaining with God for another day of life. "But I knew I wouldn't be keeping my end of the bargain. I was just lying to stay alive. . . . As if buying another day at Khe Sanh was worth all the chicanery."[51]

Barry Campbell's prayers were answered, and he returned to the World after thirteen months in-country, whole in body, if not in spirit. "I gave 110 percent the entire thirteen months and six days. I have no regrets at all, and if I had to do it again tomorrow I wouldn't even hesitate. I'd be ready to do it all over again," he said. But, as he pondered the long-term effects of his combat experience, he acknowledged: "Still yet today, I like to sit with my back to the wall." Like many veterans, he never really talked about his experience. "No one wanted to talk to me about it. People shunned me. Instead of an alcoholic I became a workaholic. Farming was peace of mind to me. With my condition I couldn't hold a job. Safety is more or less in solitude. I'm safer just by myself." Etched in Barry Campbell's nearly blank memory is a "gray" portrait of his first day in Vietnam. For years it was accompanied by what he called a "black-and-white picture" of the day he left, loaded with guilt that the people he was leaving behind might not survive as he had done. "It was about to destroy me. And I said I've got to go back to Vietnam and get something I left there or I've got to take something back that I brought home and shouldn't have. I had no clue what it was."[52]

Disillusionment with the mission and questions about the necessity and the legitimacy of the war made the combat experience worse, especially as the war dragged on to no discernible conclusion. From Vietnam, American servicemen read about the peace movement at home, young people their age burning flags, shredding draft cards, and calling them baby killers. They heard of negotiators squabbling over the size and shape of the negotiating table. Many came to wonder just what in the hell they were doing in a combat zone, laying their lives on the line in a war no one was winning. "We're in the jungle with two canteens and two C-rations, and they're arguing about what kind of fuckin' table they're going to talk around," wrote Vitt Vittorini, of Charlie Company, assigned in 1969 to the "Big Red One." In what is perhaps the classic infantryman's lament, Vittorini raged, "If those guys were walking around the fuckin' jungle, they'd forget the shape of the table and sit down right now and make peace."[53]

But for the American combat veteran—the infantryman, the grunt—peace remains an elusive commodity. Those who experienced the worst combat are generally the most reluctant to remember it. The reality of their combat experience remains hidden, cloaked, if not in the smoke and braggadocio of youth, in the strained silence of middle age.

Notes

The epigraph is taken from Samuel Hynes, *The Soldiers' Tale: Bearing Witness to Modern War* (New York: Penguin, 1997), xiii.

1. Recent scholarship makes valid comparisons between Vietnam and the American Civil War, and many analysts maintain that its similarities to other conflicts significantly outweigh dissimilarities. For pertinent examples, see Joseph A. Fry, "Going to War: A Comparison of the Combat Experiences of American Soldiers in the Civil War and Vietnam," *Halcyon: A Journal of the Humanities* 15 (1993): 161–79; Eric T. Dean, *Shook over Hell: Post-Traumatic Stress, Vietnam, and the Civil War* (Cambridge, MA: Harvard University Press, 1997); and D. Michael Shafer, "The Vietnam Combat Experience: The Human Legacy," in *The Legacy: The Vietnam War in the American Imagination,* ed. D. Michael Shafer (Boston: Beacon, 1990), 80–103. See also Harry G. Summers Jr., *On Strategy: A Critical Analysis of the Vietnam War* (New York: Dell, 1982).

2. Harry Summers, "Military Lessons Learned," in *Facing My Lai: Moving beyond the Massacre,* ed. David L. Anderson (Lawrence: University Press of Kansas, 1998), 154–55.

3. George C. Herring, "What Kind of War Was the Vietnam War?" in ibid., 96.

4. Ronald H. Spector, *After Tet: The Bloodiest Year in Vietnam* (New York: Free Press), 54–58.

5. Herring, "What Kind of War Was the Vietnam War?" 97.

6. Johnson quoted in George C. Herring, *LBJ and Vietnam: A Different Kind of War* (Austin: University of Texas Press, 1994), 37; Tim O'Brien, *Going after Cacciato: A Novel* (New York: Delacorte/Lawrence, 1978), 1, 86; Herring, "What Kind of War Was the Vietnam War?" 97.

7. Barry Campbell, Kentuckians and Vietman Oral History Project (hereafter KVOHP) interview with the authors, June 14, 1998. All KVOHP interviews will eventually be deposited in Special Collections, Camden Carroll Library, Morehead State University.

8. Ibid.

9. Gen. Tom Lynch and Charles Bracelyn Flood, KVOHP interview with the authors, April 29, 1997, Richmond, KY; Cambell KVOHP interview.

10. Grant Furnas, KVOHP interview with the authors, June 21, 1997, Louisville, KY.

11. Spector, *After Tet,* 32–35.

12. Furnas, KVOHP interview.

13. Ibid.

14. Peter Maslowski and Don Winslow, *Looking for a Hero: Staff Sergeant Joe Ronnie Hooper and the Vietnam War* (Lincoln: University of Nebraska Press, 2004), 1–6, 323, 339–42, 482–85.

15. Campbell KVOHP interview.

16. Christian Appy, *Working Class War: American Combat Soldiers and Vietnam* (Chapel Hill: University of North Carolina Press, 1993), 246–47; Arthur T. Frame, "Fragging," in *The Encyclopedia of the Vietnam War,* ed. Spencer C. Tucker (New York: Oxford University Press, 1998), 135.

17. Lynch/Flood KVOHP interview.

18. Arnold R. Isaacs, *Vietnam Shadows: The War, Its Ghosts, and Its Legacy* (Baltimore: Johns Hopkins University Press, 1997), 19–23.

19. Anderson, ed., *Facing My Lai,* xi–16.

20. Roger Sturgeon and Wes Grimm, e-mail to the authors, September 14, 2001; Michael Sallah and Mitch Weiss, *Tiger Force: A True Story of Men and War* (Boston: Little, Brown, 2006); Individual Statement of Ronald L. Vogel Concerning Investigation of Incident NAVMC 10483-GS (8-60), September, 25, 1966, 1st Marine Division, 5th Marines Command Post, South Vietnam, copy in the authors' possession; Individual Statement of Stephen J. Talty Concerning Investigation or Incident NAVMC 10483-GS (8-60), September, 25, 1966, 1st Marine Division, 5th Marines Command Post, South Vietnam, in the authors' possession; Individual Statement of James Herbert Boyd Jr., Concerning Investigation or Incident NAVMC 10483-GS (8-60), September, 25, 1966, 1st Marine Division, 5th Marines Command Post, South Vietnam, in the authors' possession.

21. Football star Rocky Blier quoted in Myra MacPherson, *Vietnam and the Haunted Generation* (New York: Anchor/Doubleday, 1984), xiv.

22. Spector, *After Tet,* 260–61.

23. Lynch/Flood KVOHP interview; David A. Wilson, *REMF Diary: A Novel of the Vietnam War Zone* (Seattle: Black Heron, 1988); David A. Wilson, *The REMF Returns* (Seattle: Black Heron, 1992).

24. Shelby L. Stanton, *The Rise and Fall of an American Army: U.S. Ground Forces in Vietnam, 1965–1973* (New York: Dell, 1985), 21; George C. Herring, *America's Longest War: The United States and Vietnam, 1950–1975,* 2nd ed. (New York: Knopf, 1986), 151.

25. Lawrence Baskir and William Strauss, *Chance and Circumstance: The Draft, the War, and the Vietnam Generation* (New York: Knopf, 1978), 5; Eliot A. Cohen, *Citizens and Soldiers: The Dilemmas of Military Service* (Ithaca, NY: Cornell University Press, 1985), 108. See also Neil Howe and William Strauss, *Generations: The History of America's Future, 1584 to 2069* (New York: Morrow, 1991).

26. Baskir and Strauss, *Chance and Circumstance,* 7–9. See also D. Michael Shafer,

"The Vietnam-Era Draft: Who Went, Who Didn't, and Why It Matters," in *The Legacy*, ed. Shafer, 68; and Paul Savage and Richard Gabriel, "Cohesion and Disintegration in the American Army," *Armed Forces and Society* 2, no. 3 (May 1976): 364.

27. Appy, *Working Class War*, 6, 15. See also Baskir and Strauss, *Chance and Circumstance*, 9. For a postwar statistical study showing that, when measured against nonveterans of the same generation, Vietnam veterans came out on the bottom in terms of income, occupation, and education, see Arthur Egendorf et al., *Legacies of Vietnam: Comparative Adjustments of Veterans and Their Peers* (Washington, DC: U.S. Government Printing Office, 1961), 142.

28. Michael Useem, *Conscription, Protest, and Social Conflict: The Life and Death of a Draft Resistance Movement* (New York: Wiley, 1973), 77–80.

29. Lynch/Flood KVOHP interview; Brewster quoted in Baskir and Strauss, *Chance and Circumstance*, 7.

30. Shafer, "The Vietnam-Era Draft," 67; Useem, *Conscription, Protest, and Social Conflict*, 77–80.

31. Ralph Hale, KVOHP interview with the authors, June 19, 1997, Louisville, KY.

32. G. David Curry, *Sunshine Patriots: Punishment and the Vietnam Offender* (Notre Dame, IN: Notre Dame University Press, 1985), 61; Peter B. Levy, "Blacks and the Vietnam War," in *The Legacy*, ed. Shafer, 211.

33. Wallace Terry, *Bloods: An Oral History of the Vietnam War by Black Veterans* (New York: Ballantine, 1984), 241–43.

34. Ibid., 256.

35. Keith Beattie, *The Scar That Binds: American Culture and the Vietnam War* (New York: New York University Press, 1998), 65–67. See also Walter L. Hixson, ed., *Historical Memory and Representations of the Vietnam War* (New York: Garland, 2000).

36. Josefina J. Card, *Lives after Vietnam: The Personal Impact of Military Service* (Lexington, MA: Heath Lexington, 1983), 120–41.

37. Marita Sturken, "The Wall, the Screen, and the Image: The Vietnam Veterans Memorial," in *Historical Memory*, ed. Hixson, 64–88. See also Harry W. Haines, "Disputing the Wreckage: Ideological Struggle at the Vietnam Veterans Memorial," in ibid., 1–16.

38. Herbert Hendin and Ann Pollinger Haas, *Wounds of War: The Psychological Aftermath of Combat in Vietnam* (New York: Basic, 1984), 16; Card, *Lives after Vietnam*, 141.

39. Ehrhart quoted in Isaacs, *Vietnam Shadows*, 29.

40. Paul Aton to Lonnie Powers, May 17, 1968, Paul Aton Collection, Kentucky Archives, Western Kentucky University (hereinafter cited as KYWKU).

41. Paul Aton to Loyd Aton, April 13, July 19, 1968, ibid.

42. Paul Aton to Loyd Aton, July 19, 1968, ibid.

43. Maj. Gen. K. G. Wickham to Loyd Aton, telegram, n.d., and Maj. Gen. K. G. Wickham to Loyd Aton, telegram, n.d., ibid.

44. David Disney to Dad, August 28, 1969, Disney Collection, KYWKU.

45. Dot Disney to Dad Disney, September 3, 1969, ibid.

46. David Disney to Dad, May 10, 1970, ibid.

47. Ibid.

48. David Disney to Dad, November 18, 1969, Disney Collection, KYWKU.

49. Tommy Mullins, KVOHP interview with the authors, April 21, 1998, More-head, KY.

50. Peter Goldman and Tony Fuller, *Charlie Company: What Vietnam Did to Us* (New York: Morrow, 1983), 67.

51. Michael Archer, *A Patch of Ground: Khe Sanh Remembered* (Central Point, OR: Hellgate, 2004), 3.

52. Campbell KVOHP interview.

53. Vittorini quoted in Goldman and Fuller, *Charlie Company,* 129.

15

The War That Never Seems to Go Away

George C. Herring

In March 1991, at the end of the First Persian Gulf War, President George H. W. Bush exulted that the "ghosts of Vietnam had been laid to rest beneath the sands of the Arabian desert." What he was saying, of course, was that America's smashing military success in the Gulf had finally overcome popular fears, left over from the war in Vietnam, of using military force abroad. "By God, we've kicked the Vietnam syndrome once and for all," he proclaimed on another occasion.

Like the rumors Mark Twain jokingly reported of his own death, President Bush's eulogy for the so-called Vietnam syndrome turned out to be greatly exaggerated. Indeed, just days before he spoke, he had refused to send his triumphant armies on to Baghdad for total victory in the Gulf War—in part, we now know, for fear of getting sucked into a political and diplomatic quagmire like Vietnam. Debates over possible U.S. intervention in Haiti and the Balkans in the mid-1990s and in Kosovo in 1999 and a disastrous involvement in Somalia in 1993—chronicled in the book and film *Black Hawk Down*—called forth repeatedly the very ghosts the first President Bush claimed to have buried. The pain and shock of the terrorist attacks on New York and Washington on September 11, 2001,

An earlier version of this essay was given as the Douglas Southall Freeman Lecture at the University of Richmond in February 2001 and was subsequently published in the *Douglas Southall Freeman Historical Review,* Spring 2001, 4–29.

South Vietnamese ambassador Bui Diem, Dr. George Herring, Admiral Elmo Zumwalt, and Douglas Pike at the 1996 Vietnam Center Symposium. Courtesy of the
Vietnam Archive, Texas Tech University, Admiral Elmo R. Zumwalt, Jr. Collection.

might have been expected to erase memories of Vietnam, but that has not
proved to be the case. Indeed, it seems clear that one of the reasons—by
no means the most important, but still significant—that President George
W. Bush launched a second war against Iraq in the spring of 2003 was to
put to rest once and forever memories of a war his father claimed to have
expunged twelve years earlier. The influence of the Vietnam War has,
thus, been persistent, pervasive, and powerful. Such is its staying power,
its hold on the national psyche, that it has become a war that never seems
to go away.

Why is this so? Why has a conflict that ended for the United States
more than a quarter century ago continued to trouble us in so many
ways? Why *is* Vietnam the war that never seems to go away?

These are questions that have intrigued me for many years. They are
questions that are particularly difficult to answer for today's students, who
have no memory of that war and little information about it except what
may be gleaned through the grossly distorted lens of film and television.
What I will try to do in this essay is to explain this quite remarkable phenomenon, to come up with some answers to the questions I have raised.

A first point to be emphasized is that Vietnam was America's longest war. Our direct involvement there spanned the quarter of a century from 1950 to 1975. From 1950 to 1954, in the name of containing communism, we assisted the French in fighting a Communist-led nationalist insurgency in Vietnam, ultimately paying something like 80 percent of the cost of the war. From 1954 to 1961, after the French had departed, we attempted to construct in the southern part of Vietnam an independent, non-Communist nation that could stand as a bulwark against further Communist penetration of Southeast Asia. From 1961 to 1965, we assisted the South Vietnamese in fighting an internal insurgency backed by North Vietnam. The real shooting war against the National Liberation Front (NLF) insurgents and North Vietnamese regulars lasted from 1965 to 1973, one year longer than the American Revolution.

The length of the war is of more than passing importance, more than simply dates in a history book. We Americans are an impatient people. We want results and want them quickly. Our preferred wars are the war with Spain in 1898, which lasted only four months, and the First Persian Gulf War, which was even shorter. That wise soldier-statesman Gen. George C. Marshall once observed that a democracy (and he was referring to the American democracy) could not fight a five-year war. And he made that comment during the midst of what the author Studs Terkel has called "the Good War"—World War II—the one American war that enjoyed near unanimous popular support. What this means is that, the longer a war drags on, the more impatient we become, and the less popular the war. Thus, by 1970, five years after the shooting war began, the Vietnam War had become a drag on the body politic, an albatross, something Americans desperately wanted to be rid of. Its staying power as a war has contributed to its staying power in our memory.

The Vietnam War was also an extremely difficult and peculiarly frustrating war for Americans to fight. It was waged in a climate and on a terrain that were singularly inhospitable: thick jungles, rugged mountains, foreboding swamps and paddies. Heat that could "kill a man, bake his brains, or wring the sweat from him until he died of exhaustion," the marine lieutenant Philip Caputo tells us. "It was as if the sun and the land itself were in league with the Vietcong," Caputo adds, "wearing us down, driving us mad, killing us." "The land is your true enemy," an NLF officer tells U.S. GIs in the veteran Tim O'Brien's classic novel *Going after Cacciato.*

At least in its initial stages, it was a peoples' war, where people rather than territory were the primary objective. But Americans as individuals or as a nation could never really bridge the huge cultural gap that separated them from all Vietnamese. Not knowing the language or the culture, they did not know what the people felt or even at times how to tell friend from foe. "Maybe the dinks got things mixed up," one of O'Brien's bewildered GIs comments after a seemingly friendly farmer bows and smiles and points the Americans straight into a minefield. "Maybe they cry when they're happy and smile when they're sad." Recalling the emotionless response of a group of peasants when their homes were destroyed by an American company, Caputo notes that they did nothing "and I hated them for it. Their apparent indifference made me feel indifferent." This cultural gap produced cynicism and even hatred toward the South Vietnamese, the people Americans were trying to help. "We're fighting, dying, for a people who resent our being here," one GI complained. It led to questioning of our purpose and produced a great deal of confusion among some of those fighting the war and some people at home.

Most important, perhaps, was the formless yet entirely lethal nature of guerrilla warfare in Vietnam. It was a war without distinct battle lines or fixed objectives, where traditional concepts of victory and defeat were blurred. It was, Caputo writes, a "formless war against a formless enemy who evaporated into the morning jungle mists only to materialize in some unexpected place." The danger was nowhere and everywhere. "We'd be expecting a huge firefight and end up picking our nose," one GI wrote. "And then one day we'd be walking along day-dreaming and—Boom—they'd spring an ambush." As many as one-fourth of the total U.S. casualties came from mines and booby traps, an omnipresent reality that was both terrifying and demoralizing. This type of war, it should not be necessary to add, was particularly difficult for Americans schooled in the conventional warfare of World War II and Korea to fight.

And there was always the gnawing question, first raised by no less than President John F. Kennedy, how can we tell if we are winning. The only answer that could be devised was the notorious body count—the daily toll of enemy dead—as grim and corrupting as it was ultimately unreliable as an index of success. In time, a strategy based on nothing more than killing enemy soldiers came to represent for some sensitive GIs and for some at home killing for the sake of killing. "Aimless, that's what it is," one of O'Brien's GIs laments, "a bunch of kids trying to pin the tail on the Asian donkey. But no fuckin' tail. No fuckin' donkey."

It was a limited war, limited in both ends and means, and that brought special frustrations to those who fought it. The United States never set out to "win" this war in the conventional sense, in part for fear that winning might provoke a larger war, even a nuclear war, in part because, at least at the outset, winning seemed unnecessary and possibly counterproductive. In escalating the war in 1965 and after, President Lyndon B. Johnson sought, rather, to apply just enough military pressure to get North Vietnam to accept a permanently divided country. "I'm going up old Ho Chi Minh's leg an inch at a time," he told Senator George McGovern in 1965. As a consequence, the United States did not use all the resources at its disposal and fought the war under restrictive rules of engagement.

The result was extremely frustrating for those who managed the war, those who fought it, and many people at home. It was especially frustrating for those in the field who in some cases could not shoot unless first fired on, could not pursue the enemy into sanctuaries in Laos and Cambodia, and sometimes felt as though they were fighting with one hand tied behind their back. "I'm flying a limited aircraft with limited ordnance and striking limited targets in a limited war fought for limited objectives and with limited popular support," a navy pilot complained. "All I've got is the personal satisfaction of doing my job along with a tangle of frustrations."

And yet this limited war in time assumed elephantine proportions, an "all-out limited war," as one official called it with no apparent sense of the contradiction: more than a half million troops, the bombing of a small country that in time exceeded the tonnage of all bombs dropped by all countries in all theaters of war in World War II, enormous destruction in all of former French Indochina, and expenditures by 1967 in excess of $2 billion per month.

In addition, and perhaps most important, it was a war where the balance of forces in Vietnam was stacked against us and where success, as we defined it, was probably beyond our reach. In seeking to establish and maintain an independent non-Communist nation in southern Vietnam we attempted a truly formidable undertaking on the basis of a most fragile foundation. The "country" to which we first committed ourselves in 1954 was a country in name only. It lacked the essential ingredients for nationhood. Indeed, had we looked all over the world in the mid-1950s, we could hardly have found a less promising place for an experiment in nation building. In addition, southern Vietnam was rent by a multitude of conflicting political, ethnic, and religious forces. It was, in the words of one scholar, a "political jungle of war lords, bandits, partisan troops, and secret societies." When viewed from this perspective, there were probably built-in limits to what the United States could accomplish there.

For nearly twenty years, we struggled to establish a viable nation in the face of internal insurgency and external invasion. But we could never find leaders capable of mobilizing the disparate population—the fact that *we* had to look for them speaks volumes about the problem. We launched a vast array of expensive programs to promote sound government, as we saw it, win the hearts and minds of the people (in the phrase of the day), and wage war against the NLF. When our client state was near collapse in 1965, we filled the vacuum by putting in our own troops. But the rapid collapse of South Vietnam after we withdrew in 1973 suggests how little we really accomplished.

From beginning to end, we also drastically underestimated the strength and determination of our adversary. I do not wish to imply here that the North Vietnamese and the NLF were some kind of superpeople. They made colossal blunders. They paid an enormous price for their eventual victory. They have shown a far greater capacity for making war than for building a nation.

In terms of the balance of forces in this war, however, they had distinct advantages. They were tightly mobilized and regimented and fanatically committed to their goals. They employed methods already perfected in their eight-year war against France. They skillfully applied a strategy of protracted war, perceiving that Americans, like the French before them, would become impatient and that, if they bled long enough, they would weary of the war. "You will kill ten of our men, but we will kill one of yours," the North Vietnamese leader Ho Chi Minh once remarked, "and in the end it is you who will tire." The comment was made to a French official on the eve of the First Indochina War, but it could as easily have been said of what the Vietnamese call the *American war* as well.

The circumstances of the war thus posed a dilemma that we never really understood, much less resolved. Success would probably have required the physical annihilation of North Vietnam, but, given our limited goals, this seemed excessive and, at best, dubious on moral grounds. It held out the serious threat of Soviet and/or Chinese intervention, a much larger and more dangerous war, maybe even a nuclear conflagration. The only other way was to establish a viable South Vietnam, but, given the weak foundation we worked from and the culture gap, not to mention the strength of the revolution in the South, this was probably beyond our capacity. To put it charitably, we may have placed ourselves in a classic no-win situation.

With the exception of our own Civil War, where Americans were shooting at each other, Vietnam was also our most divisive war. I should inject a caveat here. Dissent in wartime is as American as cherry pie, and among all our wars only World War II and the relatively brief Spanish-American and Persian Gulf wars have enjoyed near universal support, the latter, I would add, only after success was certain. Still, the Vietnam War did arouse more widespread and passionate opposition than other U.S. wars, and there are reasons for this. It occurred in a time of social upheaval, a time when Americans were questioning their own values and institutions as at few other periods in their history. It occurred in a time of generational strife. It occurred when the verities of the Cold War were coming under challenge. And, in the face of rising opposition, neither the Johnson nor the Nixon administration could ever make a convincing argument that the war was either just or necessary in terms of U.S. national security. And, in a case where the world's greatest power was fighting what Johnson himself once contemptuously dismissed as that "raggedy-ass little fourth-rate country," the methods used, especially the bombing of North Vietnam, came under increasing criticism.

The war thus divided Americans as nothing since the debate over slavery a century earlier. It divided neighbors, colleagues, and churches. Campus protest became a way of life, even in time at quiet, conservative institutions like the University of Kentucky. It divided class against class. It divided father against son, even among the families of top policymakers such as Secretary of Defense Robert McNamara and Secretary of State Dean Rusk. I have seen no more poignant example of this than in James Carroll's prizewinning book *American Requiem: God, My Father, and the War That Came between Us,* the story of a close-knit Irish Catholic family torn apart by the war: the father an air force general, head of the Defense Intelligence Agency; three sons who went very different ways, the author an antiwar priest, a follower of the Berrigan brothers; one brother an exile to Canada; the other an FBI agent whose job was to pursue draft dodgers and infiltrate the Catholic Left, in short, go after those like his two brothers. The father and the author-son split over the war and were not reconciled, even on the father's deathbed. "A noble man," Carroll concludes. "I loved him. And because I was so much like him, I had broken his heart. And the final truth was . . . he had broken mine."

The war spurred various kinds of group and individual protest. By the early 1970s, street demonstrations were a common occurrence in most American cities. There were so-called teach-ins on campuses and lie-ins at military induction centers. The folksinger Joan Baez refused to pay that portion of her income tax that went to the military budget. The heavyweight champion Muhammad Ali refused induction by the draft and thereby forfeited his title. Numerous Americans burned draft cards as symbolic acts of protest. As many as fifty thousand fled to Canada to avoid service in the war. Some young men, like a Lexington, Kentucky, acquaintance of mine, went to prison rather than fight in a war they considered immoral. Five Americans, emulating Vietnamese Buddhist acts of protest, burned themselves to death in public places, the Quaker Norman Morrison in November 1965 below McNamara's Pentagon office.

As the war dragged on, the protest mounted, and the divisions deepened, the internal turmoil itself contributed to a war-weariness that came to pervade the nation and fed a desire, even among some who approved the war, to end it regardless of the consequences. The protest and disharmony weighed heavily on policymakers as well, pushing them to extricate the nation from Vietnam. The very divisiveness of the war contributed to its lingering impact. The divisions still exist today.

The outcome of the war itself was traumatic, of course, far and away the most traumatic of all the wars the United States has participated in, leaving a bad taste in the nation's collective mouth and contributing to the longevity of its influence. It is not entirely accurate to say (as is often said) that Vietnam was the first war America lost. We did not, in a strictly military sense, lose the war. We were never really defeated in battle. Our armed forces withdrew from Vietnam; they were not forced out militarily. But that in itself is of great significance, making the outcome all the more frustrating and all the more difficult to explain and accept.

And, for those who fought there, those who supported the war, and even some who opposed it, the departure of the last helicopter from the embassy rooftop in Saigon on April 30, 1975, a glaring symbol of America's failure, came very hard. "I grieved," a Kentucky army officer observed, "I grieved as though I had lost a member of my own family." For those who had lost children in the war, it was especially painful. "Now it's all gone down the drain and it hurts. What did he die for?" a Pennsylvanian asked of his son. "It was the saddest day of my life when it sank in that we had lost the war," a Virginian added. The fall of Saigon came at the very time the nation was preparing to celebrate the bicentennial of its birth, and the irony was painfully obvious. "The high hopes and wishful idealism with which the American nation had been born had not been destroyed," *Newsweek* observed, "but they had been chastened by the failure of America to work its will in Indochina."

Indeed, looked at from the longer perspective, the Vietnam War, as perhaps no other event in U.S. history, caused us as a nation to confront a set of beliefs about ourselves that forms a basic part of the American character. This goes a long way toward explaining why the war has caused us so much pain and why its influence has lingered.

The myth of American exceptionalism holds that we are a people apart, a nation distinctly different from others. The first of its tenets, the idea of American benevolence, holds that in our dealing with other peoples we have, in general, acted nobly and generously. We have not been exploitative or imperialistic like our European brethren. When we have had to use force, we have done so only in pursuit of noble goals. Forgotten or rationalized along the way, of course, are such things as slavery and the slave trade, the extermination of Native Americans, the subjugation of Filipinos.

For many Americans, to be sure, the Vietnam War remained from start to finish, in the words of former president Ronald Reagan, a "noble cause." For many others, including some who fought there, many who opposed the war, and, ultimately, some who supported it, there was confusion or outright revulsion. Some Americans were troubled by the fact that their massive power was being unleashed against a small, backward nation, our traditional sympathy for the underdog turned against us. Others wondered whether in the absence of any direct threat to our security we could justify the level of destructiveness we were visiting on Vietnam. From that unforgettable moment in the summer of 1963 when pictures of a Buddhist monk engulfed in flames burst forth in our newspapers and on our television screens, questions abounded about the government we supported in South Vietnam and the way we were supporting it.

Those questions extended to some GIs in the field. To be sure, many—probably a majority—were not troubled. They were sent to do a job and did it. But, to an extent, and in ways that had not been the case in most earlier wars, many soldiers were troubled that what they were doing did not square with their notions of America's proper role in the world. Some GIs expected to be greeted like their fathers who had liberated Europe in World War II but found themselves sometimes looked on as an invading army. One recalls being brought up on stories of the American Revolution in which the good colonists fought the evil redcoats. After a time in Vietnam, it dawned on him that *he* might be looked on as the redcoat.

The 1968 My Lai massacre, in which an American company slaughtered more than five hundred Vietnamese civilians, including women and children, was particularly traumatic in this regard, not because it was typical, but because it raised in the most blatant and tragic way basic questions about what we were doing in Vietnam—indeed, about ourselves. It was the sort of thing Americans did not do. If that was what the war was doing to us, we reasoned with a perverse and ethnocentric kind of logic, we wanted no part of it.

Vietnam by the late 1960s, then, had become for Americans much more than a country or a war. It was a metaphor for what America was or should be. To be sure, some continued to feel that the United States was doing the right thing. But others went backward from Vietnam to rediscover a pattern of evil deeply entrenched in American history. Others saw the war as essentially a betrayal of American ideals. Thus, the journalist Arnold Isaacs has written: "[The] national argument on Vietnam was really about America's vision of itself; about conflicting ideas on who we are as a people and what we value and believe. That explains why the deep divisions have lingered in a cultural clash that still reverberates, nearly thirty years after the war ended, in America's political life, arts, and popular culture."

The Vietnam War also challenged the notion of American invincibility, the conviction that we can do anything we set our minds to. The difficult we do tomorrow, it is said; the impossible may take a while. This view also derives from history: the spectacular and unparalleled record of success the United States enjoyed from its birth; the relative ease with which it conquered a continent; its remarkable wealth; its success in war. Indeed, the late C. Vann Woodward has suggested that, among Americans, only southerners had true insight into the totality of human experience because only the South has endured military defeat.

At each step along the road to war in Vietnam, despite pessimistic estimates of the prospects of success, the United State plunged ahead, certain, or at least hopeful, that with a bit of luck it would succeed—as it always had.

When it did not, that came as a rude shock to the national psyche. Americans were so accustomed to success that they had come to take it for granted. Failure came hard, especially in the case of Vietnam, where our armies were never defeated and we were frustrated by a small, backward, and, perhaps worse, Oriental enemy.

Thus, in the aftermath of war, we concocted various myths to explain the otherwise inexplicable. The national will was subverted, it was said, by a hostile media and antiwar movement. Nightly exposure to the horrors of war via television turned the nation against the war. We failed because we did not use our power wisely or decisively. Civilians put restrictions on the military that made it impossible to win. Hence the classic statement of the 1980s film superhero John Rambo on being given the mission to return to Vietnam and fight the second round single-handedly: "Sir, do we get to win this time?" However trashy the film, the hero's statement was pregnant with symbolism—and mythology. Or, for those who follow the *Doonesbury* comic strip, there was BD's statement made to a young Vietnamese businessman: "We could have won, you know, if we had really wanted to."

The war thus ended with most of the major issues unresolved, also perpetuating its influence. Was it a good war or a bad war, a noble cause or essentially immoral? Was it necessary in terms of the national security or basically needless and senseless, the wrong war, at the wrong place, at the wrong time, and with the wrong enemy (to borrow Gen. Omar Bradley's often-quoted description of the Korean War)? Was it a good war waged poorly? Was it a war that could and, indeed, should have been won, a war lost only by the timidity of our leaders? Or was it a war that could not have been won at a price we were willing to pay? Americans were as divided on these issues at the end of the war as they were while it was going on. They have remained deeply and emotionally divided since 1975, thus again helping keep the war alive in the national memory.

Finally, and perhaps most important, the war refused to go away because for twenty years we refused to let it go away by refusing to make peace with Vietnam. The reasons for this long delay in what came to be called *normalization*—itself a euphemism for refusing to admit that we were still at war with Vietnam—are numerous and complicated. But it is impossible to avoid the conclusion that sheer vindictiveness played a major part, a deeply felt desire on the part of many Americans to make the victorious Vietnamese pay for having the temerity to frustrate the mighty United States. Bitter, and trapped in denial, the journalist Joseph Galloway observed, Americans "stubbornly refused to make peace with the Vietnamese even as they mourned the fact that somehow the war wouldn't go away and leave them alone."

Thus, for more than twenty-five years, the influence of the war has been persistent and pervasive. It can be seen in the popular culture in the sheer volume of output: as of the year 2000, 700 novels, 12,000 nonfiction titles, 1,400 personal narratives, 250 films. (In 2000 alone, 480 courses were taught on the war at colleges and universities across the nation.) It can be seen in the experience of the veterans, spurned at first, then widely stereotyped as victims. It can be seen in the so-called Vietnam syndrome, the emotional national hand-wringing on each occasion the United States has considered sending troops abroad: Central America in the 1980s, the Persian Gulf in 1990–91, Somalia, Haiti, and the Balkans in the 1990s. Even when it is not obvious and visible, it lurks beneath the surface.

Terrorist attacks on New York's World Trade Center and the Pentagon on September 11, 2001, seemed at last to bring an end to the Vietnam era. For the first time since 1814, the continental United States had come under enemy attack. In one stunning and hugely destructive moment, in an outpouring of fear and anger, much of the intellectual and emotional baggage left from Vietnam seemed buried beneath the huge piles of rubble in New York and Washington. Patriotism was suddenly in vogue again. Since 1975, every discussion of the use of military force had brought forth the ghosts of Vietnam. In the immediate aftermath of 9/11, the "V-word" was conspicuous by its absence. Speaking with a single voice for one of the few times in recent memory, Congress gave President George W. Bush sweeping authority to use military force in a new war against international terrorism. Commentators solemnly proclaimed the death of the Vietnam syndrome.

Subsequent events seemed to bear out that judgment. Remarkably successful U.S. military action against the Taliban government in Afghanistan in the fall/winter of 2001 and Saddam Hussein's regime in Iraq in the spring of 2003, with little cost in U.S. lives, appeared to demonstrate that new, high-technology methods of war fighting could win victory without pain and sacrifice for the United States, thus eliminating the possibility of Vietnam-like quagmires. Polls affirmed broad popular support for using military power abroad. The second President Bush seemed to have accomplished, with a big hand from the 9/11 attackers, what the first a decade earlier had claimed—erroneously—to have done.

Once again, epitaphs for the Vietnam syndrome proved premature. The victory in Afghanistan was, at best, incomplete. Five years later, the new U.S.-backed government teetered precariously, and the Taliban was back on the attack. After deceptively easy initial military success in Iraq in spring 2003, a woefully unprepared and badly undermanned U.S. invading force confronted the daunting and, at times, baffling political-military task of rebuilding a shattered nation and uniting a bitterly divided people. Iraqis did not welcome their American "liberators" in the "cakewalk" some Bush administration officials had foolishly predicted. Guerrilla resistance to the U.S. occupation rose immediately out of the ashes of military defeat. The number of Americans killed in action in the immediate "postwar" period quickly surpassed that of those killed in the invasion phase of the war and by early 2007 exceeded three thousand. The word *quagmire*, long a code word for *Vietnam*, again became a staple of the American political vocabulary.

From July 2003 on, the Vietnam analogy was employed more and more frequently in reference to the ongoing struggle in Iraq. Bush administration officials insisted that the two wars were totally different and the analogy invalid, but to no avail. Talk of winning Iraqi hearts and minds evoked a favorite catchphrase from the Vietnam era. Images of heavily armed and sometimes bewildered U.S. soldiers seeking to locate elusive and deadly guerrillas among people whose language and culture they could not fathom were eerily reminiscent of those that had come out of Vietnam. President Bush had gone out of his way to distinguish his conduct of the war from Lyndon Johnson's of Vietnam, but comparisons were increasingly drawn. Mounting evidence that the administration's case for war had been based on flimsy evidence, distortions, and outright fabrications opened a yawning credibility gap that brought further reminders of that earlier Texas war president. The once-invulnerable secretary of defense, Donald Rumsfeld, seemed more and more like his Vietnam-era predecessor Robert McNamara, another cocksure and arrogant defense chief who spurned military advice. Talk of training Iraqi troops to take over the war against the insurgents brought back memories of Vietnamization. Atrocities committed by Americans against Iraqis in form, if not in scale, called forth comparisons to My Lai. "We thought we had escaped Vietnam in 1975," *Newsweek*'s Howard Fineman wrote in the spring of 2004. "It turns out we never left."

The presidential campaign of 2004 seemed at times as much about Vietnam as about the issues of the day, making emphatically clear that the so-called Vietnam generation was still irreparably divided by the war that had defined it. The especially nasty charges and countercharges about the Democratic challenger John Kerry's service in Vietnam and his public criticism of the war after his return and President Bush's national guard service—or lack thereof—produced an anger and mutual recriminations that went far beyond each side's efforts to exploit for political gain a war long since ended. The debate reopened old and still gaping wounds among those who fought the Vietnam War, those who protested it, and those who avoided it. It exposed among the generation now holding political power the deep divisions that still tore them apart. "This generation will go to its grave debating Vietnam," one veteran observed.

As the war in Iraq dragged on and prospects of success increasingly dimmed, the Vietnam comparisons sharpened. Administration spokespersons continued to insist that the parallels were inexact and unhelpful, but they could not resist using them. President Bush himself, on his first trip to Vietnam in late 2006, affirmed, "We'll succeed unless we quit" (as, presumably, the United States had in Vietnam). Such bold talk had little impact. Public support for the war plummeted in 2006, dropping faster than support for Vietnam had. Bush's approval rating fell along with it. Stepped-up insurgent attacks on the eve of the 2006 elections invoked comparisons with the North Vietnamese/NLF Tet Offensive of 1968, the beginning of the end of the Vietnam War as far as the United States was concerned. An administration that had gone to war at least in part to erase lingering memories of Vietnam ended up highlighting them. An "Iraq syndrome" seemed likely to reinforce the one remaining from Vietnam. However the war in Iraq turns out, Vietnam appears even more certain for the foreseeable future to be a war that never seems to go away.

16

A Speech for LBJ with Comments on George W. Bush

Howard Zinn

In early 1967, two years after the escalation of the war in Vietnam by the United States, some of us in the movement against the war were calling for the withdrawal of American troops from Vietnam. But no major political figure and none of the major media were willing to support that idea. I wrote a book at that time, *Vietnam: The Logic of Withdrawal,* published by Beacon Press in 1967. The last chapter in the book, "A Speech for LBJ," was an imaginary speech for President Lyndon Johnson, explaining to the American people why he had decided to withdraw from Vietnam.

A businessman in the Midwest bought six hundred copies of the book and sent it to every member of Congress. The speech was reprinted in full-page ads in newspapers in various parts of the country. A columnist for the *Cleveland Plain Dealer* wrote, "Howard Zinn, a professor of government at Boston University, who served as a bombardier in World War II, has written a speech for Lyndon Johnson which, if he delivered it, would make the President one of the great men of history in my opinion."

But Johnson did not deliver that speech. The war continued, and the antiwar movement grew, and, in 1973, the United States finally withdrew. Over fifty-eight thousand Americans had lost their lives. Vietnam was devastated, and 2 million of its people, mostly civilians, were dead.

Essay originally published in *Vietnam: The Logic of Withdrawal* by Howard Zinn (Beacon Press, 1967).

North Vietnamese premier Pham Van Dong greets an American antiwar delegation, including Dr. Howard Zinn of Boston University. Courtesy of the Vietnam Archive, Texas Tech University, Douglas Pike Photograph Collection.

Today, forty years later, the United States is mired in a war in Iraq, but there is resistance in the higher circles of politics and the media to the idea of withdrawal. The reader may find this imagined speech for LBJ relevant to the policies of President George W. Bush.

My Fellow Americans:

Not long ago I received a letter from my fourth-grade schoolteacher who still lives back in the little town where I grew up. She is of advanced age now but still as she was when I sat in her class, a kindly and wise woman. She had been through depression and war, through sickness and the death of loved ones, more than most of us. Let me share her letter with you; I am sure she will not mind.

> Dear Lyndon: You know I have always had faith in you and knew you would do what is right. And you have been trying your best on this Vietnam situation. But nothing seems to be going right. So many people are getting killed. Not only our boys, but all

those poor people over there. You have tried talking peace. And you have tried bombing, and whatnot. But there is no end in sight. I hear people in town saying: "We should never have gotten in, but now that we are in, we don't seem able to get out." Lyndon, can't you get us out? I am getting on now in years and would like to see peace gain. God Bless you. Sincerely, Mrs. Annie Mae Lindley.

Now let me read just one more letter to you. It came to me from a young man fighting with the First Marine Division in South Vietnam:

Dear Mr. President: I am twenty years old and enlisted in the Marines as soon as I left high school in Massilon, Ohio. I have been in Vietnam six months now, and I have seen a lot. Three days ago my closest buddy was killed. Yesterday our outfit destroyed a hamlet that Intelligence said had been used by the VC as a base. We burned the huts and threw grenades down the tunnels. But there were no VC there. In one of the tunnels there were two women and three kids. We didn't know that. One of the kids was killed and one of the women lost an eye. We rounded up all the villagers and they stood around—children, old folks, women—crying and afraid. Of course we didn't mean to kill any kids. But we did. And that's war. I know you need sometimes to do nasty things for an important cause. The trouble is—there doesn't seem much of a cause left here in Vietnam. We're supposed to be defending these people against the VC. But they don't want us to defend them. They don't care about communism or politics or anything like that. They just want to be left in peace. So, more and more, my buddies and I wonder—what are we doing here? We're not afraid. We've been sticking it out, in the mud and in the jungle. And we'll go on like this if you ask us to. But somehow it seems wrong. I don't know what we should do, but I just thought I'd let you know how some of us feel. Sincerely, James Dixon, Corporal 1st Marine Division.

My fellow Americans, let me tell you, I have read and reread these two letters, and they have been on my mind. You all know how my administration has been concerned with the war in Vietnam. Night after night I have sat up thinking, and sometimes—I don't mind telling you—praying, that we would find a way to end this terrible war, which has cost tens of thousands of lives, American and Vietnamese, and which has caused so much pain and suffering to millions of people in that unfortunate little country.

What have been our objectives in Vietnam? I have said many times that what we wanted was for Vietnam to be free to determine its own affairs—that this is why we were fighting. We have tried every possible way to gain this objective. We have offered negotiations. And we have fought—hard, and courageously, on unfamiliar territory—with an increasing commitment of planes, ships, and ground forces, all designed to bring the war to an end with honor.

I don't need to tell you that we have not been successful. We have not destroyed the Viet Cong's will to fight. This is not a pleasant fact to report, but it is a fact.

There is another unpleasant fact to report. The government we have been supporting in Vietnam has not succeeded in gaining the respect of its own people there. No matter how valiant our men are, they cannot fight a war that is not supported by the people of the country we committed ourselves to defend. Always implied in our commitment was that if the war threatened to become our war, rather than a war by and for the Vietnamese, we would reconsider our position. That time has now come.

We have tried force, and we have offered negotiations. Neither has worked. Some have criticized us for not trying even more force. Of course we could do this. No one in the world needs to be told how powerful we are. We can stay in Vietnam as long as we like. We can reduce the whole country to ashes. We are powerful enough to do this. But we are not cruel enough to do this. I, as your president, am not willing to engage in a war without end that would destroy the youth of this nation and the people of Vietnam.

We had hoped this war could end by negotiations. But this has not worked. Pride and self-respect have often stood in the way for both sides. We are not willing to beg for negotiations. And we have too much compassion for those dying each day in Vietnam to let the war continue. In Korea, you may remember, the war dragged on while the negotiators tried to agree on terms. The diplomats talked while men died. For two years they talked, and for two years the corpses piled up in that unfortunate land. We do not want that kind of negotiation in Vietnam.

The American people have the courage to fight. We have shown this a dozen times in the past, from Bunker Hill to Gettysburg, from Normandy to Guadalcanal. We also have the courage to stop fighting, not when someone else decides for us, but when we decide for ourselves.

As commander in chief of the armed forces, I have ordered that, as of midnight tonight, our air force and our navy will halt the bombings in North and South Vietnam. We have not run out of planes, nor have we run out of bombs, nor have we run out of the determination to use them when it is wise. What we have run out of is the willingness to see more people die under our bombs. Too many have died. Too many have suffered. It is time to call a halt.

Also, I have given orders to General Westmoreland, the capable and courageous commander of our forces in Vietnam, to halt offensive operations and to begin the orderly withdrawal of our armed forces from that country.

Let us speak frankly now about the consequences of this decision.

We may see a period of turmoil and conflict in Vietnam. But that was true before we arrived. That is the nature of the world. It is hard to imagine, however, any conflict that will be more destructive than what is going on now. Our departure will inevitably diminish the fighting. It may end it.

There are many places in the world where people are going through the disorder and the violence of social change. The United States cannot interfere in every one of those instances. We do not intend to do so. To the extent that the United Nations can mediate in helping to bring tranquility to Vietnam, we will happily lend our moral and financial support.

Vietnam may become a Communist nation. The northern half of that country has been Communist for some time, and a good part of the population in the South has been sympathetic to the Viet Cong. Desperate people often turn to communism. But we have shown that we can live in peace with Communist nations, if there is mutual respect. Despite our many disagreements, we have maintained peaceful relations with the Soviet Union, with Yugoslavia, with Poland, with other Communist nations. We can certainly live in peace with Vietnam.

Everyone knows that behind our military activity in Vietnam has been our concern that Communist China shall not press its weight on other countries. Many experts on China have told us that much of China's belligerent attitude has been due to nationalistic feeling and to her fear that we intend to attack her. I hereby give my pledge that the United States will never initiate a war with China, and we will begin soon to seek ways and means of coming to a more amicable relationshp with her.

I have often said that the most effective means of maintaining a free society consists, not of armed might, but of economic development and prosperity. That will be our aim now in Asia.

To this end, I am going to ask Congress to take half of the $20 billion allocated for the Vietnam War this year and to put it into a fund—an international fund, if the United Nations will set this up—for the economic development of Vietnam and other countries in Southeast Asia. We will not force our favors on these countries. But we will stand ready to help—with no political strings attached—on the basis of their own declarations, their own needs.

The war in Vietnam was beginning to slow down many of our plans for the Great Society—plans to end poverty, to build homes and schools, to rebuild our cities, to eliminate the slums that have been at the root of unrest in various parts of the country. There will be $10 billion left unused from the war. I will ask Congress to redirect that money for purposes that I will outline in a special message next week.

We have made an important decision. It is a decision based on a fundamental American belief that human life is sacred, that peace is precious, and that true power consists, not in the brute force of guns and bombs, but in the economic well-being of a free people.

The dream I have always had since I was a boy in Texas I still have—and I want to fulfill it for America. We are about to embark on a venture far more glorious, far more bold, requiring far more courage—than war. Our aim is to build a society that will set an example for the rest of mankind. I am happy to stand before you tonight and to say that we will now build this Great Society in earnest.

I need not tell you how long I have waited for this moment—and how happy I am to be able to say that now, after so much pain, after so much sacrifice, our boys will be coming home.

My fellow Americans, good night, and sleep well. We are no longer at war in Vietnam.

Contributors

DAVID L. ANDERSON is dean of the College of University Studies and Programs at California State University, Monterey Bay; a past president of the Society for Historians of American Foreign Relations; and a U.S. Army veteran of the Vietnam War. He is the author or editor of several books on the Vietnam War, including *Trapped by Success: The Eisenhower Administration and the Vietnam War, Facing My Lai: Moving Beyond the Massacre,* and *The Columbia Guide to the Vietnam War.*

TERRY H. ANDERSON, a Vietnam U.S. Navy veteran, has written many articles on the 1960s era and the Vietnam War. He is the author of five books, including *The United States, Great Britain, and the Cold War, 1944–1947, The Movement and the Sixties, The Pursuit of Fairness: A History of Affirmative Action,* and *The Sixties* (now in its third edition). He is currently working on a book on the war in Iraq.

YVONNE HONEYCUTT BALDWIN is professor of history and chair of the Department of Geography, Government, and History at Morehead State University. Her first book, *Cora Wilson Stewart and Kentucky's Moonlight Schools: Fighting for Literacy in America,* was published in 2006. She is currently working on a book on Kentucky's participation in the Vietnam War with John Ernst, a chapter of which is included in the February 2007 issue of the *Journal of Southern History.*

ROBERT K. BRIGHAM is the Shirley Ecker Boskey Professor of History and International Relations at Vassar College. He is the author of numerous essays and books on the history of American foreign relations, including *Is Iraq Another Vietnam?* (2006).

ROBERT BUZZANCO is professor of history at the University of Houston. His published books include *Masters of War: Military Dissent and Politics in the Vietnam Era* and *Vietnam and the Transformation of American Life.*

JOHN ERNST is professor of history at Morehead State University and the author of *Forging a Fateful Alliance: Michigan State and the Vietnam War.* He is writing a book with Yvonne Honeycutt Baldwin on Kentucky and the Vietnam War, a chapter of which is included in the February 2007 issue of the *Journal of Southern History.*

RONALD B. FRANKUM JR. earned his Ph.D. from Syracuse University and is currently assistant professor of history at Millersville University of Pennsylvania. He served as both archivist and associate director for the Vietnam Center at Texas Tech University. He is the author of *Silent Partners: The United States and Australia in Vietnam, 1954–1968* (2001), the coauthor of *The Vietnam War for Dummies* (2002), *Like Rolling Thunder: The Air War in Vietnam, 1964–1975* (2005), and *Operation Passage to Freedom: The United States Navy in Vietnam, 1954–1955* (2007).

JOSEPH A. FRY is Distinguished Professor of History at the University of Nevada, Las Vegas. His most recent publications are *Dixie Looks Abroad: The South and U.S. Foreign Relations, 1789–1973* (2002) and *Debating Vietnam: Fulbright, Stennis, and Their Senate Hearings* (2006). He is currently at work on a history of the American South and the Vietnam War.

GEORGE C. HERRING is Alumni Professor of History Emeritus at the University of Kentucky. His published works include *America's Longest War: The United States and Vietnam, 1950–1975.*

GARY R. HESS is Distinguished Research Professor of History at Bowling Green State University. His research has concentrated on U.S. policy in South and Southeast Asia, including work on the Vietnam War. He is past president of the Society for Historians of American Foreign Relations and is the 2006 recipient of the society's Norman and Laura Graebner Award for lifetime achievement.

WALTER LAFEBER is the Andrew and James Tisch University Professor Emeritus at Cornell University. His books include *America, Russia, and the Cold War* (now in its tenth edition) and *The Deadly Bet: LBJ, Vietnam, and the 1968 Election* (2005).

KYLE LONGLEY is the Snell Family Dean's Distinguished Professor of History at Arizona State University. A 1994 graduate of the University of Kentucky, he has published *The Sparrow and the Hawk: Costa Rica and the United States during the Rise of Jose Figueres, In the Eagle's Shadow: The United States and Latin America, Senator Albert Gore, Sr.: Tennessee Maverick,* and *Deconstructing Reagan: Conservative Mythology and America's Fortieth President.* Currently, he is working on two books on the American combat solider in Vietnam.

LUU DOAN HUYNH is a former intelligence analyst with the Department of American Affairs in Hanoi's Foreign Ministry. He is now a senior researcher at the Institute for International Relations, Ministry of Foreign Affairs, Hanoi.

SANDRA C. TAYLOR is professor emerita in the Department of History at the University of Utah. Her works on Vietnam include *Vietnamese Women at War: Fighting for Ho Chi Minh and the Revolution* (1999). She has also contributed articles on Vietnamese and American women to *The Vietnam War: Its History, Literature, and Music,* ed. Kenton Clymer (1996), and *The Encyclopedia of the Vietnam War,* ed. Stanley Kutler (1996).

ROBERT TOPMILLER, a decorated Vietnam combat veteran, is assistant professor of history at Eastern Kentucky University, where he teaches courses on the Vietnam War. He studied under George Herring at the University of Kentucky and is the author of *The Lotus Unleashed: The Buddhist Peace Movement in South Vietnam, 1964–66* (2002) and *Red Clay on My Boots: Encounters with Khe Sanh, 1968–2005* (2007).

CLARENCE R. WYATT is the Pottinger Associate Professor of History and special assistant to the president at Centre College in Danville, Kentucky. He received his B.A. from Centre College and his M.A. and Ph.D. from the University of Kentucky. He is the author of *Paper Soldiers: The American Press and the Vietnam War.* He regularly leads study-abroad trips to Vietnam and Cambodia.

MARILYN YOUNG is professor of history at New York University. She has been teaching about the Vietnam War since 1969 and is the author of *The Vietnam Wars, 1945–1990* and the coeditor (with Lloyd Gardner) of *Iraq and the Lessons of Vietnam; or, How Not to Learn from the Past.*

HOWARD ZINN is a historian, playwright, and activist. He saw combat duty in the air force in World War II and became involved in the movement against the Vietnam War, during which time he wrote the book *Vietnam: The Logic of Withdrawal.* He is also the author of *A People's History of the United States.*

Index

Abrams, Gen. Creighton, 28, 317
Abu Ghraib, 1, 6
Acheson, Dean, 81
Adams, Gen. Paul, 197
Afghanistan, 3–4, 6, 8, 347
African American soldier experience, 321–22
Agent Orange, 159, 179, 323
Agnew, Spiro, 235, 259, 305
Aiken, George, 290
Albert, Carl, 254
Ali, Muhammad, 251, 342
Alsop, Joseph, 248, 270, 275
An Khe, 322
An Loc, 312
Apple, R. W., 3, 281
Archer, Michael, 330
Arnett, Peter, 272, 275–76
ARVN (Army of the Republic of Vietnam), 25, 130, 132, 134, 139, 147, 149–51, 153, 185, 199, 200–201, 203–4, 206, 247, 257, 261, 306
ASEAN (Association of Southeast Asian Nations), 96–97, 99
Aton, Paul, 326–27
atrocities, 6, 260, 318, 322–23, 348

Baez, Joan, 247, 342
Ball, George, 219
Bao Dai, 78, 81, 126–29
Beach, Gen. Dwight, 209
Berrigan brothers, 342
Bien Hoa, 204, 313

Bigart, Homer, 272–73
Black Hawk Down, 335
body count, 3, 174, 187n26, 323, 325, 329, 338
Bradley, Gen. Omar, 193, 196, 206, 345
Brewster, Kingman, 321
Brezhnev, Leonid, 47–48, 50–51
Britain, 23, 35, 50, 55–57, 59, 66–68, 70, 78, 84, 111
Brock, Bill, 305
Brother Howell, 313
Brown, Robert McAfee, 253
Browne, Malcolm, 272, 274
Buchanan, Pat, 258
Buddhist peace movement, 145–47, 149, 152, 156, 159–60; Buddhist Crisis, First (1964), 147; Buddhist Crisis, Second (1964), 148; Buddhist Crisis of 1966, 149–52; NLF relationship with, 152–54; School of Youth for Social Service (SYSS), 157–58; self-immolation, 154–55, 159; Unified Buddhist Church (UBC), 146, 151, 158–59, 166n63; women, 155–58
Bui Diem, 336
Bundy, McGeorge, 1, 200–202
Bundy, William, 202
Bunker, Ellsworth, 28
Burke, Arleigh, 198
Bush, George H. W., 335
Bush, George W., 1, 7, 9, 10n6, 28–29, 55, 336, 346–48, 351–52

Calley, William, Jr., 6, 260, 282
Cam Rahn Bay, 313
Cambodia, 35, 51–52, 56, 58–59, 96–98,
    102, 135, 167, 176, 180, 235–39, 258,
    260, 291, 300–302, 328, 339
Campbell, Barry, 314–15, 317, 330
Campus Commission on Student Unrest,
    260
Canada, 228, 250, 342
Cao Ngoc Phuong, 157–58
Caputo, Philip, 337–38
Card, Josefina: 1981 survey by, 324–25
Carroll, James, 341–42
Carroll, John, 280
Carter, Jimmy, 6
central highlands, 185, 315, 319
Cheney, Richard, 29
China, 14, 16–19, 22, 27, 36, 38–52,
    53n7, 57, 59–60, 65–66, 71, 76, 81–
    83, 88–89, 94, 96–97, 109, 111–12,
    153, 155, 167–69, 170, 175, 192–95,
    197, 207, 245, 284, 292, 296, 298,
    306, 341, 356
Church, Frank, 289, 291–92, 294–95,
    299–302
civil rights movement, 221–22, 225,
    245–46, 248, 250, 252, 254
Clark, Joseph, 290
Clark, Wesley, 211
Clarke, Victoria, 286
Clifford, Clark, 65, 70
Colby, William, 28
Cold War, 16–17, 19–20, 22–24, 29,
    36–39, 42–44, 46–47, 56, 71, 88, 127,
    140, 198, 230–31, 240, 245, 248, 253,
    263, 266–68, 272, 291, 341
Collins, Gen. Arthur, 204
Collins, Gen. J. Lawton, 193–94, 196, 198
Collins, Judy, 247
Committee of Six, 258
Con Dao, 176, 179
Cooper, John Sherman, 290, 300–301
Cooper-Church Amendment, 291,
    300–302, 305

Cronkite, Walter, 255

Dalat, 149
Danang, 149–51, 176, 197, 203–4, 280,
    314
Decker, Gen. George, 200
de Gaulle, Charles, 44–45, 67
Dellinger, David, 253
Democratic Republic of Vietnam,
    (DRV), 16–17, 21–23, 24, 26–27, 51,
    58, 71, 76–83, 85–88, 90–91, 93, 96,
    122, 128–29, 135, 148, 153, 172, 200,
    202–3, 248–50, 257, 259, 305, 337,
    339
DePuy, Gen. William, 203
DEROS (Date Eligible for Return from
    Overseas), 313
Dien Bien Phu, 57, 59, 127, 194–95, 292
Dirksen, Everett, 294
Disney, David, 328–29
Dodd, Thomas, 298
Dole, Robert, 304
domino theory, 17, 41, 57
Doonesbury, 345
drug usage, 261, 317
Dulles, John Foster, 40–41, 57–60, 195,
    197, 213n17
Duong Quynh Hoa, 183–84
Duong Van Minh, 139, 147, 159
Durbrow, Elbridge, 131–32, 213

Easter Offensive, 284, 305
Ehrhart, W. D., 325
Eisenhower, Dwight D., 17, 19, 40–41,
    43, 57, 60, 62, 124, 127, 193–99,
    268–69, 292
Ellsberg, Daniel, 18, 283

Fall, Bernard B., 17
Felt, Adm. Harry, 273, 276–77
Flood, Charles Bracelyn, 315
FNG (Fucking New Guy), 314
Ford, Gerald R., 28, 254, 306
Forrestal, Michael, 200

Fort Benning, 315
forward observer (FO), 328
fragging, 261, 317
France, 6, 16, 35–37, 39–41, 44–45,
    56–57, 59, 63, 66–67, 70, 76–83, 109,
    111–12, 167, 192–93, 340
Free World Assistance Program, 70
Friedrich, Otto, 267
Fulbright, J. William, 253, 256, 289–92,
    294–99, 301
Furnas, Grant, 315–16, 318, 321

Gallagher, Gen. Philip, 192
Galloway, Joseph, 263n2, 346
Gavin, Gen. James, 194–97
Geneva Accords, 58, 81, 84, 88, 90, 135,
    172
Geneva Convention, 7, 9, 124
Goodell, Charles, 234, 305
Gore, Albert A., Sr., 289, 291–93,
    295–96, 298–99, 301, 305
Gore, Albert A., Jr., 299
Gore, Tipper, 299
Greene, Gen. Wallace M., 204
Greenfield, James, 278, 280, 285
Gruening, Ernest, 289, 291, 294–95, 300
Gulf of Tonkin, 200, 246, 290, 293–96,
    298, 301, 305
Gulf War, 4, 55, 265, 335, 337, 341

Haeberle, Sgt. Ronald, 282
Halberstam, David, 17, 108, 274, 276
Haldeman, Bob, 27, 262
Hale, Ralph, 321
Hanoi, 4, 21–24, 27, 51, 79, 81, 90, 96, 99,
    119, 172, 182–83, 200, 202, 248–49,
    254, 257
Harriman, Averell, 86, 135–36, 138
Hatfield, Mark, 290, 302–4
Herring, George C., 19, 29, 36, 99, 149,
    191–92, 211, 254, 262, 336
Hersh, Seymour, 282–83
Hershey, Gen. Lewis, 253
Hickenlooper, Bourke, 298

Higgins, Marguerite, 275
Hilsman, Roger, 200
Hoang Minh Giam, 76–77
Hoang Thi Khanh, 176–77
Ho Chi Minh, 17–19, 35–37, 47–48,
    58, 75–77, 82, 85–87, 90, 92–93,
    117, 125, 127, 191–92, 194, 199,
    249–50, 339–40; *chinh nghia,* 106–7;
    Confucianism, 105–7, 108, 110–11,
    113, 115–16, 119; death of, 178;
    land-to-tiller program, 110, 116–19;
    Marxist-Leninist philosophy, 18, 79,
    81, 107–12, 114, 126, 170–71, 181;
    Vietnamese Communist Party, 85,
    87, 105, 107–8, 110, 113, 115–19,
    178; women, 113, 170–71, 178,
    181–83
Ho Chi Minh Trail, 86, 172, 300, 316
Hooper, Joe, 316
Hoover, J. Edgar, 249, 302
Hue, 111, 117, 125, 136, 143, 149–51,
    174, 178–79, 277, 312
Hull, Cordell, 291
Humphrey, Hubert, 63, 69, 227, 256, 313
Hussein, Saddam, 347
Huston Plan, 302
Huynh Van Cao, 274

Ia Drang Valley, 247–48, 280, 312
Indochina, 6, 16–20, 24, 35–36, 56–58,
    64, 67, 75–83, 94, 127, 192–201,
    204–5, 210, 303–4, 339–40, 343
Indochina Communist Party, 80–81
Iraq, 1, 3, 5–9, 28–29, 55, 98, 210–11,
    265, 285–86, 336, 347–49, 352
Isaacs, Arnold, 261, 344

Japan, 6, 16, 35, 40–41, 52, 58, 70, 73n26,
    76, 81, 126–27, 167, 192, 194, 250
Javits, Jacob, 306
Johnson, Harold K., 201, 203, 208–9
Johnson, Lyndon B., 14, 23–24, 27,
    46–48, 50, 55–56, 60, 62–71, 123,
    133, 199–204, 206–10, 257, 261–62,

278, 281, 292–93, 313, 319, 325, 341, 347, 351; antiwar movement, 219, 221, 223–24, 226–27, 231–32, 239, 249–50, 254, 256, 263; Congress, 294–97, 299; Great Society, 48, 250, 356; Ho Chi Minh, 47–49, 339; war supporters, 246–47, 250

Johnson, U. Alexis, 201

Joint Chiefs of Staff (JCS), 192–94, 196, 198, 200, 203, 206–9, 262, 282

Joint Strategic Plans Committee, 193

Joint U.S. Public Affairs Office (JUSPAO), 279

Kahin, George McT., 17, 19, 99

Katzenbach, Nicholas, 248

Kennedy, John F., 14, 19, 23–24, 44–45, 48–49, 64, 199, 206, 261, 292, 295, 338; Ngo Dinh Diem, 43, 46, 86, 123–25, 127, 129–30, 132–35, 137–40, 200, 272, 277–78, 293; press, 269, 270, 272, 275, 278

Kennedy, Robert F., 210, 231

Kennan, George, 297–98

Kerr, Clark, 221

Kerry, John, 210, 348

Khe Sanh, 14, 312, 329–30

Khmer Rouge, 96–97, 167

Khrushchev, Nikita, 41–44, 47, 88, 269, 272

King, Coretta Scott, 251–52

King, Martin Luther, 231, 250–51

Kissinger, Henry, 26, 184, 257, 261, 305, 325

Korean War, 7, 15, 17–18, 38–39, 47, 55, 65, 69, 74, 82–83, 206, 245, 294, 345

Kosygin, Alexei, 47–48, 50

Laird, Melvin, 28

Lansdale, Edward, 131–32, 163n31

Laos, 17, 35, 44, 56–59, 64, 85–87, 98, 124, 135, 197–98, 200, 261, 284, 300, 302, 339

Lausche, Frank, 298

Lawrence, David, 269

Le Duan, 84–87, 89–90, 92, 94

Le Duc Tho, 184

Le Ly Hayslip, 181

LeMay, Curtis, 256

Lemnitzer, Gen. Lyman, 198, 205

Lennon, John, 258

Liu Shao Chi, 81–82

Lodge, Henry Cabot, Jr., 138–39, 163n31, 277–78

Lon Nol, 300

long-range reconnaissance patrols (LURPs), 322

Lynch, Gen. Tom, 317–20

MacArthur, Gen. Douglas, 198, 206

Manatos, Mike, 299

Mansfield, Mike, 289, 291–93, 296

Mao Zedong, 38–39, 42, 46–51

March on the Pentagon (October 1967), 231, 252–54, 263

Marcos, Ferdinand, 63–64

Marshall, Gen. George C., 192, 337

McCarthy, Eugene, 210, 231, 234, 256, 290

McDonald, Adm. David, 206

McGarr, Gen. Lionel C., 130, 205–6

McGovern, George, 289, 291, 295, 299–300, 302–3, 305, 339

McGovern-Hatfield Amendments, 291, 300, 302–5

McNamara, Robert S., 1, 199, 200–202, 227, 239, 252, 277, 283, 293, 325, 341–42, 348

McNaughton, John, 202

McReynolds, Dave, 245, 262

"mere gook rule," 325

Military Assistance Advisory Group (MAAG), 197, 205–6

Military Assistance Command, Vietnam (MACV), 201, 203–4, 207, 209, 278–79, 284–85, 317

Mohr, Charles, 272, 276, 281

More Flags Program, 55, 62, 65, 67,

69–71; Australia, 56, 58–60, 62–63, 65–66, 70–71, 176; New Zealand, 56, 58–60, 62–63, 66, 70; Philippines, 56, 58, 62–64, 69; Republic of South Korea, 61, 63, 67–70; Thailand, 56, 58, 60, 62–65, 69, 71

Moorer, Adm. Thomas, 262

Morrison, Norman, 342

Morse, Wayne, 289–92, 294–95

Mullins, Thomas, 313, 327, 329

Murphy, Audie, 316

Mus, Paul, 77, 101n8, 106–7

My Lai, 5, 184, 260, 282, 305, 318, 344, 348

National Liberation Front, (NLF), 8, 22, 24, 86, 90–91, 93, 117–18, 143, 145–47, 149, 152–54, 156, 159, 173–77, 180, 182–85, 191, 200, 337, 340, 348

Nelson, Gaylord, 290

New Left, 223

Ngo Dinh Diem, 84, 108, 121–22, 129, 173, 191, 196, 272–73, 292; Agroville Program, 124, 130, 133–34; assassination of, 132, 139, 143, 200; birth and early life of, 125; Buddhist Crisis, 41, 43, 136–37, 143–45, 200, 277; Catholicism, 41, 175; coup of 1960, 124, 130–32, 135, 139–40; coup of 1963, 86, 123, 138–39, 143–44, 147, 277; election of 1955, 197; election of 1961, 133; refugees, 123, 128, 196–97; sects, 123, 128; Strategic Hamlet Program, 124, 134–36, 138

Ngo Dinh Nhu, 86, 125, 133–39, 198, 276–78

Ngo Dinh Nhu (Madame), 175, 198

Ngo Dinh Thuc, 136, 277

Nguyen Cao Ky, 148–49, 249, 299

Nguyen Chanh Thi, 149, 161n10

Nguyen Duy Trinh, 90–91

Nguyen Khanh, 147, 161n10, 202

Nguyen Thi Binh, 183–84

Nguyen Thi Dinh, 180–84

Nguyen Thi Hi, 176

Nguyen Thi Hong Phau, 178–79

Nguyen Van Linh, 85

Nguyen Van Thieu, 28, 93–94, 176, 249

Nha Trang, 149

Nixon, Richard M., 14, 24–29, 47, 51–52, 70–71, 92–95, 210, 256, 282–84, 320, 325, 341; antiwar movement, 219, 223, 227, 231, 233–34, 236, 238–39, 257–63; Congress, 300–302, 304–6; silent majority, 235; Vietnamization, 26–28, 71, 235, 238, 257, 261, 284, 320, 348; Watergate, 26, 284, 306

Nolting, Frederick, 132, 138, 277

Norodom Sihanouk, 300

North Vietnam. *See* Democratic Republic of Vietnam

North Vietnamese Army (NVA), 247, 249, 255, 257, 261, 300, 306, 312, 317

O'Brien, Tim, 337–39

Office of Strategic Services (OSS), 76, 192

Officer Candidate School (OCS), 315–16

Operation Chaos, 254, 258

Operation Maximum Candor, 278, 280, 286

Operation Rolling Thunder, 202, 246

Palmer, Gen. Bruce, 204, 209

Pakistan, 56, 59, 63

Paris Agreement, 90, 93–95, 97

Park Chung Hee, 70

Parris Island, South Carolina, 321

Pathet Lao, 64, 86

Pentagon Papers, 18, 250, 261, 283, 305

People's Liberation Armed Forces, 174, 182

Perry, Merton, 272, 276

Pham Ngoc Thach, 78

Pham Van Dong, 39, 88, 90, 352

Phu Bai, 177, 204, 314

Pike, Douglas, 336

Pleiku, 202, 246
Pol Pot, 52, 96, 167
post-traumatic stress disorder (PTSD), 322–24

Quan The Am, 156

racial problems, 233, 317
Rambo, John, 345
Rankin, Jeanette, 234, 291–92
rape, 8, 260, 318, 322
Rather, Dan, 281
Reagan, Ronald, 233, 236, 266, 343
Reedy, George, 295
REMFs (Rear Echelon Motherfuckers), 319
Republic of Vietnam (RVN), 16–17, 21–22, 24, 26–28, 43, 46, 48, 60, 62, 66, 71, 86, 93, 118, 121–23, 128–30, 134–35, 139–40, 143, 145–52, 154, 158–59, 180, 196, 255, 272–73, 275–79, 306, 344
Ridenhour, Ron, 282–83
Ridgway, Gen. Matthew, 20, 194–95
Rivers, L. Mendel, 253
Rolling Thunder. See Operation Rolling Thunder
Roosevelt, Franklin D., 35–36, 75–76, 132, 291
Rostow, Walter W., 14, 272
ROTC (Reserve Officers' Training Corps), 226, 228–30, 234–36, 315, 317
Rumsfeld, Donald, 4, 29, 348
Rusk, Dean, 1, 45–46, 63–64, 200, 203, 227, 239, 248, 253, 298, 341
Russell, Richard, 294, 296

Sabin, Adm. Lorenzo, 122–24
Safer, Morley, 280–81
Saigon, 23, 52, 79, 87, 91–92, 95, 105, 110–11, 115–16, 131, 138, 153, 157, 160, 173, 175–76, 179, 182–84, 195, 198, 201, 205, 209, 284, 301, 312, 319, 343

Salinger, Pierre, 272
Salisbury, Harrison, 282
Schwarzkopf, Norman, 285
Selective Service System (the draft), 224, 228, 235, 245, 249–51, 253–54, 262, 319–21, 326, 342; African Americans, 251; Hispanics, 251
Senate Armed Services Committee, 296
Senate Foreign Relations Committee (SFRC), 289–90, 293; hearings on Vietnam (1966), 296–99
September 11, 2001, 7, 36, 102n16, 335, 346
Sharp, Adm. Ulysses S. Grant, 21, 205–8
Sheehan, Neil, 271–74, 276–77, 283
Shinseki, Eric, 211
Shoup, Gen. David M., 252
Sidey, Hugh, 270
South Vietnam. See Republic of Vietnam
Southeast Asia Treaty Organization (SEATO), 56–60, 62–66, 68, 71, 200
Southern Student Organizing Committee (SSOC), 225–26
Soviet Union, 6, 16, 19, 23, 36, 38, 40–42, 44, 46–51, 57, 65, 68, 71, 77, 80–81, 88–89, 96, 102n17, 111, 170, 197, 200, 245, 266, 269, 281, 284, 296, 306, 355
Spock, Benjamin, 246
Stalin, Joseph (Josef), 37–38, 41–42, 81
Stanton, Frank, 280–81
Stennis, John, 296, 304
Stop the Draft Week, 245, 253–54
student activism: Bethel College, 234; Central Michigan University, 236; Columbia University, 228, 230–31, 233, 235, 246; Cornell University, 233–34; Emory University, 227; Erskine College, 226; Florida A&M University, 222; Florida State University, 222, 228, 236; Furman University, 228; Harvard University, 225, 227, 252–53; Iowa State University, 229, 234; Jackson

State College, 236, 238, 300; Kansas State University, 226, 230; Kent State University, 225–26, 235–38, 247, 258, 260, 300; Louisiana State University, 234; Louisiana State University, New Orleans, 225; Massachusetts Institute of Technology, 230; Michigan State University, 235; Ohio State University, 227, 235; Pennsylvania State University, 225–26; Princeton University, 235; San Francisco State University, 230; Smith College, 227; Stanford University, 227, 235; State University of New York at Buffalo, 227; University of California, Berkeley, 225–27, 229, 233, 236, 246; University of Chicago, 228; University of Delaware, 229; University of Georgia, 225, 229, 234, 236; University of Indiana, 227, 253; University of Kentucky, 229, 260, 341–42; University of Louisville, 234; University of Maryland, 235; University of Michigan, 226, 230, 246, 260; University of Minnesota, 221, 225, 234, 238; University of Mississippi, 228; University of Nevada, Las Vegas, 220, 223, 237; University of New Mexico, 238; University of Oregon, 227, 246; University of South Carolina, 236, 260; University of Texas, 225–26, 232, 234, 236; University of Virginia, 226, 228–29, 235–36; University of Washington, 229; University of Wisconsin, 227, 229, 230, 235–36, 247
Students for a Democratic Society (SDS), 223, 225–26, 246
Sully, Francois, 272–73
Sulzberger, Arthur, 283

Taylor, Gen. Maxwell D., 43, 65, 70, 148, 201–4, 272, 298

Tet Offensive, 24–25, 50, 91, 102–3n27, 176, 178, 204, 208–10, 252, 255–56, 262–63, 300, 317, 348
Thailand, 56, 58, 60, 62–65, 69, 96, 300
Thich Nhat Hanh, 157–58
Thich Tri Quang, 143, 145, 151–52, 159, 160n1
Thomas, Maj. Allison, 192
Tiger Force Unit, 318
Ton Son Nhut, 313
Ton That Dinh, 139
Tran Dang Ninh, 82
Tran Van Don, 139
Tran Van Huong, 148
Trapnell, Gen. Thomas, 195
Trieu Thi Trinh, 168, 185n5
Truman, Harry S., 16–17, 19, 36–40, 46, 52, 55, 76, 82, 193, 206, 245, 268–69
Trung sisters, 168
Tuohy, William, 281
Turner, Nick, 272
Tuy Hoa, 315, 318
Tydings, Joseph, 305

Ung Van Khiem, 86
United Nations (UN), 51, 55, 78, 83, 355–56

Valenti, Jack, 206
Vann, Lt. Col. John Paul, 274
Viet Cong, 3, 60, 67, 134–35, 138–39, 143, 148, 173, 184, 200, 204, 206, 246–47, 249, 251, 253, 255, 257, 272–74, 293, 298–99, 306, 312, 354–55
Viet Minh, 16–17, 21, 57, 76, 126–27, 140, 153, 172–73, 192–97
Vietnam moratorium protests, 232–35, 259, 263
Vietnam syndrome, 13–14, 335, 346–47
Vietnam Veterans against the War (VVAW), 225, 252, 260–61
Vietnam Veterans Memorial, 324, 326
Vittorini, Vitt, 330
Vo Nguyen Giap, 89, 91, 102–3n27, 197

Wallace, George, 256
War Powers Act of 1973, 306
Watergate scandal, 26, 284, 306
Wayne, John, 249
Westmoreland, Gen. William C., 6,
    21–22, 163, 199, 201, 203–4, 207–10,
    215n35, 217n58, 247–48, 253, 255,
    299, 305, 317, 355
West Point, 315
Wheeler, Gen. Earle, 199, 203, 209
Whitman, Bryan, 286
Williams, Gen. Samuel, 197–98
Wilson, Charles, 196
Wilson, Harold, 68
women, 167–85; Confucianism, 168–69;
    Youth Brigade, 174, 177
Women's Liberation Association, 170,
    173–75, 181–83

Women's Solidarity Movement, 175
Women Strike for Peace, 246, 252
Woodley, Arthur E. (Gene), Jr., 322, 324
World War II, 1, 4, 15–16, 18, 20, 23, 29,
    35, 52, 65, 75, 79, 171, 191–92, 199,
    221, 234, 248, 257, 268, 274, 291,
    312–13, 320, 329, 337–39, 341, 344,
    351

Yarborough, Ralph, 305
Young, Stephen, 290, 303
Young Americans for Freedom (YAF),
    223

Zinni, Anthony, 211
Zorthian, Barry, 278–79
Zumwalt, Adm. Elmo, 336